# What Do We Know?

The Carlebach Anthology

# What Do We Know?

## The Carlebach Anthology

Essays about Rabbi Shlomo Carlebach
with Selections from His Teachings and Stories

Edited by
**Rabbi Joseph Schonwald**

with
**Reuven Goldfarb**

WHAT DO WE KNOW?

The Carlebach Anthology:
Essays about Rabbi Shlomo Carlebach,
with Selections from His Teachings and Stories

Edited by **Rabbi Joseph Schonwald** with **Reuven Goldfarb**

Cover art by **Lynn Reichman**

Design and layout by **David Hillel**

Visit us on our social channels: YouTube, FaceBook, and Twitter. You can also download this volume as an e-book from Amazon.com.

To order more books please write CarlebachAnthology@Gmail.com

To order photos by Joan Roth, contact her via JoanLRoth@aol.com.

To obtain copies of the portrait of Reb Shlomo that adorns the cover, write to LynnReichmanArt@gmail.com. Her website is http://lynnreichmanart.com/

Our YouTube channel: Carlebach Book
http://bit.ly/WhatDoWeKnowBook
Zimrani Press 02-6725094

To connect with the Carlebach community see this website: http://www.shlomocarlebachfoundation.org/

ISBN: 978-965-7646-12-0

—Library Of Congress Cataloging-In-Publication Data Is Available On File

Dedicated to our beloved grandchildren,

**Ta'ir Tiferet Libi**
**Oriana Saphira**
**Rakia Ma'ayan Bina**
**Gavriel Maor David**
and
**Evan Ziv Yisrael**


and to Reb Shlomo and Neila's grandchildren

**Rafael Lev Shlomo**
**Micah Or Shalem**
**Ra'eya Ayalah Tair**
**Shlomo Liav Marom**
**Sahara Leila Miryam**
and
**Oriyah Kochav Libi**


and to all the children
who never met Reb Shlomo, *z"l*
who loves them from his heavenly abode
rejoicing when they lift their voices in song
and their feet in dance
in praise of their Creator

**Rabbi Joseph & Rolinda Schonwald**


הַטּוֹב כִּי לֹא כָלוּ רַחֲמֶיךָ, וְהַמְרַחֵם כִּי לֹא תַמּוּ חֲסָדֶיךָ, כִּי מֵעוֹלָם קִוִּינוּ לָךְ

# Reb Shlomo's Torah of the Heart

This project began some years ago in response to a feeling that we who were Shlomo's friends and followers should properly acknowledge his importance as our Rebbe. Shlomo introduced us to the Torah, philosophy, and songs of the Chassidic Masters. To us, he was like the Ba'al Shem Tov, the Ishbitzer and the S'fat Emet rolled into one. He walked among us, teaching, singing and dancing his way into our hearts and souls, opening our hearts to the deep and beautiful traditions of our forebears. He walked with us and changed our lives.

We were privileged to encounter him back in the 1960s when Shlomo reached out to university students and "flower children," and our lives changed forever. Shlomo made it his life task to reach out to the youth and bring them home, singing a new song.

He established the "House of Love and Prayer" during a time of war, protest, and alienation. He chose, above all, a Torah of the Heart.

As he taught and performed, he began each concert and class by saying: ***"Brothers and sisters, open up your hearts."*** This mantra invited us to quiet our minds and be receptive on a deeper level. He was a great *Talmid Chacham*, a great scholar. A brilliant student from his early years on, he had powerful intellectual abilities and easily mastered the Talmud and other great texts of Jewish learning. He was also well-versed in Chassidic commentaries, which provided him with an emotional richness and depth not available in most yeshivas. The ecstatic dimension of the Chassidic world provided him with the dimension he sought. This was his essential contribution — communicating the path of G-d through the language of the heart, connecting him with the needs of young people. This is what made him so present to our generation. He reached out to us in a voice we could hear.

We would like to acknowledge Reb Shlomo's family: Neila, Neshama, Nedara and all the grandchildren, for their permission to quote from Reb Shlomo's teachings in this book.

None of us would be who we now are were it not for Reb Shlomo's influence on us. He shaped the way we think, sing, dance, study, pray, and greet one another. Many of us would not live where we live, be it in Israel or elsewhere, without his opening the gates of Shabbat for us and instilling a yearning for Jerusalem in our hearts.

For those readers just getting acquainted with Reb Shlomo's world and worldview, we hope that this book gives you a taste of what it was like to be with Reb Shlomo. May the blessing of his presence in our lives continue into yours. May you live the rest of your life with your heart a little more open. May you be a blessing.

# Contents

Introduction: Speaking from the Heart ..................................... 1
by Rabbi Joseph Schonwald

## THEOLOGICAL / PHILOSOPHICAL

Shlomo's Torah .......................................................................... 9
by Rabbi Micha Odenheimer

The Existential Challenge of Brokenness:
Principles in the Thought of Reb Shlomo Carlebach .............. 21
by Rute Yair-Nussbaum

In Search of the Broken Self: Rabbi Shlomo Carlebach's
Teachings in the Context of His Life and Work ...................... 44
by Rabbi Nehemia Polen

Was Shlomo a Religious Genius? ............................................. 58
by Rabbi Alon Goshen-Gottstein

Comparing the Educational Strategies of the Ba'al Shem Tov
and Reb Shlomo Carlebach ....................................................... 70
by Rabbi Avraham Arieh Trugman

Moshe Idel and Shlomo Carlebach on Kabbalah .................... 82
Described and Transcribed by Betzalel Edwards

## POLITICAL / HISTORICAL

Shlomo and the Movement for Soviet Jewry .......................... 91
by Yossi Klein Halevi

Shlomo Carlebach: Minstrel and Rebbe ................................. 95
by Rabbi Yehonatan Chipman

## PERSONAL / MYSTICAL

The Master of Virtuous Reality .............................................. 109
by Rabbi Zalman Schachter-Shalomi

**What's the Most Important Thing for Us to Do Now?**
**We Need to Learn How to Learn** ............................................. 117
by Barry Barkan

**Multiple Lives in Bobov** ........................................................... 128
by Rabbi Dr. Reb Mimi Feigelson

**Reb Shlomo:**
**An Encounter Between the Mystical and the Practical** ........ 140
by Rabbi Sam Intrator

**A Woman's Perspective** ........................................................... 151
by Melinda (Mindy) Ribner

**Vignettes from Reb Shlomo's Life — and Mine** ...................... 162
by Rabbi Joseph Schonwald

**Torah That Opens the Heart** ..................................................... 176
by Rabbi Yoel Glick

**My Story: Excerpt from a Memoir** ............................................. 182
by Neila Carlebach

## MUSICAL

**Zion's Holy Voice at the End of Days** ......................................... 199
by Yeshayah Eliyahu ben Mishael (Charles E. Vernoff, Ph.D., *A"H*)

***Shir Hashirim Asher L'Shlomo:***
**Rav Kook and Reb Shlomo — *Zecher Tzadikim L'Vracha*** ........ 204
by Rabbi Itzchak Marmorstein

**Reflections on Reb Shlomo's Kabbalat Shabbat *Nusach*** ...... 213
The Musical Influence of the "Imrei Shaul" of Modzhitz
by Rabbi Dr. Menachem Kallus

**An Excerpt from *The Late Starters Orchestra*** .......................... 224
by Professor Ari L. Goldman

## POETRY

**Encounter at a Distance**............................................................ 229
by Chaya Lester

**A Reflection...** ........................................................................ 234
by Carol Rose

**Walking to the Kotel** and **Potiphar's Lament**.......................... 235
by Reuven Goldfarb

**Three Poems** .......................................................................... 239
by Ruth Fogelman

## EULOGY

*Hesped* **in Honor of Rabbi Shlomo Carlebach** ......................... 247
by The Chief Rabbi of Israel, Harav Yisrael Meir Lau
Delivered at Har Menuchot, Jerusalem,
19 Cheshvan 5755 / October 24, 1994

Translated by Rachel Ebner

## IN HIS OWN WORDS:
## INTERVIEW, STORIES, AND TEACHINGS

**Reb Shlomo at Yakar:**
**Interview with Harav Meir "Mickey" Rosen,** *z"l*..................... 255

**Reb Shlomo's Kislev Teachings** ................................................ 308
Temple Beth Ami, Santa Rosa, CA,
22-23 Kislev, 5741 / November 30, 1980

**Reb Shlomo Carlebach on Children and Chanukah** .............. 335

**Shlomo's Purim Teachings** ...................................................... 345
University of Florida, Gainesville,
Sunday, 24 Shevat, 5746 / February 2, 1986

**Another Purim Story and Teaching from Reb Shlomo** ......... 359

**Reb Shlomo: The Specialness of Seder Night**......................... 361
CBI, Berkeley, California, Sunday, 8 Nisan, 5754 / March 20, 1994

**German, Polish, and Jewish Intercultural Healing**................388
German Civilization class, 24 Nisan, 5750 / April 19, 1990

**Reconciliation with God** ............................................ 398
Class in Jewish Mysticism, 24 Nisan, 5750 / April 19, 1990

*Parashat Metzora* **— How Can You...?** ...................... 422

**Rabbi Shlomo Carlebach Teaching on Pesach Sheni** ........... 424
Newton, Massachusetts, 14 Iyar, 5754 / April 24, 1994

**The Doors We Go Through** ....................................... 439
Transcribed by Emuna Witt-Halevi

**Two Stories:**
**The Gypsy Musician** and **The Poor Woman's Blessing** .......... 446
Transcribed by Tzlotana Midlo

**Cry Over Every Stitch**................................................ 450
as told by Rabbi Shlomo Carlebach

**Notes on Contributors** ............................................ 452

**Afterword**................................................................ 467
by Reuven Goldfarb, Redactor

**Titles of Internet Links**.............................................. 470

# Introduction:
# Speaking from the Heart

by Rabbi Joseph Schonwald

## Our Final Meeting

When Shlomo came to Jerusalem, he liked to stay at the Ramada Renaissance Hotel. Other than the fact that it was one of the favorite venues for religious Jews, and he was well recognized by all, for the life of me I couldn't understand why he preferred it. Nevertheless, this was where he summoned me for breakfast a few months before he passed away, on his last visit to Jerusalem. It was the only time I recall that he had ever asked for something so purposefully.

When I arrived at the hotel at 10 a.m., there were throngs of people surrounding him as he exited the elevator. When he finally managed to extricate himself from all his admiring fans, we proceeded to breakfast. As we entered, Shlomo embraced each of the staff, spoke to each waitress, and inquired about her health and her family. He was a frequent guest and a well-known and beloved personality.

I waited around while Shlomo greeted everyone; then we sat down to a meal. I remember that Shlomo seemed unusually troubled. He was serious. There were none of his usual jokes. He told me that his rebbe told him that when he needs good advice, he should "speak to someone who is successful."

"Let's go find him," I replied.

Shlomo got very emotional and said, "Your humble brother needs to *mamash* talk to you straight."

"I'm here," I replied, giving him my full attention.

He told me he was concerned about his daughters. "Who will watch out for them and take care of them?" Little did I realize that this would be our final meeting.

"Of course, they will be taken care of," I hastened to reassure him. "Don't worry! But Shlomo," I asked him, "why are you so concerned at this time?"

"I owe lots of money to my travel agent," he replied.

I thought that remark to be very funny at the time.

That was the last conversation we had. Whenever we saw one another, Shlomo would say to me, "My holy Kohen friend, Rabbi Joe, bless me and I'll bless you back." Typically, he would place his head on my shoulder for my blessing, and I'd smell the familiar scent on his beard. He'd then place his hands on my head and bless me in return.

When I think back to our last encounter in the summer of 1994, I wonder to what degree he was conscious of what was going on. What premonitions did he have? He was noticeably concerned. It was a serious conversation. He had a pacemaker that needed to be adjusted. He was tired and in need of a good, long rest, but he also had a grueling schedule of performances calendared he wished to honor.

It was early in the morning in Jerusalem on October 20, 1994, when the phone rang. Awakened from a deep sleep, I jokingly said to the voice on the other end of the line, which I recognized as belonging to my dear friend, Rabbi Moshe Shur, "You were never good at math. It's 4 a.m."

"It's really bad news," he softly replied. "Shlomo passed away."

In the next several hours, the phone kept ringing. Calls came in from all over the world, calling to confirm the news.

"Can it be true? What happened? Surely there must be a mistake."

How could Shlomo die when there was so much he still wanted to do?

I recalled those late night walks in the Berkeley Marina with Barry Barkan and Shlomo after his sell-out performances, reminiscing about his trips to the Soviet Union and all the hidden Jews who came to hear him play. They came to him after his concerts asking, "Shlomo, now that I know I'm Jewish, what should I do next?" And Shlomo would encourage them to come for Shabbos and to come to Israel. Over the years, we met Soviet Jews who left Russia as a result of their encounter with the singing rabbi, who kindled a yearning for Shabbos and Yerushalayim in their souls.

"I've got to go back!" Shlomo would exclaim. "I met so many young people. I need to go back! *Gevaldt*, it's so deep!"

Shlomo visited the Soviet Union during the Communist regime. Years later, when I visited, people there still remembered the impact his clandestine concerts had on them. On one of those late nights, he had just come from Poland, where he met adults given up as babies into the hands of Polish peasants when their families were deported to the death camps.

Shlomo related that their non-Jewish, now aging, adoptive parents brought them to his concerts, saying, "I want you to see what a Jew looks like." Shlomo said that hundreds of hidden Jews are now finding out they were adopted and raised by non-Jews. They are finding out what happened to their parents. Told they are Jewish, they have no context for understanding what that is.

Shlomo told the story of one Polish Jew who came to him after a concert and said, "My parents just told me I am Jewish. They brought me to your concert. Now I need to know what to do next."

"Come for Shabbos," Shlomo said, extending a warm invitation.

After Shabbat, the man came to Shlomo again: "Now I know I am a Jew. Now I have seen what is Shabbos. Now what should I do?"

Some time later, as Shlomo and I drove to a *shiva* in the Givat Shaul neighborhood of Jerusalem, he was telling me that story. I stopped at a red light near a bus stop. Suddenly, Shlomo rolled down the window and began speaking with a young man.

"Who was that?" I asked Shlomo as we continued.

"Remember that story I was just telling you about the young Polish Jew? That was him! He made aliya! He got married and is a computer programmer. He lives in Pisgat Ze'ev."

## Arranging Reb Shlomo's Funeral

Shlomo's casket was to arrive the next morning, and we had no grave in which to bury him. Shlomo was a friend to our generation. He was a self-sacrificing person who personified *Mesirat HaNefesh*, a *tzaddik* who did more for *Am Yisrael*, for the whole world, and for each individual than anyone else I've ever met.

His final journey to his burial was left to Reb Mimi Feigelson, Yoni Gordis, and myself to arrange. We negotiated for a plot in an overfilled cemetery in Jerusalem's *Har HaMenuchot*. The cemetery is subdivided into competing areas controlled by different *chevra kaddishas*.

The official administrators of the cemetery insisted that there were no available gravesites left in the section where Shlomo's family graves were located. We disagreed, arguing that several potential spots could be found on the plot map. The caretakers insisted those spots were already spoken for. I noticed that beside the wall where the road is located, some space was available. All we'd have to do would be to remove a few old Italian cypress trees, and we'd have all the space we'd need. The map clearly showed the space was available. The managers refused to let us dig up the trees.

The plane bearing Shlomo's coffin and his mourners, including Neila and their daughters, would be arriving the next morning, and there was still no grave. At this point, we who were entrusted with making all the arrangements were frantic. Reb Mimi called Rav Lau, who was then the Chief Rabbi. Yoni and I called Mayor Olmert. They both assured us they would do what they could and were most helpful. In order to prepare the plot, the gravediggers would have to spend half a day removing the cypress trees. It was a legal plot.

Because of the large crowd, the funeral service was to be conducted in the parking lot. Arriving late (just as Shlomo usually did), his body came to rest at my feet, with the grieving family in tow. The atmosphere was one of shock. A large, communal cry went forth from the assembled crowd. Neila, Neshama, and Dari were hugging each other, weeping. It was a heart-breaking scene.

I introduced Chief Rabbi Yisrael Meir Lau, who eulogized Shlomo by first asking forgiveness from him on behalf of the People of Israel for failing to recognize Reb Shlomo's greatness during his lifetime.

The body was carried by his followers to its final resting place accompanied by *niggunim*. Much to our surprise, when we saw the trees still standing, we wondered what had happened to the plot we'd selected. It was "*gevaldt, mamash* a miracle!" — as Shlomo would have said. Somehow, the cemetery people had found an extra plot near Shlomo's brother and parents! The plot, between the grave of a Litvish Yid on one side and a Chasid on the other, was perfect! Yoni looked at me, and we both looked at Reb Mimi, and all three of us chuckled at the wondrous irony of it all.

As I looked at the throngs of people who gathered for Shlomo's funeral, people from all walks of life, religious, not religious, Jewish, non-Jewish, young, old, I wondered: how many of these people came to Israel because Shlomo had planted a seed of yearning in their hearts? Yearning for Shabbat, for *Yerushalayim,* for Israel.

We'll never know how many of the people all over the world that Shlomo hugged and spoke to had a life-altering experience that guided them in an unanticipated direction. People who made Shabbat the epicenter of their spiritual practice. People who made aliya to *Eretz Yisrael.* People whose faith was restored when they learned his melodies.

With gratitude to Reb Shlomo, this book is dedicated as a *"Nachdenk."* I only wish he were still walking among us, leading us in celebration, opening our hearts to the blessings of Shabbos, singing and dancing with us, wrapping us in his embrace, telling jokes, lifting us up like nobody else could. Only a *tzaddik* like Shlomo could touch people the way he did.

— *Yerushalayim, Ir HaKodesh,* 28 Sivan, 5776 / July 4, 2016

Memorial service for Reb Shlomo's 22nd *Yahrzeit*
http://youtu.be/Zp_U_-Mtrg0

# THEOLOGICAL /
# PHILOSOPHICAL

*Reb Shlomo accompanied by exalted musicians from the chevre, bring the Torah scroll down to congregants at the Eastern Ashkenazi Brodsky Synagogue, Kiev, Ukraine, January 1989.*

*In 1989, Reb Shlomo was blessed to be the first rabbi after perestroika whose travel to the former Soviet Union was sanctioned by the Russian government, allowing him to open the hearts of tens of thousands of Soviet Jews, who were inspired by 23 standing room only concerts.*

*Reb Shlomo then reignited the reading of Torah, obscured under Communism, in synagogues.*

*In an interview afterwards, the following edited quote was posted on Reb Shlomo Carlebach's blog:*

*"The spirituality of a Jew in the Soviet Union after 70 years of Communist rule is a miracle. You see, all the Jews there are immersed in assimilation, and they need a certain person in order to be brought close to Judaism. I come to them and I turn towards them in a very personal and straight way and I show them that I love them and want to bring them close to Yiddishkeit."*

*(Photo and text by Joan Roth)*

# Shlomo's Torah

by Rabbi Micha Odenheimer

ON A WINTER'S EVENING IN THE EARLY 1990S, RABBI SHLOMO Carlebach, in his late sixties, wearing a pacemaker that had been implanted in his heart a few years earlier, arrived at Ben-Gurion airport and picked up two heavy suitcases which held a few items of clothing, some vitamin pills, a bottle or two of cologne, and dozens of "*sefarim*" — volumes of Talmud and commentaries, Hasidism and Kabbalah. Wherever he travelled — and he was always travelling — Shlomo, as he liked to be known, carried *sefarim.* Though arriving from South Africa, where he had spent three grueling days giving concerts, visiting schools, synagogues of all denominations, and community centers, Shlomo's night was just beginning. From the airport, he rode in a taxi to a concert in Beit Shemesh, where he took the stage and moved the crowd to ecstatic dancing, weaving stories and spiritual encouragement between the songs. The show ended at 9:30, and after a half hour or so of greeting people, he rode to Jerusalem, to the home of Yehoshua and Emuna Witt in Nachlaot, arriving at 10:30. Packed into the Witt's cavernous home were more than a hundred "Shlomo *hevre*," a ragtag group of hippies, yeshiva *bachrim*, university students, and spiritual seekers of all kinds who had heard, by word of mouth, that there would be a learning at the Witt's that night. By 11:00 Shlomo was strumming his guitar, singing with the crowd, and, eventually, demanding silence, beginning to teach. The words poured out of him, hypnotic and uplifting. Couched in simple language, using everyday situations to dramatize and explain profound concepts, Shlomo taught his rapt audience until 2 in the morning. He still was not finished. With a smaller group of disciples, he took another taxi to what he called "the Holy Wall," there swaying with longing in the early morning air before finally retreating toward his hotel room. At the guard house on the way out, one of soldiers stationed there accosted him: "Shlomo, play us a song," and so he did, taking the guitar out of its case, playing one more song for a lonely soldier at 3 a.m.

Shlomo is rightfully famous for the post-holocaust revolution in Jewish music that he almost singlehandedly catalyzed. For me, however, and for hundreds, if not thousands of those who found him a source of living waters, it was his Torah, transmitted in humble settings like the Witt household, free to one and all, that fed us with hope and touched us in places inside ourselves that we did not even know existed. Shlomo's Torah is the least-known aspect of his legacy so far. But his distinctive, unmistakable teachings may yet become recognized as one of the most profound contributions to Judaism and world spirituality in the second half of the 20th century.

For this to happen, several things must occur. First of all, the primary format through which Shlomo taught — teaching sessions that lasted for two hours or more — must be transcribed and made available to scholars and seekers. While highly edited nuggets of Shlomo Torah have been published in a dozen or more books and pamphlets, and have the advantage of being easily digestible, they are no substitute for transcripts of entire teachings. Thankfully, an archives project has preserved thousands of hours of audio and videotape of Shlomo's teachings. The importance of listening to full tapes or transcripts is that, although his style might seem associative, even rambling, mixing stories with parables and interspersed with songs, closer examination demonstrates that Shlomo developed closely argued themes in his learning sessions, returning over and over again with every new turn in order to reveal deeper and more complex insights. More than that: Shlomo said that the difference between the head and the heart is that the head never thinks the same thought twice, thoughts are always moving, always changing, while the heart, deep inside, thinks one thing for an entire lifetime. My intuition is that Shlomo's Torah, while saying many things, had a coherent and singular message at its heart. Articulating that message in our own language is a task whose time has come.

Shlomo's Torah transported listeners emotionally and imaginatively, connecting them to inner states of longing and healing — to a different state of being. This state, however, was not necessarily conducive to systematic analysis: even Shlomo's closest disciples might be hard-pressed to trace his thought process in words. In his absence, though, it seems to me that it is now necessary to do just that — to begin to try to unpack Shlomo's message, to hold it, as he held it in his person.

This is not a task to be completed in a single essay or even by one person. But I would like to make a modest attempt to begin to unearth a few of Shlomo's main themes, using transcripts from several teachings, while keeping in mind the dangers involved in rephrasing, categorizing, and summarizing Shlomo's language and interpretations, thus risking disconnecting them from the rich resonance of their place within the web of tradition.

The first axiom I would like to put forward is that Shlomo's teachings, at their heart, are about human transformation. What kind of transformation? In one of his teachings Shlomo says that exile is when our life is not connected to our *neshama*. One way of articulating the transformation I sense as being at the core of Shlomo's teaching means (re) creating this connection. I must add as well that Shlomo never used the word transformation as far as I know; he had his own symbolic vo-cabulary. I am using the word in order to try in some way to translate the poetics of Shlomo's Torah by expressing it in another language; this is an exercise in interpretation and understanding, an explora-tion. To me the word "transformation," which I am sure is inadequate in other ways, indicates a spiritual metamorphosis, the reaching of a higher state of being that expresses itself both in the inner life of the person as well as in her relationship to others.

This metamorphosis is necessary because human beings are often lost, disconnected, exiled, distracted. "When God called each creature into being," I once heard Shlomo teach, "He did it with a special melody — a unique melody for each created being. And every moment, each being is still hearing that melody. Humans are the only creatures in G-d's creation that can cease to hear the melody through which G-d called them into being." Shlomo sometimes expresses this state as something inborn, a brokenness that is part of one's inner structure or state of being:

> Every person has something wrong with them inside. This is why we are in the world, because if I would be complete, then I wouldn't have to be in this world. So basically, this world is a hospital. This world is where I fix myself. The truth is that even after I fixed every *aveira* (sin) I did since I was born, I am still not fixed, because there is something deep, deep inside of me, which needs fixing.

Shlomo also addresses the fixing we need to go through and the long path human beings have to follow, including the pain we must endure, in contrast to G-d's other creatures, due to a lack of understanding of why we are in this world.

> You know, friends, imagine I would come down from Mars and I would hear that there are creatures in the world that

are just G-d's creatures and then there is a creature which is called man who is G-d's image. So I would say most probably the creatures that are just created by G-d it takes them a long time till they know what they have to do. I would say an ox has to live hundreds, hundreds of years until an ox knows exactly how to be an ox. A human being, since he's G-d's image, right away the first day we know exactly what we have to do. It's the other way around. A cute little ox, it has no problems right? You know I always say I've never seen an ox going to a psychiatrist. I'm having an identity crisis, you know. I always wanted to be a cow and now...it's hard on me...I have a twin sister, a cow, and she's always in my way. Anyway, *l'chaim*. Isn't it crazy? We're in God's image and it takes us so long, so long to find out what we are supposed to be...and not only that — you have to go through so much pain.

Deep inside of us, there is a wellspring from which the answers can come, but until we "reach that level," the inner knowledge that awaits us remains totally unconscious. Our conscious mind is clueless, and this is expressed strongly through our confusing array of desires.

G-d has carved something into us something so deep, so deep. But you know, before you reach that level...you know, friends, sometimes it can take a lifetime until I know what G-d has carved into me.... Most of us don't have the faintest idea of what we really want. We want a thousand things, but we *mamash* don't know. We don't know what we really want.

Our "wanting a thousand things" is a kind of desperate flailing about that is the result of a deep, unconscious need that lies at the root of our desires. *You know what I really want deep inside? I am missing so much that my soul should be full. You know, friends, what the most heartbreaking thing in the world is? When my soul is empty, I want to fill it with being stupid. What I want to fill it with makes my soul even more empty. What is the depths of life? That I'm here in this world to fill my heart. I have to fill my heart with something. I don't want my soul to be empty.*

By its very nature, what we truly want is unknowable until we reach a higher level of development. Thus it is not our conscious mind that creates spiritual growth, but rather our connection to our subconscious — to that which G-d has "carved into us so deep." When we have gone through a deep spiritual process, the end result, as we will see, is that we know what we truly want; we have reached the divinity that G-d has carved deep inside of us. But Shlomo underlines and emphasizes that we can't reach there only through our conscious decisions; of course, these are important, but they don't determine who we really are. The juxtaposition between the Tree of Good and Evil and the Tree of Life in the Garden of Eden story is a major theme in Hasidic thought beginning with the Baal Shem Tov and is a major axis for Shlomo's thought. Shlomo identifies conscious judgment with the Tree of Knowledge and goes far in limiting the significance of consciousness, even to the extent of saying that you can "consciously" do everything right your entire life and still be missing life's essence:

> Who are the people who have some kind of holy fragrance, paradise, right? Paradise fragrance does not come from good deeds. You know I can do right my whole life and I still don't have a good smell. And sometimes there are people who do everything wrong. And they have this kind of a holy smell, some kind of holy fragrance about them, right? Where's it coming from? It doesn't come from the Tree of Knowledge. It's coming from the deepest, unconscious, subconscious deepest deepest depths in the world. Take a piece of meat. It looks like meat, and it is meat. And it smells so bad. You know what's missing? There is no life in it anymore. Life is not a thing you

can see with your eyes. I cannot see G-d; I cannot see life. I can smell it. Life is something so deep. You know what life is? Life is this deepest, deepest depths.

How does Shlomo describe the end result of the transformational journey that he describes us as struggling to reach? This is a broad and multidimensional subject for future investigation of Shlomo's legacy, and I can only begin here with a description or two, a note or two, in what I am certain will prove to be a complex and profound melody. One way in which Shlomo describes the transformed individual is in the unity of desire and action in which there is no need for contemplation of choice because the will to do good in the world has reached a virtually instinctive level. When you are in this state of being, you do good deeds not out of duty, not because you have to, but because you want to with all your heart. Since there is no distance between your desire and the right thing to do, there is also no hesitation, as Shlomo says, "*Anything I do because I have to takes me one second to do it,*" but even this tiny second indicates distance, alienation.

Shlomo makes this idea come alive through a parable:

> You know, all our children should be well. Imagine, G-d forbid, *chas veshalom,* it should never happen, our children, *chas veshalom,* are drowning. It's clear to me that I have to jump in. It's on the level that *mamash* I don't know anything. On the level of *neshikene meneshikot pihu* — kiss me with the kisses of your mouth. It's beyond me...to jump in for my children doesn't come from my consciousness. It's not thinking. Deeper than thinking. Deeper than knowing.

Shlomo compares the actions of someone who has moved towards spiritual transformation, or, in language taken from the teaching quoted earlier, one who has reached within himself deeply enough to touch *what G-d has carved into him* to a parent jumping into the ocean to save his drowning child — there is no need for thought or decision making, no distance between personal desire and acts of goodness. His motivation comes from what Shlomo describes as consciousness's twin, what he calls "super-consciousness." It is significant, and I think a key element of Shlomo's teaching, that this super-consciousness is not abstract or disembodied, but, to the contrary, it is compared to something deeply personal — the love of a parent for a child. Speaking of the astrological sign of the twins, mentioned in the *Sefer Yetzirah* as the sign of the month of Sivan, when the Torah was given, Shlomo says:

> The twins are my consciousness and my super-consciousness, *mamash* like I told you to jump in for my children doesn't come from my consciousness. I'm not thinking. Deeper than thinking, deeper than knowing. It touches something so deep inside of me....

In another Torah, Shlomo describes Avraham Avinu (Abraham our forefather) as having achieved this super-conscious level: *The Gemorah says that Avraham Avinu had no Torah, but his very bones were teaching him...it was deeper than choice. It was not that he learned and he thought he understood....*

In these teachings, and many others, Shlomo seems to break down the polarity between conscious knowing and choice and the subconscious by describing a state that is "deeper than choice," something that is coming from our "very bones."

In another elaborately developed teaching, Shlomo describes this super-consciousness in another way, and from a different angle. Here he breaks down another opposition — that between giving and receiving. He begins with a *mashal* about soup:

And here I want you to open your hearts. You know the difference between eating soup in a restaurant or eating soup...I'm coming to somebody she *mamash* made soup for me with so much love and [she gives] it to me. We've learned it a thousand times.

It's very simple. The deepest question is: Are you receiving the outside of the soup or the inside of the soup? Is it *mamash* **your** soup or just soup. If I go to a restaurant and I pay five dollars for a plate of soup, it's not really my soup. I ate it and I paid for it. If someone loves me very much and they are giving me soup, it is *mamash* my soup. And you know, friends, when someone gives me soup, and it's *mamash* my soup, basically then I don't need anything anymore. It's so good. It's so good. So you hear, friends, the same way, the way God gives us, sometimes God gives you just soup, right, and you don't have it, and then you are unfulfilled; you are empty and you are crying, "I need more." And sometimes God gives you something and it's so deep, it's so deep.

Shlomo goes on to say that the problem with misers is not that they can't give; it's that they have never received "the inside of the soup," so to speak. Since they don't really have what they have, they can't give it. This is the first step in Shlomo's Torah. The second step is to say that, as important as it is to give, there are some things which we have no right to give away. *"The Rizhiner says there is such a thing that I'm giving something to you and then it's yours. And if it's yours, you could do with it what you want. And there is something so deep, I'm still in the middle of giving it to you...the giving never finishes."*

As in many of his Torahs, Shlomo sets up a polarity only to unify it. First he teaches that you can truly give only once you have really received the inside of what you have been given. But the most personal of gifts you can never give away because they are always in the process of being given — *"I'm in the middle of giving it to you, the giving never finishes."* This is a deeper form of receiving. Quoting the Rizhiner Rebbe, Shlomo says: *"Basically in order to serve G-d there has to be two levels. There has to be one level that you receive from G-d and you give it over to the world. But the deepest depths is if you receive from G-d that which I can't give it away. I can't."* This teaching is part of a much longer discourse, at the end of which there is a final twist: it is possible to achieve an even higher form of giving, in which you are able to give away what is still in the middle of being given, because you are receiving and giving at the same time:

> "You know I can give everything away, but I can't give my breath away. I want you to open your hearts in the deepest way. Do you know, *chas veshalom,* somebody is dead, and I say 'Hey brother, don't die yet, *khop nisht,* you know, take your time, I'm giving you my breath.' But I want you to open your hearts. How did [Elisha] the Prophet revive the...dead person? He *mamash* put his mouth to him and gave him his breath. This is awesome. You know what the deepest reviving of the dead is? That I am giving you over the deepest, deepest depths that cannot be given even. And the way I am giving it over to you, it is not on the level of giving. I am giving it to you and then it is yours. Remember, I told you before there's a certain giving, it's always mine and while I'm giving it's still mine, while you have it it's still mine.... I want you to know the deepest depths. You know when you kiss somebody, you know what you do? I'm putting my mouth on you. I'm giving you nothing, right? But you know what I'm telling you? I love you so much I could revive you with my mouth. You have to be very close for that. I can give everybody a dollar. I [can] buy everybody a house. I can give you a car. But to give you my breath, to give you

that deepest depths which I cannot give away. I can't. And yet I can.

Towards the very end of this teaching, Shlomo, in a way that is characteristic of his thought, brings us back to very basic and simple interpersonal experience, something we all know about: friendship. *"You know what the deepest depths of friendship is? Not someone who tells you [you] did right or wrong. The greatest friendship in the world is if you can revive someone. Mamash revive somebody. And reviving somebody is not by telling them what [to] do or not to do. You know it's a very little holy fragrance...."*

Here it seems to me that Shlomo is talking from his own experience and about his own aspirations. Shlomo wishes to teach a Torah that can revive us — can make us, as individuals, and the Jewish tradition as a whole, fully alive again. This is the Torah of transformation, the Torah that is not about right and wrong, about conscious decisions, but about integrating our conscious and subconscious, receiving and giving, duty and desire. How do we do this? Does Shlomo provide a map or a set of instructions? I believe that he does.

I believe that encoded within the thousands of hours of teachings that have blessedly been preserved on tape and digitized, we will find not only a vision of human transformation but a path for getting there — a path that is not a path, but a path none the less. Here is one hint, I think, at the form this path takes: Shlomo asks, in one learning session, "How do we cleanse our heart from anger?" — a fundamental question for him, a foundation of his path in Hasidism. "You can decide a million times to do it, but it won't help," he says. "The only thing you can do is at the moment you are getting angry, when your anger is so powerful you don't see any way to stop it, and then you remember, and from somewhere high above, from a place you can't even reach, from your superconscious-unconscious somehow you get the strength to be a little bit less angry.... You can only do it at that moment." You can't do it consciously. That's why it's a path that is not a path. The only thing we can do is to open ourselves, through our intention and preparation, our readiness at the moment of testing, for the gift of cleansing and transformation that comes through our subconscious from above.

I was privileged to see Shlomo embody this ideal. Though surrounded by throngs of needy souls, demanding his love and attention, I never saw him lose his temper in a personal way. Instead, his aura created a loving space, a space of inspiration and aspiration to holiness, for all that were in his presence. I believe that through the effort to understand the hidden code, the one thought, running through his Torah, we can recreate that space and activate that presence that is already within us.

Reb Shlomo tells the story of the blind Chazan in Krakow: http://youtu.be/Bs1tZ7SFntM

# The Existential Challenge of Brokenness: Principles in the Thought of Reb Shlomo Carlebach

by Rute Yair-Nussbaum

This essay is based on an article published in Hebrew in the Journal *Eretz Aheret* in 2008. It is not an academic paper, but rather a collection of thoughts gathered throughout many years. A lot has changed since this article came out. I grew, we all grew, Shlomo grew, too. — R. Y-N.

The editors of the journal prefaced my article with the following paragraph:

**Over the years, people have been exposed to the music of R' Shlomo Carlebach and to his sweet "torahs," nicely wrapped for the public's convenience. Yet many don't know that his Torah teachings constitute a viable theology. His student, Rute Yair-Nussbaum, presents some theological dimensions of his teachings.**

ONCE A MAN CAME TO R. MENACHEM MENDEL, THE REBBE OF KOTZK (known as the "Kotzker"), and asked to see his synagogue. He had heard much about the Kotzker and wanted to see him for himself. The Kotzker agreed to the visit. When the man came into the synagogue he looked to the right, looked to the left, and ran directly to the Kotzker in shock. "Rebbe! Rebbe! What's going on in your synagogue? A shirt's tossed in one corner, a pair of shoes in another. Bags are strewn all over the place — what is this? Is this what you call a synagogue?"

The Kotzker listened, and said, "I don't know if this is what you call a synagogue, but I do know that this is what I call a home. And I want everyone to feel at home."

What does it mean to be "at home"?

Anyone who knows even a little about Kotzk Hassidism knows that being at home does not just mean being in a place where I can be myself. It means being in a place where I can go beyond myself, beyond my recognized inner borders. "Home" is a place where I can touch upon my infinity.

Shlomo — who asked his students to call him simply by his first name — did not just teach the Torah of the "home," in all of its senses, but how to be at home in the "home," how to live with this "beyondness" that he spoke of so much. In the following pages I will try to relate to what may be seen as the disorder and inconsistency in the world of Shlomo Carlebach. I will attempt to frame its context and explain some of its meaning.

## The Hidden Torah

Anyone attempting to say something about the Torah (the spiritual teachings) of Shlomo Carlebach inevitably hesitates. How can one speak about his Torah? I feel a great responsibility in this regard because his Torah, unlike other branches of his life's work, is the least well known.

People have been exposed to the *niggunim* (Jewish melodies) that have passed through him, to the stories that he passed on, and to the sweet "torahs" that were packaged for our convenience whether in sound bites or in larger formats. And yet, the fact that his teachings constitute a viable theology is still not common knowledge, and for this reason his theology remains largely unknown. Personally, this has always caused me great pain.

I will address the following points in Shlomo's thought, just a few of so many that I would like to expand on:

Humor, control, intuition, the breaking of dichotomies, unpredictability, the holocaust, and the oral Torah.

I will not relate to the exceptional love Shlomo carried within him, nor to how, for him, having an open heart was the highest level of "*hachnasat orchim*" (welcoming guests). Similarly, I will not dwell at length here about the experience of learning with Shlomo, yet I will tell of the prism through which I experienced Shlomo's torah. I am aware of the fact that there are themes that I emphasize that are less significant to people from backgrounds different from mine. It is also clear to me that the music of my religious Zionist education is playing in the background.

## Humor is a plurality of perspectives

Humor is not the ability to tell jokes or the ability to laugh at them (regardless of the fact that Shlomo was a very funny man and loved a good laugh). Humor is the ability to deeply internalize the principle of multiple perspectives.

Imagine a few people sitting in a room and looking at a coffee mug. I see the mug from my own perspective, and for me this perspective is one hundred percent reality. It is difficult for me to imagine the same mug from another perspective when my own is predominant, and yet, as it appears to me, this is precisely the basis of humor. It is the ability to internalize the fact that even though we all see the same mug, still, everyone in the room sees it from a different perspective, which creates a different reality for each person. There are endless perspectives from which we can see this mug — this reality.

For the sake of clarity, let's look at the details. If there are x number of perspectives, you could say, "Fine, I will sit and examine all of the perspectives. In this way I will become both educated and a pluralist." The problem is — there are endless perspectives and you can't conquer infinity. Here you begin to undergo a complicated inner process.

From Shlomo I learned that the development of this sense, this consciousness, is called humor, and it is none other than the Holy of Holies. In my estimation, he learned it from his master, R. Mordechai Yosef Leiner, the Rebbe of Ishbitz (commonly known as the "Ishbitzer"). One can see how this humor emerges from every page of the Ishbitzer's central work, the *Mei HaShiloah*.

If you grew up with the assumption that Esau was evil and Jacob was good, that Korah was wicked and Zimri was a sinner, open up the *Mei HaShiloah* and you will completely re-evaluate your assumptions. Black will no longer be so black, and white will no longer be so white. You will go back and re-examine many truths that you had regarded as obvious. The Ishbitzer's teachings need not destroy all you hold as precious or lead you into anarchy. Although one might be tempted to use the Ishbitzer toward these ends, this is not at all the Ishbitzer's intention. And still, whosoever internalizes these "torahs of humor," will inevitably go through a period of spiritual turmoil, which brings us to the next point, that of control.

## Control

One of the deepest teachings of Reb Shlomo can be summarized in four words: "What do we know?"

The modern world is obsessed with the notion of control. It is the central issue in all walks of modern life. Technological advances have created an external form of control. Social sciences and the psychological establishment have created another, more internal one. It pumps into us the feeling that we can do everything. This notion has been discussed, and we need not dwell on it here. But the question is, "What do we do when we feel out of control?" Here we tend to get a little lost, and feelings of anger and betrayal emerge and take over.

I would like to point to some expressions of Shlomo's relationship to control:

*1. Intuition*: In my estimation, one factor that expresses Shlomo's relationship with control is his position on intuition. Shlomo, again on the heels of the Ishbitzer and his dynasty, viewed intuition as a holy device that affords us a direct and immediate connection with the Holy One, blessed be He. With intuition, we need no agents, go-betweens, or rabbis.

The Ishbitzer never uses the modern term "intuition," but in Ishbitz theology, at the end of the process of *Berur* or clarification, when this power is distilled and it becomes clear that it is rooted in a holy source, intuition is synonymous with the term he uses, *ratzon Hashem,* or God's will. This is the inner voice, the voice of the inner clarification, a pure clarification of the Divine source of human desires untainted by external agendas. It is this voice that caused various biblical characters to act in unexpected or even forbidden ways. This was only because it was clear to them that God chose to bypass the accepted *Halacha* and to speak to them in the here and now. Regarding this, the Ishbitzer quotes Psalm 119, "It is a time to do for God, they have made your Torah void," a kind of inner call where man receives a personal verdict from above. This was the teaching of the Ishbitzer, and this was the teaching of Shlomo. As I see it, this is also how he led his life.

In the Orthodox world, at least in the Orthodox world I grew up in, intuition was considered a threat. It was a power that represented a lack of control, a lack of borders. Personally, I am relieved that there has been a significant change in Orthodox circles regarding intuition. Nowadays it is more accepted that people don't need to go to a rabbi to reveal to them what their intuition is telling them.

*2. Unpredictability*: One of Shlomo's main characteristics, and not just in his torah, was his unpredictability — you simply couldn't predict what he would say at any given moment (further emphasizing the lack of control). This unpredictability was at times perplexing and threatening. However, his unpredictability was an essential part of his torah, and if anything, the dis-ease it sometimes engendered only proved how unusual it was. Following his passing and the appropriation of his legacy by various groups, this hidden aspect of Shlomo was the first thing that was stripped from him. In my experience this represented an attempt, even if not conscious, to "control" Shlomo.

*3. T'fila (prayer)*: The contraction of Shlomo's figure after he died can be felt in other realms as well, such as the realm of *T'fila*. In Israel, they're called "*minyanei Carlebach*." They're "cute" as Shlomo would have said, but they're not necessarily "Shlomo." I am grateful that these *minyanim* exist, and know they serve a real need (mine too!), but with trepidation, I dare say that what stood at the heart of *T'fila* apropos Shlomo, does not necessarily find its true expression in some of these gatherings. Shlomo viewed prayer as a journey whose end is unknown. How will we embark? Where will we land? Will we fly high, or maybe fall? The nature of the experience is in the unknown and the willingness to let go of the reins. Sometimes prayer is scratched, mumbled, and squeaky. At other times it is smooth and seemingly perfect. The heart of the matter of prayer is not in its form, Shlomo's "*nusach*" and the way it sounds, but rather in the way the form serves the prayer. Perfect *Tfila* is not necessarily beautiful *T'fila*, but the occasion of *T'fila* itself: did you actually embark on a journey?

**4. *Politics:*** Shlomo has often been claimed by various political agendas. At times he is painted as a right-wing radical, talking all day about Jews being the chosen people and how we are a light unto the nations. At others he is painted as a leftist, going on and on about freedom and peace, love and bliss, and other catchphrases from the sixties.

As someone who accompanied him on visits to both Hevron and Tel Aviv, I know that he was connected to both sides. These truths were not compartmentalized in Shlomo — each coming out in a different context. Rather, the opposing truths coexisted, taking us back to the torah of humor. In my very depths I live with polar opposites that exist at once, at all times. If we only break the dichotomy, it will reveal that at its essence there need not be any contradiction.

These are a few expressions of how the theme of control threads its way through the fabric of Shlomo. In my view, the centrality of this theme in Shlomo's thought stems from the mark that the *Shoah* left on his soul.

## The *Shoah* and the Obligation to Change

Shlomo was far less interested in graveyards than in living human beings. For this reason, when he visited Poland and Russia, he went to meet the people, and not to visit monuments and graves. I am specifically mentioning this *vis-a-vis* the notion of control because of the common theme — in death nothing is dynamic, the keys are all in the hands of the living to decide whom to remember, what to remember, and how to remember. Basically, all you are doing when dealing with the dead is erecting memorial stones. In contrast, to engage with the living is far more complicated. Where will this engagement take me? What challenges will I face?

Shlomo was the only rabbi I ever met whose confrontation with the *Shoah* was not just popular, or historic, but as part of a theological structure that is relevant in the here and now. It was a confrontation that required us to both learn the Torah differently, and to act differently, on a daily basis.

Allow me to return to the subject of Hevron/Tel Aviv. On the one hand, be completely at home as a member of the chosen people and a light unto the nations. Deeply root yourself in being that, and live in it. And on the other hand, simultaneously, be completely at home in the world of total equality, the world of humanistic values and total human dignity.

For me, as a Zionist who grew up in the chosen tradition, and as a daughter of a holocaust survivor, the two seemed to be mutually exclusive. It seems to me that for this very reason I was afraid to go with him to Poland for the first time, even though he tried to convince me, and many others, to accompany him. I felt that the intense emotions I would have felt there would have caused me to break many of the boundaries that I had grown up depending on, and I didn't even know I had grown up depending on them until I understood that it could be different.

Shlomo's statements demanded a theological resolution. It may be mentioned that when we were growing up, I for one don't remember anyone who demanded such a fundamental change in our religious lives as a result of the *Shoah*, not in grade school, *ulpana*, or B'nei Akiva. So how do we reconcile "Chosenness" and separateness from the world with normality and involvement in the world? Shlomo's answer, as I see it, is that all of humanity is holy (not equal, as in other visions, but holy). Everyone was created in the image of God and is holy, and this requires us to regard everyone as "a true brother."

Furthermore, the *Shoah* requires that we completely overturn the system.

Love becomes, in the world of Shlomo, the answer to meaninglessness. Shlomo taught complete discourses on the subject of love. What does love solve? How does love fix? How living a deep life demands love, and how it dissolves accepted notions of "good" and "evil." Suddenly you understand that in most cases there is no good or evil, but rather "inside," and "outside."

According to Shlomo, the greatest sin in our lifetime is living a shallow life. After the *Shoah*, we cannot allow ourselves to lead a shallow existence, and in particular, after the *Shoah*, the Torah needs to be explained and interpreted all over again. It is now inconceivable that a broken person could approach the Torah and not find something new in it that he did not notice beforehand, something that allows him to emerge from his darkness. Brokenness demands rectification — "fixing."

This fundamental idea, that all humanity is holy, turns out to be one of Shlomo's fundamental principles in various relations, and not just in the obvious one, our relations with non-Jews.

I would like to mention two matters that ostensibly are not connected to the *Shoah*, yet whose development in Shlomo's teachings I consider to be connected to it.

## Women and God

With all of the options that have opened up before women, the place that I have felt the most whole, as a woman in the world of Jewish prayer, was with Shlomo in the synagogue.

For years I have experienced a feeling that, against my wishes, I am trapped by labels. If I choose to do one thing, then I am making one kind of statement, and if I choose not to do it, I am making a different kind of statement. It's a maze of stickers with no exit, because whatever you do or don't do will be identified as a political statement, even if you are innocent of it, or simply tired of it. This was all irrelevant to Shlomo. Our connection as Jews was so much greater than the sum total of all the parts that made up our identity. It followed naturally that we saw each other's essence — not through the "garment" in which God had dressed us, male or female, and all the more so, not through the more external garment of pretty or ugly, successful or not. Rather, we saw straight down to the bone. It was there, after we had peeled away layer after layer of differences, that we were truly all the same. We were all created in the image of God; we were all connected to God. If I was created in the image of God, it must mean that you were, too. Hence, it is natural to give real space to all, men and women alike.

Critics may regard this as trivial, yet it was immediately felt by anyone who was present while davening with Shlomo or with him at any other religious event. The various women whom I sat next to in Shlomo's shul, from the ultra-Orthodox to the women with rabbinic ordination, always appeared to me as feeling completely at home and knowing that their contribution to the prayer was unique and essential. I think that the intensity that we felt in this regard — all people deserve space since all people are holy — was connected to the *Shoah* and the mark that it left on Shlomo.

## Confrontation and Conflict

Shlomo consistently refused to enter into arguments and withdrew from all controversy. This attitude didn't flow from an unwillingness to stand on principle, but rather from his tenacious allegiance to one principle: the obligation to elevate every person.

The fact that every person is essentially holy is meaningful not just before God, but also before mankind. I am holy means that you are holy. Just because I am connected to the truth does not mean I need to reveal the ways I think you are not. On a deeper level, every person's holiness means that at some level they are connected to the truth, even if it is not apparent to me personally.

For Shlomo, empowering people to love, honor, and believe in themselves was no less than a mission. He wanted to show everyone the good that was inside them. The core question was whether people are happy and realize the good within themselves, able to touch the holiness within, or whether the degradation and insult they have suffered has caused them to descend into darkness. Shlomo could not pass by a downtrodden person without turning over worlds to raise his spirits.

One practical way I saw Shlomo deal with confrontation was to consider that if someone says something you disagree with, or shares a word of Torah that disturbs you, then don't confront him as your opponent. Simply nod your head. Don't insult him, but rather seek areas of commonality. The danger of putting someone down as a result of confrontation, as I understand it, was inconceivable to Shlomo after the experience of the *Shoah*.

Beyond the fact that this approach requires great self-assurance, since some might criticize it as being "spineless" (*i.e.,* "if you know the truth, then fight for it!"), this approach is spiritually demanding, and my understanding is that it is a moral position rooted in theology. Our task is to bring the world to a better place, and it can only be done by elevating each individual's connection to the other.

The *Shoah* left the world destroyed. The world was broken, souls were crushed. The Six Million were burned deep into Shlomo's consciousness where they directed him to see the good and the beautiful and at times seemed to leave him no choice but to follow unconventional paths. In my view, their tremendous presence softened any tendency to be pulled into controversy.

The few times I saw Shlomo lose his balance, as it were, getting angry or even furious, were when the rules of the game changed and the person before him was revealed to be disingenuous, presenting himself in one way and yet truly being something else. This form of deceit is called by different names in Hasidic writings. One code word is "Amalek," and when Shlomo confronted a representative of Amalek, he started operating on a completely different inner level.

Once, at a "learning," a gathering with Shlomo, we were joined by a group of American tourists. They took part in the learning, and after certain members of our group were given the chance to speak words of Torah or sing near the end of the session, the Americans also asked to speak. After a few words of Torah and a few laughs, Jesus made an appearance in their words of Torah. At first it was just a small appearance which somewhat surprised us, and I remember the perplexed and uncomfortable expressions going around our group. Soon it became clear that this was a group of Jews for Jesus. I never saw Shlomo explode as he did then. He was furious, told them to leave, and had trouble calming down for a long time after. Amalek, as a metaphor, knows how to make you feel at home enough with him that you start to shed various layers of instinctive protection. You are led to believe that with him you can be completely vulnerable. On that night Shlomo encountered a form of Amalek, and I mention this in order to show that even Shlomo felt that certain circumstances demanded confrontation.

## Breaking the Dichotomy

Shlomo didn't speak the language of dichotomies that the religious world has become so expert in: intellect versus feeling (for instance, as embodied in Maimonides versus the Kuzari), soul versus body, *hesed* versus *gevurah*, good/*tzaddik* versus evil/*rasha,* and so forth.

We need only look at our learning institutions (at least as they were in my day) in order to consider the dominance of dichotomies in the religious world. Yeshivas were divided into "intellectual" yeshivas and "emotional" ones, and these divisions influenced all aspects of religious life.

Shlomo felt at home with different approaches not because he was "post-dichotomy," nor because he was "pre-dichotomy." He simply wasn't there! All of these divisions and package deals were simply irrelevant to him. Here we must note that the nickname he was given, "the dancing Rabbi," came from a perspective of dichotomy, and ruled out an appreciation of his Torah. If he dances, it must be that he has no depth, because a man with a serious world-view and theology doesn't dance! One man teaches and another man dances. Shlomo remained unaffected by such divisions. He spoke of Maimonides with the same closeness as he spoke of the Ishbitzer, and he developed new ideas about both of them. For someone like me, whose life struggle has been to negate these dichotomies, to feel that there need not be any contradiction between my being completely at home in the world of Hasidism, portrayed as a world of "feeling," and my being completely at home in the world of logical thought and Maimonides, even ardently loving it — this was deeply redemptive. Some of us live in both these worlds and do not understand the obsessive need to erect barriers between them. Shlomo enabled us to finally be able to experience a truly deep, organic, three-dimensional experience, not only in life, but also in the Torah.

In my view, Shlomo was the first to break this dichotomy and thus expand borders. He freed that which was jammed, allowing flow from one side to the other in many different arenas, not just from intellect to emotion. Here are three examples:

**1) Moment and Eternity.**

With Shlomo, "living the moment" never contradicted living connected to eternity, as we might view it in a dichotomous world. Shlomo lived the Torah of the moment and the Torah of eternity at the same time.

Shlomo's connection to the moment was influenced by the power of the verse, "It is a time to do for God; they have made Your Torah void." (*Tehillim*, 119:126) It may be necessary to go outside of halachic and cultural norms in order to save the Torah and the culture. He spoke of this at length. Shlomo was quite critical of the rabbinic establishment whose members often were dealing with trivial matters at times when Jews were losing all connection to Judaism. He spoke about this with fire and a broken heart.

He identified with the Torah of the moment, but was totally oriented to the Torah of eternity. He lived in the moment and understood the urgent need to be in the present: What is our holy intuition telling us? What is God's voice in the present? The Torah of the moment consists of knowing how to connect with people in every place, in every situation, even when the situation is as far away as one can imagine. And nevertheless, he was deeply cast in the Torah of eternity. His entire vitality and life force flowed from that source. He was deeply bound to anyone who was rooted in the Jewish *Mesorah*, and had a special emotional connection to those who claim to be the upholders of the eternal Jewish Tradition in our generation, the Haredi (Ultra-Orthodox) world in which he was raised.

I feel that this is also one of the sources of his terrible loneliness. People who understood and accepted him — and I am referring to the past when he was not accepted as he is today — were usually people who identified with the moment. Yet during his whole life, Shlomo yearned to be accepted by those who are considered to represent "eternity" in this world (*i.e.*, the Haredi world).

This conflict came up in many different situations, and in this respect Shlomo was a tragic figure who suffered intensely.

Whenever Shlomo came to Israel, even if he had just left a few days earlier, on the first night in Jerusalem we would go down to the Kotel after a long night of learning. Before we arrived with him, the rumors of his arrival had already spread through the city, and people had been waiting for him by the Kotel for hours until one or two in the morning. By the time he came there were tens or hundreds of young people gathered, mostly yeshiva students from the Hevron or Mir yeshivas. They all yearned to be with Shlomo, to pray with Shlomo — this picture is inscribed in my heart. The few women in the group stood behind the *mechitza* in the women's section and watched a surrealistic scene. It was a spot of white hair and in its middle a funny velvet yarmulke, either blue or azure — Shlomo — surrounded by a sea of black, rocking like a wave around that central point of color; praying, meditating, singing....

It was like this for a few hours until dawn broke, when, as in fairy tales, everyone disappeared, going back to their places and to the accepted attitude of their places towards Shlomo — a little disdain, a little elimination (it was then forbidden for yeshiva students even to play Shlomo's music in their dorm rooms, as I was told by a student of the Hevron yeshiva. Today it is difficult to imagine this happening because, as noted, so much has changed since he passed away). I remember well how I felt at that time. It was as if there was a shift from day people to night people. By day they scorn him, ban him, and by night they could go out of their caves, look right and left to make sure that there is no danger, and then be with Shlomo until a new dawn. Then another day breaks, and again they disappear into the distance, alienating him once again. I remember how even though we, his students, never disappeared, those yeshiva boys, representations of "eternity," so to speak, were a real source of longing for Shlomo.

To return to our subject, it isn't easy to live deeply in both worlds, the world of the moment and that of eternity. Part of the inability to fully grasp Shlomo stems from the inability to know when to characterize him using words of the "moment," and when using words of "eternity." Throughout the years, everyone who tried to turn Shlomo into a label for the moment or a label for eternity didn't understand that this dichotomy was just not relevant to him. He insisted in taking the moment on a journey to eternity, and also insisted in placing eternity in every moment.

### 2) Role Models

A second example of how Shlomo broke dichotomies was his choice of role models. Whom did he turn into a Rebbe? His role models came from different worlds. He was not just connected to the Ishbitzer and Rebbe Nachman, or to Rav Kook and all the great zaddikim he had introduced us to, but also to others, so different from him, as well (a social activist, a spiritual leader of a different religion, and so on).

This may sound obvious to someone who grew up rooted in a world of liberal values, but in the orthodox world of his time, this was a non-dichotomous stand, and sure enough, it carried its own sense of threat. For someone tired of rigid definitions, Shlomo's attitude to role models was liberating, and it allowed us to breathe in a different way. My role model doesn't need to look just like me, and I don't need to look exactly like him/her.

### 3) Relationship to sin

A third example of how Shlomo broke dichotomies was his unusual attitude toward sin.

To begin, I want to say that I feel like Shlomo wrote a whole new lexicon of key words, and gave all of them a completely new meaning, but the entry password into all of them, the password to crack them all open, is "*Ahava*" — love.

Consider Shlomo's language. His insistence, for instance, on switching the standard vocabulary of Yom Kippur from "sins" / *avonot* — to "mistakes" / *ta'uyot*. How much love is Shlomo offering here, how much "uplifting potency" is present here, just by this, supposedly semantic, change? It represents a huge paradigm shift.

The dance of our lives played out, not between two "poles": being "good" and being "bad," with the individual continuously pulled between these two forces, but within one "pole" of being "inside," close, at home, and unfortunately, once in a while, being pulled away into the distance. Even if it lasts many years, even if it lasts most of our lives, it's the principle that counts.

The classic, traditional approach to "*Avodat Hashem*" (the service of God), is such that it is all dichotomous: you are either "good" or "bad" or "a little good" or a "little bad," always in a battle, pulled between these forces. So much energy is devoted to fighting this internal war (this is all the more true if you take in the effect of the Musar movement on Ashkenazic Jewry). Shlomo changed that, and the best area to examine his effect is in what I view as Shlomo's life-changing teaching on Yom Kippur.

Shlomo taught, based on R' Nachman of Breslov, that every time we make a mistake we begin to hate someone we love. I don't want to get angry at myself, so therefore I first get filled with anger at someone else. Adam erred and got angry at Eve. Eve erred and got angry at Adam, and they both got angry at their children. What happens when you make a lot of mistakes? You no longer know what your intention is and you fall into a spiral of anger and guilt. The more guilty you feel, the farther away you spiral. R' Nachman of Breslov said that when a man does something wrong it's bad, yet to go around with guilt feelings about it, that's evil. Why? Because the guilt feelings, not the sin, ruin our lives. Guilt pushes us farther and farther away from our inner "good point," from ourselves.

Shlomo's assumption, behind his teaching on Yom Kippur, behind his teaching, at large, is the underlying existence of good, and how it shapes the idea of love: I am good, God is good, I want to do good (even if I don't always see it), God wants to do good (even if we don't always see it), and there is love between us. This is our working assumption since if in my essence I am not good, why go back to the root? If God doesn't love us, why try to be close to Him?

It seems to me that there is no greater expression of the belief in love than this underlying assumption. No greater potential to uplift.

According to Shlomo, Yom Kippur is not about God forgiving us. He forgives us every day of the year. In his view the world misses the point of Yom Kippur. After all, a few minutes from the onset of Yom Kippur we already say in the liturgy, "And God said, 'I have forgiven.'" We could have stopped Yom Kippur right there and said, "God forgives!"

Yom Kippur is not a day dedicated to asking for forgiveness, but a day of cleansing. It could be described as an inner mop. I set the sins free. I set the guilt free. This is a day when a person's true *"ratzon"* (literally, desire; the true, authentic voice, unblemished by interest or ego) seeks clarification, and forgiveness is a natural result.

Rebbe Nachman teaches on the words "with love and desire, Your holy Shabbat," when God sends us great love, as He can, only then do our desires become clear. Shlomo used to speak about people who are afraid of this great love, refusing to meet it at the regular junctures when it is revealed, such as on Yom Kippur and the Third Meal of Shabbat, times of elevated consciousness. People are afraid to meet the experience of love at these times because they are afraid of the *"ratzon"* — desire, for with such holy desire comes a time to clarify one's decisions. "What do I need to do? Where is my struggle? What should I relinquish?" In moments such as these there is no good or evil, as we have mentioned, but only inside and outside, which are more difficult to live with than the stark dichotomy of good and evil.

Shlomo spoke on many occasions about the work of Yom Kippur, and the images that he used to describe it were strong, or even crude. A man empties his bowels in the bathroom. He now has two choices. He could look at what came out of him and be disgusted. "This came out of me? What filth I am carrying around inside of me!" Or he could simply flush the toilet and feel the unusual privilege of being able to get rid of that part of him which isn't clean. Yes, I have made many mistakes, but I am holy. I am greatly valued, as I was created in His image.

Many people use Yom Kippur as a day of general whining, and thereby miss the point. This stems not just from a realization of the errors of our ways, but also from fear. This is also the reason that people engage in inner manipulations. They choose to hold on to their anger and guilt feelings in order to prevent themselves from going on the arduous journey to confront their *"ratzon."*

This teaching changed my whole orientation to Yom Kippur. In the past, if I set out to forcibly negate myself out of a great desire to be completely humble during the High Holy Days, then this teaching, together with others, returned me to myself and to a deeper and more honest approach to the day and its meaning. For this alone I am eternally grateful to Shlomo.

## The Spoken Tradition

In the interests of brevity, this section will deal with one dimension: How to transform the Oral Tradition into a true spoken Torah tradition. [In Hebrew, the term for the Oral Tradition is *Torah sh'ba'al peh* — literally, Torah "of the mouth."]

When Shlomo was teaching, I always had the inclination to glance behind the page that he was learning from, to hear the voices, the background music that was there. My inclination was to obtain a glimpse behind Shlomo: Who was standing behind him? Who was whispering into his ear?

Sometimes people would chat in the background when he was teaching. Shlomo would stop and say, *"Chevre! Chevre!* You don't know what you are doing to me!" I strongly felt how the disturbance tore him away from the active connection to Torah "of the mouth," and the chain of tradition that he was connected to. It was not just his connection to the Torah and its commentaries that was disturbed, but the awesome act of creation that was taking place before us.

I was not the only one who went home after a learning session with Shlomo and tried to re-learn what he taught from the sources that he had used. And always — always — if I succeeded in tracing the line of thought in the sources that he had used, and managed somewhat to follow his discourse, I felt as if I had experienced a miracle of the Living Spoken Tradition, the Torah "of the mouth," that had transpired before my very eyes. This concretized not just the beauty of our Torah, but also how much Shlomo hid his genius. It could be that many reading this have had this experience with other great teachers, but with Shlomo, this was my first encounter with our Torah in three vivid dimensions.

## Who Will Interpret for us Now?

The Torah has always been connected to the two-dimensional text. When a friend called me in the dark of the morning to tell me that Shlomo had passed away, my first clear thought was, "What will all those words that Shlomo used to explain in the holy books do now? They are trapped again in the books." Now that Shlomo was gone, I wondered who would be able to uplift those words out of the text and bring them back into the world.

It is as if Shlomo took those two dimensions and stretched their borders. He breathed life into them. It is as if he forced the letters to come forth, jumping off the page, and in so doing he added a third dimension to the Torah, the dimension of depth.

I saw them cry. The Ishbitzer didn't cry, but his book, the *Mei HaShiloah,* did. The Ishbitzer's son, R. Yaakov Leiner, didn't cry, but his book, the *Beit Yaakov* did. The Ishbitzer's grandson, R. Gershon Chanoch Henoch Leiner didn't cry, but his book, the *Sod Yesharim,* did. The whole Ishbitz library cried out, "Who will give us back that third dimension? Who will come and interpret us now, showing our depth to the world?"

Some explain the verse, "Moses will speak and God will answer him with a voice," by saying that the voice that answers is the interpretation of the Torah. The Ishbitzer, in his comment on this verse, emphasizes how the interpreter of the Torah, its "translator," might even be more important than the giver of the Torah. This is shown clearly by how the Holy One, blessed be He, is the one in the verse who is appointed as the interpreter, "and God shall answer him with a voice." The interpretation of the Torah, or the ability to transfer it from its source into our reality, the ability to bring forth the letters from the page, requires a rare, holy skill. I feel that Shlomo had that skill. He wasn't just a genius in his own knowledge of the Torah, as many have attested to, but he was a genius at interpretation. And we are certainly in great need of interpreters.

## In Conclusion: A Story

One night, four of us accompanied Shlomo to the wedding of the Amshinover Rebbe's daughter. The Amshinover Rebbe is known to be "beyond time," and the *Chuppah* started a little after midnight. At about two in the morning we decided to go back to the hotel where Shlomo was staying in order to part there. Three of us got into the cab: Shlomo, Mimi Feigelson, and myself. Mimi is considered one of Shlomo's top students, and is a good friend of mine. Shlomo sat in the front seat and with a holy book open on his lap, as was his custom. Mimi and I sat in the back. Even though it was dark, with only minimal light coming from street lamps, Shlomo became immersed in his learning.

Someone apparently saw Shlomo getting into the cab, and soon the cab was surrounded by young yeshiva students. They began to pound on the windows and shout, "Shlomo! Shlomo!" The knocks caused the cab to sway from side to side. Occasionally Shlomo raised his head from the book and waved a tired hand. Mimi and I were frightened. We felt threatened. "Shlomo! Shlomo! Shlomo!" We were not sure what they were saying. We weren't sure if it was voices of anger, opposition, or frustration. "Shlomo! Shlomo!" Then again, on the other hand, it might have been cries of yearning, desires for connection: "Shlomo..." "Shlomo..." "Shlomo...."

Why am I telling this story? It is clear to me that ever since Shlomo passed away such a cry is going around the world, a demand, "Shlomo!" "Shlomo!" Yet it is not always clear to me what it is saying and in which intonation it is being said. What is this cry asking for?

If we go back to the opening story about the Kotzker and the "mess" in his synagogue, even though we don't always understand what is going on, and it appears like one big mess — "a shirt tossed here, a shoe tossed there" — nonetheless, before us stands an open invitation to go "beyond," and the more we accept this invitation, the more there is a chance we will feel at home.

All of the points that we have presented here, humor, intuition, control, who we are after the *Shoah,* breaking dichotomies, the Spoken Torah, and more, are all points that Shlomo used to pave a road we can take to go "beyond," in order that through that process we can truly be at home. I want to bless us with knowing what home is, knowing how to "be at home," and how not to be afraid of going "beyond."

Od Avinu Chai — Reb Shlomo sings on an
Israeli TV show, 1973: http://youtu.be/rmWUyOBmwdU

# In Search of the Broken Self: Rabbi Shlomo Carlebach's Teachings in the Context of His Life and Work[*]

by Rabbi Nehemia Polen

THERE ARE TWO TROPES SHLOMO CARLEBACH WOULD OFTEN EMBED IN his teachings: "Everybody knows..." and "you'll never know."

"Everybody knows..." typically introduces a personality, text, or practice that in fact is not likely known by most of the audience; the phrase functions much like the Hebrew *"yadu'a"* or *"ka-yadu'a,"* used with reference to a kabbalistic or esoteric idea.

"You'll never know" is the refrain for stories from the genre of the hidden *zaddik,* the holy beggar, the marginal, outcast, or even wicked person who turns out to have a noble side, or perhaps is even a *lamed-vavnik.* It suggests that we have missed perceiving the great virtue of the individual under discussion.

As I begin this exploration of Rabbi Shlomo Carlebach, it strikes me that our task is framed by these two points of reference. There is the Shlomo Carlebach that "everybody knows," and the Shlomo Carlebach

---

[*]  Based on a presentation delivered at the Neo-Hasidism Conference, Manhattan Jewish Community Center, March 28, 2003; revised for publication.

who, I suspect, "we'll never know." It is in that indeterminate space that this exploration must proceed.

Shlomo was a man of paradoxes and contradictions, a person whom some called the first hasidic rock star, but who in his own heart never left the world of Talmud, who retained the aspiration to be not a rock star but a Rosh Yeshiva. He was a melodic genius who seemed effort-lessly to channel *niggunim* from some higher plane, who sparked a new wave of hasidic musical creativity. Yet this same person could not notate his own melodies and could barely tune his own guitar. He was a peripatetic teacher and musician who trumpeted the virtues of the Holy Beggars, who nevertheless had a deep aristocratic streak, a dignity and royal bearing, a sense of *noblesse oblige.*

Yet with all these paradoxes, it would be wrong to call him a mystery man. He was not a shamanistic cipher in the mold of Carlos Castane-da, about whose life little is known for sure, whose basic biographical particulars — date of birth, death, marital status — are blurred or in dispute.

No, we know the basic facts of Carlebach's life — his birth in Berlin in 1925 to Rabbi Naftali and Pessia Carlebach, the move to Baden bei Wien in Austria; the escape to America in 1939, his attendance at Torah Vodaas and study with Rabbi Shlomo Hyman, and later with Rabbi Aharon Kotler in Lakewood, his association and later break with Lubavitch, and finally — the launching of his independent career as spiritual troubadour, composer, performer, teacher. We know about the House of Love and Prayer, Moshav Meor Modi'im; the continual international travel and touring; the marriage, children, divorce; lin-gering questions about personal lifestyle; death in 1994; the posthu-mous popularity and belated lionization; the emergence of something resembling a "Carlebach movement."

I am thinking rather of his inner life, his motivation, how he saw his own work, what he saw as his life's mission, what sparked it, what kept him going. The wealth of hagiographic reminiscences — and I do not question their essential accuracy for the most part — shed little light on these issues. Of course he loved Jews, all people, of course his music touched hearts and spirits in a deeply moving way; of course he was a master storyteller and expositor of hasidic teachings — but the inner life remains unexplored.

Why, for example, did he leave Lakewood for Lubavitch, and what was behind his subsequent break with Lubavitch? The story one hears is that the issue was mixed seating for men and women at concerts. This has a certain plausibility, but even if true, in all likelihood the identification of such a flashpoint only masks more deep-seated tensions.

Unlike other New Age or Neo-Hasidic teachers, he remained an Orthodox Jew in belief: *Torah min Hashamayim* in the traditional sense; the documentary hypothesis was anathema to him, as indeed was the entire field of academic Jewish Studies. He had little interest in secular studies at all; Western modes of reasoning were not his forte. And his appearance at ecumenical gatherings was based on something other than serious study of other religious traditions. All of this makes his departures from traditional lifestyle and practice even more intriguing and in need of understanding.

Our inquiry is not made easier by the proximity that many of us have to Shlomo Carlebach and the debt of gratitude that we owe him. I am pleased to acknowledge that debt myself. If R. Pinhas Koretzer said, *"der Zohar hat mir gehalten beim Yiddishkeit,"* I can say, quite honestly, "Shlomo Carlebach *hat mir gehalten beim Yiddishkeit."*

We all recall his brilliant associative mind, his gifts as expositor and adapter of Hasidic teachings, his creative appropriation of those teachings and tales and his popularization of them in the service of his Judaism of the open heart.

He was blessed with a genuine love of people, and an extraordinary sense of humor. He projected delight at being alive, at being Jewish. He was totally self-confident in his Judaism, emphasizing love of Jews, of Torah, of Eretz Yisrael, of Yerushalayim, of the Holy Wall — especially after the Six-Day War. He was part of the post-1967 revival of Jewish spirit.

But there is an aspect of this work that is not often recognized. His best teachings were extended improvisational creations — entirely unplanned expositions of tropes and themes which spun biblical, rabbinic, and Hasidic motifs in a sinuously winding yet coherent tapestry of text, tale, melody, silence, and personal encounter.

If not for Shlomo, I would probably never have seen the channeling of teaching from a higher place, as the *Or Ha-Meir* describes the Maggid of Mezritch, "When you begin to hear your own voice, you must stop." Shlomo would sometimes say after a teaching, "What did I say? Did someone tape it?"

There was a strong performative aspect to the "learnings" after a concert; for the inner circle, the Shlomo *cognoscenti*, as it were, they were the center of a Shlomo appearance, so that rather than "learnings" being tacked on to concerts, it could be argued that concert bookings were ways of arranging and funding learnings.

In his world there was a spirit of openness; he never took a proprietary interest in his teachings. He empowered others and did not wish to create spiritual clones. Unlike with many charismatic spiritual leaders, there were no loyalty tests. People related to Carlebach in a diversity of ways — student, friend, admirer of the music — and it was all fine with him. I never felt pressure to move to a more intense mode of association, to join a cult of devotees. He was not entrepreneurial; he willingly, joyfully, perhaps too naively and impractically, gave away what he had.

Shlomo exemplified a robust, full religious aesthetic that included music and story. He would say, "Make Yiddishkeit even more beautiful" — meaning, do the observances, the mitzvos, in an ever-more beautiful, meaningful, tunefully evocative manner; this involved the creation of new ritual frameworks for old practices (e.g., *Kiddush Levanah* as done at Moshav Meor Modi'im).

He also embodied an ethic of interpersonal engagement: in the middle of a concert with hundreds in the audience, he would pause in mid-sentence to greet someone who had just walked through the door. His eyes having espied the new arrival from a distance, Shlomo's face would pulsate with beaming joy, a gasp of delight would emerge from his mouth, and the person would be greeted, usually by name, with "Holy brother/sister, I've been waiting all night for you to come!" And the recognition was genuine: he had an uncanny memory for names and faces, almost preternatural. Even if he only met you once, in a crowd, and years ago, he would remember you and address you by name — often your Hebrew or Yiddish name!

When someone would say goodbye, he would say, "Call me for no reason."

As my friend the late Betzalel Hamilton put it, "He sure knew how to work a room!" That is, he would walk through the concert hall starting from the back and greet every person.

This all relates to Shlomo as a master of blessing, in the sense of acknowledging and honoring the other. He emphasized the importance of honoring and acknowledging children, blessing children, especially one's own. It was especially meaningful for me to hear him say to one of his children, "Thank you for being my daughter." And he meant it.

His practice of non-judgmental, absolute love was undoubtedly shaped in part by the Holocaust (he and his family were hounded out of Germany, and subsequently from Austria; many of his family were killed in the Shoah). I recall him speaking about his first concert tour in Germany. When he came back, he gave a teaching at Boston University Hillel, during which he was asked how he could travel to Germany (at a time when many Jews were not buying German products or traveling to Germany). He replied, "If I had two hearts, I would use one for loving and one for hating; but I only have one heart, so I must use it for love...."

The practice of non-judgmentalism was deeply refreshing and uplifting for those of us disheartened by a culture of the perpetual gaze, the evaluative stare. On the other hand, we also know that non-judgmentalism can slide into a state of non-discrimination, an inability or unwillingness to set personal limits or interpersonal boundaries. And even this was not without its noble aspects, for at times the effect was courageous and redemptive, but at other times it was troubling, dangerous, corrosive. Shlomo was a teacher who did not conceal his appetites under the guise of holiness.

Much of his knowledge of Hasidic tradition came from the years 1933-1938 when his father was rabbi in Baden bei Wien, Austria. Some notable East-European hasidic rebbes had relocated to Vienna from the time of the First World War, and others came throughout the nineteen-thirties for medical consultations. It was there that Shlomo met the Tchortkover Rebbe, other rebbes of the Ryzhin dynasty, and many others. In 1936, when Shlomo was eleven, he had a special meeting with the Lubavitcher Rebbe, Rabbi Yosef Yitzhak Schneersohn. As he later recalled it, the Rebbe told him and his brother (a) *Ir zult zein*

*Chassidishe Yiden, nisht kein Deitche yinglach;* (b) always sleep in a *talis koton*; and (c) always *bentsh* from a Siddur. In fact, there was a way in which Shlomo did remain that *"Chassidishe Yingel,"* a hasidic young person, his entire life. [Based on an interview with Emunah Witt]

When he involved women in religious life in ways that outraged some other Orthodox Jews, he had no global theory of halakhic change, nor did he act, I believe, on the basis of some ideological commitment to feminism, but rather in response to the personal needs of individuals he knew and whose spiritual aspirations he nurtured. As he once said, "Maybe the Satmar Rebbetzin doesn't need an *aliya* to the Torah — that's great; but some of our ladies need to personally relate to the Torah...."

He once spoke of the great piety of one of the matriarchs of his family (I don't recall if it was a grandmother or his great-aunt). A question came from one of the women in the audience, "So perhaps we should live Judaism as your grandmother did?" He replied, "Why would you want to do that? God already has my grandmother...."

Shlomo told stories of Rebbes from long ago, of nearly forgotten Rebbes, of Rebbes murdered in the Shoah, but very seldom of Rebbes alive today or Rebbes with large contemporary followings — such as Ger or Lubavitch. Nor did he generally give over torahs from *Sefas Emes* or *Likkutei Sichos*. His favorites were perhaps Rabbi Nachman, Ishbitz, Reb Leibele Eiger. He introduced us to many rebbes and their stories, whom we might otherwise never have heard of, and their sacred practices — Reb Shaye Kerestirer; Rabbi Yisroel of Vilednik; Rabbi Shimon Yareslover. The less known the rebbe, the more marginal in the world of Hasidism, the greater devastation the lineage had suffered in the Holocaust, the more likely Shlomo was to talk about the rebbe; his project was in large measure a post-Holocaust effort of recovery, memorialization, re-awakening.

He was more likely to tell a story from the Alexander than of the Gerer; he spoke of the Piaseczner when almost no one in America had heard of him. I first heard Shlomo tell the story of the Holy Hunchback in (I believe) 1979.

For some analytic perspective, I found helpful an article by Robert Sharf entitled "The Zen of Japanese Nationalism."* Sharf focuses primarily on the work of D. T. Suzuki and notes that the idea of Zen not being a religion but a "pure experience" is a relatively recent construction, influenced by Western concerns and interests. Sharf observes, "Like Narcissus, western enthusiasts [of Zen] failed to recognize their own reflection in the mirror held out to them." Sharf notes that most of the Japanese teachers who played a key role in the establishment of Zen in the United States held a "relatively marginal status within the Japanese Zen establishment." These men were genuine mavericks, deeply dissatisfied with the current state of Buddhism in their own country and eager to establish what they saw as "true Zen" in a new domain.

Building on Sharf's research, Jan Nattier writes that we might divide all missionaries into two types — the "company man" and the "free agent," who moves to a new country of his own accord, disseminates his religion as he sees fit, and is constrained only by his own need to make a living.

Now I suspect that all of this rings a bell to those of us familiar with the literature and figures of Neo-Hasidism. Scholem's critique of Buber is

---

* Robert H. Sharf, "The Zen of Japanese Nationalism," *History of Religions* 33:1 (1993), pp. 1-43.

See Jan Nattier, "Buddhist Studies in the Post-Colonial Age," *Journal of the American Academy of Religion* 65:2, p. 469 ff; review essay of *Curators of the Buddha: The Study of Buddhism Under Colonialism,* edited by Donald S. Lopez, Jr., University of Chicago Press, 1995.

well known; and one could argue that what Martin Buber did for Hasidism was not unlike what D. T. Suzuki did for Zen, or the way Idries Shah presented Sufism. Employing Nattier's terms, one way to think about Shlomo Carlebach's career is that he moves from "company man" to "free agent."

But is it true, as we might conclude from Sharf, *mutatis mutandis*, that Carlebach merely reconstructed Hasidism in his own image? Indeed, this is consistent with the views of Joseph Dan as presented in a seminal article entitled "A Bow to Frumkinian Hasidism."[*] Dan distinguishes between the "historical Hasidism of the Baal Shem Tov" which — from the third generation — hinged largely on the hasid's relationship to a particular rebbe; and on the other hand, "Frumkinian Hasidism," essentially invented by Michael ha-Levi Frumkin, with the subsequent support of literary figures, including Y. L. Peretz, Scholem Asch, Judah Steinberg, and Martin Buber. Frumkinian Hasidism, according to Dan, involves a nostalgic evocation of an idealized culture of Jewish Eastern Europe, which bears little if any resemblance to the actual Hasidism of history. While at the end of the essay Dan is compelled to give a grudging "bow" to this movement in light of its success in capturing the Jewish imagination in the West, one is left with the conclusion that the Hasidism evoked by hasidic tales is not really Hasidism at all.

Dan notes that Frumkin (who also used the name Rodkinson) was a descendant of Rabbi Aharon ha-Levi of Staroselya, the great disciple of Rabbi Shneur Zalman of Liadi, who vied for the succession with the latter's son after Rabbi Shneur Zalman's death. Rabbi Aharon ha-Levi had a luminous mind, was a powerful and creative expositor of his master's teachings, and exercised a charismatic pull on many

---

[*] Joseph Dan, "A Bow to Frumkinian Hasidism," *Modern Judaism* 11 (1991), pp. 175-193; reprinted in Joseph Dan, *Jewish Mysticism: General Characteristics and Comparative Studies* (Northvale, NJ and Jerusalem: Jason Aronson, 1999), pp. 87-110.

hasidim, but the principle of biological lineage was affirmed as Rabbi Shneur Zalman's son Rabbi Dov Ber of Lubavitch gradually emerged as the successor to the founder. While noting this history, Dan does not comment on its significance. If Frumkin/Rodkinson was indeed a central figure in the emergence of Neo-Hasidism, it is reasonable to see his role not as an interloper or literary fabulist, but as reviving his grandfather's struggle for charismatic succession untethered from biological lineage. Frumkin's promotion of a Hasidism not linked to one rebbe or family line might have been his way to vindicate his grandfather. If so, Neo-Hasidism can on one level be seen as a legitimate return to leadership models of early Hasidism, such as Rabbi R. Aharon ha-Levi, R. Avraham Kalisker, Reb Zusia of Hanipol, Reb Hayyim Hayke of Amdur, indeed the Baal Shem Tov himself, based on personal illumination, wisdom teaching, and ecstatic experience — not necessarily dependent on biological lineage. By focusing on the forgotten rebbes, the truncated lineages, on hasidic books not reprinted or not widely known, it can be said that Shlomo Carlebach embodied and exemplified the Neo-Hasidic return to early Hasidism of the first two generations, before the ascendancy of the principle of hereditary succession. And unlike Dan's depiction of Neo-Hasidism, Carlebach's Hasidism did feature Torah and *mitzvot*; with all its innovations and deviations, it had a recognizably Orthodox face. While Carlebach often spoke against hypocrisy and hyper-punctilious observance at the expense of interpersonal sensitivities, it is nevertheless true that the central features of traditional life: Shabbat, *Kashrut, mikvah,* daily prayer based on fixed liturgy, etc., were pivotal in his communities, especially Moshav Meor Modi'im. At the same time, in good hasidic fashion, there was some boundary-testing and category-bending.

What I'm arguing, then, is that some aspects of the Carlebach legacy — especially Moshav Meor Modi'im in its early days — may legitimately be seen as reawakening the spirit and communal ethos of early Hasidism.

As Tibetan leaders spoke of some American teachers, Shlomo Carlebach's Hasidism was "spontaneous transmission arising without lineage,"* though Carlebach's intuition and creativity were undoubtedly nurtured and augmented by broad and deep text study as well as personal contact with many hasidic masters and hasidim over his entire lifetime.

He not only told stories of masters, but he modeled the life of early Hasidism. If I have some idea of what it might have meant to be in the circle of the Besht or the Great Maggid, it is by being in the chevre of R' Shlomo, at the Moshav — the idealistic, impractical, romantic egalitarian community held together by love alone, circling around one cherished figure whose true charisma and effortless gravitas bent the shape of space-time around his presence.

We are now in a better position to understand why R. Shlomo got *s'mikha* from Rabbi Yitzhok Hutner, and not from Rabbi Aharon Kotler in Lakewood, where he studied for seven years, or at Lubavitch, which was his home for at least three years after leaving Lakewood (or even at Torah Vodaas for that matter). We are told that he left Lakewood for Lubavitch because he felt the pull of Hasidism, and that later he left Lubavitch because of the Rebbe's insistence on separate seating at concerts. This has the ring of truth, but one suspects that another reason may have been Shlomo's inability or unwillingness to subordinate himself to institutional structures or the leadership directives of other powerful individuals. He was too much of an individual himself to be constrained for long by the regulations and procedures of others. So when it came time to get *s'mikha,* he sought out Rabbi Hutner for a private *s'mikha.*

* *Yoga Journal,* July 1985, p. 38.

In Shlomo's words:

> "Anyway, so everything put together, it was time for me to leave, you know. Time to check out. But the hardest thing was, I was not in Lakewood, I was not in Lubavitch, I was nowhere in the world. It takes a long time to stand on your own feet. Between heaven and earth." [Interview with Emuna Witt]

As M. Herbert Danziger wrote, "In the late 1960s, probably the only one on the American scene prepared to deal with [people struggling with their very commitment] was Rabbi Shlomo Carlebach, a Lubavitcher chasid. A charismatic personality, he was not an organizer and could not set up an institutional structure to further his work."*

And, I would add, he could not live under one, either.

His teaching was all about the individual and his or her spiritual destiny.

To be sure, community was a part of the picture, but his ideal community had little structure or hierarchy: just a group of individuals around a magnetic leader whose authority did not derive from lineage, and who did not seek to initiate one, either.

The focus on the individual comes out strongly in a lengthy teaching called "The Torah of the Nine Months," actually a conversation between Shlomo and Zalman Schachter (Shalomi) at Tannersville, New York, in 1976. This extended exploration, which went on for over two hours, sets out major themes which Shlomo would return to again and again, and it is as close to a programmatic presentation of Carlebach philosophy as we are likely to find.

---

\* *Returning to Tradition: The Contemporary Revival of Orthodox Judaism* (New Haven and London: Yale University Press, 1989), p. 85

It begins with the famous *aggadah* that the embryo is learning Torah in the womb with a lit lamp or candle over its head. Shlomo's *hiddush* is that the baby is not learning the Torah of Sinai, the Torah of law, of rules, of Mishnah, Talmud, and Codes, but the Torah of the Nine Months — the Torah of what I have to do in this world, the shape of my soul, the Torah of the individual.

Since individuation begins only after we've left the Garden of Eden, this Torah is also the Torah of making mistakes and starting over again, the Torah of the Broken Tablets, as Shlomo put it, "my *Tehiyyas ha-Meisim*" Torah, going up and down and not to give up but to stand up again. This is the Torah of "*Ein Adam omed al divrei Torah elah im kein nikhshal bah.*"

"The Torah which I don't need for fixing my soul — I learn it once (and that's enough), [but] the Torah I need the most is the Torah I learn by making mistakes — the things I am failing in, but I don't give up — in that I'm the holiest!

"*Bedikas Hametz* with a candle is the Torah of the Nine Months — looking for my *hametz*. At a wedding, the parents hold a candle to tell the child, on the way to the *Huppa*, I'm giving you the Torah of the Nine Months; and when a person dies, we light candles — giving him his Torah of the Nine Months.

"The Torah of the Nine Months is the Torah of my place in the world. This is the meaning of *Barukh ha-Makom. Barukh Hu* — Blessed is the Place — my place! *Barukh shenosan Torah le-amo Yisrael. Barukh Hu* — the highest revelation [of] Torah is the revelation of my place in the world."

## Conclusion:

Before Shlomo Carlebach, no one had ever dreamed of a German-born/ Orthodox/talmudic prodigy/hasidic/American/Israeli/world-traveling/ guitar-strumming/ songster/ story-teller/ indiscriminately loving/ God-intoxicated/ aristocratic/ hippie/ yeshiva-*bochur*.      It simply didn't exist — and if Shlomo Carlebach hadn't done it, no one would have imagined that it could exist.

Having left, in turn, Berlin, Vienna, Williamsburg, Lakewood, Crown Heights, and his own family, the search for one's place in the world had particular poignancy and urgency for him.

Shlomo Carlebach created what it meant to be Shlomo Carlebach. He not only inhabited his own place in the world, but he cleared a place where there was none before. He tried to make the whole world into a House of Love and Prayer so that he too could pray and find love. All of this must have involved enormous pain, enormous courage, inner determination, and faith. For that example alone, we owe him our eternal gratitude.

*Wedding of Rabbi Zalman Schachter to Elana Rappaport, Rosh Chodesh Sivan, May 11, 1975, in Hinkel Park, Berkeley, CA. Reb Shlomo was Mesader Kiddushin.*
*Photo by Rabbi Joe Schonwald.*

# Was Shlomo a Religious Genius?

by Rabbi Alon Goshen-Gottstein

WE HAVE ALL BEEN TOUCHED. WE HAVE BEEN TELLING THE STORY, MANY stories, of who Shlomo was, what he meant for us, what he has brought into the world. We will continue to tell stories, just as he did; so will I. But this moment is not one of storytelling. It is one of reflection. I seek in the following reflection to get a handle on how Shlomo might be presented, especially to those who did not know him and who seek to understand why he was important to so many people. Stories are one way of gaining understanding. Shlomo's music opens a window into his soul. But here I would like to think of the category by means of which we think of Shlomo and to propose a new category.

What (indeed what, rather than who, as I seek to think through a category, rather than simply describe a person) was Shlomo? Surely a talented musician. Also a teacher. An interpreter of sources? Sure. Perhaps a spiritual master. Was he a *zaddik,* a saintly person? What other categories do we have available to us, by means of which we can understand the truly unique contribution of a man who touched so many thousands of lives, and did so in forms unique to himself and through structures, patterns, and a lifestyle that he developed beyond the norms and framework of conventional Jewish expression? I would like to explore the usefulness of a category that is on the whole novel, but precisely because it is not commonly used might provide us with a handle for appreciating Shlomo's greatness. The category is "Religious

Genius." I have been working on this category over the past year, and have recently received support from the John Templeton Foundation to explore its usefulness in relation to saints in world religions. The invitation from the Templeton Foundation and the subsequent opportunity it offered to reflect on Shlomo, found me after the Foundation had brought together a group of scholars who explored how this category might help us to better understand saints in world religions. With those discussions fresh in my mind, and the novel category at hand, I would like to apply it to Shlomo, putting forth the suggestion that he might be appreciated as a Religious Genius.

What, then, is a Religious Genius?

## Introducing Religious Genius

All religions recognize that there are outstanding individuals whose spiritual insight, presence, and power by far surpass those of others. These individuals help create, define, drive, reform, and inspire their traditions. To a large extent they are the models that provide the basis for emulation for others, and they are the ideal of the tradition in its concrete manifestation, in the lives of humans. What makes these individuals more than the ordinary teacher or the successful practitioner is that they bring something novel to the religion and thereby facilitate a regeneration of the tradition and a spiritual renewal in the lives of its adherents.

The Religious Genius has the capacity to apply intuition and intellect in bringing about a new understanding of reality, grounded in awareness of a broader existential dimension, one that leads to deep transformation of the person. The new understanding offered by the Religious Genius provides creative and constructive solutions for religious and spiritual problems of a particular community or tradition. A religious genius will accordingly have high positive output, effectively addressing challenges and issues that are fundamental to a tradition, or, speaking more universally, to being religious.

The contribution of the Religious Genius may be a creative presentation of the tradition in ways not previously known, rather than the discovery of a new truth. Much of what Religious Genius is about is vivid realization of aspects of reality or of tradition not previously appreciated. Such realization is a major expression of creativity and is closely associated with creativity in related areas — intellectual, artistic, and so on.

The creativity of the Religious Genius comes as a response to something problematic. The old ways lose their savor, they no longer work; conditions change. The creativity of the Religious Genius comes in response to that problematic situation. The problem could be focused intellectually, emotionally, or in relation to ritual. Unlike the common teacher or saint who ordinarily interprets according to existing canons, the Religious Genius offers new ways of understanding. When old ways of interpretation no longer work, the Religious Genius may find new means of engaging tradition or the existential issues it addresses. Because the Religious Genius addresses a problem that is related to contemporary conditions, there will be some interaction between the being and contribution of the Religious Genius and the historical and sociological context within which he or she is being appreciated.

A religious genius would have habits of heart, mind, and will that conform to the broader vision of reality that he/she perceives and that consequently define the manner of being and the contribution of the Religious Genius in an ongoing way. This is why a Religious Genius might be considered a subset of sainthood. Ideally, the Religious Genius' actions and orientation conform to his/her view of reality. However, we must also make room for the flawed Religious Genius, one who has a core vision of reality and who brings forth a teaching in accordance with it, inspiring others in light of that teaching, but whose actions may not be fully commensurate with the vision and teaching he offers. Indeed, if it is difficult to talk of a flawed saint, inasmuch as the terms "saint" and "zaddik" suggest perfection, it is easier to conceive of a flawed Religious Genius. Religious Genius evokes creativity, originality, vision, an outstanding contribution to the life of religion, but it does not connote perfection in the same way that "saint" or "zaddik" do. Indeed, geniuses as such often have complicated personalities that are the flip side of their talent and creativity.

## Characteristics of Religious Genius

Our work on Religious Genius as a category suggests several characteristics are fundamental to the Religious Genius as an individual, though not all religious geniuses have all these characteristics in equal measure. Differences between religious geniuses may stem from the varying distribution of these and other characteristics. The following characteristics are deemed important to saints and religious geniuses:

A. Love — Love is a central defining element in any portrait of Religious Genius. Love is manifest as altruism, the supreme expression of love offered selflessly in service of the other. It may be superfluous to add that love is a reality, a state of being, and that therefore the question of its recipient is almost secondary. A loving heart and presence extends to God, to the fellow person, to the entire world. The more expansive the love, the higher the state of being that is manifested, the greater the expression of religious genius. We might go as far as considering a notion of genius of love, that is: an interpretation of the higher meaning of reality expressed through a life of love and a way of being in the world (rather than through a teaching). The centrality of love accounts, in part, for descriptions of the heart of the saint as a liquid heart, a heart of butter, and similar expressions, that convey a particular quality of the heart of the saint or the Religious Genius.

B. Expanded awareness of reality — This seems to be a key element in Religious Genius and one of the main features that distinguishes it from ordinary piety and even from many expressions of saintliness. A Religious Genius lives in more than one plane of existence. He or she is simultaneously present to the physical order of life and to the alternative order, to which he or she is increasingly drawn. The latter redefines one's way of being in the physical plane. It establishes priorities, provides meaning, and reorients all of one's actions. The genius of Religious Genius comes from the fact that all actions, engagements, and teachings, indeed, all expressions of the religious life, are experienced from an awareness that transcends the physical plane, even as the individual seeks to transcend his or her sense of a limited personal self.

Broader awareness of reality need not be limited to the heavenly, other-worldly, sphere. If we consider broadening awareness horizontally, then we can consider the expansion of awareness to others, to the world's suffering, to the entire world of social relations that cries out for healing. Perhaps herein lies an important key to the altruism of saints. Their altruism is neither a mandate, nor simply an expression of love. Rather, it expresses a broader sense of their identity and their own sense of expanded awareness that includes the other, the world at large, as part of their own awareness.

C. The Logic of Imitation — Awareness of higher or broader reality does not simply provide meaning and reorientation to physical existence. It leads to an inevitable dynamic wherein one seeks to conform one reality to the standards, vision, or perfection of the other. The Religious Genius is not only in touch with a higher vision of life; he seeks to incorporate and implement it in life, or, from the other end, make life on this plane attuned to, commensurate with, harmonious with, that higher reality. Only those who are aware of the tension implied in living in multiple worlds and the suffering, struggle, and continuing effort to harmonize and attune our world to another order of reality truly deserve to be called religious geniuses. Here we have a pinnacle of genius — intuiting another order of reality, seeking to ground it, transforming oneself and the entire world in a movement of totality and harmony toward that higher perceived reality. Religious Genius is the bridge between two realities, and the primary means of constructing this bridge is imitation. The Religious Genius seeks to implement the higher form of living, the model of a life made available through contact with an alternate reality, by imitating that reality or the examples, models, and forerunners who have lived that reality and who continue to uphold it from another plane of reality.

D. Purity — Purity is the core of the struggle that is common to all who are on the spiritual path. It is born of the recognition of the tension produced by an awareness of multiple realities in which the aspirant dwells. What is perceived as the higher order, the ultimate, beckons and invites the individual toward greater conformity with its perspective, with its way of being. To attain that, purity is required. Purity is indispensible for the spiritual life and must therefore occupy a prominent position in any description of Religious Genius. Religious Genius thrives on, aspires to, and is ultimately realized through the increase and assimilation of purity into the life of the religious genius.

E. Humility — Humility may be understood as proper recognition of one's position in the great scheme of things. Such recognition is quite distinct from the ways in which the ego seeks to assert itself in order to boost one's sense of personal worth. Humility is thus closely related to de-centering of the self and its reorientation in a larger view. In many traditions this is understood as ultimately leading to some form of annihilation of the self, *bitul hayesh*. It is also the basis for continuing self-inspection, leading one to identify faults and to become aware of one's own imperfections. These in turn drive the quest for purity.

F. Self-surrender — If humility situates the self in its proper place, self-surrender defines a particular attitude and relationship of the self to the higher reality that it seeks to identify with. The personal ego decreases in significance as one increasingly is identified with the greater reality or goal towards which one is making his or her way. Self-surrender is closely related to the capacity to serve others, as one's view of oneself is transformed, and as one increases in loving capacity. But more is involved in self-surrender than simply transcendence of self. Self-surrender assumes growing in awareness of that larger presence or reality of which one is but a part. As awareness shifts, the question of the true author of our actions increasingly comes to the forefront. Is it the self or the greater Self — the divine, the absolute — that is the true actor?

Other characteristics of the Religious Genius may be suggested, but for present purposes I will limit myself to these core traits. The question that those of us working on this project have been asking ourselves is whether one must have *all* of these characteristics (and some others) or whether there are some fundamental traits or some basic combinations that allow us to recognize certain individuals as outstanding paragons of the religious life who in turn bring such creativity and novelty to their tradition that we can recognize in them Religious Genius. How demanding we are in the application of the category and how much perfection in the attainment of these characteristics we demand would affect whether we chose to describe Shlomo as a Religious Genius or not. I would like to argue he is certainly a worthy candidate for consideration as a Religious Genius, and that even if we decide to apply the category very strictly, thereby limiting it to great founders of religious movements and ultra-great teachers who have redefined tradition for ages, still a consideration of Shlomo in light of this category is enriching both for our appreciation of Shlomo and for the possible uses of the category. Let me then proceed to consider in what way Shlomo might be considered a religious genius.

## Shlomo as Religious Genius

Let me begin by stating what I think Shlomo's singular contribution to *Yiddishkeit* was: Shlomo taught us a new way of being Jewish. While that way had all the components of classical Judaism — *mitzvot,* Torah, *ahavat Yisrael,* prayer, *Shabbes,* and more — there was something unique in how he put it all together. And that uniqueness allowed people to revisit and re-experience their Judaism in ways not available elsewhere, and possibly never previously available. Because his way of living Judaism was novel, those who came to Judaism through him and who established their lives in accordance with his vision of what it is to be Jewish ended up being Jewish in ways that are different from how Judaism is practiced in other groups and sectors. The nuances are fine, in the same way that the sound of one musical tradition may be different from that of another. But there is something about how the *"chevra"* are Jewish that makes them different from other groups. This difference is not simply a carryover of a former hippy identity. It is an expression of a way of being that Shlomo brought through that marks the community he created.

Shlomo was able to address a core problem of Judaism today and to offer it a new solution — the problem of alienation, including the alienation of those who are already steeped in the practice of Judaism. He was able to bring back to Judaism an entire generation that had been far removed by providing a new way of being Jewish and restating the meaning of Judaism. At the very least, it was, and is, a Judaism of love, a Judaism where loving relations within the community, and between the individual and God, take on a new form and fuse the entire religious life of the individual and community in ways we may not have seen for generations.

What makes Shlomo a serious candidate for Religious Genius is his ability to see another way of being in the spiritual realm and to translate it into the life of a community. A vision beyond, translated into the here and now, made Shlomo more than the typical teacher who hands on the classical texts and values to the next generation. Surely, he did that, too. But in doing so, he completely reframed the meaning of religiosity by grounding it in those particular characteristics that make a religious genius. Let us look at those more closely.

Love is the single characteristic that more than any other describes what Shlomo brought to the world. To truly understand this, one had to taste and experience the depth of his heart, its profound softness, a softness typical of the hearts of great saints. His love went way beyond the open heart and the loving embrace he made available to one and all. It was a love that provided a new reading of tradition. It is as though Shlomo was able to read all the classics and to hear in them the unified message of love. Those who did not experience teach-ins that went on for hours and hours, wherein Shlomo would creatively weave readings of *hassidic* sources with tales and songs, cannot appreciate the hermeneutic revolution of this great teacher. I am repeatedly frustrated by all the compilations of teachings that have come out since his passing away. The words may be correct, but broken down into small fragmented units, they fail to convey the grandeur of the majestic vision of love that informed Shlomo's reading of Judaism. It was the magic of a dreamer who was able to take others into his dream world. But this dream world was not just words. It was another state of being, another state of consciousness, tapping into the divine presence, and making it accessible through teaching-performances that somehow provided a bridge between heaven and earth. What Shlomo was able to achieve as a teacher was to bring the listener into the whole, into the expanded vision of spiritual reality that is the foundation from which the Religious Genius draws inspiration. The task of the Religious Genius is to convey that reality, and Shlomo did so by telling us what the meaning of the *Mey Hashiloach* and *Likutey Moharan* was, as these were read as statements of divine love, weaving for us an image of ultimate reality as a mandate for our lives here and now.

Anyone who knew Shlomo knew he lived in another world not only because his eyes were always set to heaven, as the famous pictures of him rolling his eyes up and looking skyward suggest. His sights really were set on another world, seeking and drawing from it constant inspiration, bringing it to bear on the concrete teaching that he was transmitting. Indeed, if Religious Genius joins intellect and intuition to a message of love that redefines the meaning of being religious and thereby offers a response to a contemporary need, then with the possible exception of the Lubavitcher Rebbe, there is not a figure in the past 50 years more worthy of the title than Shlomo. But Shlomo lived not simply in the other world of "heaven." His "heaven" was populated with very specific personalities, and it is those whom he somehow imitated, and whose teachings he sought to convey. His attitude to the hassidic masters is difficult to describe in conventional terms of either mere respect or as sources of knowledge. The great hassidic masters were alive for him. It is as though he constantly looked to them as models, while his task was to carry forth and to translate their spiritual reality into the here and now of the circumstances of his followers and their life conditions. If Religious Genius is founded on a logic of imitation, I believe it is correct to argue that Shlomo lived in constant imitation of the hassidic masters, following their way outwardly, but, more importantly, imitating in his overall orientation how they lived, who they were, how they related to God, while seeking to extend this orientation to his concrete relations and to communicate it to his disciples. And I believe it is fair to say that all this also translated into a deep sense of humility, wherein Shlomo recognized the greatness of those who had gone before, the enormity of his mission, and also the frailty of his own human condition. His humor and showmanship may have covered up what I believe was a very deep characteristic of his person, a humility born of a proper perception of his place in reality.

Shlomo's expanded awareness of reality was not exhausted by awareness of spiritual life; it extended to awareness of *Klal Yisrael,* with whom he deeply identified, selflessly so. His broader awareness and his power of love found concrete expression in a life of selfless service, ultimately offering his life for his work, sacrificing his health and well-being as he travelled, preached and made himself available to one and all day and night. His ceaseless giving of his own person extended to his material belongings, in a movement of love that often knew no boundaries. Indeed, Shlomo's genius was a genius of love that went beyond the patterns of behavior of anyone within the Jewish world. Consider his love for non-Jews. Consider his openness to teachers and aspirants of other religions. Consider his offering a testimony of love by dancing in Poland with individuals that others in the Jewish world would have considered as enemies. A gospel of universal love, extending beyond any conventional boundary, was the driving force that led him to extend his reach to all, whether within or without the Jewish community.

But Shlomo was not perfect. No one is. And, given our description above, a Religious Genius, too, can be flawed. Shlomo also had his struggles. He was not simply grounded in the supernal world, seeking to describe it to his followers below. He struggled to attain it, to connect to it, to remain faithful to it. And that struggle, of necessity, is the struggle for purity — purity of action, purity of motive. I have encountered voices, most often of women, who, especially since his passing away, have been turned away from his example and his model because they considered some aspects of his person to be incommensurate with the ideals of sanctity that he, and the tradition, teach. Many of us have struggled with how to address this challenge. It seems to me "Religious Genius" can provide us with a way of tackling this challenge. A Religious Genius is closely related to sainthood, but he is also something other than a saint, and therefore may be flawed in particular ways. Perhaps overcoming flaws might have made Shlomo's genius greater or more potent. But his humanity as it was also provided the foundation for a life that, so I suggest, manifested Religious Genius. With and through various life circumstances, through which he had to struggle, he was able to articulate a vision of what it means to be religious in today's world that has so many of the markings of Religious Genius that we may consider him as one.

If genius involves creativity, Shlomo's genius was founded on a coming together of intense originality and creativity in numerous fields. It manifested through his music. It came through his teaching and storytelling. It expressed itself in a life lived in original ways. But all these different expressions of genius and creativity were at the service of a greater unifying genius — Religious Genius. To appreciate Shlomo, I submit, we must go beyond appreciation for his contributions in so many areas, we must go beyond the powerful memories of how he shaped our lives, we must go beyond the inspiration of his teachings. To appreciate Shlomo, we must appreciate how all these aspects came together in a powerful and unique personality that is worthy of consideration as one of the rare instances that our generation, our century, can call Religious Genius.

# Comparing the Educational Strategies of the Ba'al Shem Tov and Reb Shlomo Carlebach

by Rabbi Avraham Arieh Trugman

IN THIS BRIEF ARTICLE I WILL COMPARE THE ESSENTIAL TEACHINGS AND educational philosophy of the Ba'al Shem Tov (1698–1760) to those of Reb Shlomo Carlebach (1925–1994). Although they were born 227 years apart, the spirit of their respective generations, their life missions, and the specific strategies they used to impart their messages reveal uncanny resemblances.

The Ba'al Shem Tov is universally acclaimed as the inspirational figure whose teachings launched the Chasidic movement. Although he never committed his fundamental teachings to writing nor left an organizational paradigm upon which to build a movement, the charismatic force of his living example was enough to ignite the enthusiasm of his closest students. They subsequently spread his teachings far and wide, creating one of the most successful movements in Jewish history.

Although some might claim that the Ba'al Shem Tov was guided by pure inspiration and spontaneous religious fervor, he undoubtedly developed a firm set of beliefs and was, in fact, quite deliberate about the message he wanted to impart to his students and to his wider audience. Not only was his message unique, but the means by which he imparted his teachings were also; in fact, they were part of his message. The very same can be said about Reb Shlomo. Both the Ba'al Shem Tov's and Reb Shlomo's "educational philosophy" determined the parameters of their lives' work.

The Ba'al Shem Tov was born into a dispirited Jewish world that was about to be shaken by the forces of modernity. He was born approximately thirty years after the debacle of the false messiah Shabbetai Zevi and fifty years after the massacres perpetrated by Chmielnicki and his Cossack armies. Both these events, coming at the end of nearly 1700 years of exile, left the Jewish people distraught, discouraged, and drained of hope for the future. The Ba'al Shem Tov gave the Jewish people hope and strengthened them to withstand the sweeping changes about to occur.

The Industrial Revolution began in approximately 1760, the year the Ba'al Shem Tov died, and the American and French Revolutions followed soon after. In addition to the monumental changes these revolutions wrought, the winds of the Enlightenment began to challenge basic Jewish beliefs in Europe. Within a relatively brief time, both the world at large and the Jewish world changed almost beyond recognition. The Ba'al Shem Tov's teachings prophetically intuited these events and were geared to address this rapidly changing world order, as he clearly believed that he had come to inspire and rejuvenate the Jewish people at a crucial point in history.

Reb Shlomo also seems to have been born into a similarly dispirited and chaotic world and followed a similar philosophical path, which has led him, as it did the Ba'al Shem Tov, to ever-increasing posthumous greatness. Reb Shlomo came of age during and following the Holocaust, which left the Jewish people decimated numerically and traumatized psychologically and philosophically. Assimilation, intermarriage, and Jewish illiteracy grew by unparalleled leaps and bounds among the remaining Jews, while cultural and political upheavals shook the world. The changes occurring over the twentieth century left the Jewish world reeling and confused, seeming to have lost its direction and having no notion of how to stem the rising tide of assimilation. Reb Shlomo, like the Ba'al Shem Tov, clearly responded to the disastrous developments in Jewish life, crafting his worldview and message to the analogous realities of his time. Like the Ba'al Shem Tov, Reb Shlomo left no writings or directions for how his followers should proceed without him, but they took up the torch and have very successfully spread his Torah. The one poignant difference between the Ba'al Shem Tov and Reb Shlomo's eras was the rebirth of the State of Israel in 1948, which for the Jewish people provided a true glimmer of hope in a sea of darkness.

\* \* \*

I will now summarize the Ba'al Shem Tov's cardinal teachings, which reveal his educational strategy, and demonstrate how Reb Shlomo adopted these same ideas and a similar approach to impart his message. Due to the brevity of this article, only an overview of these ideas can be provided. An entire book would be needed to do them justice.

The most important document in our possession from the Ba'al Shem Tov is the letter he wrote to his brother-in-law, Rabbi Gershon of Kitov, describing a mystical elevation of his soul. During this elevation, the Ba'al Shem Tov's soul was in contact with the soul of the Mashiach. In response to the Ba'al Shem Tov's question as to when he would come, the Mashiach replied: "When your teaching will become public and revealed in the world and your wellsprings [of Torah wisdom] burst forth to the farthest reaches...." In other words, the Mashiach conditioned his arrival on the Ba'al Shem Tov disseminating his innovative interpretations of the Torah and his educational initiatives throughout the world. The Ba'al Shem Tov, aware of this mission, trained a small cadre of Torah scholars by personal example so that this objective would ultimately be reached.

Reb Shlomo, following in the Ba'al Shem Tov's footsteps, was also driven to spread the inner light of Torah to the farthest reaches of the globe. Thus he traveled around the world nearly non-stop for forty years, bringing the joy, depth, and relevance of Judaism to communities everywhere. Like the Ba'al Shem Tov, Reb Shlomo also inspired scores of talented and learned individuals by his personal example. These men and women carried out his mission, both during his lifetime and after his passing.

It is no surprise that the sixth Lubavitcher Rebbe, Yosef Yitzchak Schneersohn (the Frierdiker Rebbe), who first sent Reb Shlomo out to college campuses in 1949, was likewise inspired by the Ba'al Shem Tov's mission of disseminating the wellsprings of Torah to the farthest reaches of the globe. His successor, his son-in-law Rabbi Menachem Mendel Schneerson, continued and increased these efforts. (In fact, the Chabad movement and its thousands of dedicated emissaries serving Jewish communities all over the world can only be understood in terms of the Ba'al Shem Tov's mission.)

The Ba'al Shem Tov famously used stories as a means of imparting the very depths of Kabbalistic wisdom, and he did so in a manner that everyone could understand. Just as Rabbi Yitzchak Luria, known as the Arizal, had probed the depths of the *Zohar* and revolutionized its study by revealing its true inner meaning, the Ba'al Shem Tov took the teachings of the Arizal and revolutionized their study by presenting them in new and simpler language. In a revolutionary move, he opened the door of Kabbalistic wisdom to the masses for the first time and infused every word of Torah with deep contemporary meaning that was relevant to each and every person.

Reb Shomo continued this Chasidic tradition of storytelling during his countless concerts and in his many teachings, crafting a laid-back yet heart-opening language that combined Yiddish parlance with the hip language and style of the 1960s. He infused the words he fashioned with deep Torah insight so that all who heard him, no matter how connected to or estranged from their Jewish roots, felt he was speaking directly to them, to their hearts, to their inner souls.

When the Ba'al Shem Tov was five years old, his father, on his death bed, instructed him to follow two imperatives: to fear nothing other than God and to love each and every Jew with his whole heart. He followed these instructions meticulously and forged ahead despite great opposition, creating a new path in the service of God and a refreshing worldview based on rectifying Creation. He reached out to the downcast masses as no one else had before and treated each person, especially the "simple" Jew, with the utmost respect and love.

This love led the Ba'al Shem Tov to formulate one of his most important teachings: the soul is "an actual part of God above." Not only is man created in the image of God, but, according to this fundamental Chasidic teaching, the soul is an actual part of God. Therefore, the Torah's commandment to love one's neighbor as one's self becomes the most effective way to love God.

Expanding upon this notion, Reb Shlomo used to say that while every Jew may not be holy, every Jew is the Holy of Holies. In other words, though Jews may make all sorts of mistakes and act improperly on the outside, they are still fundamentally connected to their inner essences, their Holy of Holies. This hidden inner essence is in fact the part of God above that dwells within. This perspective allowed both great teachers to look beyond the petty inadequacies and superficial exteriors common to all human beings and instead focus upon peoples' inner Godly spark and treat them accordingly.

Reb Shlomo's love of every Jew — and every human being — was legendary. Like the Ba'al Shem Tov, he thought and acted "out of the box" and brought upon himself the wrath of the religious establishment. Despite this, he forged ahead, inspiring his students to create the House of Love and Prayer in the 1960s in San Francisco and Moshav Meor Modi'im in the 1970s in Israel. Both of these places, along with the Carlebach shul in New York City, which he inherited from his father, became platforms to draw in Jews of every persuasion and level of commitment. He used his infectious love and stirring music as a means to inspire and to touch hundreds of thousands around the world.

Reb Shomo's decision to emphasize joy in his teachings and concerts drew directly upon the teachings of the Ba'al Shem Tov. In response to the despondent state of Jewry in his time, the Ba'al Shem Tov's emphasis on serving God with joy and living life joyously was both refreshing and revolutionary. Similarly, in the 1960s, following the Holocaust and under the constant threat to the young State of Israel's continued existence, the sound of music was not exactly "in the air." Yet in this atmosphere of existential doubt and angst, Reb Shlomo burst onto the scene, bringing with him a new spirit and a message of great hope for his generation.

Perhaps one of the greatest contributions these teachers made was teaching their students that prayer was not only an obligation but also a unique opportunity to undergo joyous, meaningful, spiritual experiences. Many of the teachings preserved by the followers of the Ba'al Shem Tov relate to his philosophy and customary practices concerning individual and communal prayer. His great-grandson, Rebbe Nachman of Breslov, carried these teachings about individual prayer to their logical conclusion by teaching *hitbodedut* (literally, lone meditation), a unique spiritual practice that combines prayer, song, meditation, introspection, and intimate dialogue with God, all taking place amid the wonders of nature.

Reb Shlomo's ever-increasing influence is perhaps most apparent in the phenomenal spread of "Carlebach davening," quite literally all over the world, since his passing. The seeds he sowed on Shabbat during his forty years of constant travel have come to fruition as congregations everywhere have not only adopted his melodies but also have attempted to emulate the deep spirit of prayer he tried so hard to instill.

The students of the Ba'al Shem Tov used to relate that when he taught, they were certain they heard the sound of the shofar blown at Sinai. Another tradition reports that when the Maggid of Mezritch, the Ba'al Shem Tov's eventual successor, first came to see him, he was initially unimpressed. In their first private meeting, the Ba'al Shem Tov asked him to learn a section of *Zohar*. The Maggid did so in a dry, uninspired manner. Then the Ba'al Shem Tov learned the same piece and not only did it come alive, the room filled with angels! The Maggid, who was already a great Torah scholar, realized immediately that he had found his teacher.

These two traditions exemplify how the Ba'al Shem Tov revealed Divinity as an immediate and personal experience. He did not just tell stories — he drew people into a living experience of the teachings hidden within, of the Divine.

Likewise, Reb Shlomo was a master at "creating a moment," a deep temporal experience that would move his listeners to the cores of their being. He did this through music, story, prayer, and learning, sometimes fusing them all into a profound moment that could change one forever. He was looking for lost, estranged souls, and he would use this method to bring them back to their Jewish roots.

Another major element of the Ba'al Shem Tov's educational philosophy was the importance of building community in both the spiritual and material senses. When at an early age he became head of a society of hidden *tzaddikim,* his first "campaign" directed them to empathize with and attend to the physical hardships of their fellow Jews, most of whom lived in abject poverty and oppression. A true community could only be built on the basis of its members' mutual caring for one another's most basic needs. His concept of a spiritual community was one in which the members feel a true love and loyalty to one another and a sincere desire for real personal growth in the context of and in harmony with the larger community. This paradigm has successfully served a wide variety of Chasidic communities to this day. It was this spirit and orientation towards practical organization that enabled decimated Chasidic communities to rebuild after the Holocaust with a speed and to a degree that no one imagined possible.

Reb Shlomo, by the sheer power of his personality, created a worldwide network of like-minded people. He used to call his close followers the *chevra,* "the group [of friends]," a term very close linguistically and philosophically to the *chevriya,* Rabbi Shimon bar Yochai's intimate group of students over 18 centuries ago. Even though it was clear that he was the undisputed leader of the group, Rabbi Shimon bar Yochai made everyone feel like they were equal, bonded together in their intimate community of spiritual seekers. Reb Shlomo also created such a feeling and would often say that even more than we need rebbes today, we need good friends.

One of the Ba'al Shem Tov's most important, though lesser known, teachings, is that each person contains within him or herself a spark of *Mashiach* that needs to be revealed and developed. This spark contains a person's pure potential and leadership qualities. (Rabbi Yitzchak Ginsburgh teaches that when enough individuals realize their own personal sparks of *Mashiach*, a critical mass will be achieved which will then draw the energy of the Messianic era into reality.)

This teaching was intrinsically tied in to the Ba'al Shem Tov's overall Messianic vision. The Arizal had taught that the inevitable march to the Messianic era had begun, and the Ba'al Shem Tov felt that it was time to accelerate that process and focus upon the central role *Eretz Yisrael* would play in this unfolding drama. The Ba'al Shem Tov's famous attempt to reach the Holy Land was at that time practically unheard of, and despite his failure to reach his destination, he began a trend that was championed by his students. They, as well as the followers of the Vilna Gaon, helped form the backbone of the Jewish communities living in Israel's four holy cities: Jerusalem, Hebron, Safed, and Tiberias. In truth, this was the first *aliyah* movement of modern times.

Despite the fact that Reb Shlomo traveled around the world for over forty years, performing concerts, running Shabbat programs, and teaching, he, too, placed *Eretz Yisrael* at the epicenter. Notwithstanding his travels, he always spent approximately three months each year in Israel, and during the last twenty years of his life he was based in Moshav Meor Modi'im. At concerts all over the world he played the role of Israel's ambassador, beginning many an event with the words: "I bring you greetings of peace from Jerusalem, the holy city." He always spoke of how the world was constantly improving, despite what many people thought. No matter where he was or what situation he found himself in, he, like the Ba'al Shem Tov, attempted to arouse people's innermost spark of potential and goodness, their individual spark of *Mashiach*. Likewise, he constantly reminded his listeners that the Messianic era was approaching and that the contemporary reality in Israel is a fulfillment of the ancient Jewish prophecies.

Both during and immediately following the many wars the State of Israel has endured, Reb Shlomo would go to play for the Israeli soldiers on army bases and visit hospitals to cheer up the wounded. He brought hope and strength to those on the front lines as no one else could. He told stories and spoke constantly about the awesome holiness of Israel's soldiers and their commitment to the Jewish people and the Land of Israel.

In conclusion it would be highly instructive to apply the various teachings and practices of the Ba'al Shem Tov and Reb Shlomo more systematically to construct an educational paradigm that is desperately needed today on a wide scale. In general, we can safely state that the educational models being used in formal Jewish education — the religious school systems and the non-Orthodox pluralistic day schools and supplementary education tracks — are too formal, cold, and emotionally detached from the student. Independent thinking, hands-on experience, and a feeling of community are not emphasized enough, and creative alternatives to frontal classroom teaching are not experimented with sufficiently.

Just as problematic is many students' sense that what is being taught is boring and unrelated to contemporary reality, and even more disastrously, that it does not relate to their own personal experiences and inner lives. A frequent complaint made by those not raised religiously is that the little they were taught almost always boiled down to what to do and not why we do it. This approach ultimately breeds frustration and disdain. Unfortunately, many students in Orthodox day schools, yeshivot, and seminaries can make a similar complaint. It is quite shocking, for example, how many products of the Orthodox educational system pray by rote daily yet possess very little understanding or feeling for the beauty and depth of the prayers. The *mitzvot* are generally taught with little emphasis placed on their personal relevance or spiritual beauty.

By systematizing the core strategies of the Ba'al Shem Tov and Reb Shlomo, a holistic educational model can be created that will reveal the spiritual underpinnings of Jewish belief and practice. By delving deep within Jewish learning and tradition, the diverse levels of understanding can be made available. It is no longer sufficient to teach only the superficial aspects of Torah. Today's youth are seeking much more than some authorities seem to give them credit for. Unless our students feel a real spiritual depth to Judaism, they will simply look elsewhere for answers to life's deepest questions, or stop looking altogether. The Jewish soul longs for meaning and purpose and if it cannot find it in Judaism it will look elsewhere to fulfill that longing.

Today, this longing is expressed in part by the explosion of interest in Kabbalah, as Jews rebel against the lack of spirituality in the mainstream Jewish world. The amazing spread of Carlebach davening also speaks volumes about this spiritual void. Ongoing Carlebach minyanim have been established on campuses and in communities throughout the Jewish world, filling an obvious need.

Notably some of the most successful programs in Jewish education today — and, indeed, there are some highly successful ones — are adopting the model described in this article. This success — in building vibrant youth groups and summer camps, involving students in community service, and conducting study in Israel, Birthright, and March of the Living type programs — should be built on, as these educational paradigms also use the Ba'al Shem Tov and Reb Shlomo's formula: more creativity, more hands-on experience, and all in all a more spiritual and joyous approach to Judaism.

Ultimately, to a large degree, the success of any educational endeavor depends not just on the material taught but on the teacher's attitude toward and method of approaching the students. Thus, it would make a tremendous difference, if, in addition to focusing on spirituality and creativity, teachers adopted the interpersonal practices of the Ba'al Shem Tov and Reb Shlomo: relating to their students with consummate love and respect; envisioning the Godly potential within each and every student; and committing themselves to assisting each and every one to realize his or her latent potential.

It is within our power to continue to build upon the direction and initiatives the Ba'al Shem Tov and Reb Shlomo pioneered: to fearlessly extend our hands out to every Jew and to the entire world by revealing the inner depths of the Torah in a joyous and easily accessible manner; to treat everyone as an image of God with limitless potential; to build community spirit and sharing while simultaneously developing our own unique connections to the Creator; and to do our parts in bringing the Messianic era and consciousness closer, especially by being connected to *Eretz Yisrael.*

The Ba'al Shem Tov and Reb Shlomo, in their respective generations, took the ancient traditions and forged new pathways relevant to their times. Their wisdom, courage, and creativity are needed now more than ever to meet both our contemporary and future challenges.

Rare Footage of Shlomo Carlebach in the 1970s — Le'ma'an Achay Ve're'ay: http://youtu.be/B1Upx9e40I8

# Moshe Idel and Shlomo Carlebach on Kabbalah

Described and Transcribed by Betzalel Edwards

IN 1992, AT THE OPENING OF YAKAR IN JERUSALEM, A SYNAGOGUE AND educational institution dedicated to Jewish spirituality and creativity, Moshe Idel, one of the top professors of Kabbalah in our generation, and Rabbi Shlomo Carlebach, of blessed memory, spoke before some 50 people about Kabbalah. They each spoke from their own world and hearts. There was barely any common ground between the two presentations.

Moshe Idel described four worlds, not the higher worlds of traditional kabbalah, but four directions taken by four groups or even movements that invest much time and energy in the pursuit of Kabbalistic knowledge.

## *Haredi* Kabbalah

The first direction is found in the Ultra-Orthodox Haredi world. There he described "an intolerable phenomenon" *(bilti musbelet)* that he claimed did not exist ten years previously. The external evidence for a massive Haredi interest in Kabbalah was the prevalence of Kabbalistic books on the market. The internal situation was only accessible through conversations with a number of Haredim who, though apparently members of the extremely traditional and conservative norm, would actually take great risks with Kabbalah. These Kabbalists were, "learning one kind of Kabbalah in the day and another kind of Kabbalah at night." On the one hand they learned the traditional Kabbalah of the Arizal in the "Eight Gates," while on the other they delved into different kinds of kabbalistic books, some of which had even been banned by the religious establishment. The Arizal taught a way of *tzimtzum,* constriction, limitation, with many fasts and a strict adherence to the law. These Kabbalists were involved in a Kabbalah that spreads out into the physical world.

Just what Idel meant by this, except for a plethora of publications, is unclear. Whereas the 19ᵗʰ century was a time when great efforts were made to put a halt to the study of Kabbalah, the end of the 20ᵗʰ brought with it a tremendous resistance to this conservatism and a great blossoming of deep interest in the esoteric mysteries.

## Intellectual Kabbalah

The second direction is in the "outside" world of academia, where there is a great interest in Kabbalah with little or no connection to Jewish tradition. Some of the greatest intellectuals alive today, from Umberto Ecco to Harold Bloom, are all learning Kabbalah. They find a different understanding of culture through Kabbalistic texts. "The interest in the Kabbalistic library as a source of inspiration is only growing stronger and stronger," said Idel. These intellectuals are not trying to return to their traditional roots: Ecco is not even Jewish. Rather, they see Kabbalah as a refreshing alternative to the Greek world-view that has predominated from ancient times until the present. They see Kabbalah as a release from a world-view that was forced upon them. They feel that the Greek intellectual hegemony has reached a dead end. It seems that they have no intrinsic love for the Kabbalah, but are using it as an ancient system that has survived the ages in their fight against the Greek view that has perhaps been blindly accepted and barely challenged.

These two directions are from completely different worlds, yet they find commonality in that they both constitute sudden upsurges of interest in Kabbalah over the past twenty years in opposition to the accepted norm. Idel does not see either movement waning in the near future.

## University Kabbalah

A third direction is a strong new interest in Kabbalah in university curricula by professors, most of whom do not even know Hebrew and cannot decipher a kabbalistic text on their own. And still, Idel was willing to gamble that there are more lecturers in Kabbalah today than there were university students learning Kabbalah ten years ago. He claims that nowadays a major university, both in the Jewish and non-Jewish world, that does not have a good lecturer in Kabbalah is simply lacking. This whole interest began with the late Professor Gershom Scholem. Idel notes that just ten years ago [*i.e.,* 1982] you could barely find a series of academic editions published on the subject of Kabbalah. It is the claim of the Christian academics, who have no spiritual connection to the world that brought forth Kabbalah, that Kabbalah is not just a part of Jewish culture, but of Western culture. This is a claim of Christians, and Idel added, "regardless of whether it is true or not, that is their claim."

## Messianic Kabbalah

There is a great resurgence of interest in Kabbalah among a number of Messianic religious groups. It is Idel's contention that throughout history, whenever there has been a Messianic resurgence of Kabbalah, it is not the study of Kabbalah that caused these groups to want to bring the Messiah, but rather that the Messianic fervor is the source of their Kabbalistic endeavors. The study of Kabbalah was drawn on by the Messianists in order to explain or justify their Messianic goals. Idel claims that today the Messianists are studying Kabbalah with greater intensity than the other three groups and are perhaps more influenced by it than are the other three.

Idel said that if he had more time he would discuss other groups, such as the popular Kabbalah of "HaRav Dr. Berg," which have a "kind of new understanding" of the study of Kabbalah. The Haredi world also has developed interesting new paths in the understanding of Kabbalah and is conducting a massive publishing campaign hitherto unknown in the world of Hebrew publishing. It will be interesting to see the particular kinds of spiritual awakening that all of these movements will stimulate.

## Shlomo Carlebach on Kabbalah

Shlomo got up and teased Moshe Idel about being concerned with keeping to the ten minutes he was given to speak. Many women laughed, and Shlomo said, "He is a great professor, and I am just a simple Jew." There was more bubbly laughter. Then Shlomo realized that he had crossed the line and tried to save it by saying, "It's not a joke; he really is a great professor." Shlomo then continued:

"We are not living in a generation of people who are interested in the Kabbalah. We are living in a generation of Kabbalists. I see one Jew who knows the Talmud by heart, and then he learns Kabbalah, and it's clear that he is not a Kabbalist. Then there is another Jew who eats *treif* on Yom Kippur, never cracked a book in his life, but you feel that he is a Kabbalist. The infinite is inscribed in his heart. Most people learn Gemara; fewer are going with the Zohar. Reb Hatzkele Kuzmir said that Gemara is like bread, and the mysteries of the Torah [are] like wine. If you just drink wine, you get drunk. You also need the Gemara.

"I merited being in San Francisco with all the Hippies. With all of their drugs and all of their faults, they were the true Kabbalists — Kabbalists from the depths of their souls. But they didn't know what to do. Their neshamas broke forth in all directions. They were looking for the deepest depths, and thought they could find it in drugs, but they didn't find it there. Still, they opened up the doorways to Heaven.

"I just read a book by a very religious Jew about what it will be like when the Messiah comes. He writes that the police will arrest anyone who doesn't keep Shabbat. That is his Messiah. There are thousands of people who think the same. They think that the time of the Messiah means every man will have a long beard and *peyos*, and every woman will go with a black kerchief. Do you know why they think that way? It's because they are not Kabbalists. Even if people who think this learn Kabbalah night and day, they are not Kabbalists.

"May we merit to really see the Messiah. 'And all flesh will see as one.' May we truly merit seeing God with our own eyes. 'And our eyes shall behold Your majesty.' When the Messiah comes, everyone will look at everyone else with the eyes of the Messiah.

"You know what the Kotzer said about how the Torah describes Moshe Rabbeinu, 'And he beheld the form of God.' It doesn't mean that Moshe saw God's holy name. It is that he would see a Jew just in the same way God would see a Jew.

"I want you to know, there is Kabbalah from books. And there is Kabbalah that is truly given from Heaven at each and every moment. In this way there is an abundance of Torah scrolls given from Heaven at every moment, the secret of all secrets, the mystery of all mysteries. And if only we had the sense to receive it.

"The Tzidkat HaTzaddik tells us what a secret is. For instance, let's say I went at 4 in the morning to the Kotel to pray that the Messiah would come so I would not have to meet with the professor and say what I am saying. I was *mamash* praying and turning my *peyos* green and black. Let's say I didn't tell anyone what I did. Do you think that that is a secret? That's not a secret; it's just information that I didn't tell anyone. A secret is something that even if I tell it to everyone, it still remains a secret. Reb Tzadok says that a secret needs to be between two people [such as in the phrase in the Psalms, the *sod ye-sharim,* or the council of the upright, where *sod* means both secret and council, that the secret is shared in the council of friends]. A true Jew is one who shares a secret with the Holy One, blessed be He. It's not so simple. I could be a complete Jew, doing *mitzvot* day and night, but I may have not yet reached the secrets of the Torah.

"Do you want to know how to love another person? It's where every-thing I tell the one I love, and everything the one who loves me tells me, is a secret between us. I could sit with someone I love, we could be speaking on the radio for the whole world to hear. But I don't care. Everything is a secret between us. It's deep, deep."

For Shlomo, Kabbalah was a direct experience of Godliness that was beyond one's observance or non-observance of *mitzvot.* One gets the feeling that he was reacting to the academic intellectual approach of Idel, as if to say, "What you and the professors are doing, what many orthodox or even ostensibly Hasidic Jews are doing, is walking around the palace but never actually going in." For Shlomo, the depth of the ineffable secret, a defining aspect of true love, is the true experience of the Kabbalists in our generation. It may be noted that we know nothing about Moshe Idel's inner world. That is to say, just because he is a professor who lectures about the subject but does not reveal the essence subject itself, we cannot know anything about his own personal experience. After all, according to traditional Kabbalah, it is something that is supposed to be concealed and only revealed to the rare initiate. Yet in the exchange between the two at Yakar, Idel was giving a short lecture about historical and social phenomena, and Shlomo was showing us what it is to feel.

*Teaching in Jerusalem, 1990. Photo by Rabbi Joe Schonwald.*

Rabbi Shlomo Carlebach - In Concert Toward *Slichot*
http://youtu.be/rdKtfKcg5rA

# POLITICAL / HISTORICAL

*At Rebbe Nachman's graveside in Uman, 1989. Photo by Joan Roth.*

# Shlomo and the Movement for Soviet Jewry

by Yossi Klein Halevi

THE EXODUS MARCH [PASSOVER 1970*] WAS HELD ON A WARM SPRING day. The area around the Soviet UN mission was filled with Jews. Instead of posters with slogans, we held large white cards, each naming another Soviet Jewish letter writer, covering Manhattan's streets with names.

The march ended at the UN. On a platform in the middle of First Avenue stood Rabbi Shlomo Carlebach, troubadour of the Soviet Jewry movement. Shlomo — that's what everyone called him — wrote songs of longing for redemption. A Shlomo melody could be so compelling, so obvious, that after a single hearing one seemed to have always known it. His songs seeped into the Jewish people almost anonymously, becoming instant classics, as though transmitted from a distant, vital past.

Shlomo was the poet of the lost Jews. He traveled the world, inspiring miracles of Jewish renewal. In communist Prague he danced all night with young Jews surrounded by secret police and then in exhausted ecstasy wrote the SSSJ theme song, *"Am Yisrael Chai,"* the people of

---

\* The Exodus March took place in New York on Sunday, 20 Nisan, 5730 / April 26, 1970.

Israel live. He danced in the streets of Haight-Ashbury with the hippies, whom he called by his own Yiddish endearment, *"holy hippelach."*

Shlomo taught that Jewish redemption would come not from the self-satisfied Orthodox with their three-piece Shabbos suits and kosher Chinese restaurants but from the periphery — the hippies looking for God in material America, the Soviet Jews and the SSSJ kids throwing themselves against either side of the Iron Curtain, all those trying to tear down walls and staking their lives on a miracle. At concerts he told a story of a young woman in Moscow who summoned him into an alley and then whispered the first five letters of the Hebrew alphabet, the only Jewish sounds she knew. "Her holy letters will *mamash* — really — help bring the Messiah," he said.

Shlomo had a big gray beard and long curly gray hair in which were tangled his Hasidic side curls; a large belly; a fleshy, sensuous face; and intense, charismatic eyes. A giant Star of David hung on a chain across his shirt, as if he could be mistaken for anything but a Jew. He seemed to remember everyone he ever met, as though he'd decided to embrace the whole Jewish people by befriending each of its individual members.

I had met him at a Soviet Jewry rally when I was a boy and requested his autograph; he pulled me toward him, kissed my forehead as though blessing me, and laughingly called me "holy brother Joe," insisting on the English name for "Yossi" as a private joke between us. Afterward he would greet me at rallies with a hug and a mischievous smile and, rolling his eyes in feigned ecstasy, shout, "Hey, holy brotha' Joe, *mamash* the highest Jew in Borough Park!" sounding at once like a hipster, a Hasid, a Baptist preacher, and a parody of Shlomo Carlebach.

Though I knew Shlomo only from those fleeting embraces, I cherished him like an old friend. Shlomo created his own messianic reality through exuberant good will, turning passing acquaintances into instant intimates. Other Orthodox Jews measured their spirituality by the thickness of their walls, while Shlomo sang his Hasidic songs in prisons and Indian ashrams and black ghetto schools. In Shlomo's world there were no strangers, no borders between people or nations, certainly no enemies, only souls waiting to be revealed. In Chicago he gave a mugger his wallet and then hugged him; the mugger broke down weeping and returned the wallet. In Moscow he waved to KGB agents who were tailing him, and they waved back. It didn't matter whether every detail happened exactly as Shlomo said it did: for Shlomo was saying that this could be the time of redemption, of the triumph of good, if Jews used the miracle of their survival to help heal the world.

Shlomo stood before the "Exodus" marchers gathered at the UN and said, "Friends, I want you should know that the two holiest Jews in the world are Yankeleh Birnbaum* and Glenn Richter**. I know a lot of rabbis who won't be sitting on the dais when the Messiah comes. But Yankeleh and Glenn will be up there with the highest."

With a sudden vigorous strumming, his voice deep and sure and sweet, Shlomo sang, "*Am Yisrael Chai.*" He began slowly, prolonging each word. Then he paused. Before the song could really begin, the words must be properly introduced, their power acknowledged: "*Am — Yisrael — Chai.*" Again. He held each word until it swelled, then released it, not breathless but reluctant.

---

* Jacob Birnbaum, British-born activist and founder of the Student Struggle for Soviet Jewry in 1964 (SSSJ). It was he who asked Shlomo Carlebach to compose a song in support of the movement. "*Am Yisrael Chai!*" was the result.

** Glenn Richter, Birnbaum's colleague, whom Rabbi Avi Weiss called "the *tzaddik* of the movement."

"Holiest friends," said Shlomo, interrupting himself, "I want you to really sing, our souls should go straight up and tear apart Heaven until God opens the gates of Russia for our brothers and sisters."

Then the song broke through. *"Am Yisrael Am Yisrael Am Yisrael CHAI!"* Shlomo jumped up and down and shouted, "Come on, let's go!" The random crowds organized into circles. We braced each other's shoulders and spun. I was instantly breathless, unable to sing. Someone stood in the center of our circle and waved a giant blue-and-white Israeli flag on a pole, and it looked as if the blue glass monolith of the UN and the white river behind it were absorbed by our flag. We spun until the ground fell away, nothing left but ecstasy, miracle, the certainty of flight spiraling to a place without borders.

— excerpted from Yossi Klein Halevi, *Memoirs of a Jewish Extremist: The Story of a Transformation* (New York: Little, Brown & Company, 1995; Harper Perennial, 2014), Chapter 8, pp. 113-16.

Reb Shlomo with Reb Yehuda Katz in Leningrad 1989:
http://youtu.be/cKME7mmh7CA

# Shlomo Carlebach:
# Minstrel and Rebbe

by Rabbi Yehonatan Chipman

A FEW WEEKS AGO MY WIFE WAS LISTENING TO A EULOGY ON YOUTUBE in memory of Rabbi Mickey Rosen, rabbi of Yakar. The woman who made the presentation began by strumming a Hasidic *niggun* on her guitar and singing it; later she said a few words, telling a Hasidic story and saying over a Hasidic *vort*. Suddenly it occurred to me: over recent decades, there has been a total weather change in Jewish religious life, in the United States and elsewhere. When I was growing up, in the late '50s and early '60s, the synagogue, the Jewish schools, even the youth movement, was dominated by words: by lectures, by talks, by books and articles. There was a sense that one made people better Jews, or would bring people to Jewish commitment — be it Orthodox, Reform, Zionist, secular-cultural, or whatever — by means of rational persuasion and well-reasoned argumentation. Thus, one of the early prominent rabbinic figures in the nascent *Ba'al Teshuvah* movement offered "eight proofs of the existence of God" and "eight proofs of the divine origin of Torah."

All this has changed. Today, wherever you turn in the Jewish world, one finds teachers trying to address the heart. There are those who will begin a lesson text by singing a *niggun,* by telling a story. More and more frequently — at weddings, at synagogue *divrei Torah*, in certain kinds of *yeshivot* — one hears teachers quoting Hasidic teachings. Spirituality and an appeal to the emotions seem to be the call of the hour. Someone wrote a book called *Spiritual Judaism*; one hears talk of "spiritual rabbis" who are expert, not in *halakhah* or Talmud or in teaching texts, but in inspiring people spiritually and emotionally, in guiding them towards an emotional, spiritual experience of Shabbat or *davening*. Kabbalah and Hasidism are amazingly popular everywhere; there's even a course in Kabbalah offered at the adult education program of Temple Emanuel in New York City, which sixty years ago was the flagship synagogue of classical Reform: anti-Zionist, anti-Orthodox, a bastion of Western rationality and decorum.

In writing for this volume, I was confronted by the question: eighteen years after his death, what was Shlomo Carlebach's lasting contribution to the life of the Jewish people in our day? Who was this man? What are we to make of him and his life? I found myself thinking that, if the soul of every human being is in some sense a mystery, that of Reb Shlomo is a total enigma. But then, suddenly, I had my answer: first and foremost, Shlomo was the "granddaddy" of this profound change — the first one to realize the deep emotional and spiritual needs that were not being met by the Jewish establishment, and to attempt to do so; a paradigmatic figure who, through some thirty-five years of public activity, of traveling and teaching and singing and meeting people, literally till his dying day, served as an example and influenced tens of thousands of people, including scores if not hundreds of teachers who have adopted his path.

I don't know whether these things might have happened without him, for there are others who have also contributed to this movement: whether he in some sense was the one who introduced this mode into Jewish life, or whether through powerful intuition he sensed the *zeitgeist* which was just beginning. But in either case, he was the trailblazer: he was the first one to consciously reach out to the heart, from the very beginning. I can personally testify that, already the first time I met him, at Camp Tel Yehudah in the Summer of 1963, over fifty years ago, his approach was essentially the same as it was in later years: *niggunim*, stories, and a simple message, an affirmation of Jewish faith and of joy in being Jewish. From the earliest years of his "mission," one might describe him as a one-man movement to reach out to as many Jews as possible: travelling the world, giving concerts, singing songs, getting people to sing with him, to dance with him, to be joyous.

Shlomo's basic message, repeated over and over again in a variety of ways, was love: love of God, love between man and his fellow, love between man and woman (he saw weddings as the holiest, highest conceivable occasion). All this was very much in keeping with the *zeitgeist*, the mood of the times, particularly the youth culture of the '60s (*e.g.,* the Beatles' "All You Need is Love"). Indeed, one of the criticisms leveled against him by mainstream Orthodoxy is that he gave too much emphasis to *ahavah*, love, without the counter-balancing role of *yirah*, the fear or awe of God.

Traditionally, Judaism spoke of a fine balance between these two as defining man's posture before God. But in point of fact, Orthodoxy as taught in most places seems to have placed excessive emphasis on *yirah* — on strictness in observing the law, on the fear of sin, and on the need for extra strictures or "fences" to keep one from transgression. Shlomo did not have patience for this type of thinking; he felt that the love of God and the love of one's fellow were not emphasized enough. Hence he spoke of the joy of Shabbat, of its holiness, of Shabbat as a door to the infinite, as a day in which the ordinary boundaries of the world fell away — and not so much about the restrictions on various acts, that one may not do X, Y, or Z. Somehow he seemed to feel that if one felt the greatness and holiness of Shabbat, they would come almost as if by themselves — and for many of his followers they did. If you like, Shlomo's approach may be understood as a kind of Maimonidean corrective to the over-emphasis on fear, going to the opposite extreme in order to create, in the end, a healthy middle.

In an "outline of a biography" I wrote some years ago* — essentially a list of questions that need to be answered in order to understand Shlomo's life — I pointed towards what I see as two central turning points in Shlomo's life. The first was his embrace of Hasidism (made together with his twin brother, Elyah Hayyim): the transition from the somber, sober style of Talmudic Orthodoxy, whether that of his *Yekke* (German Jewish) parents or of his Lithuanian mentors at yeshiva, to the emotional richness, intensity, and ecstasy of Hasidism. Elyah Hayyim was to remain an "Orthodox" *hasid* the rest of his life, becoming one of the closest disciples of the Bobover Rebbe, under whom he served *inter alia* as editor of a major publishing project, *The Encyclopaedia of Hasidism*. But Shlomo continued to seek, to search, and to move on.

At a certain stage Shlomo seems to have realized that in mainstream Hasidism, too, something was missing. Somehow — and I see this as one of the great mysteries of Shlomo's life — he came to the realization that there were hundreds and thousands of Jewish youth in colleges all over America, and thousands more of Jewish "flower children," who were yearning for something; he made it his life task to reach out to them and show them the way of Torah. I call this the second great turning point in his life: the break with institutionalized Orthodoxy (though not with observance), including what was by all reports a very painful break with the Lubavitcher Rebbe, who was like

---

* See my essay, "Rebbe and Minstrel," at http://hitzeiyehonatan.blogspot.co.il/2006_10_10_archive.html (Lekh Lekha [Supplement]).

a second father to him*; and his decision to reach out — but not as a "missionary" who has all the answers, but "at eye level," one soul to another — to the hippies who were creating their own ambience in San Francisco. There, sometime in the mid-'60s, he created the House of Love and Prayer — part-commune, part-synagogue, part beit-midrash, part-hippie crash pad — which was to become the center of his activity. It was a daring move. He thus invented his own path, created his own mission in life and his own *modus operandi* — something very few people do. The fact that so many people revere him as their rebbe and teacher and friend suggests that he was doing something very right.

## Shlomo and Music

Although it is clear to me that Shlomo saw his life work as bringing Jews closer to the Torah and to their Creator, he is best known to the majority of people as a musician, both as composer and performer. Hence, a few words about his music are called for. Since his death in 1994, his music has conquered much of the Jewish world, especially among the younger generation, and in a great number of synagogues the so-called "Carlebach *Nusach*," a certain set of melodies for Kabbalat Shabbat, has become *de rigeur*, whether every Friday night or once a month.

---

* An interesting memory about this: once, during my college years, I went to the great farbrengen at 770 Eastern Parkway on *Yud-Tet* Kislev, the "New Year of Hasidus" — the most important day in the Lubavitch calendar. At one point in the evening, I noticed Shlomo, who had quietly slipped into the huge hall, almost surreptitiously, and was standing quietly by himself all the way in the back. It was as if he felt that he was not really welcome there and was regarded as a kind of black sheep, but that he couldn't stay away from "being with the Rebbe" on this day.

At the time that Shlomo began singing publically, in the middle of the last century, Jewish religious/synagogue music was dominated by *hazanut,* by the traditional cantorial art (which was itself not so "traditional," but, as practiced by such great cantors as Yossele Rosenblatt and the two Koussevitzky brothers, was essentially a nineteenth century creation). *Hazanut* was basically a performing art, in which the cantor-soloist sang elaborate compositions for certain selections from the *tefillah,* at times accompanied by a trained choir, while the congregation-audience sat passively and listened. Some have criticized Shlomo Carlebach and his simple, catchy tunes for undermining *hazanut* as a high art form — but the truth is that for a long time *hazanut* had been speaking to fewer and fewer people. It will no doubt continue to exist, appeal to certain individuals, and even thrive; in recent years, there are even some dedicated composers and choir directors who have devoted great efforts to its preservation and revival. But by the post-war era many young Jews were looking for something different, and Shlomo presented an exciting alternative. To begin with, his music was centered, not on the cantor as a performer, but on the community singing together, on public prayer as a collective outpouring of joy, of enthusiasm in Jewishness, even to the point of getting up and dancing (something for which there is a certain precedent in historical Hasidism). Secondly, traditional Ashkenazic Jewish music had a sad and melancholy note; typically, it was set in a minor key. Shlomo's music was more often in a major key, full of joy and a more positive feeling (although, if one listened carefully, there was a certain melancholy note in Shlomo's own singing voice — but I attribute this to Shlomo's own profound loneliness as a person, rather than to any statement about Jewishness).

I do not think that Shlomo was the only one to bring about this "weather change" in Jewish music, although he was certainly a central catalyst. I see his music as reflecting three main influences: first, American folk music, which flourished in the 1950s and '60s (he certainly did not adopt the rock idiom of later decades, despite its ubiquitous presence in the hippie milieu within which he moved). Second, the creation of the State of Israel and the emergence of an indigenous Israeli style of folk music; the sense of security and at-home-ness that came from living in one's own natural environment, and the concomitant feeling that it was okay to feel happy and to express happiness, which also found an outlet in the musical realm. In addition to "secular" folk music, the Zionist religious community — the religious kibbutz movement, B'nai Akiva, the *yeshivot hesder*, and ordinary Israeli synagogues — began over the course of time to create new melodies for prayer and for the Shabbat table, which reflected these same positive moods — and these, too, by and large, were also set in a major key. Third (or perhaps first in terms of Shlomo's biography): while reflecting these influences, Shlomo's music was also deeply influenced by authentic, indigenous Hasidic music, which he absorbed in his youth and young adult years when he and his brother Elyah Hayyim made the rounds of various Hasidic courts. Some of his *niggunim,* such as the "Krakover *Niggun*," which he composed when he first visited the former Torah center of Krakow in Poland, is a real Hasidic *niggun* in every sense.

One more important point: Shlomo was an auto-didact in matters musical. To the best of my knowledge, he never received formal training in music theory or composition, never studied in a musical conservatory, and it's unclear whether he even knew how to read sheet music (certainly in the early years). Yet he was amazingly prolific, writing over his lifetime hundreds if not thousands of eminently memorable melodies. The following passage, although written about Paul McCartney, could equally well have been written about Shlomo Carlebach:

A gift for melody is so rare that, in revenge, critics call it a craft. Of all the great songwriters, few have had the gift so distinctly as [he]; even fewer, perhaps, have seen it last so long. ...like Irving Berlin, [he] has managed to produce memorable tunes for a span of more than forty years. (It is probably no coincidence that [they] are among the least trained of the great songwriters: neither could read or write music.) ...his melodies have never stopped coming, and they all still have the self-sustaining "Whistle me" quality they had when they first appeared, so many years ago.[*]

On one or two occasions I had the privilege of being present at the birth of a new Shlomo *niggun*: suddenly, he would stop whatever he was doing and tentatively sing the new melody a few times; he might then go over to the piano, if there was one, feeling out the basic melodic lines — but he did not write it down or ask for sheet music paper.

## Shlomo and the *Teshuvah* Movement

Shlomo played a formative role in what has become known as the *teshuvah* movement. He and Zalman Schachter, as young rabbis connected with the Lubavitcher movement, were reportedly the first two emissaries of the Lubavitcher Rebbe to college campuses, in 1949 — and, as such, among the few emissaries sent by the *"Freirdiker Rebbe,"* (Rabbi Yaakov Yosef Schneersohn (1880–1950), the sixth Rebbe of Chabad, who brought this Hasidic school to America in 1940). Some people have even hinted that Shlomo and Zalman were the ones who first suggested the idea of outreach to the Rebbe.

---

[*] Luke Nicholson, "Music Man" (Showcase by David Bailey), in *The New Yorker,* Nov. 10, 1997, p. 116.

The idea of *teshuvah*, of outreach or *kiruv*, of "missionizing" Judaism to assimilated Jews, is so familiar, and in many places has been so successful, that we forget that is a relatively recent phenomenon. To start with, one must be able to imagine the possibility that American-born, assimilated, secularized Jews, particularly young people, could and might wish to return to traditional Judaism. During most of the modern period, what came to be known as "Orthodoxy" was so focused upon bolstering its own communities, and keeping those who were still faithful to the tradition within its walls, that it could not or did not reach outwards. It was only after the Second World War that things began to change. Part of Shlomo's genius lay in his recognizing the spiritual longing, the need, nay, the hunger for religious and spiritual meaning in life among the second and third generations of Jews born in the United States — the so-called "baby-boomers," born after the war, who came of age in the mid-to-late 1960s. This was a generation of young people who no longer needed to struggle for economic survival and success as did their parents's generation, who began to ask questions of meaning and, in the Hippie movement or the anti-Vietnam War movement of the '60s, to rebel against social convention.

Shlomo's approach was dramatically different from that of just about every other Jewish "outreach" teacher, whether that of the Lubavitch movement which he left during the 1950s, of the Lithuanian yeshiva world, of other Hasidic groups such as that of the Bostoner Rebbe or Rabbi Shlomo Ben-Zion Twersky of Denver, or from the Modern Orthodoxy of Rabbi Shlomo Riskin and Yeshiva University's JSS program. First, in terms of the people towards whom he directed his message: Shlomo reached out to the hippies, setting up a House of Love and Prayer in the heart of San Francisco, whose doors were open to all. In this by itself his approach differed from all the teachers mentioned above, who worked within the established Jewish communities and their synagogues, which were by their very nature part of the middle-class milieu which most of the hippies so decisively rejected.

Somehow, Shlomo found a common language with the hippies. The fact that a man like himself — someone a full generation older than most of the hippies (he was born in 1925), European born and bred, who had personally experienced the beginnings of the Nazi persecution of the Jews in Austria; someone steeped in traditional Orthodoxy, who had spent his youth engaged in intense Torah learning and Hasidic *avodah* — a life of divine service through meditative prayer, Torah study, and mitzvot — was able to reach these "kids," is little short of remarkable. How he did this, from whence he drew the powers, the understanding of how to talk to them, what words to use, how to translate the Hasidic message into their idiom, is one of the mysteries of the human soul.

A partial answer lies in two areas: a) music; b) something in Shlomo's personality. Quite simply, he acted as if he was one of them; there was no distance, no sense of him preaching, or that he had all the answers, that he was speaking from above to below. Rather, he seems to have seen himself — dare I say it? — as a broken human being like themselves. In the end, he felt more at home among his "hippie Hasidim" than anywhere else in the world. He, too, was anti-middle-class; he was too foot-loose for the typical bourgeois home with dining table and sofa with plastic covers and a breakfront with glass doors to matter to him. One also had the sense that he understood the hippie kids's problems, specifically, with their parents.

## Shlomo and Hasidism

But Shlomo not only reached out to young people; he created a new type or school of Hasidism. He was, in a very real sense, a Rebbe — a Rebbe of a new type. His "hippie Hasidim," unlike most of the *ba'alei teshuvah* in mainstream Orthodoxy (including that of Lubavitch, in which he'd been deeply involved during an earlier stage of his life), did not assimilate into existing models of piety — whether that of Lithuanian Talmudic scholarship, traditional Polish, Galician, or Hungarian Hasidism, or (here in Israel) the new models of Sephardic Haredism. Rather, they created their own model, which took its inspiration from the unique personality of Shlomo. In terms of dress, they wore coarsely knitted, big woolen *kippot*; informal, colorful, American-style "hippie" dress, but with long *peyot* and *tzitzit* hanging out. The style of worship was unique — very emotional, intense, enthusiastic. Shabbat was sometimes described as an endless "high." Some have even suggested that the feeling among Shlomo's Hasidim may have been the closest thing to the feeling in the original circle of the Baal Shem Tov. But, withal, he also conveyed the Hasidic message to the "second level" of those he influenced, in concerts and teach-ins, where he would talk and sing for hours, weaving together Hasidic stories, teachings, and songs or *niggunim*.

During his years in the yeshiva, and later, travelling among various Hasidic groups — including not only Lubavitch, but also Vizhnitz, Bobov, Modzhitz, and many others — Shlomo acquired encyclopedic knowledge of Hasidism. These experiences, coupled with his phenomenal memory, made him a walking treasure-trove of knowledge of Hasidic highways and byways. He was expert in all aspects of Hasidism: the formal teachings of Hasidism, as recorded in hundreds and thousands of books; Hasidic song and melody; Hasidic folklore and legends; and the traditions related to the multitude of various Rebbes, including genealogies and teacher-student relations of all the major and minor dynasties over the generations. All these he absorbed and learned and shared with his disciples — reshaping them and filling them with a kind of energy that made them attractive and spell-binding.

## Unanswered Questions

There are many unanswered questions about Shlomo. First, how did he make the two transitions mentioned above and, more important, what motivated moved him, psychologically, to do so? Here one enters into the realm of the secrets of the soul, which no person can ever know about another — all the more so of a great person like Shlomo. How did he find the language, the way to bridge the gap between himself and his "hippie" disciples, so as to "turn them on" and excite them about Judaism? Music, as a universal language of the soul, was part of the answer, but not the whole answer.

A second group of questions: What did he know about Western thought? Was he what we would call an intellectual? He was clearly blessed with an extraordinarily powerful and quick mind, as well as a retentive memory — but, offhand, he seems to have been the type of the pure Torah scholar, who was not interested in philosophies outside of Judaism; his path was not that of "synthesis," in the style of Soloveitchik. His knowledge of the world was far more "down-to-earth," even "street smart."

Third: What were his views on the "issues of the day"? He did not exist on the usual continuum of Left/Right; Haredi/Modern Orthodox; liberal/conservative. On a gut level, he had a very open approach to things like women's participation in prayer — he didn't require a *mechitzah*, he agreed to give women *aliyot* — but he did not do so out of reasons of "Orthodox feminism," but simply out of an intuitive sense that this was the right thing for the situation of time and place in which he found himself.

PERSONAL / MYSTICAL

*Reb Shlomo davening in 1990 with chevre at the "Synagoga Remuh," located in the once glorious Jewish quarter of the Kazimierz district in Krakow.*

*As far back as 1495, King Jan I settled pious Jewish refugees from the then-European diaspora here; it subsequently grew into the center of world Jewry and remained so for centuries. The synagogue, built in 1558, was adjoined to the Remuh cemetery, one of the oldest in Europe. Both structures are named after the holy Rabbi Moses Isserles Auerbach, the Maimonides of Polish Jewry, referred to as the RaMa or "Remuh."*

*The Nazis wiped out the whole community during WWII, but when the war ended, the Remuh's matzeva remained, giving rise to stories of his miraculous powers, as well as to stories of Yossele the Holy Miser.*

*And, it was here, inside this historic, restored, "Synagoga Remuh," that Reb Shlomo memorialized the thousands upon thousands of Jews who had marched across the Krakow bridge, hauling household remnants to an unknown destiny. Harrowing visions brought down from heaven soon channeled their way into the Krakow Niggun — a heart-rending ode of joyful surrender to redemption, a Shlomo melody beyond words.*

*(Photo and text by Joan Roth)*

# The Master of Virtuous Reality

by Rabbi Zalman Schachter-Shalomi

WHAT CAN I SAY ABOUT REB SHLOMO, MY BUDDY? I WAS TEN OR ELEVEN years old when I first met him in Baden, near Vienna. I had to go and ask his father, Reb Naftali, a question about a chicken that I had brought along with me on the trolley from a neighboring town called Voeslau.

He and his brother, Reb Eliya Chayyim, were twins. And Eliya Chayyim was a wonderful person in his own right who sought to be close to Hasidic Rebbes and Hasidim in both his demeanor and his garb. And if Reb Shlomo was like buckshot, then Reb Eliya Chayyim was a sharp-shooter. He would pick individual students and would train them to become rabbis and scholars. He also traveled around to collect money for Zekher Naftali, which printed wonderful volumes of Hasidic materials that had gone unpublished or fallen out of print.

When I met Shlomo again, in the United States, I urged him to come join us in the Hasidic *yeshiva*. He refused at that time. He was studying under Reb Aaron Kotler, of blessed memory, who was one of those amazing *geonim,* prodigies of Talmud, the commentaries, and the codes. So I asked him then, "Why do you stay there?" And he told me, with a tear in his voice, "The reason I stay is that if I go, there won't be anyone to take over where Reb Aaron left off."

I think to his dying day, Reb Shlomo kept with him little notebooks in which he would record, while on the plane, going from place to place, beautiful Torah *novellae* that he didn't have customers for. Several times he had tried to open up something like a *yeshiva* in Brooklyn, but never with great success. And shortly before he died, he had organized a gathering of descendants of Hasidic Rebbes and wanted to re-infuse them with the fervor and the light so that they might be able to carry out the chain of transmission. That meeting never happened. Reb Shlomo passed on.

On another occasion, later, after Reb Shlomo had left the Lakewood Yeshiva for the Lubavitcher Yeshiva, I asked him a similar question. By now Shlomo was considered one of the most promising young Talmudists in the country and pronounced an *illui,* a Torah genius, by Reb Aaron Kotler. So this time I asked him, "Shlomo, Reb Aaron treated you as his own son, your future was sure — how could you leave that?" And he looked at me penetratingly and said, "Don't you see, the Jewish world has been destroyed! The leaders of our people are gone — who will guide us? Somebody has to take their place. From Lakewood come scholars, but from Lubavitch come outreach workers. At Lakewood I could expand my own soul, but at Lubavitch I'll learn to expand the souls of thousands! I did it, Zalman, for the six million." He was an amazing being!

But that was also part of his music. He designed that into his melodies. He wanted to have melodies that would go so quick that people would learn them with great ease and then join in the harmony and in the sharing. Singing with Shlomo would open up the heart for his teaching. But if you asked people later on, "What did he say?", hardly anybody remembered. It was a quality that was experienced.

Recently, on Reb Shlomo's *yahrzeit* (the anniversary of his death), we had a meeting at my home, and people brought some of Shlomo's melodies that they had transcribed. One melody is from the *Kedusha,* from the *Sanctus* of the *Shabbos* morning liturgy, which is so complex and beautiful (very different from Reb Shlomo's later melodies). One person sat down at the piano, another was at the clarinet, and I sang along with them. And we made that old melody live, that melody which will probably fade into obscurity. Most people don't sing it anymore because it isn't as easy to learn as the later ones. And what we then discussed is how Reb Shlomo gave up even his genius for making more complex music, much as he had given up his genius for Torah scholarship, in order to be able to make the music that people would be able to get very fast and to sing along with.

Shlomo was also known as a great storyteller, and I like to say of him that he was a "genius of virtuous reality." Not virtual but virtuous reality. When he would tell the stories, they would come out in such a way that they would give you a great longing to live the life of the person whose great virtues were being talked about. You aspired to that holiness. He always told stories about the hidden ones, despised by people on the outside, who were unaware of their real value and true saintliness. And I think that was also a description of Reb Shlomo himself. For it happened that on the thirtieth day after his passing, there was a meeting at the synagogue, and when the people came out, they found some homeless people standing crying. And the people said, "What are you crying about?" And they answered, "Who will come to us now that Reb Shlomo is gone?" It turned out that there was a place where many of the homeless would go "bunk out" (before Mayor Giuliani drove them away), and Shlomo would come to them laden with food and with his guitar, and he would sing to them and tell them stories. They said, "Even if you will give us the food, who will come in the middle of the night and tell us stories and sing and help us?"

✳  ✳  ✳

One of the great teachings of Reb Shlomo was the teaching of the "Torah of the Nine Months." The Talmud states that there is an angel who teaches the fetus while in its mother's womb. A candle is burning at the fetus's head (obviously, this is not to be understood as a physical candle), and there the angel instructs the fetus in the Torah that she or he will need throughout life. At birth, that same angel touches the child under the nose, creating the cleft, and all the teaching that was learned in the womb is forgotten. And so the question is raised, "What is the point of the teaching if it is only going to be forgotten?" And the answer is that the teaching is indeed forgotten, but it gets restored, resurrected. This is the source of the *déjà vu* phenomenon. Someone teaches us something, and we feel as if we knew it all along. Reb Shlomo was fond of saying, "How do you know that you have met your true teacher? Whatever this person teaches you, you knew it all along." And it is the Torah of the other three months that gives us trouble; other people have to handle that for us. And when Shlomo and I were discussing this teaching, my daughter Shalvi was in the womb, and so was his daughter Nedara. So you can imagine how excited we were about this teaching of the "Torah of the Nine Months" at this time. And both of us were eagerly awaiting these babies to make their appearance, thinking, could they possibly remember?

That is an example of one of Shlomo's popular teachings. They are fun and helpful, but he could also teach in such a way that he could penetrate to the core of one's heart with great skill. And in a way, I have been leading up to the teaching with this long introduction so that you will get a sense of what a complex and magical person has given this teaching based on the words of Reb Zakok HaKohen, one of the great students of Reb Mordecai Yosef of Ishbitz. Shlomo glossed these teachings with a depth of insight all his own.

So in the text, when the world says that the "world is getting less and less religious," Reb Shlomo via Reb Zadok says, "On the contrary, the souls are becoming more and more refined." And notice that he doesn't make the distinction between religion and spirituality. When we look at the issue of spirituality, which many people are into as opposed to religion, we have to ask, what is it that they don't like about religion? One thing is the hierarchical and patriarchal language, the antifeminist sentiment that goes all the way through the Vatican to the Taliban, *Meah Shearim* to the Laws of Manu, and that is a big part of the problem.

The other thing is that most of the religious traditions have wanted to draw a distinction, saying that nature is tainted, nature is fallen, and spirit is elevated. *Hasidut* always makes the claim for the supranatural, saying that the name YHVH represents the supranatural, while the name *Elohim* represents the natural, and that we see ourselves as being in a supranatural situation. The Church has done the same thing, and I think that when orthodox Islam looks at itself, it can see the same trend. There is a sharp vision that comes with monotheism that wants to say there is good, which is Divinely ordained, and there is evil, which is all that is against the good. And this is what people who are into spirituality don't like so much and why philosophies that come from the "export East," which is very monistic and shorn of its obligations and cultural attachments, are embraced so quickly.

However, this dissatisfaction is quite natural when our worldview, our paradigm, has shifted to an organismic way of looking at the universe. Because then it looks to us as if all those other paths, which create that sharp surface tension between good and evil, are definitely not where we want to go. The *Tanya* of Reb Shneur Zalman of Liadi talks about the "middle domain," which he calls the *K'lipah* of *Nogah* — Venus is the way we translate that — and this comes close to Freud's libido theory. *Nogah* is basically neutral in and of itself but can go either toward the holy or in the other direction. If an action is done selfishly and for one's own sake, it tends to go for the evil side, but it can also be raised to the holy because it is basically translucent — light passes through it — which is why Venus, *Nogah*, also means "shining."

So Reb Shlomo keeps the definition of religious even when he means spiritual so that there is not an unnecessary divorce. And maybe, he says, on the outside it looks like many people are breaking away from God, meaning that they are breaking away from formal religion, but on the inside they are becoming increasingly holy. On the exoteric level, there seems to be a shriveling up, but on the esoteric level, a lot of strengthening is going on. People are getting some distance so as to be able to discern the chaff, which is necessary periodically.

Some years ago, Pir Vilayat Khan organized a meeting in Berkeley that was held on a weekend, including Shabbos. And for Sunday, since so many other people were going to be at that meeting, we organized a special meeting of Jews that we called "Torah and Dharma" (while a protester walked around outside with a placard that said, "Torah versus Dharma"). It was at the Pauley Ballroom, and some wonderful things happened at that meeting. First, we walked the room before the meeting, dedicating the space, because the Pauley Ballroom was used for secular activities previously, and we had to make it a sacred space. On the platform there were about ten panelists and a moderator, Murshid Moineddin Jablonski, the only non-Jew. All the rest were of Jewish birth. One wore a Sikh turban, another was the prior of a Zen monastery, and others were Sufis, but each had a different kind of belief, and I turned out to be the only "Jewish Jew" on the panel. And we had come together to deal with the relationship between Torah and Dharma. So I asked Reb Shlomo if he could come and join me on the panel. And he said he couldn't because he was already committed on that date. But we were in my car during this conversation, and since I had a tape recorder with me, I asked if he could record something for the meeting. And here is how he began:

"The Torah spells out that a *kohen,* a priest, is not to defile himself unto the dead. He must not be in a place where a corpse is and must not be under the same roof with a corpse and so on. Elsewhere it says, *Siftey kohen yishm'ru da'at v'torah yevakshu mipihu*, 'The lips of the *kohen* guard knowledge, and teaching you will seek from his mouth'" [Malachi 2:7].

So it is clear that one of the functions of the *kohen* is to teach people. Thus the Ishbitzer, Reb Mordecai Yosef, in his *Mei HaShiloach*, points out that the reason why a *kohen* must not defile himself unto the dead is not so much for reasons of physical purity and impurity as for reasons of emotional response, for the existential feeling of the situation. Often a person who is confronted by a corpse cannot help but be angry at God — "Why did you do this? You give people life and then they have to die. Why do you take that life away from them?" And this anger turns people off from being able to say a good word about God. So since the *kohen* is supposed to be speaking to people about the knowledge of God, and you are supposed to seek Torah from his mouth, he must not defile himself unto the dead in order to avoid that anger.

After the Holocaust, Shlomo said, we all became defiled by death. We all were in touch with so much death that even the teachers who were supposed to be teaching us, like the *kohanim*, were in some way angry at God. The anger wasn't even conscious with many people. It was unconscious, and therefore it even contaminated the teaching that they gave. And so the souls of people weren't quite able to absorb the teachings, nor were they quite open. It was as if people had been impregnated — and this is my interpretation of what Shlomo was saying — by an attitude that was "doing Judaism" in an angry, reaction-formation way, doing the *halakha* as if saying, "See God, we keep our word. Where were you?" That is the unconscious motivation. So what did God do at that time? Since there were some people in the Far East, in India, Japan, and Tibet, who could teach us about God Most High and were not then contaminated, they came to America and many Jews turned to them in order to have a connection with God.

That was a wonderful teaching, and it touched us all a great deal to hear that little bit of tape from Reb Shlomo. Many of the people who were on the panel spoke afterward of how their souls had taken them to spiritual paths and what a pity it was that they didn't have anyone in Judaism to teach them at that time. Now this was in 1974, and you figure that fifteen to twenty-five years before, many of them were around Bar Mitzvah age in the 1950s and 1960s. And that way had been closed to them after the Holocaust. They didn't have a sense of juicy spirituality in Judaism then because at the time everything spiritual was considered to be an aberration of mind or superstitious in the normative traditions.

When I came to Manitoba in 1956, another rabbi there called my board and said, "You must fire him!" "Why?" "Because he's teaching the kids how to meditate, and don't you know you can go crazy from meditation?" That is where we stood at that time. But from the place in which we now stand, it looks quite different and some things have come full circle. My wonderful compensation after all these years is that one of my students is now the rabbi of that congregation. So now they have someone who is an expert meditator.

— from Rabbi Zalman Schachter-Shalomi, *Wrapped in a Holy Flame: Teachings and Tales of the Hasidic Masters,* edited by N. M. Miles-Yepez (San Francisco: Jossey-Bass, 2003). Used by permission of the author.

Eulogy for the Rebbe of Lubavitch:
http://youtu.be/E9_d1eVkwSE

Teaching at the Carlebach Shul in New York,
October 1988: http://youtu.be/9S9eLR-Tubo

# What's the Most Important Thing for Us to Do Now? We Need to Learn How to Learn

by Barry Barkan

Alter Shoresh Ben Tsion Moshe Ben Reuven HaKohen v'Shoshana

It's midnight, January 1, 2013, as they reckon time here in Berkeley, California, on the West Coast of North America. I am making yet another attempt to write this article, to bring down Torah in honor of Reb Shlomo Carlebach's eighteenth *yortzeit* that will convey the same light that my teacher of blessed memory conveyed. It's a cold clear night. Yesterday's full moon is on the wane but still bright. The cloud formations dance with the moonlight.

In my mind's ear I hear Reb Shlomo singing, *Rebbe Nachman says, Rebbe Nachman says the greatest sin in the world is to be sad...is not to be filled with joy.* I reflect on how the sky above is the same sky beneath which Rebbe Nachman danced across the very narrow bridge. The air we breathe is the same air that Adam and Eve breathed. If we foul the air, there can be no other for the grandchildren. May they grow up in a world where wholeness and harmony flourish. It's all so very deep and so very real and so very urgent.

I have such deep intention to write something that is worthy of the love and gratitude I hold in my heart for my teacher, something that will make life better for all of us everywhere who are created in G-d's image. It's obvious to me that the only way I can write something that is worthy of Reb Shlomo is to ask my Holy Rebbe to tell me what to say and be his scribe.

I am part of the Aquarian Minyan *chevra,* a community that was seeded by Reb Shlomo in the San Francisco House of Love and Prayer days and brought together by Reb Zalman Schachter-Shalomi. Our community is a true hybrid of these two greatest *shluchim* of Reb Yoseph Yitzchak, the sixth Rebbe of Lubavitch. Together, each in his own way, they wove a bridge for those of us who were in the counter-culture of the sixties — the earth-loving, feminist, tai-chi-ing, yoga-sitting peaceniks — to find our way home in the mysteries of Shabbos and Kabbalah. We may not be so strong on Halacha, but we are strong on nurturing and amplifying the spirit that our two Rebbes brought to us as they cultivated the Chassidic soul in our American experience. I think of what emerged in this land as "native American Chassidism." Each place has its unique spirit and the spirit of this place is infused with the spirit of the people who were here before us, and it has mixed well with the Chassidic essence that our teachers gave over to us to help make us more whole.

Many of us in this community take seriously the permeability of the membrane that separates the higher realms from the world that is. In my heart I believe that even from his place in the world of wonder, it is possible to learn with Reb Shlomo. Being his scribe under such circumstances is not easy. Reb Shlomo is somewhere that is not here and at the same time is more real than all the greed and fear and violence and sadness and hopelessness that seem to be everywhere. From his place beyond *Chochmah,* the voice of the Master can only be heard in profound, yet muted impressions that come and go quickly. And so I apologize in advance for any inaccuracies or inconsistencies in what I write.

I close my eyes and envision Reb Shlomo. His face is luminous in my mind's eye. My mind drifts to my mantra, repeating the special configuration of G-d's names with which I ground myself in the ultimate reality. Shlomo comes in and out of focus. Snippets of his golden wisdom that I have heard from his mouth over the years travel across my mind at the speed of thought as variations of his themes that have inspired me so many times come to me.

> Shalom to you wherever you are.... We want so much, we need so much. We ask so much from heaven. You know when they deliver the good? When we are filled with joy, the heavenly mailman can't wait to give us what we need. When you are filled with joy we can do anything. We can carry the whole world on one finger.
>
> We don't have peace because we don't have enough joy in the world. People only hate because they are sad.
>
> Friends, the biggest problem in the world is that everyone is against. Even the good people are against. Against war. Against sickness. Against hate. We need to become for. For peace. For health. For war. We need to be for.
>
> It has to be so strong, this Jewishness, that nothing in the world can move them from it. On the other hand it needs to be connected to every other human being in the whole world.

"Yes, my Rebbe, my teacher, my friend, I thank you for all you have given over in your journey here on earth," I say speaking in my imagination, "but please, can you give me a piece of Torah I haven't heard before for me to share now in your name, with anyone who will read it and perhaps pass it on. I'm kind of desperate. I need to write something in your holy honor today so I don't let down my holy friend Rabbi Joe Schonwald who has taken on the mitzvah of creating this celebration of your teaching."

I have received transmissions from the other side of the veil before. Years ago, at a time when Reb Zalman came to Berkeley to teach about the Tree of Life, I sat under a live oak tree and had a vision that seemed to come from the mouth of the Sacred that called me to the mission of restoring the role of elder in the world for the sake of the future generations. The voice was so powerful that I took on the mission as my life's work.

Shlomo's stories have taught about communications between the world that is and the world to come when great rebbes among the early Chassidim communicated with their students after they left this world. On the other hand, I'm not on the level of the great students of great rebbes in the nineteenth century who were themselves great rebbes. But Shlomo taught that even though we are far less worthy than our grandparents, we have to be even greater than they were. This teaching may be the root source of what Reb Shlomo called "holy *chutzpa*." Coming from the movements of the sixties, in which we believed that not only could we change the world but that it was our birthright and duty to do so, the concept of holy chutzpa resonated with me and sealed the deal for my tribal return.

In times of need, when my heart was breaking, I have called on Reb Shlomo for guidance, and I received what I experienced as clear instructions from him. Once, in the midst of a conflict that was tearing our community in half, I said, "Okay Shlomo, I don't know what to do. This situation is beyond my ability to fix, tell me what to do next." Seven years after he left the planet I heard his voice say as clearly as if he were right here with me,

> Whoever you disagree with the most, that's the person you should agree with the strongest.

Who else but Shlomo could come up with such a teaching? Imagine if the right-wingers and left-wingers would do such a thing.

When I re-entered the over-heated conversation, I voiced support for the position of the person I had been disagreeing with the most. Our hearts had become so hardened and our ears were so closed, that it took her a while to hear that I was actually agreeing with her. The results were unbelievable. In a few minutes the whole energy shifted as she gladly moved over to fill the space between us and meet me in the middle.

So, Reb Shlomo, here we are, today, at the start of the year 2013 of the Christian Era. Things seem to have gotten even worse than they were when you walked among us. The whole world seems to be going *mishugge* with conflict and hatred and selfishness. We need help, Reb Shlomo. All over the world, we need to hear a deeper, more profound voice to relax the fear that keeps us from grounding ourselves in G-d's abundance.

"What's the most important thing we can hear from you now to change everything?" I ask.

I breathe deeply, repeating G-d's holy names again and again. It's cold outside, but I bundle up and sit on my porch, waiting hopefully and expectantly for the words of the master, gone from this world for over 18 years, to give over a piece of Torah that can change the world.

I begin to hear Reb Shlomo's voice, and I rush inside to write down what my mind can hold onto.

> Whatever the tzaddik can do, anyone can do. The tzaddik opens doors, liberates spaces, so that each of us can come through the door if we have the right intention. Inside of each

one of us is a tzaddik that grows when our actions and our intention to do good become one.

Once in San Francisco, in the seventies, I had the privilege of being Reb Shlomo's driver. I was waiting for him in his room at Mary Ann's guesthouse not far from the House of Love and Prayer on Ninth Avenue. We were running late, and Reb Shlomo asked me to wait so he could daven Maariv. He stood near the window, swaying and praying. I could feel a field of holiness both surrounding him and emanating from him. The whole energy in the room shifted. It felt like the very atoms themselves were energized. Through the experience of being near him and on the level that I occupied, I had a taste of entering into what Reb Zalman, may he live and be well, calls the G-d Field. Reb Shlomo opened the door for me, and to this day, during moments when I am really blessed, I can go through the door he opened.

> Our ability to do good comes from our unity. Our unity comes from the Holy Shekhina. When we connect to one another, we connect to heaven.

> Friends, we need to be bigger than we are. We are bigger than we think we are. We are all, each of us, more than we are. This is the time for us to be more than we can imagine. To rise up. To fill new spaces.

> What's the most important thing for today? (*When he speaks of today, I'm sure Reb Shlomo is speaking about this moment in earth time, not heavenly time, which I cannot begin to imagine.*)

> What is the deepest and holiest thing we can do?

> We need to learn how to learn.

Why is it so important to learn how to learn?

*We need to learn how to learn so we can be holy peacemakers, so we can fix the world. We have to learn how to learn so we can become new, because if the old knowledge was enough, Mashiach would have been here long ago.*

Reb Shlomo was a peacemaker who dared to do what no one else had the chutzpa to do. When he went to Germany and said on the radio, "I'm here to hug every German I meet and tell them that the Jewish people are alive and well," he went into a territory of redemption that no one had entered before. Do you think it was easy for this rebbe, who carried the six million in his daily burden, to go to Germany with his heart wide open to embrace everyone he met? To do this, he had to be the most radical tzaddik on the planet, maybe the most radical tzaddik who ever lived.

Why did he do it? Because it was in his nature to make peace. His name and his mission were the same. The source of his peacemaking came directly from the Holy Energy Field I felt him connect to on that evening so many years ago in Mary Ann's Guest House.

Although it seemed effortless, his path was not easy. It was lonely to open the door to the future. He had to make a break with the holy outrage and hardened hearts that came with our survival. I glimpsed how hard it was on the YouTube video "Shlomo Carlebach on the Road"* which showed Reb Shlomo standing in the gas chambers at the Majdanek Death Camp during his first trip to Poland. You could feel his broken heart. You could feel that he was there with the six million. And then he left Majdanek to reach out to the Polish people in a concert. "When I walked the gas chambers," he chanted that night, "it was clear to me — dawn is breaking. I want you to know, my beautiful friends, don't ever give up on the world. Don't ever give up on any human being. Because we are all G-d's image."

---

* See p. 334 for internet link to "Shlomo Carlebach on the Road."

Friends, I hear him saying in my imagination this secular New Year's eve, *Now we have to be more chutzpadik than ever before. We can only fix ourselves and the world by being more than we are. We can't get to being more than we are by being the same way we always have been.*

Why do we need to be peacemakers? Because there is so much pain in the world. The heart of the world is about to burst from anger and hatred and violence. Love can save us all. There can be no peace unless we love. And there can be no love without joy. So we must be joyful. That's the holiest, the deepest thing we can do.

What does it means to be a peacemaker? We need to spread joy.

And this is what we must be learning right now, how to break from the past and become peacemakers. How do we learn how to be peacemakers? How do we learn to grow into the person we are becoming?

We need to start by learning how to learn. Before we can learn, we need to ask the question, what do we know, what do we really know? We know so little about bringing G-d into the world. We need to learn so much. We need to be aware every moment that we are learning how to learn. That's the only way we can know what we need to know.

We need to learn how to learn faster and deeper. Brother Satan is busy making trouble. The troublemakers never rest. We need to learn how to change very fast. Our grandchildren's grandchildren need us to wake up now. They are waiting to receive the gifts only we can give them. G-d forbid we should fail them.

We need make a new kind of yeshiva with branches all over the world, every place where people come together. In the new yeshiva every one will learn to be a peacemaker, to bring joy and hope in every situation.

We need to learn to forgive. Not only our enemies. We need to forgive ourselves and to forgive the people we love the most. We need to forgive G-d — but unless we forgive ourselves, we can't forgive one another. Without forgiveness we can't be joyful and without joy we can't change. Oy, do we need to change.

We need to learn in community. We can't change by ourselves. And if only I change, what's the good? Together we must learn to be bigger than we've ever been before. This is the time when the light can break through. This is the time when the light must break through.

In the peace yeshiva, we need to learn how to bring the light. We need to learn how to be the friend to the light.

Don't have any doubt, we are learning faster than we can imagine. We just need to learn together more. We need to learn every day to do teshuva. We can't learn without teshuva. Without teshuva there can be no peace. To heal the world, we need to heal ourselves. Each of us needs to learn how to become a baal teshuva. And we have to do it joyfully. We have to do be kind to ourselves. We have to do teshuva and let go. There is no longer enough time to hold on to what we have done yesterday that is bad.

We need to train our eyes to see each other with kindness. We need to see ourselves with kindness. This is what we need to learn at the peace yeshiva. All of us. Together. Learning how to love one another. Learning how to heal one another. Learning how to love ourselves.

We can't hold on so tight. We need to learn to be giving when our past screams at us to hold on. We need to trust. G-d is with the peacemakers. Peacemaking must be our Torah.

The peace yeshiva needs to be so, so radical. It needs to be so holy. We need to be as radical as Shlomo haMelech when he put 70 gates for the 70 nations in the Bet HaMikdash. Our peace yeshiva should have 70 gates and people from all the nations should come and learn together how to be peacemakers. For the sake of the Holy One, the One and the Only One, we need to respect each other. Together we can learn how to learn, how to be joyful.

Don't have any doubt. Mashiach is here. Now. Waiting for us to build the bridge to one another so she can dance with us. This is the time to eat the fruit from the Tree of Life. Our ancestors yearn for us to do it. Our grandchildren are depending on us.

When in my mind, I hear Reb Shlomo say we need to be "radical," there is a cognitive dissonance. I never heard Reb Shlomo use that word. I realize that my imagination is growing tired and Reb Shlomo's voice and my own thoughts are beginning to blur together. So it is time to end.

I have been blessed to be one of Reb Shlomo's countless best friends and have sought to embody him with every hug and every blessing I give.

I hope that what I have heard and what I have tried to transcribe is authentic and that my consciousness is in alignment with Reb Shlomo and that no harm will come from any flights of fancy or inaccuracies in what I have written down.

The tzaddik is eternal. I invite all of us to open our hearts to the Rebbe and to listen to what he has to tell us about fixing our own lives and our own relationships. If we can't hear him when we are awake, and our yearning is real, sleep deeply and invite him into our dreams. He will speak to us in our sleep. It was never in Shlomo's nature to refuse anyone at any time. Learn this and our grandchildren will rejoice in our legacy.

*At Temple Beth Abraham, Oakland.*
*From left: Reb Zalman, Rabbi Joe Schonwald, Barry Barkan, Reb Shlomo.*
*Photo by Rolinda Schonwald.*

Barry Barkan on meeting Shlomo for the first time:
http://youtu.be/GkIJEU7nrBw

# Multiple Lives in Bobov

by Rabbi Dr. Reb Mimi Feigelson

I WANT TO WRITE ABOUT BOBOV. I WANT IT TO STAY WITH ME. IF NOT everything now, then just a part and later another part and another part.

Here in Yerushalayim, during the evening of the holy Shabbat, all the pieces of the whole were woven together: Bobov/Poland — that night of Tevet 1989; Rechovot/Israel — during the second half of the 1970s, Bobov/Bat Yam, 1972, Bobov/Brooklyn on the second night of *Chol Hamoed* Sukkot 1991. A question a generation old.

It all fell into place during the evening of the holy Shabbat, *parashat Noach,* in the midst of the *niggun,* ״יָהּ רִבּוֹן עָלַם וְעָלְמַיָּא, אַנְתְּ הוּא מַלְכָּא מֶלֶךְ מַלְכַיָּא, עוֹבַד גְּבוּרְתָּךְ וְתִמְהַיָּא, שְׁפַר קֳדָמָךְ לְהַחֲוָיָא.״ 'Master of the World and All Worlds, You are the King of All Kings, It is beautiful to declare before you Your powerful and wondrous deeds.'

When we arrived at the Rebbe's sukkah the second night of *Chol Hamoed* Sukkot 1991, in Brooklyn, he was still not there. He was still inside the *beit-midrash.* I was heavy-hearted. Although I knew that when he was in the *sukkah* I could barely see him, maybe only a glimpse of his hand as it waved hello (and at the same time opened the gates of heaven), but even so — to see the Rebbe in his *sukkah,* as the concept of the surrounding light and the immanent light being one, is always a divine vision in my eyes. Sammy entered the building and returned saying that the Rebbe is inside and that there is a place that I can stand and at least see something. We agreed that we would meet fifteen minutes later and in my heart I thought that even fifteen minutes was too long to try to see what is impossible, as a woman to see in a man's world, and to peek into a world that is not mine — in more than one way. I almost wanted to give up on the whole ordeal, but, even so, I went in. It was past midnight, and it was raining outside. If we reached this far, I thought, we should go in.

Sammy led me to one of the side halls in the *beit-midrash*. Tables, benches, and a large grey space. There were another two, maybe three, women who within moments left me standing alone to see the sight.

I had never seen the Rebbe from so close. In front of me was a wall, chest high, and above the wall iron bars — reaching up to the ceiling. I held onto the bars and peeked into a world that did not belong to me. Into a world that I knew I belonged to.

The Chassidim danced and danced and I knew that "there, inside" was the Rebbe. I could almost see him, but the Chassidim danced and danced, only allowing me to see his golden *kapota* (long coat) spar-kling though their black bodies that moved in an unchanging rhythm round after round. I was frustrated and happy all in one. Frustrated, because it was so hard to see Him. Happy because the Chassidim were dancing and dancing and I had never seen them dancing and dancing.

Sammy crossed the gate of the partition that separated our worlds and told me that if I stood on a bench I could actually see the Rebbe. This was the second time in my life that I found myself standing on a bench trying to see the face of a Rebbe. Only hours before I was standing on a bench of the women's section of the Chabad *beit-midrash* in order to see the Lubavitcher Rebbe, as he addressed his holy flock and gave out charity — a means with which to spiritually enrich them. Now, when I stood on the bench, here in the Bobover *beit-midrash*, everything changed, quickly, into many different worlds. Once on the bench, watching the Chassidim dance and dance I met "her". I did not know this, however, until I returned to Yerushalayim.

As I stood on the bench I saw everything — even beyond what I was capable of comprehending.

The Rebbe stood still and he "danced his Chassidim," who danced and danced. He was standing exactly opposite me! I had never really seen him: I had never seen him without plastic partitions that painted his white skin a dull brown; I had never seen him in a manner that the rays of light that hit his skin and soul were reflecting directly into my eyes and penetrating directly into my soul — without vessels or foreign objects that split the impact of the rays in the process. The Rebbe stood, his arms spread to the sides. Moving them up and down, elevating earth towards heaven and lowering heaven towards earth. His face is glowing. White light pouring in every direction. Is this the manner in which the face of Moshe Rabbeinu, "*Ish Ha'Elokim*" (the man of God) was illuminated after his encounter with the One and Only?

The Rebbe's hands and smile, expanded from one end of the world to the other end of the world.

I look and see how there is not one muscle or limb in his body that isn't saturated with happiness and joy, or better yet, joy and happiness. And I ask myself, "How?!" How can a person who lost his whole family in the Shoah (holocaust), except for one son, be immersed totally in complete joy and happiness? I return to Rebbe Nachman of Breslov's torah that teaches us that the *Tzaddik* is always in the continuous present. For him every moment is a point in the continuous present that embodies within it all of past and future. And so I see the Bobover Rebbe standing here, totally present in the present, and yet simultaneously there, in the past, and there in the future, in the time of Mashiach. Alas, an encounter with the Rebbe is in itself an encounter with the infinite in the midst of the finite.

And the Chassidim dance. They dance and dance. All the time. I observe the Rebbe, I observe them, and they dance and dance. They sing again and again: ״אַתָּה בְחַרְתָּנוּ מִכָּל הָעַמִּים אָהַבְתָּ אוֹתָנוּ וְרָצִיתָ בָּנוּ וְרוֹמַמְתָּנוּ מִכָּל הַלְּשׁוֹנוֹת
וְקִדַּשְׁתָּנוּ בְּמִצְוֹתֶיךָ וְקֵרַבְתָּנוּ מַלְכֵּנוּ לַעֲבוֹדָתֶךָ וְשִׁמְךָ הַגָּדוֹל וְהַקָּדוֹשׁ עָלֵינוּ קָרָאתָ.״

'You have chosen us from all the peoples; You loved us and found favor in us; You exalted us above all the tongues and You sanctified us with your commandments. You drew us close, our King, to Your service and proclaimed Your great and Holy Name upon us.' — from the *Yom Tov Amidah*

They sing and dance, dance and sing.

And they pass by me. There are those that see me and there are those that for them I'm not there, completely non-existent.

And the feet. Dancing and dancing.

They dance and dance in perfect order. Not in circles around the Rebbe but like a rattlesnake, like an endless chain of people, they dance and dance. I hear their feet encountering the floor again and again, over and over again. In an unchangeable rhythm.

I see them reach a certain point in the room and turn left, and I ask myself, "How do they know to turn at this exact spot?" Can it be that for generations and generations they have been dancing in this room and turning exactly at that spot?

I hear their feet again and again — just as I always hear the feet, since then, since the ceremony on the Memorial Day for the Holocaust, in Rechovot.

At the ceremony in Rechovot/Israel, some fifteen years ago, the theatrical youth group prepared a skit for the ceremony. The main theme was the feet. Between scenes the room was darkened and Israeli children, dressed as Nazi soldiers, marched across the stage, with strong, organized steps. Steps in an unchangeable rhythm.

Every scene in the skit was connected with the feet: the feet of a mother running to protect her children, feet of children climbing a ladder to hide.

Since then I always hear the feet. I listen to the feet.

It was in such a way, also then...at the end of Tevet 1989, when we walked alone — just us — Reb Shlomo and a few of us — alone through the paths of the Majdanek concentration camp. I heard from within the silence the sound of our feet on the stones — some new stones, and some, perhaps from then.... Stones that our families walked on towards their death. I heard our feet from within the silence and I heard their feet swirled with fear and fright. I knew at that moment that maybe I was the only one who heard this **now**, but I also knew that **then**, they all heard the feet.

And the Chassidim dance and dance.

And the Rebbe claps his hands, completely immersed in bliss, connecting the above and below; bringing the edges, the *Nidchei Yisrael* (the forgotten ones of Israel), into the center, into the middle. He brings the scattered pieces of each and every one of us to a sense of focus. When his hands meet and embrace each other he is centering us, and with us the whole world.

I am standing on the bench and see all of this, but not only I see this. Sometimes I am not really me. In juxtaposition to the Mimi that wants to be involved, to be part of the scene, does not want to stand on the side and observe how others dance and sing, but she herself wants to dance and sing, now, as I'm standing and watching the Chassidim dance and dance, my hands are holding on to the iron bars, and I feel that they are guarding me, protecting me. I feel happy that I am here, on the other side, only watching and not a part of the dancing and dancing. At times, there were moments when I stood on the bench like a little girl, whose father was a Bobover Chassid who had taken her with him to see the Rebbe. With my eyes I could see the child but I didn't know who she was. But every once in a while I was not me on that bench in Brooklyn. I was her glancing into my eyes.

At that moment I did not know who this little girl was. I thought perhaps she was something from within me. I was happy because she, the child, was happy and I was happy that because she was happy to stand, embracing the iron bars and watching the Chassidim dance and dance, then I was also happy to stand and watch the Chassidim dance and dance.

And the Chassidim are dancing and dancing.

Each one, at his turn, passing by the Rebbe. They turn their faces towards the Rebbe as they pass him. Each one wants the Rebbe to acknowledge him, to smile at him, to look into his eyes and wash them clean of any evil or illness that they have seen or experienced in the past.

When the Rebbe glances into your eyes, the windows of your soul, it is not only your body that is immersed in a *mikvah* (holy waters) like no other, but your soul is immersed in a *mikvah* like no other. And you rise from within the *mikvah*, within your eyes that are within the Rebbe's eyes, a different person than you've ever been before.

And the Chassidim are dancing and dancing.

Turning their faces towards the Rebbe as they pass by His Holy Presence. As they pass by me and don't even see me, I know what they do not know. For I know that I was **there**, in Bobov/Poland, at the gravesite of the previous Rebbe, and also at the site of the mass grave at the top of the hill next to the "*ohel*" (burial structure over the graves) of the Rebbe — the mass grave in which most of the Bobov Chassidim lie! In mere days a wondrous Chassidic community, with glorified Chassidic men and women and children, vanished from the world. Vanished, but yet did not vanish, for behold, we were standing **there**! One day, instead of joining Reb Shlomo at his concert in Cracow, as part of his trip to Poland, in January 1989, we rented a car and went off to Bobov and Tzanz. We decided that better than standing outside the *beit-mid-rash* in Tzanz that was now functioning as a factory, we would head to the cemetery in Bobov. We stood waiting near the gate of the cemetery. Someone went to get the key for the gate and we turned to open the gates of heaven with our prayers. We stood in the piercing cold at the top of the hill. The winds whistled as from the flute of the Shepherd who knew not how to pray. We tried to bring life to the dry bones that lay at our feet. We sang Bobov *niggunim.* We sang: יָהּ רִבּוֹן עָלַם וְעָלְמַיָּא, אַנְתְּ הוּא מַלְכָּא מֶלֶךְ מַלְכַיָּא, עוֹבַד גְּבוּרְתָּךְ וְתִמְהַיָּא, שְׁפַר קֳדָמָךְ לְהַחֲוָיָא. 'Master of the World and All Worlds, You are the King of All Kings, It is beautiful to declare before you Your powerful and wondrous deeds.' Sammy told us some Chassidic tales about Bobov. We were surrounded by a vast darkness and even though it's only close to seven p.m. we feel like we rose in the middle of the night to partake in *Hitbodedut* (meditation with God).

In the "*ohel*" we sang some of Reb Shlomo's *niggunim.* Trying, unconsciously, to connect ourselves, with the deepest elements of our souls, to the *Tzaddik* (the Righteous Master) that was lying in front of us and smiling above us.

We tasted a bittersweet taste of newness. For who, before us, brought Reb Shlomo's *niggunim* to this site? We stood long-short minutes. We sang, we offered a silent prayer for our loved and dear ones.

Sammy said, half joking but very seriously, that we — Barbara, Barbara and I — were definitely the first women, the first Chassidic women, to make "Aliya" (pilgrimage) to the grave site of Reb Shlomo Halbershtam and Reb Ben Tziyon Halbershtam, of blessed memory; the first Chassidic women to stand at the mass grave and recite in a demanding tone: שִׁיר הַמַּעֲלוֹת מִמַּעֲמַקִּים קְרָאתִיךָ ה'. ה' שִׁמְעָה בְקוֹלִי תִּהְיֶינָה אָזְנֶיךָ קַשֻּׁבוֹת לְקוֹל תַּחֲנוּנָי: אִם עֲוֹנוֹת תִּשְׁמָר יָהּ ה' מִי יַעֲמֹד. 'A song of ascent, from the depths I call to you God; God hear my voice, may your ears be attentive to the voice of my pleas. If you preserve iniquities, oh God, God, who will survive?' (*T'hillim*/Psalm 130)

And the Chassidim are dancing and dancing. Brooklyn, Sukkot, 1991.

They pass me by as if I don't exist.

They pass by the rebbe as if only he exists.

They don't know that I was **there**...

They don't know that I live their dream.

They don't know that I have something in common with the Rebbe that they possibly never had and never will have.

And I stand in silence.

\*   \*   \*

Sometimes I am me, and sometimes I'm her, the little girl, that holds on to the iron bars of the *beit-midrash* in Bobov, whose father brought her to shul so she should see the Rebbe, so she should see the Chassidim dance and dance.

In such a manner I stood there, peeking into a world not mine, into a world that from the inside of the inside is all mine, till the Chassidim danced the Rebbe into his *sukkah*. Did they understand as they danced, that he who understands the concept of *tzimtzum* (contraction) according to the literal approach also understands that God, so to speak, "jumped" so to speak, "danced" in order to create an empty space to create the world in?! Did they, as they led the Rebbe into his Sukkah-of-Peace, on the level of Yerushalayim, on the level of the unity of the surrounding and immanent light, did they understand that as they dance they must raise both feet to enable the creation of a new world?! That the meaning of creation for us, now, of a new spiritual plane for our souls, is by hanging in mid-air for a split second and believing that God will guide us to land peacefully on the exact spot that is right and worthy for us?! Did they understand this the way their Rebbe understands this?!

When the Rebbe disappeared from our sight and left the *beit-midrash*, I did not want to leave. I wanted to stand there for hours and hours and see the Chassidim, in the eyes of my mind, dancing and dancing.

Sammy and I returned to the car. Outside, it was pouring. I always say that when it's raining God is crying. Sometimes happy tears, sometimes tears of pain and sorrow. Nevertheless, rain is always "God crying" to me. Inside, in the dry car, I started to cry. I did not exactly understand why, I did not exactly understand where these tears came from. But I sat and cried more and more. Deep, quiet cries. The tears dropped from my eyes. Each tear an entity and essence of its own.

Sammy tried to calm me, to quiet the bubbling fountain that burst from within me, and I couldn't even explain to him why, how, and from where this was coming, and when it would stop, and what would stop it. I myself did not know why, how, and where.

I only understood that I didn't understand what had happened there. I only understood that once again I had seen something that was beyond me, beyond my understanding. I only understood that, again, I had received a gift that I desperately wanted to understand but didn't have the capacity to. Sammy took me home, and I cried till I fell asleep.

The next day he asked me to explain the meaning of my "holy cries" as he called them. I promised him an answer, but I didn't know clearly what answer he was expecting. I didn't know what answer I could offer him. I promised him that at the right moment I would indeed answer him.

But the truth of the truth is that I didn't understand a thing until I returned home to Yerushalayim (may She be rebuilt and restored quickly, in our days, amen), till I sat, on the evening of the holy Shabbat in the home of my friends Alan and Ruth, surrounded by loving friends, friends of my everyday reality in Yerushalayim, and we sang, like we sang **there**, in Bobov/Poland, on that cold winter night of Tevet 1989, with Barbara, Barbara and Sammy: יָה רִבּוֹן עָלַם וְעָלְמַיָּא, אַנְתְּ הוּא מַלְכָּא מֶלֶךְ מַלְכַיָּא, עוֹבַד גְּבוּרְתָּךְ וְתִמְהַיָּא, שְׁפַר קֳדָמָךְ לְהַחֲוַיָּא." 'Master of the World and All Worlds, You are the King of All Kings, It is beautiful to declare before you Your powerful and wondrous deeds.'

Only at that moment did I understand what happened at Bobov/Brooklyn on Sukkot 1991.

Only at that moment did I understand who was that little girl that I felt was a part of me while standing on the bench, holding on to the bars, observing the Rebbe, observing the Chassidim dance and dance.

Only at that moment did I understand and receive the answer to my question a generation old: who / what was I **there**, in Europe, during the Holocaust.

Only at that moment did I understand that when the Nazis entered Bobov I was a little girl, whose father was a Bobover Chassid, who would take her with him on the evening of the holy Shabbat to the Rebbe, Reb Ben Tziyyon's (of blessed memory) *Tish* (table/gathering). A little girl who would stand in the women's section and observe how her father, with the other Chassidim, were dancing and dancing as the Rebbe stood with his hands spread out from one end of the world to the other end of the world, with a smile that reached from one end of the world to the other end of the world.

Only at that moment did I understand why the first Chassidim that I encountered when my family made "Aliyah" in 1971 to Bat Yam were Bobover Chassidim.

Only at that moment, on the evening of the holy Shabbat, in Yerushalayim, were all the questions, answers, places and pieces of my life woven together.

Only at that moment did I understand what I saw that night in Bobov/ Brooklyn, and what had happened.

Only at that moment did I understand why I cried.

The third of kiss-lev, 5751 / 1991, Yerushalayim

\*    \*    \*

## Epilogue

Dear Reb Shlomo,

It is twenty-five years since we danced together through the streets of Poland and the Former Soviet Union, shedding light on Divine Sparks waiting to be ignited. It is twenty years now that we are dancing and dancing without your physical presence to bring heaven and earth together. You taught us that we were all from **"there"**... You said that whoever was born after the Shoah was a reincarnation of a soul taken then. I always believed you until I learned the truth of my identity. It was then that I not only believed you but was called to live the magnitude of the truth of your teaching. This is not the only time that you've changed my life in such a manner. You have taught us all to live with these multiple identities. To never let go of where we come from, and yet to never cease to see where it is we are called to go and how we are meant to Serve. You bequeathed us, in your being, and in the way you danced through God's world, with a taste of what it means to be a *Tzaddik*, standing in the present, bound to past and future.

You have taught us to dance in God's world. You have taught us that the meaning of creation for us, now, of a new spiritual plane for our souls is by hanging in mid-air for a split second and believing that God will guide us to land peacefully on the exact spot that is right and worthy for us. And when you blessed us with the courage to continuously, a million times a day, take that leap of faith, you were there standing in the midst of our life's chaos, promising us that God loves us and trusts us with His/Her world.

✳ ✳ ✳

Dear *Heilige* (holy) Rebbe,

There is not a day that I don't share your torah with others; not a class that I teach where you are not present; not a person I sit with, laugh with or cry with that isn't a reflection of what you've taught me; not a prayer I offer or *niggun* that I sing that isn't cloaked with the belief in God that you instilled in me.

Not a step that I take without thanking you for giving me my life back and enabling me to serve our Creator as the Rav that I am.

I pray that you and I, along with the six million, and those yet to be born, dance together in the streets of Yerushalayim. May it be soon!

באהבה רבה ובאהבת עולם, with great love, with eternal love,

Mimi (Miriam Sara) bat Frada Leah u'Moshe Refael

*photo by Joan Roth*

# Reb Shlomo: An Encounter Between the Mystical and the Practical

by Rabbi Sam Intrator

RABBI JOE SCHONWALD ASKED ME TO CONTRIBUTE TO THIS ANTHOLOGY by describing what it was like to work for Reb Shlomo as his manager and Assistant Rabbi and what unique understandings of him I might have gleaned from those combined experiences. Those experiences were profound and life altering. They included both tremendous challenges and great privileges, the story of which could easily occupy a volume of in-depth study and analysis. I believe, however, that even in recounting anecdotes based on a few episodes I was a witness to, a striking dualistic pattern emerges that reveals an important lesson in both the complexity and simplicity with which Reb Shlomo led his life. His example influenced me as well as thousands of others, and will, I believe, continue to inspire people who are seeking to lead a meaningful Jewish spiritual life. Through his music, teachings, stories, and distinctive style in leading prayer services, Reb Shlomo's mystical and deeply compassionate public persona is inspirationally displayed. However, having observed and worked with him up close, I saw him leading his life in a way that was not impervious to pragmatic necessities, even though he was steeped in the mystical. In working with him, I felt that both of these were present in much of his life and that an awareness of both was part of his vision for his life's work. This is not to deny that his natural inclinations and personal preferences were directed toward the mystical but that he saw the importance of the practical in life as well.

I believe that such context is important because Reb Shlomo is more popularly remembered as a dreamer and idealist who, coupled with what appeared as counter-cultural, new age-like influences, was marginalized by many in academia and the Jewish establishment's leadership as at best a fine entertainer but not as one who offered a spiritual approach that the mainstream community could emulate. Such a critique points to the fact that during his lifetime he was not viewed as mainstream and that therefore his legacy will carry that stigma. There are, of course, many great innovators who, during their lifetimes, were regarded as radicals and underminers of established order, yet history has shown them to be forerunners of new perspectives.

Reb Shlomo once said to me that Van Gogh's art was terribly under-appreciated during his lifetime, but that his artistic legacy has shown how far ahead of his time he was, and how mainstream art and culture would eventually, though posthumously, embrace him. In reflecting upon Jewish history, he would cite Rabbi Yehuda HaNasi's radical act in transcribing the Oral Torah and Maimonides' attempt at approaching Greek philosophy from a Torah perspective as examples of great spiritual masters who were much criticized during their lifetimes and were only later embraced. He understood that his vision of a Judaism that is all loving, profoundly joyous, that touches both the mind and the heart in a powerfully meaningful way — that respects the depth of the tradition and at the same time is open and sensitive to contemporary challenges — was something that in his lifetime the world did not yet have vessels to properly receive. The fact that in the years since Reb Shlomo's passing, both his music and his style of prayer have grown significantly in popularity — and across denominations throughout the Jewish world — demonstrates the lasting power of his spiritual message. I believe that in his case, too, as his teachings and stories gain wider recognition, history will show how far ahead of his time he was. Thus, his spiritual vision will continue to be embraced by mainstream culture for years to come. Those of us who had the privilege to be close to him and observe his erudite brilliance, deep heartfelt compassion for others, and innovative, charismatic approach to spreading Torah consciousness, felt certain that history would judge him far more kindly than his contemporaries did.

The juxtaposition of the mystical and the pragmatic is most highlighted in Reb Shlomo's life when one takes a deeper look at his life mission and his greatest musical, liturgical, and intellectual contributions to Judaism. He may have begun his musical career as a spiritual singer, but he quickly evolved as he introduced joyous participatory singing and dancing into the service. He correctly foresaw that such an experiential approach would not only make the prayer service and Judaism in general more open to the mystical but that it would have pragmatic utility in popularizing the service and helping to broaden Judaism's appeal, especially to the alienated younger generation. His approach showed, counter to popular thinking at that time, that merely shortening the service would not increase synagogue attendance, but making it more meaningful through song, dance, and brief running commentary would, even though the service might run longer. He also believed that the loving compassionate message of Judaism needed great amplification in order to reach the younger generation. Reb Shlomo understood the importance of recognizing the needs of the time, an idea that is powerfully and radically developed by his greatest Hasidic influence, Rabbi Mordechai Yosef Lainer, the Rebbe of Ishbitz. Thus, even in regard to his spiritual work, a merging of the mystical and the practical was essential.

I gained my perspective on how he melded the mystical and the practical in much of his life because although my formal relationship with him was based on the practical details of his professional life, he was my Rebbe — the greatest spiritual influence in my life — and his teachings, stories, and music inspired me no end. The thick veil that separates the spiritual from the practical was constantly being lifted for me to observe and gaze in awe at how he achieved the seemingly impossible. He may have developed a reputation for coming late to concerts or studio recordings, but few knew or even cared to know about the infinite multi-tasking in performing good deeds he was involved in daily. Stories of the friendship and support he provided to lost souls all over the world, who were in desperate need of his counsel and assistance, could occupy multiple volumes of amazing testimony to how he was personally involved in bettering countless lives. If you add to that his immense achievements as a brilliant musical artist, teacher, and storyteller, even while he helped create and guide communities as a spiritual leader in Israel and the United States — with practically no professional staff support to assist him in all these endeavors — the evidence mounts that he must have had some pretty well-developed pragmatic skills to relate to and excel in all these disparate worlds. You can maintain this conviction even if you correctly accept the notion that his career was guided by a much higher force.

He also tried bringing into his daily life tasks the warm and meaningful atmosphere he created at his concerts and Torah classes. The underlying theme in much of what he studied and taught was an infinite love for G-d and fellow humans. The challenges for a finite human being seeking to live life with a consciousness of infinitude are endless. To be candid, during my early days of working with him professionally, having simultaneously to cope with his spiritual infiniteness and artistic temperament was quite frustrating.

It was not until I spent significant time learning Torah with him and watching his interactions with others that I realized that instead of my seeking to change Reb Shlomo, I should instead be looking at changing myself. When I allowed his sometimes seemingly chaotic pace and approach to set the tone of our working relationship, I began to see how his infiniteness had some hidden order to it. When I asked him for a phone number, he would often turn to his daily planner book, and within a relatively short time he would find the number he was looking for. That book looked like it had names and numbers written haphazardly all over the place, but Reb Shlomo somehow had mastered the randomness of his daily planner book and knew where to find whatever details he was searching for.

His daily itinerary was largely set by the needs of those who called upon him regularly. If I needed to speak to him earnestly about a work-related matter, I would need to patiently wait my turn. I often joked with him and said that if I would tell him that I had a serious personal problem, I would probably get an audience with him sooner than if I told him I needed to talk shop. It was not that earning a living was unimportant to him, but he responded to all the infinite needs that came his way, and his practical business needs were just one of the many callings that he felt the need to respond to. However, when we did get to talk shop, he would always make me feel that he understood the importance of the work I was doing for him, and there were even times that he gave me very sound advice on how to do my work better. Yet hovering over almost any such conversation were the infinite other callings that he was also engaged in.

While his livelihood was very important to him, he did not lose perspective on other equally important things in his life. I remember a few months before his passing he called a prominent performer from an airport phone. Evidently, the man's mother picked up the phone and told him her son was not in. I can still hear his loud and painful instructive words to the mother: "Please tell your son that by not paying me royalties for singing my music on his albums he is not only cheating me but he is stealing my children's inheritance." Then he added, "Please tell him to stop singing my songs the wrong way." He was always deeply troubled when people took liberties with his music and sang it in whatever manner felt comfortable to them. After he completed the phone conversation, he said to me, "You know, I really should take him to a *Din Torah*." I said to him, "But he knows I know and you know that you won't do that," to which he expressed his agreement with a smile. Suing was not his way, but being cheated by others was also not something that he would tolerate, nor could he accept people altering his melodies.

While he wanted to get paid his going price for his bookings, he made countless private exceptions to his price for those who said they could not pay. There were times when those who paid his regular price found out that others got reductions and were troubled by it. Reb Shlomo would empathize with them and recognize that his approach could cost him future bookings or result in not getting paid his proper amount, but it still did not lead him to change his ways.

In many of my encounters with him, as in the vignettes that I relate here, one could see that his quest for the infinite was often challenged by the finiteness of life. Indeed, Reb Shlomo taught much on the subject of how the infinite interacts with the finite. He once gave an in-depth teaching on this subject to Hillel students at the University of Florida. I accompanied him on that trip, and the Torah portion being read that Shabbat was *Yitro*. From it, he derived a profound take on the story of revelation. He noted that the Jews needed to meet Yitro, the pagan high priest, before they could experience revelation. Yitro tells Moses, his son-in-law, that he will wear himself out if he tries to teach all the Jews the laws of the Torah by himself. He advises Moses to appoint men capable of judging minor disputes while reserving for himself the most difficult cases. (*Sh'mot*, 18:13-26)

G-d, in His infinite wisdom, before He reveals Himself at Mount Sinai, emphasizes the absolute need to establish borders separating various segments of the Jewish people. According to Reb Shlomo, the reason for these seemingly odd limiting preparations prior to receiving in-finite revelation is because G-d wants the Jewish people to bring their earthly finite limitations with them when they will experience the most infinite divine revelation ever known to humankind. This great transcendent experience would last but a fleeting moment in the lives of those present at Mount Sinai. In order for it to have a lasting effect, they would need to experience it with the finite limitations of this world. One can see Reb Shlomo's approach to understanding the deeper message of revelation in the way that Reb Simcha Bunim of Pe-shishka explains why after the Ten Commandments were given, G-d finds it necessary to tell Moses "Go tell them to return to their tents." (*Devarim*, 7:27) Why would they not return to their homes after the revelation experience is over? Reb Simcha Bunim explains that G-d is really telling Moses the true test in how well the Israelites received the revelation will only be determined after it is completed. If, when the Israelites return to their homes, they maintain some of the elevat-ed consciousness they experienced at Sinai — that will be the greatest sign that its message permanently affected them. The finite needs to be infused with infiniteness in order for it to be transformed, but its expanded vessels will still not be boundless.

Perhaps this defining teaching on how Jewish spirituality is to be received and spread can help us gain a better understanding of the way Reb Shlomo led his life. He lived his life in the fullest and most meaningful way he knew how. He did not spend much time preparing to live his life but sought to live every moment with all that it offered. Even in his professional life, he resisted rehearsals before shows. To him, such preparation should have innate significance and not serve solely as utility for the future. Ironically, he told me that one of his rehearsals was recorded unbeknownst to him and released without his authorization and went on to become a leading album without him realizing the royalties he was entitled to.

Reb Shlomo sang with the same enthusiasm and taught with the same vigor to a group of ten poor "holy hippies" as he did when he appeared in a grand ballroom for thousands of upper-class concert-goers. Making artificial distinctions between classes of people and discriminating against some while favoring others to him represented pagan finite value judgments. He opted for the infinite in life. He felt that is the root of authentic Judaism. It therefore followed that no challenge was too great for him to not try to overcome, and no task was too difficult for him to not try to accomplish, and no worthy deed was too inconsequential for him to attempt. To Reb Shlomo, if man is truly created in the image of G-d, we must always strive to realize the divine infinitude that resides in each of us. Pragmatists may find such an approach to life too demanding, almost superhuman, while idealists may find it too action-oriented and liable to prevent one from experiencing bliss and serenity. Reb Shlomo would probably view these criticisms as products of our Western pagan influence, which seeks to rob us, and to keep us from meeting our greatest challenge: the challenge of discovering our infiniteness. He would often say, "The whole world says live up to your potential — I say reach beyond it."

In spite of leading his life with such an openness to the infinite and stretching his own finiteness to the outer limits, as the above synopsized Mt. Sinai teaching illustrates, he understood that the human condition had limitations even if his inclination was not to dwell on them. He did, however, want his teachings, and even his life example, to be viewed as a study in reaching for the infinite through the prism of the possible. To him, everyone on his or her own level must have an awareness of the great importance of reaching for the infinite and transcendental in life as we work our way through our finite existence and its limitations.

In the end, you do the best you can in reconciling these two opposing perspectives, but ignoring one for the other is not being faithful to the human-divine image we all bear. The divine in us should always encourage awareness of the divine infinitude that stirs in us. The human being in us should always be sensitive to the finiteness of the human condition. The attempt we make at reconciling the two represents the distinctiveness of the human-divine image. Reb Shlomo's life represented a constant sacred dialectic of these opposite pulls. From his perspective, by seeking to be faithful to both, he found a sacred synthesis of these two complementary opposites, both in his teachings and in daily life encounters, even though his attraction to the infinite was probably greater than most of ours.

His skill at connecting the infinite to the finite parallels another great paradox that resided in his soul and was always on public display. Perhaps one of the greatest contradictions he seemed to integrate naturally was between the traditional Orthodox world he was raised in, and was deeply steeped in, his regular appearances at synagogues of other denominations, and his profound connection to a counter-culture whose universalistic peace-loving spirit he deeply embraced.

The truth is that among his followers today, those that tend to the right may have embraced much of his deep loving message; however, they filter it exclusively through their world view, while those who tend to the left and have also embraced much of his loving message filter it exclusively through their world view. Unfortunately, the two world-views do not really meet in the way they did in Reb Shlomo's life. This is perhaps one of the greatest challenges the Carlebach legacy faces today.

Professor Shaul Magid has argued that Reb Shlomo was a mirror and that people saw in him what they wanted. [*Tablet Magazine*, November 1, 2012.] While I agree that Reb Shlomo certainly sought to achieve commonality with people, that empathic identification was only the beginning of his journey of friendship. He then sought to transform those people by introducing a transcendental component that he often called the "infinite" or the "beyond." If you connected with him, he would take you to a very special window, and then he would, as it were, place a telescope and a mirror outside the window; then, through his teachings, music, and stories, you could hear him ask you to look deeply "through" one and "at" the other instrument simultaneously. With one eye you see yourself, but with the other eye you see the vastness of the world beyond you. As you gaze at infinity you never lose sight of yourself, and as you stare at your own image you never disconnect it from the beauty of the great world beyond you. It is at such a window that the infinite and the finite meet, and that is where our divine image must glow with the great light of both of those visions.

While such a view may reveal the complexity of life, and it would appear that only an enlightened visionary can truly grasp it, Reb Shlomo's brilliance in his music, stories, and teachings always showed how the simple can inform the complex. If you sing and you dance with others at a Carlebach Friday night service or wedding, the joy you feel is immense, but at same time you are connecting with others who also feel immense joy, and the joy generated in such an experience is infinitely greater than what any individual can feel, for both the personal and collective joy are profoundly experienced by all. Likewise, for Reb Shlomo, expressions of love, deep mesmerizing Torah study, and life in general all offer similar personal and transpersonal experiences, encourage group bonding, and create an awareness of a vast infinity that Kabbalists might call the *Ein Sof* (the limitless).

Reb Shlomo's approach to music, and the metaphors in his teachings and stories, are all tools he gave us that help to simplify life's complexities, yet he leaves us knowing very well that there are further complexities that are beyond us. When he would take us to that transcendent consciousness, he would often use the phrase, "to give you a taste." There you hear the pragmatist in him helping us access mystical ideas or spiritual realities that are usually beyond our reach.

So, yes, the infinite and the finite, the duality and the unity, the simple and the complex, and the mystical and the practical all met in his life and coexisted with one another. His life offers a profound lesson in the great range of human potential and how with deep faith one can accomplish the seemingly impossible. As many debate his legacy, irrespective of how diametrically opposed they may be to one another, the greatest tribute they can offer to Reb Shlomo would be to listen to each other and attempt to learn from one another and then seek to find a shared commonality. That commonality should not be represented by the lowest common denominator but should emerge from a quest to find the highest common denominator.

Boi B'Shalom — Reb Shlomo sings on an Israeli TV show, 1973: http://youtu.be/ITstpCVtDN8

Pe'er VeChavod — Reb Shlomo sings on an Israeli TV show, 1973: http://youtu.be/Kfn_SG7Z3Ys

# A Woman's Perspective

by Melinda (Mindy) Ribner

*"If the women are good enough to hold our babies,
they can surely hold a Sefer Torah."*

REB SHLOMO RESPONDED WITH WORDS LIKE THESE TO EXPLAIN HIS decision to grant a *Sefer Torah* to the women on *Simchat Torah* sometime in the early 1980s. This was a radical move on the part of Reb Shlomo. Giving a *Sefer Torah* to women may not have been done before in an orthodox synagogue. Reb Shlomo surely received disparaging remarks from many of his orthodox rabbinic colleagues at the time, but that did not discourage him. Once, members of the Carlebach congregation, along with Reb Shlomo, were even asked to leave a Simchat Torah celebration we were sharing with another synagogue when the *Sefer Torah* was brought to the women's section.

Though Reb Shlomo is best known for his revitalization of Jewish prayer through his beautiful *niggunim*, his brilliant Torah teaching, and his spiritual activism in visiting numerous countries, such as Poland and South Africa, little is said about his unique legacy to women. As a woman who was with Reb Shlomo constantly for more than twenty years, primarily in New York but also in Israel, and who also received *s'mikha* from him, I am in a good position to state that Reb Shlomo was a trailblazer for women.

In the early days, that is the late 1970s and 1980s, when I came to the *shul* — Shlomo's shul on West 79th Street in New York City — Kehilath

Jacob was primarily a women's shul. Unusual, to say the least, among orthodox synagogues, women outnumbered men in numbers and influence. The disparity between the men and women was most apparent during the High Holy Days. During these holidays, when seats were purchased for around two hundred dollars a ticket, the women's section was almost twice the size in width and length compared to the men's, and extended to the door by the entrance of the shul. The men would be crowded in a small section on the left side of the shul. It was very peculiar, but powerful. When it came to buying *aliyot* for holidays, the women often outbid the men and purchased the honor for Reb Shlomo or other men. Though the women may not have participated in service leadership, their presence in the shul was quite strong and made an impact on Reb Shlomo as well.

In most orthodox synagogues, the women look at the action happening in the men's section. The men are singing and dancing in circles around the synagogue. The women are generally silent, peering over the *mechitza,* the room divider, to the men's section or talking among themselves. In the Carlebach shul, it was the opposite. The women sang and danced fervently and ecstatically on their side, perhaps even more than the men. There were times when I noticed that some of the men would be looking across the *mechitza* toward the women rather than dancing themselves. It was clear to all that the women carried the light and joy of the *Shekhinah.*

One of the reasons that there may have been so many more women than men was that Shlomo's heart-centered and experiential approach to learning and prayer, which emphasized singing and dancing, had particular appeal to women. Feminine spirituality is more about experiencing the direct revelation of God within one's heart and body than analytical learning. In all his learning and *davening,* Reb Shlomo was a teacher of the feminine and sought to do what he could to meet the spiritual needs of his women congregants. He even created a tunnel of *talaysim* that extended from the *bima* to the women's section so women could also receive an *aliyah.* I know personally that Reb Shlomo would have done more for women, but he was restricted by others within the shul who did not understand the *halacha* in regard to women in the same way that he did.

In the very early days of the shul, there was even more ecstasy in *davening* because Reb Shlomo was not pressured to complete services on time. He listened to the spirit of God flowing through him rather than complying with the constraints of a clock. The members of the *chevra* then were similarly not limited to time. In most synagogues, the *davening* is scripted and always ends around the same time. *Davening* with Reb Shlomo was always thrilling and spontaneous. One never knew which *niggun* would be sung and for how long. I loved the vitality of the services. As a general rule, we completed morning services in the early afternoon. Friday night services would also be long and particularly joyous. Sometimes, we would sing a *niggun* for half an hour at a time or more, dancing and even jumping most of the time. When Reb Shlomo would create a new *niggun* before us or share a *niggun* that he created elsewhere with us for the first time, we could go even longer with extra joy for the gift of this new *niggun.*

Shlomo's weekday Torah learnings were also quite wonderful. "Please open your hearts; I do not know what I am going to say." With these words, Reb Shlomo would usually begin these learnings as he gently strummed his guitar strings and sang a beautiful soul *niggun,* a wordless melody. Then he would speak softly, seeming to channel the very words people listening to him needed to hear. In a very romantic setting, a darkened room illuminated with the light of candles, Reb Shlomo transmitted his Torah to us. As Rashi states, "Words that come from the heart enter the heart." The Torah that Reb Shlomo taught was always beautiful and sweet.

For the most part, the women in those early days with Reb Shlomo were an unusual group of creative, accomplished, deeply spiritual and beautiful women. Many of us had had spiritual experiences outside as well as inside of Judaism, so we enjoyed the intensity of prayer that Reb Shlomo offered us. Though most of the women had a strong Jewish identity, we were not initially observant or knowledgeable. Reb Shlomo was a door into the spiritual riches within Judaism for each of us.

The spiritual sisterhood among the women in the shul, nurtured by Reb Shlomo, was very vibrant and important to the women. Though we were each there because of the awesome light we experienced in the davening and learning of Reb Shlomo, for the most part we had fun with each other. Life-long friendships between the women formed during that special time. I am still good friends with a few of the women from that era.

We women at the shul may have been feminists in our profession-al and personal lives, but it would initially appear that we were not feminists in the synagogue. Unlike other Jewish feminists, we did not feel demeaned to not be counted in the minyan nor by the separate seating mandated in the shul. I would even venture to say that the women were relieved to not be counted in the minyan and actually preferred separate seating. Not being counted in the minyan meant that no additional responsibilities to be on time would be placed upon us. Besides, most of us were mystics and more concerned with the higher worlds than this world. It was not really important to us that we were not counted in this "lower world" minyan. We were sure that we were counted in the higher planes where it mattered more.

Sitting exclusively with the women helped me to bond with them and open more directly to the love and beauty of the *Shekhinah*. For my part, I was mainly interested in what occurred within me during prayer than what was externally happening around me. Knowing that I would not be called to receive an *aliyah* or to lead davening gave me the freedom to focus more intently on davening or Torah reading. "Let the men carry the burden of the external service," I would say to myself, so the women could do the more inner, demanding, and important work of prayer. I actually grew to appreciate the *mechitza* in the shul because it clearly provided the safety needed for men and women to go more deeply into prayer. One time I inadvertently glanced at the men's section and witnessed a man in the most deep moment of *devekut,* clinging to the divine. I really did not need to see that. It was just too intimate.

Out of curiosity, I once attended an orthodox women's prayer gathering where the women led the services for other women. Women even read from the Torah and received *aliyot.* I did not stay too long because I did not feel the *"ruach"* there as I did when davening with Reb Shlomo. I wanted to experience the light of God more than anything else, so I hurried back to the Carlebach shul where I would pray and sing the *niggunim* that connected me to my soul.

Reb Shlomo often referred to me as his "right hand." I actively worked to support the shul and his ministry by cooking meals, editing newsletters and designing flyers, accompanying him to concerts to hand out these flyers, and even helping him attend to personal matters. It would seem that it was my karma, my fate, so to speak, to work for the shul. The first time I came to the shul to purchase tickets for Rosh Hashanah and Yom Kippur was in 1976, when Shlomo's mother was alive. She put me to work right away to prepare the shul for the upcoming holidays. I spent two weeks working with her. When I was not running around on errands that took me outside of the synagogue, she loved talking about Reb Shlomo. She delighted in showing me many of the albums composed of pictures and articles about Reb Shlomo as well as sharing those little anecdotes about a son that give a mother particular joy and pride.

When I finally began attending the shul regularly in 1977, I found myself spending a considerable amount of time in the kitchen directly above the shul. If I had gone to a more egalitarian synagogue instead, I would have surely been called up to the *bima* for an *aliyah*, and possibly even acquired such skills as reading from the Torah and leading davening. At the Carlebach shul, I learned how to shop and cook for a hundred people each Shabbos. I learned the laws of *kashrus* in Shlomo's holy kitchen, often directly from him. Rather than feel demeaned by doing "women's work," as my feminist sensibilities might have dictated, I actually felt honored and blessed to serve Reb Shlomo and the community in such a direct and intimate way. The meals with Reb Shlomo were extraordinary. Quite frequently, these beautiful meals would last six or seven hours. Often I was walking home at 4 a.m. on Saturday, only to return to the shul at 9 a.m. for learning with Reb Shlomo prior to *davening*. I am grateful that I had the opportunity to be with Reb Shlomo when I was young and had lots of energy.

After being observant for several years, I journeyed to Israel to learn in a yeshiva. Reb Shlomo did not encourage me to do so and even expressed concern about my going. I delayed going until I felt some urgency within myself to learn more Torah than I possibly could with Shlomo, due to seeing him only on Shabbat and occasionally during the week. He must have known that the yeshiva would be a very challenging experience for me. Within a few days of being there, I totally understood why he had discouraged me from attending. Reb Shlomo had spoiled me. The yeshiva teachers did not have his charisma, and the Judaism they were teaching seemed so different from Shlomo's Judaism. In a short time, I dropped out of yeshiva. "You can't always get what you want, but if you try some time, you just might find, you get what you need," as the Rolling Stones song goes. I was soon invited to join a very small private experimental Jewish meditation group. There I found my spiritual calling and joy.

Upon my return from Israel, Reb Shlomo invited me to teach meditation before Shabbat morning and afternoon services in his shul. My meditation sessions were well attended and served as a wonderful preparation for prayer. I was later invited to teach at other synagogues on the West Side of Manhattan. Within a few years, I left my employment with the New York City government and went on to make my livelihood teaching Jewish meditation and working as a spiritual therapist and counselor. I formed my own organization, Beit Miriam, and offered meditation and spiritual healing classes three times a week, as well as at holiday and Shabbat gatherings after Reb Shlomo left this physical world.

My 13 years of *davening*, learning, and serving Reb Shlomo and the synagogue led to Reb Shlomo offering me *s'mikha* to show his support publicly for my work in Jewish meditation and healing. Giving me *s'mikha* was entirely Reb Shlomo's idea. Even though he had given *s'mikha* to a number of men, as a woman it never would have occurred to me to ask him for it. Reb Shlomo chose to bestow *s'mikha* upon me during the *yahrzeit* celebration for his father when there would be a large gathering of people present. Knowing that it was controversial, he asked me to keep it secret and only invite a few close friends and family. When he announced it during the learning, several people were upset and stormed out of the room. Those who remained received a treat. Reb Shlomo was in his rebbe mode in a way I had never experienced before or would ever again. The *s'mikha* ceremony was most powerful, as Reb Shlomo became a conduit for the blessings of all the holy rebbes he so frequently talked about. In that fleeting moment, I became a Jew and a teacher on a different level. Judaism entered my cells, the pores of my body. I was plugged in, connected, in a new and deeper way. My *s'mikha* document was signed by three orthodox rabbis.

In establishing the House of Love and Prayer in San Francisco in the 1960s, Reb Shlomo introduced a model for outreach that served as a prototype for Chabad houses all over the world. In giving me s'mikha in 1989, I believe that Reb Shlomo wanted to pave a way for observant women to be empowered to teach Torah in the manner that they were personally called upon to do. He wanted the spiritual empowerment of women to be a part of his legacy. While being totally respectful of halacha, Reb Shlomo always sought many different ways to honor women and help them to recognize the important and unique contributions they make in the world. Other than the Lubavitcher Rebbe, who empowered Chabad women to serve alongside their husbands in their outreach efforts, I do not know of any others in the Torah world who did something similar. When Shlomo and his twin brother Eli Chaim were alive, I was even invited to speak my "heart of the feminine" Torah to the congregation many times. Reb Eli Chaim even had me do morning b'rachot several times. It was very powerful for me to have all the men say "Amen" to my bracha. That invitation to speak before the congregation was unfortunately rescinded when they were no longer in the world because I was a single woman. During their reign, it was not necessary to be a "rabbi" to share words of Torah or even to lead morning blessings. In the old days, the shul was more like a family than an institution. If viewed in this way, it really was not so radical to have one of the daughters speak at the table or from the bima.

I suspect that most women who gravitate to becoming a rabbi do so because that is the primary way to have a voice in the synagogue. The rise of feminism as a socio-political movement demanded equal job opportunities for women. As a result, women could move into positions that had previously been occupied solely by men. The non-orthodox Jewish world responded to this plea and began to ordain women along with men. It is quite possible that because the Torah world failed to carve out pathways for Jewish women to be empowered as spiritual teachers, as Reb Shlomo did (and wanted to do even more), the non-orthodox had to do it. I surmise that had the Torah world done this, there would most likely have been less of a need on the part of women to become rabbis.

In my humble opinion, women could and should be empowered to teach the "wisdom of the feminine." The world is in dire need of this kind of wisdom. Just because women are engineers, doctors, lawyers, or even rabbis, it does not necessarily indicate they do so as women. It does not demonstrate a "rise in the feminine," but rather it only shows that these women have sufficiently mastered the wisdom of the masculine to publicly teach. For example, female rabbis often give the same kind of *D'var Torah* as their male counterparts so as to demonstrate their mastery of Jewish texts.

Isaiah's prophecy, "The light of the moon will become like the sun" [Isaiah, 30:26], anticipates a time when women and the feminine spirit within all will rise to transform the world for the better. According to Kabbalah, the body of ancient esoteric Jewish wisdom, there is a primal drive in the universe to restore the Divine Feminine on High and return the woman on this earthly plane to her proper place as well, so that the feminine, both divine and human, is in proper balance with the masculine in both the spiritual and physical universes. Because the external world is already quite adapted to the dominance of the masculine, the values and wisdom of the feminine will have to rise to create the balance needed for peace and harmony. As long as the feminine presence within each person and within the world is not honored, there cannot be peace between men and women, between various groups of people, and with our mother earth, our common home.

My newest book, entitled *The Secret Legacy of Biblical Women: Revealing the Divine Feminine*, is a guide to the "rise of the feminine," offering vistas into the new paradigm beyond feminism. Through an imaginary interview format, keys to the knowledge and practices of feminine spirituality that are sourced in the wisdom of the Kabbalah and embodied by biblical women are revealed. These women did not imitate their male counterparts; they made courageous and independent choices that changed the world. They bequeathed a legacy to generations of men and women that has been largely hidden but will be revealed more in the coming times.

By way of summary, it has taken me many years to understand the difference between women's empowerment due to feminism and the empowerment that is rooted in Torah. I believe that this important difference will become increasingly significant and more obvious to people in the future. As I understand the matter, succinctly stated, feminism promotes egalitarianism and wants to eliminate the difference between the masculine and feminine, as well as between all people, so there will be fairness for all. That is one reason why it is essential that women have the same opportunities as men. On the other hand, Kabbalah, the esoteric wisdom within Judaism, highlights the differences between the masculine and feminine, between the Jewish people and other nations, and seeks to restore a harmonious balance between them all. One is not based in Torah and the other one is based entirely in Torah.

Today's men and women are often confused by what is meant by masculine and what is meant by feminine. Kabbalistic ideas are quite different from secular ones. In my therapy practice, one of the challenges that I have seen for women today is that the problem-solving and negotiating skills that women have acquired in the workplace and that have made them successful there may not serve them in their personal relationships with their husbands or lovers. It usually backfires and actually dampens the love and passion between them. Many women need to learn how to embody the beautiful and receptive qualities of the feminine without becoming a doormat or defensive.

Men, on the other hand, need to embody the beautiful bestowing and directional qualities of the masculine without becoming domineering or insecure. I work with men and women to help them to relearn and reclaim the unique differences between them. When they learn to do this, they restore harmony and passion to their relationships.

Over the years, I have come to understand myself more as a teacher and proponent of the feminine rather than a feminist. This perspective guides me in my work as a therapist, in my teaching of Jewish meditation and Torah, and in my personal life as well. My time with Reb Shlomo, years of Torah and Kabbalah study, and the teaching of Jewish meditation and spiritual healing helped shape my thinking on this important subject.

*Reb Melinda Ribner with Reb Shlomo at her s'mikha signing, 1989.*
*Photo by Joan Roth.*

# Vignettes from Reb Shlomo's Life — and Mine

by Rabbi Joseph Schonwald

## I
## HOW I MET SHLOMO

IT'S A FAIR QUESTION TO ASK HOW I MET SHLOMO — AFTER ALL, IT'S A question often asked whenever the *chevre* meets.

"Holy Brother," Shlomo would exclaim when I made an omelette for him, "you *mamash* saved my life." He said it with such conviction you'd have to stop and reconsider what it was that you did. Although Shlomo always traveled with a suitcase full of vitamins and books, he often overlooked basic needs like eating when he was on the road performing, and his health suffered for it.

My friendship with Shlomo began in the sixties, soon after the Six-Day War. The program director for our overseas students program, R. David Zeller, *z"l*, brought Shlomo to Herzliya, where the foreign students were housed. I had tried to make my way to Israel to help with the war effort but had to wait until a day after the war ended. Tel Aviv University's overseas student program attracted many students, many away from home for the first time. We were housed at the old Dekel Hotel in Herzliya Pituach, on the beach near the ancient port of Appolonia. Some of the luckiest students were housed in villas that had been vacated by the Cuban delegation shortly after the failed Bay of Pigs invasion. One night, the entire Cuban delegation and staff, housed in four villas, surreptitiously left the country in the dead of night. Later, the American students took them over.

It was here that I met Shlomo for the first time. Reb David, *z"l*, thought we needed a spiritual uplift. He had met Shlomo before. I can only say that Shlomo's appearance that night forever changed the direction of my life. June of 1967 was an epic time. The spirit of redemption was in the air. If the Messiah had come, he would have been easily recognized.

*"Let there be peace. Let there be light. Let there be Shabbos. Let there be love."* We all yearned for peace, for Shalom.

In a conversation with Shlomo that evening, I mentioned that I was studying Bible with a Biblical scholar, a wounded general who treated the subject as literature.

"Brother," Shlomo said, "you came all the way to the Holy Land to study Torah like that?" He told a group of us about a new yeshiva just opening up in Jerusalem for newly religious students who'd later become known as *ba'alei teshuvah*. It was the very beginning of the movement. The yeshiva was called the Diaspora Yeshiva. It was located on Mount Zion in Jerusalem.

That night, Shlomo sang, "Come back to *Yerushalayim,* sing the song of *Yerushalayim*." His music penetrated my soul and touched me in a way that no other experience had ever moved me. I knew then that I wanted to learn with my heart. Shlomo awakened me to new possibilities and my life took a new direction.

The next day, a vintage stretch limo Mercedes with Jordanian license plates rolled up to our dorm in Herzliya. What a scene! Five of us got into the limo with all our bags. We were escaping this surreal hippy university beach enclave for Jerusalem.

We arrived at Mt. Zion and the Diaspora Yeshiva and were warmly greeted by Rabbi Dr. Mordechai Goldstein, z"l, who, in the style of Reb Shlomo, embraced and kissed each of us. He said: "We have been waiting for you."

The yeshiva, set up shortly after the war ended, was situated in one of the most sacred places for all religions, King David's Tomb. The only private residence on Mt. Zion was occupied by the Rose family, and a dilapidated building called "the Nachal Building" housed two former soldiers who had defended the mountain and then taken up residence there. We all shared the buildings and space. Mt. Zion was a place from where you could get a glimpse of the Old City. Since 1948, it had been no man's land. A small band of Nachal recruits were guarding the mountain. The area was located on the other side of the wall between the Old City and Zion Gate.

Our soldiers who shared space with the yeshiva dorms were defenders who had held off a large detachment of Jordanian Legionnaires. They did so by running up and down the trenches, firing as they ran to create the impression of a large contingent of defenders. They succeeded in keeping the Jordanian army at bay.

Also with us on the mountain was an interesting array of spiritual seekers who came to Israel and ended up studying at the Diaspora Yeshiva, linking up with Rabbi Mordechai Goldstein to form the first student body. There were established students who came from other yeshivot, and academics, who were taking time off from their university studies to deepen their appreciation of Judaism.

I was entrusted with inviting potential students to come spend Shabbat with us at the yeshiva. My fishing trips for new students took me as far away as Eilat in search of likely candidates. In those years, Eilat was a teeming watering hole for young people. It wasn't hard to find people who were tired of the free lifestyle scene on the beach and realized they were wasting their time. Interestingly enough, I found many youths from fine, religious families on the East Coast of the USA, some even from rabbinical families. Their parents thought their kids were in yeshivot. By the end of the month of Elul, just before the high holidays, we welcomed a group of 28 to our beginner's program, in addition to the dozen or so regular students from other programs who had enrolled in our yeshiva program over the summer.

The Mount Zion Diaspora Yeshiva had become the grand-daddy of all the *"ba'alei-teshuva"* returnees programs sprouting after the Six-Day War. We were the "in" place to be, studying with Rabbi Goldstein and listening to great music with cool people. Rabbi Goldstein warmly embraced all of his students with great care and attention.

Shlomo visited regularly. We had the hottest band around, the Diaspora Yeshiva Band. They created a music scene on Mt. Zion and a whole new wave of Jewish music unheard of before.

Many of us had found our way to this yeshiva through the good counsel of Reb Shlomo. It's no exaggeration to say he was saving lives every day. Rabbi Freifeld's yeshiva in Far Rockaway was his address in the States for directing young people to study Torah. Har Tzion was his choice in Israel, and he sent all of us there. So we were privileged to see Shlomo often, whenever he came to Israel, which was several times a year. Mount Zion became his place to teach, officiate at weddings, conduct workshops and give concerts. His large concerts were given in bigger venues in Jerusalem. Shabbatot he spent with chevre in Migdal and in later years at Moshav Meor Modi'im. His Motzei Shabbat Nachamu concerts were legendary.

In the spirit of an embracing orthodoxy, we at the seminary were afforded a breadth of learning experiences, including nighttime study at the original Kabbalah Center in the Old City. We studied the Torah of Rav Kook from his students, and best of all, we learned with Reb Shlomo. He had a close relationship with Rabbi Goldstein.

Rabbi Goldstein's method for teaching Talmud was systematic and unique, and he also taught Musar literature. I remember spending several months on the introduction to Moshe Chayyim Luzatto's *Mesilat Yesharim,* "The Path of the Upright." Chasidic texts were readily available in our library.

My friendship with Shlomo deepened, and he was ever a source of encouragement and friendship. His Torah of the Heart touched me as no other experience did.

I received a religious deferment from the United States army in 1968, during the Vietnam War, which I opposed. My aim was to receive rabbinic ordination and then go into Jewish education. My upbringing was filled with choices. My parents were Holocaust survivors. My mother came from a long line of rabbinic luminaries, stretching back to the Chatam Sofer, in Pressburg (Bratislava). My father was from a more liberal tradition. My brother and I were given freedom to choose. I came to terms with some of my questions about the Holocaust, and my parents' survival became a cause for me in a very personal way. Why did my mother survive? I wondered. To what purpose? As my faith began to deepen, I began to see my birth and choice of career in the rabbinate as a significant way to serve the remnant of the Jewish community in a focused way.

The period immediately after the Six-Day War was an electric time, especially in Jerusalem. The whole country was elated. I actively participated in the reunification of Jerusalem by affixing the mezuzah on Zion Gate. Redemption was at hand. You could feel it in the air. It was the dawning of a new era, a hopeful time for the end of hostilities and the new age of peace. Shlomo's concerts were packed. Wherever he went, people of all ages came out in droves. He embraced everyone and was often seen in hospitals and schools. He was scheduled around the clock. He often performed and taught until 3 a.m.

||
## AFTER THE YOM KIPPUR WAR, 1973

When I returned to California after receiving *smicha* (ordination) in Jerusalem, I held several educational positions, as headmaster of a Jewish Day School, principal of a large afternoon Hebrew School, and teaching in a Jewish high school program. It soon became clear to me that I could better serve our community as a congregational rabbi.

Throughout the years when I held rabbinic posts, in California, Kansas, and Arizona, I always found time to host Shlomo. I organized concerts for him in my synagogue and arranged for teaching opportunities throughout the broader community. I felt privileged to present Shlomo as a national treasure of the Jewish people.

*Rabbi Joe and Rabbi Goldstein, z"l, affixing mezuzah on Zion Gate, July 1967.*
*Photo by Yisrael Lev.*

It was my usual practice to make sure he was paid with two checks. One, marked "for deposit only," was for his family. He'd cash the other and distribute the proceeds to the band of "Holy Beggars" (disciples) who followed him. It was known in his inner circle that Shlomo was a terrible money manager. Generous to a fault, he gave to every out-stretched hand. It wasn't unusual for Reb Shlomo to give away all his concert earnings before the evening was over.

In many ways, he was oblivious to the ways of the world. I saw him sign contracts hastily written on paper placemats at restaurants. His trust in people left him vulnerable to unscrupulous individuals who took advantage of his naïve trust. If I pointed out to him that someone was stealing him blind, he'd say: "He's only a small *gonif* (thief)." I was left with the impression that it was pointless to bring the matter up in the first place.

III

## *"MAMASH* A MIRACLE"

You can read about Shlomo and Neila's courtship in Neila's chapter in this book, "My Story." Shlomo was an "old *bocher.*" His mother was always trying to marry him off.

The scene I wish to describe for you is the last few days before Shlomo and Neila's wedding. Chevre from all around the world assembled in New York for their December wedding. Many of us stayed with Shlomo at the Esplanade Hotel in Manhattan. Everything was set for a Sunday night *chuppah* at the site of the World's Fair pavilion.

There were three different sets of invitations. One got people into the *Kabbalat Panim.* The second one got people into the *Chuppah.* A third got people into all three, including the dinner dance reception. As one of Shlomo's "top friends," I felt privileged to have all three invitations.

Thursday night at midnight, a dozen or so of the *chevre* accompanied Shlomo to the mikvah at 770 Eastern Parkway, Lubavitch headquarters. Dr. Josh Ritchie entered first, as steam escaped and he declared the water temperature to be just right. Some of us dared to dip our toes into the very hot water. A most intense mikvah experience for all of us.

Late Friday morning, Shlomo rang me and said: "Listen brother, I *mamash* have a problem. You have to save my life. In order to get married Sunday, I need a little piece of paper, you know, a license. We've got to go to City Hall and get a wedding license. Please meet me downstairs."

In the lobby, I find Shlomo and his worried-looking bride. Off we go to the subway station, with Ian Grand in tow. He keeps us laughing despite the tense situation. The subway is standing room only. We arrive at City Hall as they are preparing to close for the weekend. Many clerks have already left. Shlomo runs in and finds a Jewish judge on his way down the main corridor.

"Brother," Shlomo calls out, "I'm Rabbi Shlomo Carlebach. I need the biggest favor in the world from you."

"I know who you are," the judge replies. "What can I do for you, Rabbi?"

"Well, I'm getting married Sunday."

"*Mazel Tov,*" says the judge.

"I need a license."

"Okay," the judge says. "Do you have your blood test results?"

"I didn't know I need a blood test," Shlomo answers.

"Go to the clinic at the hospital. They are closing in 45 minutes. Try to get the tests. Meanwhile, I will fill out all the necessary forms and sign them. When you get the blood test, come show my clerk and you'll have the license you need to get married in New York."

Once again, we're on our way. When we arrive at the hospital clinic, the doors are already closed. Shlomo finds a doctor on his way out.

"Brother," he says, "you *mamash* have to do me the biggest favor in the world. I need a blood test so I can get married."

"I wish I could help you," the doctor replies, "but I haven't drawn blood since my days in medical school. Let's see who is still available. Most people have already left to go home for the weekend. Oh, look! There's one person still cleaning up in the lab. Maybe she can do the blood test for you."

The doctor leads Shlomo and Neila into the lab. Shlomo asks the nurse to do him the biggest favor in the world.

"Rabbi!" she exclaims. "You need a hematologist, not me! I don't do that." She picks up the phone, and two minutes later, as we are all sweating, a nurse comes in and takes Shlomo's and Neila's blood.

"Thank you a thousand times!" he exclaims. "You saved my life!"

Now, with proof of the blood test in hand, we catch a cab back to City Hall, where the blinds on the windows are drawn, and a clerk approaches us on her way out.

"Holy sister!" Shlomo exclaims.

"Rabbi Carlebach," she says as she looks up at him, "I have your license right here on the table. You just have to sign it and you're kosher."

Shlomo is shaking his head. "It's *mamash* a miracle."

Then he turns to me and says: "Brother, I couldn't have done it without you."

Neila, looking noticeably relieved, says: "This is *mamash a gevaldt*."

"Our angels are looking out for us, darling!" Shlomo exclaims.

IV

## LEADING KABBALAT SHABBAT AT
## THE CARLEBACH SHUL

Shlomo asked me to lead services Friday night at his father's shul. I found myself in awe, standing where his father stood, at the Bima where Shlomo himself often led services.

This experience was the most emotionally charged davening I had ever done and the biggest recognition I had ever received from my dear friend, now a bridegroom — the privilege of conducting Shabbat services in his own Beit Knesset.

I couldn't find the right key to sing in. I started out too high. Neila's father, Cantor Glick, z"l, was standing next to me, looking aghast. He reached over and put his hand on top of mine as I clutched the reader's table, as if to say: "Relax, it's not your bar mitzvah." Neila's father was a kind and reassuring man, advanced in his years. He had a beautiful voice, with which he graced us that Shabbat and at the wedding.

V

## SHLOMO'S WEDDING WEEKEND: AN ATTEMPTED
## SHABBAT AFTERNOON VISIT TO A.J. HESCHEL

On Shabbat afternoon, a few of us ventured out to see if we could stop and say "Shabbat Shalom" to Rabbi Professor Abraham Joshua Heschel. When we knocked on the door, his daughter Susanna greeted us and told us that her father had just passed away. If there was ever a clear message that if you are going to do a mitzvah, don't put it off, that was it.

VI

## BOBOV TISCH

After Shabbat, some of us went with Shlomo to Bobov, where a *farbrengen* was going on. The hall was filled to overflowing with chasidim, filling the room on rows of bleachers, awaiting the Rebbe's every word.

Imagine the scene as Shlomo arrived with his colorfully dressed followers in tow. To the chasidim, we must have seemed like Martians! There was a great commotion. You could feel the consternation in the room as we entered. I wore a flowered shirt and light brown suede jacket. My hair (I still had some then!) was long, and I was carrying some of Shlomo's books.

As we entered, we were confronted by the chasidim, who wanted to know about the flowers in our hair, the beaded necklaces we wore, and most of all, were we all Nazarites? What with the length of our hair, it was a legitimate question, to which we calmly attempted to reply!

Meanwhile, the Bobover Rebbe motioned Shlomo to his side. Shlomo, holding my hand, approached. I found myself standing next to the Bobover Rebbe alongside a table filled with his most trusted disciples. It was getting late. Shlomo was noticeably tired. He was standing up, leaning on a stack of books. The rebbe lovingly encouraged us to come closer to him. He spoke, uninterrupted, for forty minutes, in Yiddish. Then he turned to Shlomo, who had been standing there, and asked him: "What do you think?" You could have heard a pin drop in the hall as Shlomo recounted everything the Rebbe had just said. What I will forever remember was the long, deafening sigh from the throngs that flowed through the capacity-filled hall.

As is the tradition at *Farbrengen* gatherings such as this, plates of kugel were then distributed, and not in the most orderly fashion. The chasidim were attacking the plates as they were being borne on the shoulders of the waiters. The kugel disappeared before it hit the table. The Rebbe handed Shlomo and me some kugel, to the noticeable dismay of the more prominent members of the community.

After receiving the blessing of the Rebbe for long life, good health, ample sustenance and every manner of blessing, our group got ready to exit. We passed a large crowd of chasidim who were a little bit friendlier than when we entered, still asking questions.

After the reception accorded us by the Rebbe, they were still curious as to why Shlomo wore a huge Star of David on a gold chain. He said to the chasidim that it helps him communicate with the young people. He said to them, as I recall: "Where I go, you cannot go. That's why I have to look the part."

VII

## THE WEDDING

Shlomo and Neila's wedding was held on December 26, 1972, at Terrace on the Park in Flushing Meadows-Corona Park, the site of the 1964/1965 New York World's Fair. Originally built as a heliport for the Fair, the venue was a wooden building that seemed to expand as more and more people arrived. At the *Kabbalat Panim,* Shlomo was nowhere to be seen. I was concerned, because there had been a serious altercation at the door with people claiming to be Shlomo's best friends but lacking printed invitations. They had moved, so they didn't get the invitation in the mail. People were shoving and shouting; it was a major fiasco. Shlomo had for sure invited them, and they had traveled halfway around the world to be there, but he had either forgotten to send them an invitation in the mail, or the mail had been misdelivered or not forwarded or not forwarded in time.

Neila emerged from the bride's private room looking noticeably shattered. Someone had stolen the white kittel she had worked for months embroidering. *Ribeno Shel Olam!* (OMG!) Brother Itzikel offered to drive out and buy another white robe for Shlomo to wear as a replacement. I felt so sorry for all of Neila's work. The bride was sobbing in disappointment. Seeing Shlomo's beautiful bride so distraught was devastating to behold.

By this time, the extra guests had managed to crash into the first reception, the *Kabbalat Panim*. The building was so filled with people it felt like it was buckling apart.

Brother Itzhak Eisenstadt came in with a new white kittel for Shlomo to wear to his *chuppah*. Shlomo said to Neila: "Darlin,' you worked so hard, *mamash*! Maybe the person took the kittel by mistake."

So many of Shlomo's closest friends crowded beneath the *chuppah* that Neila almost fell off the platform. As they all jostled to be close to Shlomo, there was no room left for the bride!

There were delays waiting for people honored with one of the seven blessings but who couldn't get under the *chuppah* to give them. But what was lacking in decorum and *derech eretz* was made up for in *ruach*. What dancing! What *simcha*!

As I stood beneath the *chuppah* holding the wine goblet waiting for the important guests to arrive, the building began to shake with the additional weight of the celebrants.

Shlomo's close friends included some of his old study partners (*chevruta*) from yeshiva days as well as his family. In sharp contrast to the San Francisco hippies who journeyed to their rebbe's wedding, there were suits and ties beside the bell-bottoms and the beads.

## VIII
## CHEN V'CHESED: GRACE AND LOVING-KINDNESS, A STORY ABOUT SHLOMO AND THE BOBOVER REBBE

Rabbi Shlomo Halberstam was the third Rebbe of Bobov. He re-established the community after World War II. He lost his wife and seven children during the war. Only one son, Naftali, survived the Holocaust. Reb Shlomo told me he was invited to this young man's wedding. What a bittersweet wedding it was. The Rebbe must have ached for his wife and children.

"This was the highest wedding in my life," Shlomo told me. "Highest is not enough to describe this wedding. Before the wedding, whoever wanted a blessing walked up to the rebbe and gave him a *kvitl*, a note, with your name written on a piece of paper. You asked for a blessing. There was no time for lengthy discussions. You just handed him the note, stopped for a blessing, and took your leave.... I remember the whole scene. The Rebbe sat on a large chair. He held my hand and said: '*Chen v'Chesed.*' At that moment, he pierced my *neshama*. My body shakes when I remember this blessing."

The Rebbe's blessing stayed with Shlomo throughout his life, defining Reb Shlomo's essence, his most cherished qualities: *Chen v'Chesed*, Grace and Loving-kindness.

*Reb Shlomo with* Arba Minim *at his shul in New York,* Hoshana Rabbah *1990.*
*Photo by Joan Roth.*

# Torah That Opens the Heart

by Rabbi Yoel Glick

REB SHLOMO HAD AN AMAZINGLY CREATIVE WAY OF TEACHING TORAH. His way of looking at a text was unique. The more I learn, the more I appreciate the greatness of Shlomo's *chidushim*.

For Shlomo, the purpose of learning was to take you to God — to connect you with your soul. His teachings were meant to inspire you and raise your consciousness.

Reb Shlomo never tried to be "clever" in his teaching. He never tried to show off his vast learning. He always focused on providing people with teaching that was meaningful and uplifting. His teachings were very personal and intimate.

Learning was also about bringing you closer to people. Shlomo believed that holy books provide insight into the nature and purpose of life in this world. They enable us to understand the hearts of other human beings. They empower us to overcome our own challenges and support us in our struggles.

Shlomo loved to learn. He would always want to know what I was learning. Sharing a teaching was the mode of personal communication where he was most alive and at ease. "Holy brother, listen to this *gevaltik* Torah" was a common opening line to any meeting between us.

Learning was like breathing for Shlomo. He always had a *sefer* with him and would use every spare moment to glance into the *sefer* and learn. Standing on a street corner, waiting in a restaurant, or getting ready to board a plane, Shlomo was always either learning or interacting with someone else.

I would like to share several examples of Reb Shlomo's teaching that express something of the *derech* — the spiritual path — that he taught, as well as his amazing capacity to draw living Torah from mere words on a page.

Shlomo's teachings were, more often than not, about the relationships between people. He saw the stories in the Torah as paradigms for the hopes and dreams, the desires and fears, of all human beings.

One teaching of his that always stayed with me was based on a torah by Rebbe Nachman of Breslov about the spies who entered the Promised Land. The Torah portion of *Sh'lach lekha* tells the story of their failed mission and the subsequent banishment of the Children of Israel to forty years of wandering in the desert. At the end of the Torah portion, God gives the people the commandment of wearing *tzitzit*. Rebbe Nachman explains that the purpose of *tzitzit* is to transform our vision, to change the way we look at the world and ourselves. Shlomo built upon this idea from Rebbe Nachman to speak about what it means to have "*tzitzit* eyes."

For Shlomo, the failure of the spies was an inability to see the beauty of the land, to love the country that God had given to them. To have *tzitzit* eyes, then, is to see the beauty in the world around you — to see the beauty in every human being.

According to Reb Shlomo, the problem with the world is that people look at each other with "snake eyes" — the eyes of judgment and heartlessness that is symbolized in the tradition by the serpent that tempted Adam and Eve. To have *tzitzit* eyes is to love people with all of their failings, to see their special qualities — to turn to them with love and acceptance.

Parents need to look upon their children with *tzitzit* eyes, and not judge or condemn their mistakes and failures. Life partners need to see each other with *tzitzit* eyes, rather than assessing which attributes the other has and which qualities he or she lacks. Each person is blessed. Each person is beautiful, if only we have the eyes to see.

This theme was echoed in another favorite torah of Shlomo's from the Ishbitzer Rebbe. In his *sefer, Mei HaShiloach,* the Ishbitzer has an innovative interpretation of the third part of the first line of the first paragraph of the *Shema.* "*Ve'ahavta eht Adonai Elohaikha, bekhol le-vavkha, u-vekhol nafshekha, u-vekhol me'odekha*" 'You shall love the Lord your God with all of your heart, and all of your soul, and all of your might.' The Ishbitzer translates the last part of this phrase — "*vekhol me'odekha*" — not as 'with all your might' but as with your "*me'od, me'od*" 'your very, very.'

What the Ishbitzer is telling us, Shlomo explained, is that each of us has a quality which is uniquely our own. Each of us has a special beauty that belongs to our soul and to no one else. We need to love and serve God with the special gifts that He has given to us, to reveal our Divine spark in the world.

Reb Shlomo spent a lot of time trying to help people see their special beauty — to discover their "*me'od, me'od.*" He was always compliment-ing and uplifting those around him, telling them what a deep and radiant *neshama* they had. He profoundly believed in the beauty of each person and truly saw their "*me'od, me'od.*"

This thought leads me to another of Shlomo's poignant teachings about Yitzchak's blessing of Yaacov and Esav. In this teaching, Shlomo was not interested in discussing why Yaacov received the blessings of the firstborn. He wanted to know why Yitzchak wanted to bless Esav in the first place. For Shlomo, Yitzchak was not a blind and feeble old man who had a soft spot for his first-born son. He was someone with a deep understanding of human nature and of the brokenness that we all carry in our hearts. Yitzchak wanted to bless Esav, Shlomo explained, because he knew that Esav really needed his blessing. Yaacov was an ideal son; he had all the right attributes and did not need Yitzchak's help to thrive. Esav, on the other hand, was really struggling. He was disconnected from his neshama and only cared about his physical needs. Without his father's blessing, Esav would be lost. Yitzchak understood that it is the broken souls of the world who most need our love and blessings.

This teaching infused the whole of Shlomo's *avodah*. He spent his life working with broken souls. But it was a different type of brokenness that was the central focus of his labors. Shlomo worked with individuals who were searching for something more than just a material existence and were unable to adjust to a so-called "normal" life. These sensitive souls lacked the hard exterior needed to succeed in this world, the steadiness and will power necessary to find their way on their own. Shlomo strove to support and uphold them, to heal their wounds and uplift their spirits. He filled them with his love, wisdom, and strength.

In the Torah portion that follows Yitzchak's blessing of Yaacov, the Torah recounts the story of Yaacov's twenty-one year stay with his uncle Lavan in Padan Aram. Upon his arrival in Padan Aram, Yaacov falls in love with Lavan's daughter Rachel and works for seven years to win her hand in marriage. But Lavan tricks Yaacov, and sends his eldest daughter Leah to Yaacov on the wedding night, instead of Rachel. Yaacov wakes up in the morning and finds himself married to the wrong woman.

The rabbis were incredulous as to how such a thing could happen. How did Yaacov not discover that he had the wrong sister? *Chazal* solve their dilemma by explaining that Yaacov, who was afraid of Lavan's trickery, arranged special signs ahead of the wedding with Rachel. Rachel, however, did not want her sister to be humiliated by Yaacov, so she gave the signs over to Leah. As a result, Yaacov was deceived.

Once again, Reb Shlomo used this teaching to create a vision of how we should live in the world. Think of how much Rachel loved her sister, he would say. Think of the courage it took for her to make such a sacrifice. Imagine the pain Rachel felt that night. If she had kept the signs to herself she would have been married to Yaacov, but she could not bear to see her sister dishonored and spurned.

For Reb Shlomo, this was the heart of the story of Yaacov, Leah and Rachel — not Lavan's trickery, or even Yaacov's perseverance in working another seven years for Rachel's hand. It was Rachel's love for her sister that really touched Shlomo — her willingness to sacrifice herself and her own well-being to prevent another's pain.

This sense of self-sacrifice was at the core of Shlomo's life of service. He gave away everything he had to help others — his energy, his love, even his own belongings. He would do anything he could to protect another person from being shamed or embarrassed. He gave over his "signs" to everyone that he met.

Rebbe Natan, the disciple and recorder of Rebbe Nachman's teachings, teaches that Rachel is symbolic of the path of Torah, the revealed and external world of study and learning. Leah is symbolic of the path of prayer, the hidden moments we spend pouring out our heart before God. The beauty of Rachel, someone who has learning, is easy for all to see. The beauty of Leah, someone calling out in the privacy of the night, is more difficult to discern. Lavan, Rebbe Natan says, felt the need to trick Yaacov because Lavan did not see the inner beauty of Leah, the value of a life of prayer and contemplation. But he was wrong, Rebbe Natan asserts. Yaacov's marriage to Leah was essential for Israel. Without their marriage, there would be no twelve tribes and no Jewish people. Without Leah nothing could have occurred.

Rebbe Shlomo transformed this torah of Rebbe Natan into a discourse on the so-called "beautiful people" of the world, with their fake smiles and plastic exteriors. These individuals draw a lot of attention due to their beautiful facades, while the people who shine inwardly, like Leah, are shunned and ignored. We should not judge others by their external appearance, Rebbe Natan is telling us, but by whom they are inside.

Shlomo saw the hidden beauty of the "Leahs" of the world. He recognized their inner light and heard them crying out for God. These young men and women were precious to him. He believed that they were special souls who would help to revitalize the Jewish people. He believed that their sincerity and profound yearning would make Israel whole.

Reb Shlomo's teachings reflect his wide-open heart and his great love for people. He loved all of humanity and was happy to encounter seekers of any faith. His teachings also express Shlomo's own sense of brokenness, his struggles to try and make his life complete.

Shlomo's teachings are a source of inspiration for all of us who want to open our hearts, a well of wisdom to deepen our souls. They are a support for us in our moments of anguish, a gift of love when we feel all alone in the world.

Reb Shlomo's teachings urge us to love and cherish every single person. They encourage us to see the beauty in everyone we meet. Reb Shlomo's teachings provide us with a *derech* to fix the brokenness we see around us — a way that each and every one of us can repair the world.

— Southern France, Chanukah, 5775 / 2014

# My Story: Excerpt from a Memoir

by Neila Carlebach

SHLOMO IS GONE.

Not like he usually is.

Travelling.

He has died.

Through the pulsing, the open mouth frozen in some strange contortion, the whirring of space, an intrusion pinpricks a hole in the already fortified air.

Someone is screaming. My daughter. She is here with me.

The phone is still in my hand, attaching me to where Shlomo is, in some anonymous hospital, my call to find out what his condition is since he collapsed on the airplane, to the voice that says, "Sorry, madam, but your husband has expired."

Dari is waving her arms and screaming.

Moving slow motion from this no place, trying to touch her with my hand that is not attached to the rest of me.

Her voice follows with our contact as we finally manage to reach each other like two drowning souls, gasping, finding a tenuous lifeline. Our insides are exploding, and I hear her *"Nooo!"*

Did I say something, anything that made sense? Did I offer her motherly comfort? Was I there?

Shattered particles, one frame at a time, sometimes two or three, mostly frozen moments. Dari and I reduced to one loud wail that drifted into moments of silence, an instinct for survival to keep breathing.

Somehow we materialize downstairs. My older daughter, Neshama, has just returned from the airport where she was to pick up her father...and we all are collapsed in the front hall, a puddle of unbelieving, lost, scattered parts all over the floor.

✳   ✳   ✳

Dear friends,

With great humility I offer some pages of a book I am in the process of writing about Holy Reb Shlomo, *zt'l*. It is a personal story filled with love, life, heaven and earth, sweet friends, and great learning and awakening.

Bless me to finish soon and do great honor to one of the greatest men to have walked among us.

With uncountable blessings for peace, love, joy, health, parnassa. and to be connected to the source. May Hashem shine from the all, with the all and the all on all of us.

Neila

# Chapter One

*The Premishlaner Rebbe told his disciples that the
only way he ever could make it through this perilous
journey of life on earth was to hold on to Above.*

This afternoon I bought a new dress in the Arab shuk. Haggling comes easy to a long-time plea bargainer. Being the youngest child in a family of grown-ups has made me a pro in the art of finding a loophole or winning a point. Any argument based on an obscure notion of why the reality of things usually written in stone had to be bent, maneuvered, or out and out rejected has become my forte. So I was pleased that the white frock with huge red flowers that reached respectfully halfway down my thigh was had for 25 shekels less than the asking price. With my hair swinging down my back and my stacked shoes, which lifted me to a much more rarefied viewpoint, I was ready to meet God. And I wanted to do it alone.

The flow of old buildings around an open courtyard is filled with ingredients that stir into a strange pie. Devout, bearded, and black-garbed righteous, swaying and bowing in rhythmic motions, stopping periodically to kiss the wall, to lay a hand upon some stone that they made claim to through the years just by being present. These stone blocks were heaved into place by the builders of Herod and bear the imprints of millions of possessive worshippers. There are guards that scrutinize all who approach and hand out *kipot,* skullcaps, to men who wear no head covering, and draped material squares to women to cover immodestly bare shoulders. I am given a square to tie at my waist, to cover the rest of my legs. In patches of color stand diverse groups from all over the world, testimony to the sanctity, the need to be in this place.

It takes time, or maybe it takes to be in no time, but I finally approach.

I am at the Holy Wall and a light, cool darkness drifts through the ancient city but doesn't touch the stones. It has taken me two weeks to prepare myself, to approach and touch. My thoughts skip from here to inside ruminations, and I wonder how it is that I forgot there was a God for so many years.

When my fingers finally caress the stones in an all too awkward advance, like from a tenuous lover, shy of the first overture, how shocked I am at their warmth, at the discovery of the heartbeat beneath my finger-tips. I pray first from the Siddur, the offered prayer book, from a deep well of my collective memories and from generations of wailing here at this very spot. "Hear O Israel, God is God, God is One!" bursts from my lungs. It is a different kind of alive I feel. New air, potent air, and I don't quite have a handle on what to do with it, but I can't leave. Not yet. There are too many secrets that I sense, some new book that needs reading, some key that needs jiggling. The prayers I utter are a begin-ning. I feel a door open, and I pass through without thought and join the universal expression of my Jewish brothers and sisters repeating ancient words that echo through time and space. The night becomes lighter, and I then become aware of the pressure of the shoulders next to mine, keeping rhythm to this ancient rocking. I come back to where I began, touching stones. It is only a beginning. I pull away with the promise to myself and to the wall to come back soon.

Several French students sit around with a guidebook. I join them, glad that my university French still works for me. We share experienc-es and offer new possibilities to see and feel in this land of so many sights. One girl, studying art and architecture at the Sorbonne, tells of a rabbi who plays the guitar, sings, and through stories and teaching brings a new kind of Judaism to young people. I wonder whether it is the same rabbi I heard about in Toronto and chose to decline tickets to his concert. Her friend heard him sing in Paris, and she mentions that he sometimes comes to the Wall to pray late at night. They are waiting, just in case. I wait, too, but not for the rabbi. I am not quite ready to move in that direction yet. The months of re-acquainting myself with my roots through study and some rituals have been good ones. The timing to move deeper has to be my own. Wafting in and out of my thoughts, I laugh at their stories and jokes and wait with them, unable to leave: there is a stillness and yet a gentle wind stirs the flag swaying beside the square.

Suddenly there is a definite shift in the floor of the courtyard. Everyone is moving, being sucked toward some invisible vortex. And I am stone still and yet reel with the tilt.

A shapeless group of bobbing heads attached to one large shared body progresses down the dark stairs that lead from the Arab marketplace to the courtyard, a dark grey shadow juxtaposed on grey stone. Following the pointing fingers, I blink when a head atop a white shirt bathed and glowing in light appears. And I stand transfixed, wondering if the halo surrounding him is real.

Some two hundred people slowly merge in the courtyard. The waiting group insinuates itself and melds into the wave of humanity pulsing with anticipation. I stand at the outside of the perimeter and hear a gentle melody that wafts over the group and sets everyone to swaying. I can't see the center, the force. I only feel the light, the bond snaking around and attaching each of us by some invisible energy as the song is drawn into our mouths and as quickly expelled, fully formed, as we become part of its melody. Then the word spreads — a hiss, "Sit down, sit down, sit," and the circle of people, as if choreographed, slides to the ground in silent waves. I, unthinking, stay standing, too fixated to move.

And then he is totally visible. His halo is real, and it shines with pulses of light, keeping some magical time with the music. He sways slightly, and looking around, meets my eyes. It is a look unlike any other I have known before. His eyes don't pierce but they look right into me, seeing something I don't know yet. His full black beard is flecked with grey and his face shines, his eyes twinkle, and I can't look away. He covers his eyes with his hand and sways again, and after a million years, he speaks. "Good Shabbos," he says, and then louder, "Good Shabbos!" People respond, saying "Good Shabbos." And then again, even louder, he calls out, "Good Shabbos!" and this time everyone calls back to him, meeting his words in mid-air, strong and loud, bumping syllables, "Good Shabbos!" He covers his eyes again, and he seeks my eyes again. Turning to a red-bearded man at his side, he whispers, and the man looks at me. Again he covers his eyes and finally he begins speaking: "Shabbos is so special. Shabbos is back to paradise. Paradise is a place where everything is good, everything is holy, everything is beautiful. Paradise is a place where suddenly it's clear to me that I can fix all my mistakes. And even more so, everything I thought was a mistake, every street I thought was the wrong street, was the only way to get here. One second before Shabbos, purity and holiness descend to the world, cleaning our vessels so we can pick up the bliss of Shabbos. And what a strong vitamin Shabbos is, this new energy that comes down from Heaven. *Gevalt!*"

I want to be in his Paradise, his Shabbos. He sings again; his melody is so contagious and uplifting, everyone sings. He looks up, stroking his beard gently, a caress from ear to chin. He seems to be seeking heavenly inspiration, stroking his beard, swaying and silent. "My beautiful friends, I am sure you all know that Shabbos has two faces. There is keeping Shabbos holy, the 39 laws of Shabbos, the withdrawing from the everyday world. And then there is the bliss of Shabbos, the inside of Shabbos, which is a gift from Heaven. The bliss of Shabbos is even deeper than Paradise. It's a secret between me and God, between me and the people I love so much. Shabbos is peace because peace is secrets, secrets of the depths, of the deepest depths. Secrets are the deepest God revelation. A true Shabbos person is someone who walks the streets of the world and every human being they see, they seem to have a secret with. And with those they love, they have the secret of all secrets."

He then covers his eyes with his hand again and continues swaying. The crowd of people is so still I can hear the gentle wind. I want to tell him my secret, and I don't even know what it is yet. He becomes still, opens his eyes, and looks at me again, and then turns to the man with a black beard standing at his other side and whispers to him. That man looks at me. I suddenly feel self-conscious, connect to my body again, and look around, wondering whether there are others at whom his friends are staring. Suddenly I become aware that I am the only person in his circle of observers that is standing, and it then makes sense; they want me to sit down, and I do.

He continues singing and speaking for another while. I don't know what he says, I only think that maybe it is time for me to have a rabbi after all, to guide my spiritual awakening that is now so strong that it burns my eyes, my heart, my feet. The tears are hanging on, just beyond expression, when I hear everyone moving, going back to the wall to pray. Or as the rabbi was calling out, "Time to welcome the Holy Sabbath and pour out our hearts." And then he walks straight to me, his eyes again holding mine, exotic eyes, large, slightly tilted upward, soft eyes, strong and soft. He extends a hand. "My name is Shlomo," a soft melodious voice purrs at me, "And what is your name, Miss World?" he asks, mischief in his eyes, his hand warm, holding mine. "Elaine Glick," I answer, and quick to be less self-conscious, I tell him how much I liked his words, his songs.

"Ah," he answers, "Elaine Glick, and what's your Hebrew name?"

"Aliyah," I tell him.

"Ah, and where can I find you if I want to invite you sometime?" he continues, still holding my hand.

"I am staying with my uncle in B'nai Brak."

He prods, "And does your uncle have a telephone, maybe?" He tells me he has a good memory, and I reply that the number is easy, 747-747.

"What a number!" he exclaims, "Double jumbo! You know, I love flying. Why don't you pray with us and come to *Sheva Brachas* afterwards? Sweet friends of mine just got married, and I am making a little feast for them."

I want to go. Something about him is so compelling, so sweet. Even though it is already after midnight and I had been tired, his presence wipes away anything real. It is a faraway land I now inhabit of washed white stone, people kissing a wall and holding onto the warmth of it, each other, the night, to Shabbos. All in one bubble, like my smiling snowman in a globe, where the glass always reflects peace, and he is always jolly as the snow swirls around him.

And I am in a swirl of women, dancing and singing again, songs I don't know but seem to be singing, praying prayers that come to life because everyone is praying them and singing them and clapping to them and dancing. Oh, the dancing! Without feet, without steps or patterns, we just dance, float in each other's circle, our different colors blend into a shifting white blur of light and inside laughter. I love everyone, and trickling through my smile I taste my tears and finally catch myself, look at myself from somewhere outside and am stupefied as to who I am, lost in a dance, wanting to never stop, and yet wondering what is happening, how these feelings could grab me without my even knowing it. I give into it all. There is no concept of time experiencing this kind of Shabbos. And I don't even notice when the prayers end.

I am walking towards Shlomo, who comes to find me. He takes my hand, and holding it leads his group away from the crowd. "We are going to the Artists Colony for the feastele," he informs me, as he gently pulls me along. The questions begin: how was the davening for me, where am I from, what do I do, what do I like, how long will I be in Israel, what does my father do, where is my family from originally, and he punctuates each of my answers with his own commentary.

He has friends in Toronto and has sung there and teaches there often. He is living a little bit in New York, a little in San Francisco, a little in Israel, but his watch is always set on Israel time. "I am always in the Holy Land no matter where I go." He holds my hand firmly, almost possessively. I wonder about him, this magical man, different from any rabbi I have ever met, different from any person I have ever met. Is he flirting or sensing my new resolve to ask him to be my rabbi and taking me into his fold, much to my surprise. And does he hold other women's hands like this as well?

The wind in Jerusalem at three in the morning is different from all the winds in the world. This wind carries secrets, moves me along not just by pulling on my hair but by making movements, one tug, two tugs, do you know why you are here yet, three tugs. It's a soul wind, moving from all directions at once and still gentle, coaxing me along. This wind is carrying me along the path in the old Artists Colony. Perhaps it is even keeping my feet from touching the ground every few steps. The movement is step once, twice, float three, four, and maybe five. Shlomo is my anchor and another kind of wind. He whispers stories, his voice singing to me as he tells me about the night having so much light and the miracle that two people met each other and married and that we will celebrate with them.

"Are you married, sugar?" he interjects. Since I am on a third or fourth levitation, I look at him and wonder whether I have landed yet or whether his song is carrying a message. I should feel awkward because I didn't catch the words, but the wind is so cool and his voice so sweet that I don't feel it. "Maybe it is too personal to ask," he says.

"Ask me again," I say, as if I am the type that needs prodding. Doesn't he know I would tell him everything?

"Are you married, sugar?" he asks, his eyes undaunted, twinkling even more.

"Oh," I say, as if the question needed to be asked twice. In response, all that comes out is one shy, "No." I then believe he is flirting.

One of his people comes alongside and asks for a moment of his attention. He releases my hand with a squeeze and croons to me to come sit with him at the *Sheva Brachas.* I fall behind and start walking with a girl named Chaya. We tell each other where we come from and what we do. She has been a follower of Shlomo for years. She had been at the House of Love and Prayer in San Francisco. I nod and think that it must be something special to be at the House, but I don't ask her what it is. I guess I want to look more 'in' than I feel. We continue to follow, and I wonder if she floats. I meet others, Ruchale, Sarah, Tzipporah, Osnat, and Ruthie, and I attach names to the faces that were blurred with the dance. They are all welcoming, carrying an extension of Shlomo's warmth.

Candles flicker within the studio's cave-like appearance. Seated upon the dais are Ruthie and Amnon, the bride and groom. Shlomo is beside them. He beckons and makes room for me. On the table are two bottles of wine, some soda, two cakes, and sunflower seeds. He tells me it is a Holy Beggar's feast. I again nod as if it makes all the sense in the world. But I want to disappear into the group. To take a place beside him and the bride and groom seems so strange, so intimate. I have just met him. So pulling some reality back, I whisper — it feels like I have to whisper to him — I whisper that Chaya has a headache and I will sit with her. "Ah, good," he says, understanding everything. So I sit at a distance with Chaya, who really does have a headache, and as Shlomo offers blessings and stories, I massage her shoulders, trying to release my own tension, singing those old new melodies again, wondering about the eyes that keep seeking me out and soften even more when I look back through the light of twenty dancing candles, all in their own rhythm.

"You know," he tells us, "when the groom covers the face of the bride, he is telling her, 'There is so much more to you than I can ever see or know. You are so deep, so holy, so hidden. I am covering your face to tell you that I will always be in awe of you, that I will never think I know you, and always be filled with joy when you show me another secret.'

"*Chevra*, do you remember the story about the Seer of Lublin and the wedding of the orphans? No?

"So the story goes that one day the Chozeh of Lublin, who had clear vision and prophetic eyes and could see from one corner of the world to the other, called his Chasidim, his followers, together. He said, "We are going to make a wedding for two orphans who have nobody in the world. So take this money and buy everything they will need for the wedding and the feast, and also buy for them a bed, pillows, and pots to start their home.

"The orphans worked in a little inn in the countryside, several hours away. The owner of the inn was not a kind and loving man. Quite the contrary; he was harsh, demanding, and un-caring. When the orphans announced their wedding plans to him, he said they could marry only after the guests had been fed and the cleaning done.

"When the Seer of Lublin arrived with his followers and three wagons of gifts, the youngsters were so moved by the first generous gesture to them in their lives, their fatigue left them. They put on the beautiful white garments they brought for them and were transformed, shining like angels.

"The Seer married them under the stars, and after singing and drinking the wine, they sat at a table laden with wonderful food. Finally, the Seer said, 'It is time to give blessings to the new chasson and kallah. I'll start. I bless you, *mamash*, that you become your own masters and own your own business. That even this little inn has to be yours.'

"The young couple couldn't imagine such a leap of fortune, but as the Rebbe rocked and spoke the words to his blessing, they began to believe it could happen.

"The Chassidim followed their Rebbe's lead and blessed them that the windmill on the top of the hill, several miles away, and that all the land in between be theirs. And they began laughing. Next they were blessed that all the land they could see all round the inn, the forest, the hills, and the farms be theirs. They were blessed with children, long life, and joy. The night turned to day and the laughing and singing grew with every minute.

"Finally, the Chozeh announced that it was time to leave.

"As their wagons passed through the forest, the Seer held up his hand and halted the procession. Everyone was silent as he listened intently. Finally he said, 'Someone is crying for help. Let us go quickly!' They ran through the forest and came to a pool of quicksand where a young man was up to his face in the mire and at the end of his strength. Miraculously, they pulled him out, bundled him into a wagon, and drove with him to his home. His father was a wealthy landlord who owned most of the area. He and his wife had been sick with worry over their only son's failure to return home from an afternoon ride. When the Chozeh of Lublin and his followers brought him home, their joy and gratitude was so great they didn't know what to do for them. Finally, when they heard where they had been, the landowner said, 'I know what I'll give you. I own that inn. I hereby deed it to you.' His wife added, 'Why just the inn? Give them the mill and all the land in between the two as well. We have our son back and have so much more than that.' The landowner said, 'You are so right, my dear, and let's add all the land you can see from the inn and the mill — forests, farms, and hills.'

"The Chozeh answered, saying, 'My friend, your generosity is overwhelming, and I thank you so much. But I have no need of your gift. I live in Lublin. But I would be so happy if you gave this gift to the orphans I told you about. They merit your generosity.

"And it was done.

"So, *chevra*, don't hold back. Bless the sweetest bride and groom with everything."

And it is done. The blessings touch an even deeper core, and I know that everything is indeed possible. I wonder where the wind will take me now.

I don't go back to my cousin's apartment near the university as planned. Shlomo suggests quietly that I consider not traveling on

Shabbos and stay instead at the President Hotel where he has taken a room for the women, one for the men, and one for himself. It's 3 am, and I think I may be able to sleep for a few hours, even on a mattress on the floor in a room with ten other ladies. He holds my hand all the way back to the hotel. Others walk and talk with us as we wind our way through the silent streets of Jerusalem, the night air cool and my hand very warm. We all say good night, and I linger while Shlomo still holds on, and finally saying something like thank you and sleep well, I head for the washroom. When I return to the lobby, the rabbi, still wide-eyed and alert, is waiting for me. "Are you tired?" he asks, "or do you want to go for a little walk?"

There is no choice as he holds out his hand. I go for a walk around the hotel grounds and finally sit with him at the edge of the pool, where the stars reflect and the night almost gives up its darkness. "I love swimming," he says. "Do you have a bathing suit? We can swim after Shabbos." He puts his arm around my shoulders to ward off the chill. And then he slowly leans towards me, slower than slow motion, watching my eyes, and he kisses me. Soft, soft lips barely touching me and yet sinking deeply into my being. I am surprised. "What kind of rabbi are you?" I ask. And he replies without hesitation, "A rabbi who loves you."

I have no words. I have no understanding of how I have been catapulted from a chance meeting to a romantic poolside interlude with a man, no, not a man, but a rabbi who sings and whispers and lulls me with each word. He tells me that I am so special and he has been waiting for so long. I am out of my element. My male encounters have never been like this, and I feel young and childlike in my embarrassed response. "How do you know?" I ask, in utmost innocence. And he, the wise sage, the man of the universe, says, "Because I know." No secret powers divulged, no explanation, he just knows. I can't even offer a rebuttal, a bargain, or a response. He knows.

So I return to my world of reference, my safe stories, and tell him about my parents and brothers and my life in Toronto. And he tells me about the House of Love and Prayer and his shul in New York and his father, who passed away in 1967.

"I wish you could have known him," he says. "He was a prince and he would have loved you."

"How do you know?" I chance, a second time.

And his answer leaves me again wordless, breathless: "Because you smell so good, and my father loved good smells."

My frame of reference for life so far has been very simple, and I think I have been able to anticipate and handle myself in most social encounters, most discussions. I do not know what land I have journeyed to, but I am at a total loss. I hear his words and they strike chords, but I don't know how to become involved. What do I say about my smell, his departed father who would love me, his knowing, and especially his kiss? I try to seem really cool and mature, but I feel like a mass of new brain cells, not knowing the language. What is 'mamash,' and how does he know Nina Simone?

And who am I?

Someone he loves.

# MUSICAL

*In Wroclaw, Poland — formerly Breslau, Germany. Photo by Joan Roth.*

# Zion's Holy Voice at the End of Days

by Yeshayah Eliyahu ben Mishael
(Charles E. Vernoff, Ph.D. *A"H*)

Reb Shlomo Carlebach, the sweet singer of Zion during the second half of the secular 20th century, grew up as a performer together with the State of Israel. From his artistic origins as a gifted beginner in 1950s St. Louis, when Israel was also just getting started, he has left a worldwide legacy of music and teachings that show every sign of having a permanent impact on future Judaism. There was no coincidence in the fact that both his music and his career acquired their true character and momentum after the Six-Day War. Shlomo's music at that time became perceptibly more oriented to *Moshiach* and *Ge'ulah*, to the triumphant divine culmination of history. Shortly after the war, Shlomo's astounding success at a Berkeley, California, folk festival resulted in the establishing of San Francisco's House of Love and Prayer that effectively became the epicenter of the Jewish branch of the 1960s counterculture. After two moves within Marin County and two in San Francisco, many of the residents of the House moved to Israel and established the still thriving Moshav Meor Modi'im.

As with not a few great men, Shlomo's most resplendent fame has come after his passing from this world (in 1994). Controversial while he was alive, so that the very devout would not listen to his music, in the aftermath of his earthly life his music attained unique popularity amidst every segment of Jewry, including the most devout. Rabbi Israel Meir Lau, a former Chief Rabbi of Israel, wept at his funeral and asked Shlomo's forgiveness for the disdain of the most pious. With the clarity of hindsight, it has became evident that Shlomo was sent into this world to inaugurate a new musical spirit, a sound that would accompany and celebrate the return of the People of Israel to their Land. Although drawing upon Hasidic and other Jewish musical sources, Shlomo's thousands of melodies were instinct with the feeling of imminent *Ge'ulah,* Redemption, that was roused by the return to Zion — representing a unique musical departure, although still profoundly and indelibly Jewish.

His melodies could touch deep places in the Jewish soul that had seldom been reached before. At his concerts, young and old would often be moved to tears. Although sometimes he did push back the boundaries of tradition, it was always in a way that looked toward the Redemption. In 1969, for example, I spent an unforgettable Shabbat at the first House of Love and Prayer. Shlomo himself was not present, and the service was led by two hippie followers who had fully absorbed Shlomo's spirit and manner. The singular high point came on Friday night when, after the davvening was finished, one of the leaders explained that in a traditional Jewish home before the meal, it was customary for the parents to bless their offspring by placing their hands on the children's heads. But here in the House of Love and Prayer, he continued, we are all parents and children to one another.

Upon this cue, there ensued for half an hour or more one of the most remarkable spiritual experiences I ever had — truly *Me'en Olam Haba,* a foretaste of the world to come. In complete silence, your eyes would meet those of another and you would approach one another, each of you placing your hands the other's head. The feeling was one of utter spiritual transparency, of a soul contact so deep it seemed you had known one another in the angelic realms forever. The whole thing was moving beyond words. Never had I felt so complete an absence of barriers between me and others. Although both genders participated — thus pushing the boundaries of tradition — the emotions were those of pure love, devoid of and far beyond any sensuality. And Shlomo was not even present in the flesh! Yet his presence permeated the room. It was truly a taste of heaven.

In his teachings, many of which have been recorded and distributed or soon will be, Shlomo brought many sublime Hasidic insights down to easy intelligibility. His style directly addressed the souls of his audience with a disarming intimacy. In his own way, he aided in the transmission of Jewish traditions that might otherwise have been lost. That is not the least of his gifts to us.

Perhaps the most remarkable aspect of Shlomo's personality was his utter availability and accessibility. It is said he knew more Jews by name than anyone on earth. Knowing Shlomo as I did since the early 1960s, I in due course became "Holy Chuckeleh" — a term of playful endearment that no one else could probably have gotten away with. And, indeed, it seemed he was everyone's friend. Although everyone knew he was surely one of the most famous and influential Jews in the world, he neither cultivated nor projected a "celebrity aura." He was just plain Shlomo, your loving friend. No more authentic mark of sanctity could be imagined. He was so much who he was that one could at the same moment realize he was one of the greatest, most celebrated Jews on earth and yet interact with him as just plain Shlomo, your heart-to-heart friend. His life carried the imprint of his incredibly soulful, intimate music. It is said that most of his earnings were given away as charity, often to unfortunate non-Jews as well as Jews.

And yet the legacy of Shlomo has yet to be realized. The key to that legacy, I believe, was my 1969 Shabbat at the House of Love and Prayer. Too often, too easily, we fall into the repetition of Shlomo's exceedingly inward music, as though his melodies were just part of the standard repertoire of Jewish music. But that sublime evening, when strangers exchanged blessings and in doing so became intimates, is what Shlomo is really all about. Shlomo embodied an opportunity to begin preparing the messianic transformation of the world. In addition to adapting his melodies for liturgical and concert use, we need leaders capable of opening their innermost souls to Shlomo's music and its message of messianic love. We need to learn to sing his melodies in a meditative way, perhaps repeated many times, that opens the soul and moves it to embrace other souls. We need pioneers of the spirit, moved to bless and be blessed. Shlomo's music has the power to open a soul like a blossom and share its innermost essence with other such souls.

The next step in developing Shlomo's legacy should be retreats, perhaps just Shabbatot, perhaps whole weekends or longer, during which mature leaders will guide others into the kind of spiritual simultaneous giving and receiving that Shlomo's music invites and facilitates. No fees should be charged and each participant might bring food to share. The aim must be purely spiritual. The Shlomo community needs to follow the light of inner guidance to learn how its members can help one another grow and blossom in spirit. The entire world, including the Jewish world, is parched by an inner drought for which Shlomo's gift can provide cooling waters. So let us not be content simply to record and publish the inheritance left for us by this messenger from heaven. Let us recognize it as living seeds to be planted in the open furrows of prepared souls so as to bring forth a rich harvest that can spread the first dawning of the light of Moshiach to many corners of the world.

One of Shlomo's greatest triumphs was his visit to Poland where many gentiles, in the most anti-Semitic of countries, were moved to tears with everyone else. Shlomo anticipated the time when the House of God would be a house of prayer for all peoples. At this moment of deep pre-messianic darkness, it may be time for the People of Israel to magnify Shlomo's light and begin to draw the whole world toward it. Thus, far more than being a legacy of the past, Shlomo's truest greatness may be as a light for the future. So let us not continue with business as usual. We each must open our souls as fully as we can to the sound of heaven that Shlomo bore to this earth. And then we must let it teach us to start building even now the community of the soon to be redeemed.

Interview with Neshama Carlebach:
http://youtu.be/edjZFK90WEk

"Over the course of her five-CD career, Neshama Carlebach has emerged as one of the premier female singers in the genre of jazz/pop Jewish soul music. If that sounds like a big fish in a small pond, it is. But the daughter of the late Jewish mystic and music legend Shlomo Carlebach certainly inherited both the DNA and the pipes to dominate the field.... Indeed, one need not even be Jewish to love the music of Neshama Carlebach, though after hearing her sing, one might want to be."

— Dan Pine, *j. the Jewish news weekly of Northern California,*
*December 24, 2004*

# Shir Hashirim Asher L'Shlomo: Rav Kook and Reb Shlomo — Zecher Tzadikim L'Vracha

by Rabbi Itzchak Marmorstein

"The great souls feel in the depths of their being their connection to all existence, to all creatures and especially to all humankind...they announce the lights of new life...The Godly song is awake in the souls of the great tzaddikim...the delight of song overwhelms all. They draw the delight of the supernal song to the world of action and to the practical Torah...The higher a soul the more it feels the unity that is in all...and these souls are full of love and compassion and their desire is filled with good." — *Orot Hakodesh 1:203, 206, 708*

Rabbi Avraham Yitzchak HaKohen Kook (1865-1935) was the spiritual revolutionary whose teachings, illumination, and leadership offered the most holistic and enlightened understanding of the Torah that has ever been presented in Jewish history. Inspired by Lurianic Kabbalah, he integrated all that preceded him as he led and enabled the spiritual return to Israel and the world stage.

"The Baal Shem Tov says that whatever you think of yourself is what you think of God. What we have to do is to stop being so small. We have to have a heart as big as the world, and also a soul which is shuffling back and forth between heaven and earth, and then deeper than our heart and soul, our life has to be filled with something, so deep, so heavenly and so sweet, because there's so much bitterness in the world. The world just needs one drop of sweetness." — *Rabbi Shlomo Carlebach, in an interview in 1988*

Rabbi Shlomo Carlebach (1925-1994) was the spiritual revolutionary whose teachings, stories, songs, and activities offered a sweet taste of the Garden of Eden to a world largely wracked in suffering. He traversed the world, sharing the light of Torah and its loving and hopeful song with multitudes of Jewish and non-Jewish people.

I am blessed to be a student of both.

I first met Reb Shlomo at the Kotel on a Friday night in early 1974. He began to sing *"L'cha Dodi,"* and I felt my spirit rise and my heart open. From that moment, he was an important and joyful part of my life. His visits, teachings, and concerts, in whatever city I was living in at the time, were beloved highpoints in my spiritual growth and experience. One of the great blessings (and responsibilities) of my life was receiving *s'micha* from him in 1992. His passing was one of the saddest days of my life. His songs and teachings continue to teach and inspire me, and many others, profoundly.

I first met Rav Kook in the summer of 1980 in a sunlit cottage in Winnipeg Beach, Canada. I sat down to read from the "Kook book" — Rabbi Ben Zion Bokser's wonderful translation. Rav Kook wrote in a state of illumination, and as I read his words, I experienced an internal expansion, an inner recognition. I felt my soul stirred, touched by an extraordinary consciousness. His grasp of the brokenness and wholeness of existence and the possibilities for perfection were breathtaking and clear. I felt I was tasting the Torah of Eden.

Since that light-filled afternoon, I have often been inspired deeply by the writings of Rav Kook — known by some as *Baal Ha'Orot*, The Master of the Lights. One of my greatest blessings is to learn and share his teachings at his historical home, Beit HaRav Kook, in Yerushalayim. I have dedicated my life to sharing his song with the world.

As my learning of Rav Kook's Torah deepens, I have come to the conclusion that Reb Shlomo was perhaps the most profound exemplar of Rav Kook's teachings in our time. His connection to Rav Kook is profound both historically and spiritually. In 1915, when Rav Kook was exiled in Switzerland, he and his son, Rabbi Tzvi Yehuda, stayed at the house of Shlomo's grandfather, Rabbi Dr. Asher Cohen, the Chief Rabbi of Basel. There was consideration of arranging a *shidduch* between Tzvi Yehuda Kook and Rabbi Cohen's daughter, Pessia. It did not occur and she ended up marrying Rabbi Naftali Carlebach and giving birth to Shlomo Carlebach, his twin brother Eli Chaim, and his older sister Shulamit.

That is why when Rabbi Tzvi Yehuda Kook, z'l, first met Reb Shlomo, he told him, "I was supposed to be your father." Rabbi Tzvi Yehuda understood and supported Reb Shlomo. Rabbi Yochanan Fried, the director of Beit HaRav Kook, was a main student of Rabbi Tzvi Yehuda.

He recounts: "Rav Tzvi Yehuda very much valued Reb Shlomo. Very much. A few times I remember him saying very clearly, 'Reb Shlomo is reaching to *merchakim* (distant places) that no one is able to get to. To people that no one else is able to talk to/with. And to distant souls...I know what people may think about him — they don't understand him. I will not accept any *lashon hara* about him. I really know the value of what he is doing. There is no one else in the world doing anything like that.'"

After the first House of Love and Prayer in Kiryat Yovel began and didn't go so well (it was burnt down a number of times), Reb Shlomo came with his students to see Rav Tzvi Yehuda. Rav Tzvi Yehuda later told his students, "Reb Shlomo is taking people to the *mikveh* so that they'll be clean and this is something very important."

Another story: "Rav Tzvi Yehuda had a Wednesday night *shiur* with his main students — Rabbi Chaim Druckman, Rabbi Eliezer Waldman, and [several] others every Wednesday night at his home. One time we were all kept waiting outside his door for over an hour. This was very unusual. Suddenly Rav Tzvi Yehuda came out with Shlomo and accompanied him to the street, though it was very hard for Rav Tzvi Yehuda to walk at that point. They parted with hugs and kisses. When we came in together, he explained in very strong language that 'you don't yet know who Reb Shlomo really is, how much Reb Shlomo really is.'

"In Elul 5720 (1960), Shabbat *Parashat Ki Teitzeh/Re'eh* at Beit HaRav...it was the *aliyat l'Torah* of the children of two important students — Rabbi Yaakov Ariel, who is today the Chief Rabbi of Ramat Gan, and Rabbi Yaakov Friedman, founder and Rosh Yeshiva of Yeshivat Tifrach. I brought Reb Shlomo from the Melachim Hotel. All the important rabbis were there... When Tzvi Yehuda saw him he said, 'he'll *daven* Musaf.'

"And so it was. All the rabbinic families had great *chazanim* there, but Tzvi Yehuda insisted that he daven...and it was there that he composed the *Keter/Shma Israel* — '*Mimkomo Hu Yifen b'Rachamav....*' After the *tefilla* (Rav Kook and his son davened Nusach Ashkenaz), Rav Tzvi Yehuda said how much he appreciated that Shlomo brought the *Keter*...."

Reb Shlomo had a deep appreciation of Rav Kook and his importance. As he said in a talk to Yeshivat LeZeirim — the Youth Yeshiva connected to Mercaz HaRav Kook: "There is no tzaddik and holy person in the world who speaks of love of Israel like our holy rabbi HaRav Kook... and there is no tzaddik in the world who explains that through love of Israel we come to love the entire world.

"Everyone disregards this. A Jew has to love the entire world, to repair the world...and how can you repair the world without love.... Rav Kook was the greatest in relation to love.... There is no tzaddik in the world who ever exhibited the qualities of being of Avraham Avinu like our holy Rabbi, Rav Kook.... Rav Kook believed in perfect faith that it is possible to speak to the lowest Jew, the Jew of S'dom, and to make them into a complete tzaddik, and he also believed this about the entire world.... I would say the closest to a Rebbe I would come to would be Rav Kook. To Rav Kook I would definitely go.... Rav Kook is one of the only people who *mamesh* had prophecy for today. *Mamesh* prophecy...."

Spiritually, Shlomo was an inheritor of Torat HaRav Kook in many significant ways. There is much that they shared. Without comparing their level of Torah knowledge, as Rav Kook's was incomparable, they both emerged from deep Torah learning (Volozhin and Lakewood) to bring to the world a unique illuminated blend of the Jewish and the universal. Their commitment and dedication to Jewish survival, growth, and learning was legendary. "Our people will be rebuilt and established and be renewed in all aspects of its life through the expansion, vitalization, and perfection of its religious faith...the divine dimension of its life." (*Orot HaTshuva* 15:11)

They both taught the Torah of love. Their caring for the well-being of all peoples and nations was outstanding and a tremendous contribution to the renewal of Jewish participation in *tikkun olam*. As Rav Kook wrote, "The heart must be filled with love for all. The love of all creation comes first, then comes the love for all humankind, and then follows the love for the Jewish people.... All of these loves are to be expressed in practical actions by pursuing the welfare of those we are bidden to love and to seek their advancement." (*Midot HaRayah*: Love 1,2)

They both taught that kindness, understanding, and a deep commitment to fixing the broken — inside and out, personal and universal — must accompany all our ways and means. In Rav Kook's words: "The higher holiness abounds with love, compassion and tolerance, as the mark of its most radiant perfection. Hatred, sternness and irritability result from forgetting G-d and the extinguishing of the light of holiness." (*Orot HaKodesh*, 3:317)

They both rose high and pointed us to a greater future. Again, Rav Kook: "The understanding that dawns on a person to see the world, not as finished, but as in the process of continued becoming, ascending, developing — raises one from being 'under the sun' to being 'above the sun,' from the place where there is nothing new to the place where there is nothing old, where everything takes on new form.... In this luminous perspective one looks at all the world, at general and human development, at the destiny of each creature, at all the events of all times." (*Orot HaKodesh* 2:220)

They both expressed the depths of their inner understanding in new and original ways that continue to teach and inspire the generations that follow them, such as in this passage: "Understanding reached by one's own mind is the highest expression of spiritual progress.... The uniqueness of the inner soul in its own authenticity is the highest manifestation of the seed of divine light...from which will bud and blossom the fruit of the tree of life." (*Orot HaKodesh,* 1:180,177)

They both taught and creatively demonstrated in many ways that the free unfettered song of the inner soul is our divinity in expression. Rav Kook declares: "The soul sings always...a person must raise themselves to the height of meeting their own soul, of recognizing its spiritual imprint, the rushing of its wings that abound in the majesty of the holy of holies. Then one will always be ready to listen to the secret of its holy discourse." (*Orot HaKodesh,* 174)

Shlomo's holy discourse integrated Torat HaRav Kook; he was one of the first to speak of Rav Kook publicly in English and outside of Israel. He taught pieces of Torat HaRav throughout his life. Someone who accompanied him regularly told me that sometimes if he saw Haredi Jews in the group, he would make a point of teaching Rav Kook. As one of the final major teachings of his life, he taught a series of classes at Jerusalem's Yakar on Rav Kook's *Orot HaTshuva* — "The Lights of Return." He told his students there, "I want you to know that every word that Rav Kook wrote touches on the deepest secrets of Kabbalah, Midrash, and Talmud."

Shlomo embraced the *Dati Leumi*/Religious Zionist movement that emerged from Rav Kook, and [its members] embraced him. He often performed for them all over Israel, including in Yehuda and Shomron. At the previously mentioned talk to the Yeshivat LeTzeirim, he said to the students: "I bless you that you be true *chasidim* of Rav Kook." Reb Shlomo was a true *chasid* of Rav Kook and his largest and most universal teachings. We and the whole world were blessed by his song.

In his honor and in dedication to his great light, I'd like to conclude by sharing one of Rav Kook's most famous and poetic teachings. I offer it as a tribute to Reb Shlomo's multifaceted gifts to the world. The piece is based on the Tikkunei Zohar teaching that the Divine four-letter Name YHVH (Yud, Heh, Vav, Heh) is a שיר מרובע — a fourfold song.

"Yesh sh'hu sha'ar shirat nafsho" 'There is the one who sings the song of his soul…'. The violin (or perhaps guitar) of Reb Shlomo's soul brought him to *Olam HaNiggun* / The World of Song. *Tehillim* was his ladder, David *HaMelech* his mentor, and his guitar his loyal friend. He told me that he only learnt a few chords, but as his first teacher later admiringly said to him: "You're my best student because nobody ever did so much with 3 or 4 chords."

"VeYesh sh'hu shar shirat ha'uma." 'And there is the one who sings the song of his people.' *Am Yisrael Chai* — those 3 or 4 chords became hundreds of songs. Reb Shlomo began to sing and the Jewish people began to sing with him.

He never stopped. Airplane after airplane. To wherever he was invited — synagogues, summer camps, youth groups, JCCs, Hillel Houses, kibbutzim, settlements, and living rooms. Inviting everyone to Israel and inviting everyone in Israel to sing and dance with him.

And we still are. Every Friday night tens, if not hundreds, of *minya-nim* welcome *Malkat Shabbat* with his *niggunim.* His spot at the Kotel is stronger than ever. We have recently started a 'Carlebach Minyan' at Beit HaRav Kook. Hundreds of holy *hippelech* with happy hasidim and everyone in between is drawn to "sing a song of Shabbos."

And not just on Shabbos. Weddings have not been the same since he showed us how to sing with *"kol chatan v'kol kallah" 'the voice of the groom and the voice of the bride.'* Everyday, his songs are sung, his stories are told, and more and more of his torahs are coming out. He continues to be a major Jewish inspiration for many young people.

*"Ve'Yesh"* — *'And there is the one who expands their being beyond the bound-ary of Israel' "la'shir et shirat ha'adam" 'to sing the song of humankind.'* He truly sang with all humankind. In concert halls, churches, ashrams, festivals — all over the world. He predated the World Wide Web with his own Whole Wide World singing harmony. He sang in Germany and Austria and sent children and grandchildren of Nazis to volunteer in Israel after they tearfully approached him at concerts. When asked on Israeli radio how he could return to sing in those countries, he answered, "If I had two hearts, one of them could afford to hate...."

*"Ve'Yesh"* — *'And there is the one who rises toward wider horizons, uniting with all existence, with all creatures, with all worlds' "v'im kulam omer shira" 'and he sings his song with all of them.' "HeHarim ra-k-du kh'eilim, g'vaot kiv-ney tzon."* Reb Shlomo led us in singing and dancing with the mountains and the rams, the high places and the lambs — *"b'yemini Michael"* — with the angels on every side — *"v'al roshi, Shechinat El"* 'and above all, above all, the Shining Face of *El.'*

*"Ve'Yesh"* — *'And there is the one who rises with all these songs together in one ensemble, there all join their voices together, harmonizing their melo-dies.'* He invited all to "Give me harmony" and brought so many to sing together.

He gave us so many songs:

"*Kol sasson v'kol simcha*" 'songs of joy and gladness';

"*Kol tzahala v'kol rina*" 'songs of jubilation and celebration';

"*Kol chedva v'kol kedusha*" 'songs of ecstasy and holiness.'

As a Holy Rebbe, he truly integrated:

"*Shirat HaNefesh*" 'the song of the soul,'

"*Shirat HaUma*" 'the song of the people,'

"*Shirat HaAdam*" 'the song of humankind,'

"*Shirat HaOlam*" 'the song of the world.'

Showing us how ישראל — *Israel* — is truly שיר אל
**"Shir El" 'the Song of God.'**

He gave us:

"*Shir pashut*" — one-chord songs,

"*Shir kaful*" — two-chord songs,

"*Shir meshulash*" — three-chord songs,

"*Shir meruba*" — four-chord songs.

**Shir HaShirim Asher L'Shlomo —**

**The Song of Songs of Holy Reb Shlomo**

**L'Melech Sh'HaShalom Sh'lo — To The Holy One of Shalom**

How many songs have you composed, Shlomo?
http://youtu.be/HlsXS4DPZpw

# Reflections on Reb Shlomo's Kabbalat Shabbat *Nusach*:

## The Musical Influence of the "Imrei Shaul" of Modzhitz

by Rabbi Dr. Menachem Kallus

THE USE OF LITURGICAL CHANT AND SONG AS A MEANS OF INTERPRETA-
tion has a long tradition in Jewish prayer, and anyone who *davened*
on Shabbat eve with Reb Shlomo would be brought thereby into
the energy of Shabbat. When Reb Shlomo put words to melody, one
essentially significant feature inherent in how his liturgical *nusach*
'worked' was his inspired attention to *"perush ha-milot"* 'to what [or
how] the words mean' — or can mean — and a foremost concern
of the *Shaliach Tzibur*, the Prayer Leader, has always been how to
project a holy space, conducive to being within the inner-unity of
enunciation, emotional presence, and meaning. When Reb Shlomo
was in this role, he seemed to hand over his charisma to the fueling
of communal sacred joy. Countless times I came to where he was
*daven*ing Kabbalat Shabbat — on the Moshav, in NY, in Jerusalem,
in Berkeley — dejected from the alienations of the week, and by
his tremendous genius in combining holy presence with chant and
community, I was effortlessly transformed to being in touch with the
entry and presence of Shabbat. It is this intent, in which his *nusach*
is soaked, that continues to enable the various "Shlomo Minyanim"
to fulfill such a function when the world needs it so much, and so,

the significance of the overriding principle of precision in this inner unity remains vital for one who aspires to be a Prayer Leader in a Reb Shlomo Minyan.

Reb Shlomo's *nusach* for Kabbalat Shabbat begins with the majestic tune he composed for the opening words of Kabbalat Shabbat (Psalm 95): *"L'chu Neraninah la-Ha-Shem..."* 'Let us all go-on-together, Sing Praises to the Holy One...' that seems to evoke an invitation issued already "before the beginning," to join the terrestrial Shabbat with the Celestial One:

*Music for Psalm 95 verses 1-2*

This tune is then used as a refrain for the last sentence of this and of each of the next three chapters of the Psalms (96-98) sung during this prayer. And whereas the opening words-and-melody of this Psalm extend an invitation, the repeat of the melody at its end — especially when placed in the context of the words sung in that psalm (95:10-11), *"arbaim shanah"* 'For forty years I was wearied with that generation, and I said: "Oh, what a people with erring hearts...for I swore in My anger...."' — serves as a reminder to make peace with Ha-Shem, so that any lingering anger between the Shabbat celebrant and Ha-Shem is dissolved.

After letting go of the past, we launch into the second psalm (96): *"Shiru La-Ha-Shem Shir Chadash..."* 'Sing to Ha-Shem a New Song...', the first of two psalms in this service with such a beginning. Reb Shlomo would sing this psalm to a tune he composed for words in another psalm (102:14): *"Ata takum terachem Tziyon..."* '[May] You arise, be compassionate to Zion, for this is the period to be gracious, because the appointed time has arrived' *"Ki Va Mo'ed."* It is at the same time a beseeching and a joyous celebratory melody, reflecting the hopeful and supplicatory spirit of the words of that psalm. The meaning of the second psalm of Kabbalat Shabbat, its "explication" through Reb Shlomo's *nusach* and its musical origin, is what I'll be discussing here.

But as part of entering into this discussion, I feel a kind of obligation to offer a corrective note, mandated also by the fact that Reb Shlomo himself would occasionally attempt to correct — even in the middle of the singing — a musical-*kavanah* error (and this one, in fact, continues to this day). I remember a parable from my friend Yossi Chajes, in the spirit of Reb Shlomo, about this. Here is the gist of it. Imagine you're on the subway and you meet the most beautiful person in the world. Convinced that this person is your soul-mate, you strike up a conversation, and then, just as the person is making preparations to get off at the next stop, the person shouts a phone number, but apparently it's copied incorrectly. You're off by one number. Okay, you check it and dial variations of it.... Eventually, finally, you get to the right number, and *Mazal-Tov!* May all parables end so well.

The point of the parable is that a tune and its applications — especially with reference to Reb Shlomo's *nusach* — is as precise as a phone number, so that if it is misapplied, one may not reach the intended place. There is a big difference between a song emerging from a prayerful joy-of-faith, and one emerging from the very midst of celebration. And to replace the emotional register of a tune calling for beseeching joy with one expressing confident celebration would count for an esthetic misdemeanor — displaying a kind of over-confident *chutzpah.* And the case in point is the singing of the musical refrain of Reb Shlomo's: *"Bo-i Kallah..."* 'Come, O Bride' from his march for the final verse *"Bo-i b'shalom..."* — the culmination of the *"L'cha Dodi"* refrain, 'Come in peace, O Crown of Her Husband, Come, O Bride' —

*Musical notation for "Ki Va Mo'ed"*

instead of Reb Shlomo's tune for: '...for this is the period to be gracious, because the appointed time has arrived' *"Ki Va Mo'ed."* The joyous and carefree musical flavor of the refrain *"Bo-i Kallah,"* rather than the sincerity-within-the joy, embodied in *"Ki Va Mo'ed,"* if sung at this point in the gradual unfolding of Kabbalat Shabbat, is premature.

*Musical notation for "Bo-i Kallah..."\**

This mistake, which bothered Reb Shlomo during his lifetime in this world, unfortunately still persists in the vast majority of Reb Shlomo Minyanim with which humble-me is familiar. And I'm sure that its correction will add deeper joy to the Kabbalat Shabbat, both Above and Below — just as getting the phone number of the beloved right the first time would hasten the ultimate joy.

Indeed, the function of this, the second Psalm of Kabbalat Shabbat,

---

\* This notation reflects the two mistakes frequently made in the popular singing of Psalm 96: (1) people substitute the tune for *"Bo-i Kallah"* for the second part of *"Ki Va Mo'ed,"* and (2) they sing this tune with a wrong affect: the sixth bar should be sung the same as the tenth bar.

as indicated in the words of the psalm, is to gather together *"b'hadrat kodesh"* 'in the beauty of holiness' — the entirety of the worlds and all their sentient inhabitants — all plants, animals, nations, people — for a kind of prequel to: "The Whole World is Waiting for the Great and Holy Shabbos." This is because the aspiration for cosmic-unified joy is common to all levels of existence.

Beginning with the second psalm and onward until — and after — *"Lecha Dodi,"* Reb Shlomo introduces different Hasidic-*Hazzanut* elements that precede the repeated refrain from *"L'chu N'raninah."* As is well known, Reb Shlomo's greatest self-acknowledged influence in this regard is the great Modzhitzer sacred-musical tradition, to which he was introduced by his high school buddy, Reb Ben Zion Shenker — may he live long in good health —Reb Shlomo's life-long friend, the other great luminary of the post-WW II Hasidic music revival, his classmate from Yeshivat Torah v'Da'as (the location of Reb Shlomo's stories about himself and Reb Shlomo Heiman, *z"l*). Reb Ben Zion introduced Reb Shlomo to the previous Modzhitzer Rebbes, and — as I heard from one of Reb Shlomo's "minstrels," the holy French horn player Reb Dovid Steinberg — Reb Ben Zion said that he can "quote chapter and verse" with reference to the specific Modzhitzer influences on particular "musical riffs" that Reb Shlomo would use in his own *hazzanut.* This assertion was later confirmed to me by Reb Meir Fund, a long-time mutual friend of both Reb Shlomo and (*l'havdil bein chayim l'chayim*) Reb Ben Zion. It was a statement that was made matter-of-factly, and I'm sure that Reb Shlomo would gladly concur. Reb Shlomo used to say similar things about himself and Modzhitz — and also, I remember Reb Shlomo recounting how at one point during the inter-war years, the great musical conductor (and *ohev Yisrael* — lover of Israel) Arturo Toscanini was brought to a Modzhitzer *tisch,* and upon hearing their melodies (some of which run even longer than 25 minutes), he pronounced that this music is no less sophisticated than that of Beethoven.

So in the spirit of our sages who said [BT *Megillah* 15a] that when something is mentioned in the name of the person who had said it originally, one brings the redemption of the world that much closer, I'd like to positively identify one such direct influence. It's a piece of *hazzanut* composed by the great Rebbe and composer, Reb Shaul of Modzhitz (1886-1948), for one of the verses of *"b'Motzaei Yom Menu-chah,"* a sacred poem sung for the *Melaveh Malka* — the holy meal at the other end of Shabbat — escorting Shabbat away and greeting the beginning of the week. Reb Shlomo adapted it very closely, for use in the liminal transition at the preceding side of the sacred spiral of time — saying farewell to the week and greeting the Shabbat anew with the same tune. This "riff" was something I remember hearing again and again while growing up, from a record owned by my grandparents, *z"l* — the 1956 Ben Zion Shenker Modzhitzer *Melaveh Malka* — which was, if I'm not mistaken, the very first post-WW II LP record of authentic Hasidic music produced in the U.S. In Reb Ben Zion Shenker's rendering, this verse takes nearly a minute to sing; in Reb Shlomo's slightly less-ornamented *hazzanut,* it takes around 45 seconds. I also assume that because the record was so widespread (Polish Hasidic music, even into the homes of Hungarian Hasidim in Brooklyn), Reb Shlomo assumed that 'everyone' recognized it [as Reb Shlomo would often preface something he was saying with: "Everybody knows..."].

The entire tune of *"B'Motzaei Yom Menuchah"* 'At the Time of Bringing-out the Day of Rest,' by the great Hasidic composer, Reb Shaul, the Modzhitzer Rebbe known as the "Imrei Shaul," was composed in about 1932, according to a Modzhitzer Hasid, and recorded in the Jerusalem National Library Music Archives in 1966. According to the notes on the CD jacket, *circa* 5694/1934 — and based on information gleaned from Rabbi Dr. Natan Ophir's excellently researched biography — it is quite likely that Reb Shlomo heard this from the Rebbe himself! The entire tune runs about eight and a half minutes. It is from the fourth section of this hymn that Reb Shlomo takes this interlude for the words following in Psalm 96 the last words of *pasuk* 10: *"Yadin amim b'meisharim"* 'He shall judge nations with righteousness.' Those last words would still be sung with the tune of *"Ki Va Mo'ed"* by the *hazzan* — whereas for this song the congregation actually sings that tune till the end of the psalm; however, the section adapting the original tune for the *Motzaei Shabbat* hymn is initiated by the *hazzan's* repetition of the words of the last three verses of that psalm. So whereas the 13th and last verse of the psalm is sung with the *"L'chu N'raninah"* refrain, the two previous verses were sung by Reb Shlomo to the music originally composed for the words:

קְרָא יֶשַׁע לְעַם נְדָבָה,
אֵל דָּגוּל מֵרְבָבָה
יְהִי הַשָּׁבוּעַ הַבָּא,
לִישׁוּעָה וְלִרְוָחָה

|מפזמון "במוצאי יום מנוחה" למוצ"ש|

'Announce Salvation to the Generous Nation,
O all-Powerful-One, Thronged by Myriads.
May the next week be
for Deliverance and for [arriving at] Wider Vistas.'

As we said, in Reb Shlomo's Kabbalat Shabbat *nusach,* this tune served as an interlude between the words/tune for *"Ki Va Mo'ed"* and the standard refrain, and was adapted for the words:

יִשְׂמְחוּ הַשָּׁמַיִם וְתָגֵל הָאָרֶץ
יִרְעַם הַיָּם וּמְלֹאוֹ.
יַעֲלֹז שָׂדַי וְכָל אֲשֶׁר בּוֹ
אָז יְרַנְּנוּ כָּל עֲצֵי יָעַר.

|תהלים פרק צו: יא-יב|

May the Heavens rejoice and the earth delight;
May the sea and all within it roar.
May the fields and all in them celebrate;
Thus shall all the trees of the forest offer praise.

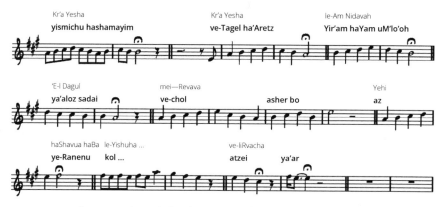

*The original words for the Motzaei Shabbat Modzhitzer tune,*
*and below the words of Reb Shlomo's Kabbalat Shabbat Nusach*

In putting these words to song, I always continue to be struck anew by the precise correspondence between Reb Shlomo's musical emphases and the symbolism of the mystical *kavanot* of those words in accordance with the Lurianic tradition of mystical correspondences in contemplative practice, as we will attempt to illustrate below. These *kavanot* need to be understood in the context of the principle that whereas during the week our service to the Divine is expressed in the movement from Below to Above, for the Shabbat our main service is in accepting and in being a conduit for the Union, proceeding from Above to Below, and here in this psalm, recalling the intent of the ultimate celebration of a unified Cosmos, the unification begins in the unified realm of Divine Emanation and proceeds to the lowest world, the material world, encompassing ALL.

The *kavanah* with musical expression for these two verses can thus be summarized as follows. In the first phrase of the verse "יִשְׂמְחוּ הַשָּׁמַיִם וְתָגֵל הָאָרֶץ" 'May the Heavens rejoice and the earth delight' (96:11) — which comprises the first two sections of the first line of the music — the first letters of those words form the Tetragrammaton, symbolizing the unified realm of Divine Emanation, where the first two 'heavenly words' flutter, and the second two seem to glide as if taken along.

The next three words ending the first line of the music: "יִרְעַם הַיָּם וּמְלֹאוֹ" 'May the sea and all within it roar' — whose first letters comprise the first three letters of the Tetragrammaton, without the final *Hei* — refer to how the final letter, denoting the Divine Attribute of Sovereignty in the realm of Emanation, descends to manifest the Divine Presence within the World of Creation — the highest of the created worlds, corresponding to its processes of thought and understanding, and occupying the third section of the first line of the music not as a statement-in-itself, but as a segue "יִרְעַם הַיָּם וּמְלֹאוֹ" to the next world, the World of Formation — emotion, energy, creative blooming, and purposeful order — the realm of the Tree of Knowledge, whose Archangel is Metatron (the Angelic teacher of Moshe, from whom we received the Torah, whose purpose is to transform the Tree of Knowledge), also called *S[h']Dai* (the same numerical value as Metatron) and also *"haSadeh"* 'the Field' (referring to the six terrestrial directions) and also the "Small Tetragrammaton." All this is reflected in the next words: "יַעֲלֹז שָׂדַי וְכָל אֲשֶׁר בּוֹ" 'May the fields and all in them celebrate.' The musical placement of the words that occupy the first two sections of line 2 of the music echoes the reference to fluttering and gliding and mirrors that of the previous verse; and the word "v'chol" 'AND ALL' receives an 8-note emphasis, as if to say that in our very singing of this word, all the denizens of "the field" are thereby unified.

And then, given that the essential intent in creation is that all — including the lowest realms — shall be unified in Divinity, even from the points of view of these lower realms, follows (in the sections occupying the end of line 2 and all of line 3 of the music): "אָז יְרַנְּנוּ כָּל עֲצֵי יָעַר" 'thus shall all the trees of the forest offer praise.'

Here, the words *"Az Y'raninu"* 'thus shall [the plurality] praise,' is sung as the beginning of a crescendo that again embraces the word "Kol" 'ALL' — sung as ten notes — referring to the symbol of ultimate diversity in the manifestation of *"Atzei Ya'ar"* 'the Trees of the Forest' [sing]. The word *"Ya'ar"* 'forest' — with its numerical value of 280=MNZPKh (the five letters that change their appearance at the end of words) is used as a Kabbalistic symbol for the Archangel of the Material World of Action, whose spiritual progress is especially assigned as the responsibility of Elijah the Prophet, who in the end unites the higher with the lower and is seen as the essence of embodied creativity, which is expressed by the special uniqueness of each created being brought to fruition. Then we return to the *"L'chu N'raninah"* theme for the final verse: "לִפְנֵי ה' כִּי בָא כִּי בָא לִשְׁפֹּט הָאָרֶץ יִשְׁפֹּט תֵּבֵל בְּצֶדֶק וְעַמִּים בֶּאֱמוּנָתוֹ".

"[All shall be] facing HaShem who has arrived — who arrived to adjudicate the Land. He will judge the world with righteousness, and nations with His faithfulness,' where the reiteration of Divinity's 'arrival' indicates such an advent in its ideal form as a gradual process, not as a sudden shock. Likewise, may the Universal Liberation arrive in our day, by means of peaceful creative integration rather than by apocalyptic wars, Amen!

This essay is also dedicated to the memory of Reb Yitzchok Eizik Eizenstadt, *z"l* — a great friend of R Shlomo and of all the *chevra* — who passed away on 6 Kislev, 5772 / December 2, 2011 — someone about whom Reb Shlomo said that he knew more of Reb Shlomo's *niggunim* than he himself did. His proficiency in the long and complicated Modzhitzer *niggunim* was also legendary among the Modzhitzer

Chasidim in Bnei-Beraq and in Brooklyn. May the singing of these two great friends in *Shamayim* add holy power to our own sacred singing here on earth. And a warm thanks is also due to my friend Steve Peskoff, who transcribed the music for this essay, may HaShem grant him all he longs for. Amen.

We are sad to announce that during the final days of editing this article, on 19 Ram-Cheshvan 5777, Reb Ben Zion Shenker, *z"l*, passed on, at age 91. May his memory be an eternal blessing.

*R' Micha Odenheimer, R' Michael Golomb, z"l, and R' David Herzberg, z"l.*
*Photo by Rabbi Joe Schonwald.*

Modzhitzer tune for B'Motzaei Yom Menucha including "Kra Yesha": http://youtu.be/kNVTrsSiqCw?t=209

Shlomo Carlebach - Singing Modzhitzer Rebbe's Hallel http://youtu.be/amBNrDASKpg

# An Excerpt from
# *The Late Starters Orchestra*
by Professor Ari L. Goldman

EVEN AS A BOY I WAS DEEPLY MOVED BY THE MUSIC OF CARLEBACH, A German refugee who revolutionized Jewish music in the decades after the Holocaust. Shlomo, as I knew him, emigrated from Berlin as a teenager with his parents on the eve of the Second World War. While the understandable reaction to the Nazi horrors was mourning and sadness, Shlomo picked up a guitar and gave American Jews songs of hope, joy, and redemption. He produced some wonderful early LPs, which I listened to again and again in my youth. There were songs like *"Od Yishama"* ('May It Be Heard'), which became a standard at Jewish weddings, and *"Am Yisrael Chai"* ('The People of Israel Live'), which was sung at rallies in support of Soviet Jewry and the young State of Israel. These were catchy anthem-like songs that were easy to learn. But Shlomo also wrote several intricate and majestic cantorial pieces. And I sang one of them, *"Mimkomcha,"* at my bar mitzvah. Soon after my bar mitzvah, which was held in Queens, my mother, my brothers, and I moved to the Upper West Side of Manhattan. It was there that I finally got to meet my idol, whose father, Naftali Carlebach, was the rabbi of a synagogue just a few blocks from our apartment.

The older Rabbi Carlebach looked and acted like a proper European Torah scholar. He had a formal, distinguished manner about him and a wispy white beard that seemed to hang around his face like a cloud. By comparison, Shlomo was a rebel. He was warm and physical with all those he met. He favored vests over his white shirt but rarely wore a jacket. In California's Bay Area he established The House of Love and Prayer, something of a hippie shul. He once quipped, "If I called it Temple Israel, no one would come."

I met Shlomo on his frequent trips to New York and, as a teenager, I became his part-time "roadie," accompanying him to concerts, carrying his guitar, and trying to keep him moving toward the stage when he'd stop to hug and greet fans. For me as a teenager in the 1960s, Shlomo gave me a chance to grow my hair long and rebel without ever leaving the bosom of my traditional community. I was singing protest songs but they were from the liturgy of the synagogue, and I was marching for causes like Soviet Jewry and Zionism that were part of my legacy.

I lost touch with Shlomo for many years, but his music and his spirit of Jewish activism deeply influenced me. Toward the end of his life, I had an opportunity to travel to Morocco with him and a group of American doctors who had arranged a tour "in the footsteps" of Judaism's most famous doctor of the Middle Ages: Maimonides. The doctors engaged Shlomo to travel with us as a teacher and singer.

A master storyteller, Shlomo performed for the small Jewish communities of Fez and Casablanca as well as for our Muslim hosts. He was also featured at a banquet organized by the Moroccan Ministry of Culture. There he sang Hebrew songs with a 12-piece Arab string and percussion band. It was a remarkable and hopeful moment.

I sat with him on the flight back from Casablanca to New York. He was exhausted and weak from the journey. In a moment of candor, he told me that he was not afraid of death. "When I die, I will go to Heaven and there I will meet many wonderful people. I will meet my mother and my father. And I will meet Johann Sebastian Bach."

"And what will you say to Bach?" I asked.

"Well, first I will finally find out if we are related. Bach and Carlebach. How could we not be? Then I will tell him, 'Mr. Bach, you wrote many wonderful symphonies and concertos, but I, Reb Shlomo Carlebach, wrote something great, too. I wrote *Mimkomcha.*'"

*Mimkomcha* starts very low, down by the cello's low C string, but then it settles for a sweet and soft lyrical section in the comfortable middle range of the male voice. The song suddenly becomes strident as the prayer gets louder and louder and asks of God: "When, O when, will you rule again over Zion?" And then it climbs inexorably higher as it demands: "May our eyes see your kingdom as you have promised us." The last notes are confrontational yet so hopeful. The prayer holds God to a standard and yet embodies a faith that God will deliver his people. By using the full range of the human voice, Shlomo is expressing a vast range of human emotion. For me, the song was never just about Zion. It was about making demands of life, of fighting for what we need, even when it seems beyond our reach.

I told Shlomo that, given *Mimkomcha*'s musical range and intensity, it was the perfect song for the cello. "Yes, the cello," he said with a smile. "It was a favorite instrument of Bach — and of Carlebach, too! How I love the cello. It must be the instrument that they play in heaven."

— First published by Algonquin Books, June 2014

The Soulful Melodies of Shlomo Carlebach with Neil Seidel: http://youtu.be/ Z0Eov3ji1wg

*Reb Shlomo, Neil Seidel, and Rabbi Joe Schonwald.*
*Photo by Rolinda Schonwald.*

# POETRY

## A Brief Historical Background

*There is a poignant irony in this photo of Shlomo accepting flowers after a 1992 concert in Wroclaw (pronounced "Vratzlav"), today part of Poland's western region.*

*Since its founding, the city has changed hands many times. It has been ruled successively by Bohemia, Hungary, the Austrian Empire, Prussia, Poland, and Germany, when it was renamed Breslau. Likewise, Jewish fortunes in the city have waxed and waned, periods of flourishing being followed by expulsion, return, revitalization, centrality and influence, then pogroms, destruction, and murder.*

*Consistent with Wroclaw's recycled Jewish story, in the 1980s the community again experienced a revival. In 1992, the city invited Rabbi Shlomo Carlebach, z"l, to give a concert during his whirl-wind tour of Poland and the Ukraine. Shlomo, of course, was not merely an entertainer. His true mission was to re-connect every lost Jew in the world to his/her heritage, as well as to one another, and to quash a hatred that he believed must not be passed on.*

*"The most important thing today," he told his audience, "what every person has to do, is to cleanse their hearts from anger. And the only way to get rid of anger is to fill your heart with joy!"*

*Hundreds of unidentified Jews went wild. Clapping their hands and singing without really knowing who they were, women, men, and children jumped out of their seats inside the great concert hall as they danced to Shlomo's song. Through all of its diverse historical extremes, such magic had never before been seen in Wroclaw.*

*"Everyone has to be strong in their Jewishness! Nothing in the world should move the Jewish people to ever again un-Jewish themselves," Shlomo shouted, as he accepted the flowers presented to him.*

*(Photo and text by Joan Roth)*

# Encounter at a Distance

by Chaya Lester

I NEVER HAD THE Z'*KHUT* OF MEETING REB SHLOMO. BUT I DID GET ONE encounter-at-a-distance. It was sort of like smelling the bakery without really tasting the challah...though that *shmek* sure did open my neshama.

It was the summer of 1994. I had just finished my freshman year in college, and I spent the summer in Israel. Those were my first days of falling in love with Torah, truly one of the magical chapters of my life. On one of those honeymoon nights, I was walking with friends from the center of town to the Old City. Apparently there was some big concert happening in Safra Square. It was right there in front of the municipality where I now make my regular treks to register my kids for school and pay my city taxes. But in those days it was just the site of a concert I didn't have the money to get into.

My friends and I loitered around at the entrance, listening wistfully. The music was upbeat, engaging, and the folks entering seemed to be of kindred spirits. We were not alone in our loitering. Apparently there were lots of other young Jewish hipsters who, like ourselves, didn't have the spare change to buy a ticket. We were the party of the "can't-pays," getting a contact high from the vibes that wafted over the gates. We were on the outside, but making the most of it.

Suddenly, though, the music stopped. We heard the mysterious singer call out to the powers-that-be, "Hey, you guys at the gate! Forget about the money. Just let everybody in!" Was it a joke? Was he talking about us? Sure enough, they opened up the gates, and we all started gleefully streaming in. It was the first and only time I have ever been suddenly let in to a concert for free! And, of course, it was Shlomo.

We flooded in to find a world of hundreds of circle dancing, Hebrew singing, funky and *frum* members of the tribe. I recall being shocked that there was a split between men and women, a phenomenon I could have never imaged at a concert. It was so pure, yet wild. It was fresh and new and yet old world, old style.

I looked around and knew I had found my home in the homeland.

I had no idea who Shlomo was. Little did I know that he was about to change my life, even from a distance. I would later learn that this was the last concert that Shlomo did in Jerusalem before his untimely death a few short months later.

It was not long after that concert that I ended up formally falling in love with the Shlomo chevra. I became a devoted groupie of Ein Safek, and one of the many who made the Moshav my home for the holidays. I lived in the Old City and had the enormous merit of davening under the arbors of song that was the Dovid Herzberg-led Shlomo minyan at the Kotel. Manna from heaven! Actually, it was feeling like a part of the Shlomo chevra that enabled me to eventually move to Israel after college and make aliya a year after that. The Shlomo chevra gave me an invaluable anchor of community. For once I had family in Israel.

As I think back to that magical night at the concert, the thing that most stands out from my singular slice of "meeting Shlomo" was the moment the gates were opened; the moment that we realized that we were being let in. It was a totally unexpected, seemingly unearned gift. I was filled with a sense of, "Yes, the universe is friendly. Yes, I am welcome. Yes, I have value beyond the cash in my pocket. Yes, I belong here in this city, with this people." After all, as a *ba'alat-teshuva*, I sometimes have this creeping fear that I just got too shmutzed up in my life to ever really be an authentic *frum* Jew. I couldn't possibly ever really deserve to be let in the front gates of this palace of God. But then it happened. I was on the outside and making the most of it. But then, Shlomo let me in. It was nothing short of Messianic.

That was the gift that Shlomo blessed us all with. That sense that we are all invited — and we don't have to pay admission when we're coming home. He gave us a sense, a knowing, that we do belong to this Jewish millennial dance party. And in fact, it really isn't much of a party without us.

So I owe enormous thanks to Shlomo and to the holy brothers, sisters, and shleppers who have been my surrogate family of gate-openers to the Holy Land. The poem below tries to capture that "ecstasy of entrance," that sense of being newly turned on to Torah, and that sense of the wonder that comes with being invited to enter into the gates of Jerusalem.

✳   ✳   ✳

THE LIVE TREE

So this is what it means to be a Jew —
Who knew?

Who knew that Torah was
ancient and yet progressive,
mystical, intellectual, and impressive,
grounded yet elevating,
paradoxical and penetrating.

Suddenly I am plumbing depths and thumbing through texts
that have been thumbed and plumbed
for generations past and more to come.

Here in these courtyards of holy Yerushalayim,
filled with Torah wisdom and higher vision,
living the return of Judah's long-lost children
— so far gone, so far hidden —
now come home to the old books
of our own venerable tradition!

Here in the study halls of Rehov Beer Sheva,
in *hutzot* Yerushalayim,
in Nachlaot, in Bat Ayin,
crawling on *berkayim*
just to kiss these stones — and make a home
in Yerushalayim's now-revived old bones.

We Jewish children are coming home,
coming streaming like four-cornered gleanings,
clamoring with higher calling,
cleaving to deeper meaning,
shining with persistence
and a 3000-year-old commitment —

Commitment to the Torah, to something more
than the mores & norms of the Western world
with her hordes of the immoral and the impure.

Committed to something more than a Manhattan latte
and a pumped-up paycheck to "provide for the family"
that may smile wide for the cameras
but weeps inside, for their bankrupt neshamas,

famished for a richer truth
than the loose change of material gain,
famished for the fresh fruit of the living tree,
stamped with God's name!

And so I pace myself with the stealth
of a leopard on the chase for the truth,
which darts like a gazelle
through these hills of Yehuda
and tomes of Gemara
I will come to know so well.

With a fire hotter than 1000 degrees,
from the cool Ivy League,
my ivy climbs the Western Wall —
a beanstalk tall to which I cleave.

For it's a living tree of Torah, Ketuvim, Neviim.
I'm a member of the band belting songs of the Leviim!
We have returned to these streets
to breathe these books,
to dream these dreams.

If Torah is a Tree of Life,
then I will gladly change my life,
that I may sit amongst her leaves and read....

Neshama Carlebach — "The Krakow *Niggun*"
at March of the Living 2013:
http://youtu.be/tDZpufU8oDg

# A Reflection...

### by Carol Rose

Asking if Shlomo had anything to do with my knowing
that G-d is eternally present
is like asking if eyes have anything to do with sight!
While eyes don't always guarantee sight,
they make that skill infinitely more possible!
So it was with Shlomo.

Although I carried a vague sense
of the Mysterious Holy Presence (always),
Shlomo was like an amplifier — an enhancer —
magically transforming felt sensations into language;
providing image, sound, and texture
for what had always been so elusive.
His were the words that my heart could hear;
the melodies that stoked my soul.

Over the years many have shared their ideas of G-d.
Shlomo held my hand and walked the path with me,
telling stories, singing songs, remaining unafraid,
even through the dark.

# Walking to the Kotel

by Reuven Goldfarb

I have some rough edges. I go down
to daven to smooth them out, sometimes
with the grateful refuge of a minyan,
sometimes with the melting fires of a heart
open to G d.

                     The center of my heart
beats a steady pulse, but my mind races
this way and that, following after
every sensual and mental vagary.

I long for sanity, for peace, for inclusion;
I stir the embers of passion
and blow on the fires of controversy.
I am a counselor and a mediator,
yet I cannot govern myself completely.
Voices well up, demanding to be heard,
insisting on their right to direct.
I calm them with cautionary tales
and advice from scripture. I sing to them
with a *niggun* from my rebbe.

I stand
in the Holy City, every stone a monument.
My own aspirations are linked
to their history, my destiny
to their future. Since we are — or will become —
dust, what does it matter how we build today?

What we leave behind, we leave for others
to build on. Let the foundations be strong!
And let the place where I stand to daven
support me well as I climb to the peak
of my soul and link her to the gracious G d,
who blesses me with her Holy Presence
and lifts me up to realms of being
I cannot reach alone.

Jerusalem
27 Sivan, 5758
June 21, 1998

The Rizhiner *Niggun*:
http://youtu.be/WQz_jMc_wFw

# Potiphar's Lament

by Reuven Goldfarb

*"Yosef HaTzaddik — everyone knows — was mamash — he never did anything wrong. Mamash holy. The wife of Potiphar — he held out— and I want you to know, the Gemora says, it was not just a little affair. For twelve years she came three times a day to prison, and there was no way for him ever to get out of prison. And three times a day she came and said, 'Listen, just one time, and I'll let you out of prison.' Twelve years."*

— Shlomo Carlebach

A dry wind is blowing
across the desert sands
from where the sun embarks each day
astride his scorching chariot.

And I marvel that the gods have made it
easy for a man to judge the pattern
of the changes in the sky and on the earth
that bring a benefit or curse to those who dwell on it,
that bring life-giving rain,
that drive the ships across the sea,
that bring their cargoes to my master and to me.

And yet, in the affairs of man,
such patterns are not clear.
Deception, hidden motives, greed and lust,
bend a man's will and teach him treachery
to those who call him friend.

When my wife
first cast her eyes on Joseph, I felt helpless.
The gods do what they will, and women lead
the dance.

I scan the sky for omens,
and even if I know what will occur,
I cannot change the heavenly decree.
So also, in the life of man, I see,
and yet I cannot order things or change
an order sent us by the gods, who rule at will
and squeeze our petty kingdoms drop by drop.

Tomorrow, when I order him to jail,
my wife will weep and wail.
The young man did no harm;
she could not resist his charm.
But he did hers,
although she demurs,
and yells in anguish,
forfeiting her wish.

If she pursues him there,
I trust his god will spare
him from her urgent wiles
and incandescent smiles.
It may be he will yet emerge
when all of heaven's twisting paths converge.

Shlomo Carlebach - Yehi Ratzon:
http://youtu.be/mndM-pi7P9M

# Three Poems

by Ruth Fogelman

## The *Niggun*

You heard the *niggun*
before you were born,
when your grandmother's grandmother
sang it as she rocked her child,
and when your grandfather's grandfather
hummed it on his way to prayer.

Like a lost princess, the *niggun* awaits
your yearning, your desire.
The melody waits near wells of water,
on river banks or by the sea,
for you to hold it, return it
to the palace on the mountain of myrrh.

Do not delay, lest the *niggun*
take flight, like a frightened gazelle,
far beyond the wells,
beyond the river banks and seas,
and when you reach out to receive it
it cannot be found.

# The Words of the King's Son and a King's Daughter

I

The king's son writes stanzas in the wilderness;
A king's daughter pens lines on a mountain-top.
They dip their quills — feathers from the same phoenix —
In the same fountain of ink.
His words stretch forth their hands and enter her soul.

Her words stretch forth their fingers, pry open and enter his heart.
The phoenix flies between the wilderness and the mountain,
Perches on a lily in the dunes,
Rests in a cypress on the mount,
And carries their phrases, like pollen, one to the other.

II

The phoenix rides the rolling winds far beyond the wilderness
And spreads its wings, carrying their words, far beyond
        the mountain.
Their words' song is heard in the corners of the world.
They stretch forth their arms,
Embrace the children of Eve and open their hearts.

The phoenix carries the words, which stretch forth their legs
And form a ladder standing on earth and touching heaven.
From the ladder's peak the phoenix flies into the light from the lost
        palace.

The words unlock its gates of pearl and enter its courts,
And the phoenix sets them, phrase by phrase, in the scepter of the
        king.

## Brothers-in-Law

I

Jonathan
When my father stabs me with his jibes,
I shrink away, like a stream deprived of water —
I walk with David in the vales,
For only he can hear the words beneath the ones I say.

> *David*
> *When I am nothing but a clod of earth,*
> *At a loss for melody and psalm,*
> *And fear that G-d may not receive my thoughts,*
> *Jonathan hears*
> *The words I cannot express.*

Jonathan
When my father's melancholy turns to rage,
I escape the palace for a breath of air —
I walk with David through a wadi in the wilderness,
For only he can hear the scream that barely leaves my lips.

> *David*
> *When enemies encircle me as fields of thorns on fire,*
> *Jonathan finds me praying in a cave.*
> *Though I fear G-d may not listen to my prayer,*
> *Jonathan hears*
> *The scream refusing to leave my throat.*

II

Jonathan
When courtiers nag me for an audience with the king,

And a myriad requests invade,
I walk with David in the hills,
And he gives me his melodies and psalms.

> *David*
> *When nightmares plague my sleep*
> *And I have none with whom to share the pain,*
> *I walk with Jonathan in the hills,*
> *For only he can hear*
> *My melodies and psalms.*

Jonathan
When parents' expectations grate and make me flee,
And I have none with whom to share my dreams,
David listens as we walk together in the hills,
And he gives me his melodies and psalms.

> *David*
> *When the palace seeks my life and I know not where to hide,*
> *Jonathan comes and finds me shelter from the night.*
> *We sit together in the hills,*
> *And even in the storms he stays to hear*
> *My melodies and psalms.*

\* \* \*

It was Reb Shlomo who introduced me to the stories of Rebbe Nachman, especially stories about the son of the king and about the daughter of the king, and stories of The Lost Princess, which is a major theme in his stories, from the time I first met him in the House of Love and Prayer in Kiriat Yovel, Jerusalem, in 1970, and ever after.

It was Reb Shlomo who gifted me with his *niggunim*, inspired by Rebbe Nachman and other Hassidic Rebbes. I'd never heard their names before Reb Shlomo gave over stories about them and sang their *niggunim.*

Moreover, it was Reb Shlomo who introduced me to the Psalms of King David in the deepest way — through his putting David's verses to music. So, in a very deep way, it's Reb Shlomo who inspired all three of these poems. And it was Reb Shlomo who taught me about opening your heart and listening in the deepest way — which is a theme of "The Words of the King's Son" and also "Brothers-in-Law."

Reb Shlomo opened my heart to "return again, return to the root of [my] soul" — to the lost world of *niggun* and of the lost princess.

All three of these poems previously appeared in *The Deronda Review.* "The *Niggun*" and "The Words of the King's Son and of the King's Daughter" also appeared in *Kol Chevra.*

Some of these poems can be found on my website: http://jerusalemlives.weebly.com

# EULOGY

*Once at a Shabbat dinner in the New York City Carlebach
shul, Shlomo invited my sweetest — then college-age — daughters,
Melanie and Alison, to spend successive summers with his beloved
family at Moshav Modi'im. With Shlomo and Neila's daughters,
Neshama and Dari. OMG!*

*The most precious of precious beings in our hearts + in those days,
cutest of cuties in our eyes. It took Neila's approval to make it
happen. To spend summers with the Carlebach family was beyond
an honor. It was as if the Holy of Holies opened up for us.*

*The treasure of eternal friendship was bestowed upon Neila and
me, and our daughters, a vow we've kept through thick and
thin all these years. And for all the good that happened to all of
us under Shlomo's lion's wings, for us, my family, our love for the
Carlebachs, as well as all the holy Moshav families, remains the
most meaningful of all our prayerful aspirations that did in fact
materialize. Wow!*

*Immediately drawn into this welcoming joyous spiritual realm of
delicate devoted souls, who yearned for nothing more than learning with Shlomo. Once among them, one cannot resist yearning too.*

*As such, summer visits were not only filled with laughter, fun &
love + maybe a little stress from time to time, but with the poetic
justice of Shabbos — when the whole moshav, everyone present,
davened their hearts out to the tunes of Shlomo's ever-invigorating
God-evoking melodies and prayers.*

*And Shlomo channelled the deepest, most vital torahs, precisely
brought down to each as one.*

*So how could I not be there to receive the Torah too? At least for
one summer Shabbat in 1988.*

*That's how I got to be at Shlomo's holy abode, visiting his family
with my camera, at the time our Rebbe returned from the mikveh.*

*Right before the onset of Shabbos, when our Rebbe's heart and
mind was always and only filled with faith, his focus on observance
and books, having traveled from one end of the world to the other,
intending to schlep us along, as he stormed the gates of heaven
with his knowledge, to swear to our holiness as reality and draw us
closer to Hashem.*

*(Photo and text by Joan Roth)*

# *Hesped* in Honor of Rabbi Shlomo Carlebach

by The Chief Rabbi of Israel HARAV YISRAEL MEIR LAU
Delivered at Har HaMenuchot, Jerusalem,
19 Cheshvan 5755 / October 24, 1994

Translated by Rachel Ebner

I BELIEVE THAT I WILL NOT HAVE FULFILLED MY DUTY IF I DO NOT HERE SERVE as spokesman for many who need to beg forgiveness and pardon from HaRav Shlomo Carlebach. We did not relate to him with enough respect, we did not value him sufficiently, we did not stand strong enough to guard the honor which he never sought but was truly entitled to.

I ask forgiveness and pardon in the name of those who are present here and in the name of the many who should have been present here but did not come. They will come, however, and they will come to value this great soul who moved among us: a soul from the world of nobility and purity, the world of awe, of melody, and of intimacy with the divine.

Perhaps the name Carlebach is not familiar to the young among you, but those of us who are older know R. Shlomo's roots: he came from one of the most aristocratic families in the world of Torah, the world of Judaism before the *Akeda*, before the destruction.

[R. Shlomo] belonged to all worlds, even though sometimes it appeared he belonged to none — sometimes he was so isolated and so lonely. More than once, when we'd meet on an airplane, it seemed that he had no ally but his guitar. But he belonged to all worlds. He was a true ben-Torah in the world of the Lakewood Yeshiva, alongside R. Aharon Kotler, who today stands ready to greet him. [R. Shlomo] was a household member in the home of the Lubavitcher Rebbe, who today stands ready to greet him. And [R. Shlomo] was a Bratslaver, and, no doubt, Rabbi Nachman rejoices today with this great soul arriving in the secret, lofty places.

[R. Shlomo] was a member of a very illustrious family, a family of deep believers. His uncle, R. Yosef Zvi Carlebach *z'tz'l*, wrote one of the last postcards of his life — perhaps the very last — to my father. Both of them, friends in heart and soul, rose heavenward in the storm in Europe fifty years ago. [R. Yosef Zvi Carlebach] wrote to [my father]: "As for me, I am amidst my congregation." He had been advised to embark for the safety of America, and he answered my father — we have the postcard — "I am amidst my congregation; I shall not leave my congregation." Such devotion for the community of Israel.

I see Shloimele in Russia, before any of us had the chance to get there — [Russia,] where souls were being lost at the murderous pace of a thousand a day. And this young man showed up with his guitar. They'd [not] seen anyone looking like this in a long time — a beard and *payot, tzitzit.* And from these encounters was born that song that the whole Jewish world knows: *"Od Avinu Chai"* (Our Father still lives). [Shlomo] came to them as if to tell them: The people of Israel lives! Why? In what *zechut*? Because our Father lives. They didn't understand his words, but they understood his soul. They absorbed him without understanding his texts — no dictionary is needed for the language of feelings. They understood and absorbed [R. Shlomo's] language more than they did our rabbinic speeches. R. Shlomo had a language called the language of the heart.

You just sang *Mizmor L'Dovid*, a Psalm of David. More than twenty years ago, I had the honor of hosting [R. Shlomo] until four in the morning in my house on Vermiza Street in Tel Aviv. And he said to me, "R. Yisrael, you are a child of the Holocaust. I want to sing you a melody." And there, on the spot, he composed a melody which has never been published anywhere, to the words of one Torah verse. And that verse was — and it is with it we accompany him today — "Even when I am walking in the valley of the shadow of death, I fear no evil, for You are with me." This "You are with me" is what sustained [R. Shlomo] all over the world: on the campuses of Berkeley; all the campuses of the east and the west; the campuses of England, France, Austria, Germany, South Africa, and Australia; in places so far-flung that the name of Israel was barely remembered there. R. Shlomo stood up and returned so many people to the embrace of Judaism and helped so many turn back from distorted lives. I remember the first time [R. Shlomo] appeared at Zion-America House, which at the time still had no ceiling and was wide open on top. He began with the song *"Essa Einai"* ("I lift my eyes to the mountains"), and we answered him with *"Shomer Yisrael"* ("Guardian of Israel, guard the remnant of Israel"), and, as if in a message appropriate for this last week [which included the kidnapping and murder of Nachshon Wachsman and the terrorist bombing in Dizengoff Center which took 22 Jewish lives], he sang for us *"Yisrael, Betach BaHaShem, Ezram uMaginam Hu"* ("Nation of Israel, trust in the Lord; He is [Israel's] Help and Shield"). And then he promised us the promise of *"Od Yishama Kol Sasson veKol Simcha"* ("There will yet be heard the voices of joy and gladness"), then *"Vehanchilaynu Hashem Elokeynu beahava uveratzon Shabbat Kodshecha"* ("In love and grace He has given us His Holy Sabbath"). He made us all take a leap into the holiness of the Sabbath, and today we accompany him into the day that is all Shabbat and peace, to the life of eternity.

R. Shlomo was a great soul, a quintessential soul. Only once in a generation does such a soul turn up — who knows from whence it was drawn? From the roots of higher worlds.

I want to tell you something. There are four species: the *Etrog*, the *Lulav*, the *Hadas* (myrtle), and the *Arava* (willow). Their initials spell out *"A'aleh"* (I shall go up). [R. Shlomo], this is the day of your going up. The *Hadas* is called a branch of interwoven foliage. What is special about the *Hadas*? Three leaves in a row emerge from the stalk at the same spot. The three leaves are three hearts. These are the three loves about which we have been commanded. First of all *"Veahavta et Hashem Elokecha"* ("You shall love the Lord your God") — this is one leaf of the *Hadas.* Secondly, *"Veahavta leReacha kamocha"* ("Love your neighbor as yourself") — this is the second leaf. And the third is *"uverachta et Hashem Elokecha al ha'aretz hatova asher natan lach"* ("Bless the Lord your God in the good Land which He has given you") — the love of the land of Israel. Now it is not the case with all of us that the three leaves line up. For one person, love of Torah might be stronger than his love of the Jewish people. Another person's love of the Jewish people might be stronger than his love of God. And there are those whose love of the land might be stronger than both other loves. The Rambam calls a *Hadas* of this type — one whose leaves are not equal — a *"Hadas shoteh"* (a foolish Hadas). [R. Shlomo], you were a wise *Hadas,* whose sweet fragrance was widely diffused. You were a *Hadas* who possessed all three leaves, and all of them suckled from the same inner point that is in all of Israel, who is hewn from the Rock. [You had] powerful love for the Holy One, Blessed be He, boundless love of Torah, and an unparalleled love for Israel. R. Shlomo's love of Israel, and love for every grain of dust of the land of Israel...how to put it?...he was connected to every letter of Torah, to every soul in the nation, and to every clump of dust in the land. Today, as with a good name you go to the higher world, surrounded by the love of your friends, your students, and people who esteem you, the clumps of dust of the Holy Land that you so love will sing sweetly for you....

And your prayers at the Western Wall, your Friday nights at the Western Wall...it is into your own Sabbath eves of *"Rav lach Shevet"* ("Enough dwelling in the vale of tears, come arise from the ruins"), into your own *"Mikdash Melech"* ("Temple of the King") that you are entering today in the higher worlds. I can see in my mind's eye the Tzaddikim and higher Holy Ones who are right now greeting your soul. You brought the spirit of Jewish life into so many Jewish souls who were on the threshold of danger, of getting lost, of disappearing.

May your pure, refined soul be bound up in the bouquet of life.

Alas, alas for those who are gone, no longer here.

You had a soul the likes of which is only seen once in many generations, and it had the power to sustain numerous souls in Israel.

May you be granted in the higher world enjoyment from your daughters, whom you always praised so highly; may you attain faithful "houses" to carry on your name in Israel with honor and splendor. Your songs are living monuments, unlike a stationary tombstone. [Your music is] a living, ongoing monument. The entire Jewish world — in this generation and for generations to come — are building up for you a memorial of sons and daughters — "I shall give him an eternal name which cannot be cut off." Every song, every letter, every note, is a living monument to the great soul whom we were privileged to know, the soul of HaRav Shlomo Carlebach, may the beloved Tzaddik be remembered for blessing, for eternity.

Shlomo's funeral in Jerusalem:
http://youtu.be/SiHHizQpN4w

# IN HIS OWN WORDS:
# INTERVIEW, STORIES,
# AND TEACHINGS

*Reb Shlomo hanging out at home on Moshav Meor Modi'im with kids.
He was always happiest while learning Torah with them. Summer 1988. Photo by Joan Roth.*

# Reb Shlomo at Yakar: Interview with Harav Meir "Mickey" Rosen, *z"l*

## Summer 1994

### Transcribed by Betzalel Edwards

Reb Shlomo (arranging the microphones): Here's for you, Reb Meire'le, and here's for humble me.

Rav Rosen (R): At Yakar, for the past month or two, we start *Kabbalat Shabbat* with a certain consciousness that we want to make some kind of offering to the Rebbe. We would sing something that was for us an offering to the Rebbe. I'd like to ask Reb Shlomo to start with something that is his personal offering to the Rebbe.

Reb Shlomo (S): What are we going to sing? I was thinking the whole time of a Skulener *niggun*, "Hasdei Hashem Ki Lo Tamnu" 'For God's mercies have never ended' — *Eichah* (Lamentations) 3:22. (Shlomo starts singing, 'Hasdei Hashem ki lo tamnu, ki lo chalu rachamav.' Afterwards, Rav Rosen starts the Chabad *niggun*, "Eli Atah Ve'odeka" 'You are my God, and I will thank you,' from *Tehillim*, 118:28.)

S: *Heilige* (holy) Reb Meir, you are the master of the world!

R: Rav Shlomo, there is learning, there is teaching, and there is singing. Where is your *shoresh neshama* (the root of your soul)? Here you are...it is correct to say that you are, excuse the phrase, the father of modern Hasidic music. I didn't mean that you are responsible for all the jazz it's produced, but it was you who more than forty years ago started it. But you also function as a Rebbe, as someone who wants to convey a certain *hashkofa* (a way of looking at the world, a philosophical or theological perspective). It comes up in your teachings; it is a certain part of your view. So where is your *shoresh neshama,* where is your soul? Is it in your learning, your teaching, or your singing?

S: Reb Meir... (Shlomo gives a wry smile and the audience chuckles) I mean it, you didn't warn me enough. But now it's too late to back out! I could say I'm double-parked. Remember I told you that the *Heilige* Reb Chaim Brisker and Reb Zalman Sender were learning together when they were seven or eight years old? Once Reb Chaim Brisker's father, the Beis HaLevi, came in and asked, "Which one of you learns better?" So Reb Chaim Brisker says to his father, "Should I brag or should I lie?" So Reb Chaim's cousin Reb Zalman Sender says, "You are bragging and lying."

You know, whenever a person asks you something about yourself, you have to brag and lie, otherwise you can't answer, right? So I'll tell you something, if you ask me, without really bragging too much, my *shoresh neshama* is in depth. I cannot stand shallow talk. I can't stand shallow people. I forgive them and I love them, but I can't stand them. I can't stand shallow ideas, I can't stand anything shallow. It makes me sick. And especially since I had the privilege of learning by the deepest and the sharpest [rabbis]; Rav Shlomo Hyman and Rav Aharon [Kotler] were deep but sharp deep. And I can't [praise] without bragging; my songs are really deep. It's really good music.

Do you know what deep is? It's [that] the second part is not just one more note, another note, another note, but it's getting deeper. And deeper and deeper. And you know, when I take a *niggun* (melody) and look for words, I don't just choose words I can get by with; the depth, the *niggun* brings out the depth of the words. So I'm looking for the deepest, deepest learning, the deepest singing, and I hope I have the privilege of making the world just a little bit deeper, to make *Yiddishkeit* (Jewishness) a little deeper. Also for me the words deep and sweet go together. Because if it's bitter, it's definitely not deep. Bitter is when you put something in your mouth and you want to spit it out. Sweet is the other way — you want to take it in. I'm craving sweetness. Anyway....

R: It may sound childish, but you have to choose. Let's put it another way. Where is your sense of being drawn to *HaKadosh Barukh Hu* (the Holy One, Blessed be He)? Is it in learning, is it in teaching, or is it in music?

S: I'll tell you something, if the *Ribono Shel Olam* (Master of the World) were to tell me, "You can play your music, but don't ever open up a Gemara, or if He [were to say] you can learn, but you cannot sing," I would say, "*Ribono Shel Olam,* You have to choose for me." (Laughter) I mean, if He talks to me He might as well...[choose for me also] do the whole thing! Rav Meir, you are a *gevaldt!*

R: When you sing, how does it come to you? Is there some sort of context? Could you describe some sort of creative process? How does a *niggun* come to you?

S: First of all, a *niggun* always comes by heavenly federal express. It could come any time during the day or during the night. Sometimes at night I dream of the most unbelievably beautiful *niggunim* (melodies), and sadly enough [they're] forgotten. Again, without bragging, I walk around with new *niggunim* in my head day and night. Let's say Friday night when I begin to *daven* [and here Reb Shlomo hums his own melody] "*Lechu Neraninah.*" Then ten *niggunim* in major are hitting me already. But what can I do? There is no tape recorder on Shabbos. But you see, Reb Meir'ele, it's clear to me that the *niggunim* don't come to me because I deserve it, it's just that maybe I heard them in my last *gilgul* (reincarnation). You know, I have this *niggun*...I don't know how many people pay attention to those so-called spiritual people who have visions, maybe they are a little bit high and hear things we don't...but I have this *niggun*, *"Yehi shalom b'cheilech shalva b'armenotayich"* 'May there be peace between your walls, prosperity in your palaces' — I'll sing it to you in a second — and there was a woman there who was a really high spiritual person. I would say that her soul was very developed, and she told me that the night after she heard that *niggun* she dreamt and saw herself standing by the *Beis HaMikdash* (Holy Temple), and the *Levi'im* (Levites) were singing this *niggun*, and all of Israel was singing with her. So maybe it's true, you know?

R: Let's sing it.

(All sing *Yehi Shalom B'cheileich...*)

R: You know, Shlomo, there is something very unsatisfying in being told that it just comes to you. (Laughter) Let's try to understand or put it into a context, rather than some kind of *yesh me'ayin* (creation out of nothing) or vacuum, [by saying] it "comes." My impression is that the Carlebach family is a musical family. But actually they were musical in a way that you were making fun of this morning, in the Mozart and Beethoven way.

S: *Chas v'shalom* (God forbid)! I'm not making fun of Mozart and Beethoven, I'm a big hasid of Mozart. What I'm making fun of is a Yid who only likes Mozart but doesn't like anything Jewish.

R: I'm putting my head on a line now, if I were to try to imagine the kind of music you grew up with it would either be classical music or some very heavy stereotypical German Jewish music. (Reb Shlomo nods in the affirmative.) I wonder, excuse me, what kind of *"Kah Ribon"* your father used to sing. Like the *"Yom Zeh L'Yisrael"* (R. Rosen starts singing an old version) — that's my image.

S. That's already the Polish version. My father sang it like a *Yekke* (German Jew). (Laughter)

R: My attempt…it seems to me that you've gone east, you've gone into Eastern Europe. This is a theme of Jiri Langer, and Dr. Marcus before him, of western Jews who've gone east.

S: It's a privilege from Heaven.

R: How? How?

S: You see, what it is —

R: Why that type of music?

S: *Heilige zisse* (Holy and sweet) Rav Meir, obviously if you ask me about the roots of my *neshama,* the roots of my *neshama* are in this kind of music, and again, what do I know what I did last lifetime? What do I know what I did the last time before?

R: Did you hear that type of music?

S: No, you see, at home it was always German music, but then I went to Mesivta Torah V'Daas [in New York] where there was *Hasidishe* music, and you know, in Vienna, with my father, there were two synagogues in the same courtyard. My father was the Rabbi of the Oberlander, Hungarian Oberlander, which was German, and then there was the Shinover Kloise, Shinover Beis Medresh [Polish Hasidic], and there my brother and I first got a taste of *Hasidishe niggunim.*

R: So you left your father's shul?

S: I didn't really leave it; it's just that I didn't really go there. (Laughter) And my father used to say that if he didn't have to go to his shul he would also go and *daven* in the [Shinover] Beis Medresh.

R: I'd like to ask a little more, not *chas v'shalom* to hurt you, but…

S: Reb Meire'le, you are the sweetest.

R: I'd like you to sing for us the *niggun* of the Rema (R. Moshe Isserles of Krakow) because I want to suggest to you a little analysis of your *niggun*.

S: Reb Meir is a *gaon adir* (an exalted genius), so this is a little bad for me! If you permit me...you're right, it was not such a satisfactory answer. The truth is that the really good *niggunim* are coming to me when I'm *mamesh* heartbroken. That means that sometimes for me if I wouldn't have been so completely broken, I would have no vessels for this melody. And a lot of times, when something happens to me, I think, "*Oy gevaldt*, I gotta have the tape recorder with me." Without bragging again, you know I went to Poland, some of us went to Poland. It was actually the first time there was like a Jewish concert tour in Poland. And you know that a lot of Yidden, a lot of people go to Poland just to go to Auschwitz, to Majdanek, and have nothing to do with the living people in Poland. But I'm not a cemetery person. We were really invited by the government, and we played for thousands and thousands and thousands of Polish people. And there was so much love between us, it's not to be believed. I mean non-Jewish kids. I mean, the old people didn't show up; I would say most people were between the ages of 15 and 40. You know, I think the best *niggunim* I ever made up, it must have been at Majdanek.... You know, there is one room with 80,000 shoes. And the craziest thing is, I had a tape recorder with me, a micro-tape recorder, Mimi remembers...and you know that I am a little bit of a maven of my own music, and the craziest thing happened, the next day I put the tape recorder on the piano, and it was stolen. Obviously [the *niggun* that came to me at Majdanek] was not for me to remember.

The morning after Majdanek we davened at the Rema's shul, the only shul left in Krakow. And for me it was so special, because my great-great-great-great-grandfather was the Bach [R. Yoel Sirkes, the "Bayit Hadash"], who wrote the first commentary on the *Shulhan Aruch*, and he davened in the Rema's shul, because he eventually took over [for] the Rema. The Rema was the Chief Rabbi of Krakow, and then about 60 or 70 years later the Bach was the Chief Rabbi. And again, as Mimi remembers, it was awesome, it was *mamesh* like Kol Nidre, *mamesh* like Yom Kippur. Not only we (30 or 40 Jewish people came with me) cried, the television crew, non-Jewish people, who came with us, were crying like...*gevaldt!* It was a very high moment, so — I made up this *niggun*.

R: It's so much more real to me when you say that there are moments when you are broken-hearted, and in that context some sort of creativity in the *niggun* takes place. Let me say this, I say it with love, and you can tell me it's absolute rubbish. I think when people listen to the *niggun* that you are about to sing, I would suggest that you are not allowing yourself to dwell too long on the broken-heartedness aspect; as soon as it gets just a little too much you will deliberately change the mood in quite a dramatic way. And my theory is, consciously or unconsciously, you are not letting the *devekus* (lit. cleaving, "heavy" or "deep," and in this context, "sad") parts get too dominant. Let's listen to your *niggun,* and let's present it to the *tzibbur* (congregation).

S: Reb Meir, you are a *gevaldt!* Why didn't you come with me to Krakow? (Reb Shlomo sings the Krakover *niggun*. He sings the *devekus* part 3 times as he usually does, and then instead of going into the *simcha* (joyous) part of the *niggun*, he adds in a singing voice) "*L'koved* (in honor of) R. Meir, let's sing it [the *devekus* part] one more time!"

R: (Excited) Now that's not fair, you NEVER do that!! (And R. Meir jumps in and starts the *simcha* part of the *niggun*.)

R: (*Niggun* ends) And even then, it's that aspect (the second "*simcha*" part) which becomes the mantra! It is never the slow, *devekusdik* aspect of your *niggunim* which is repeated over and over. I suggest two possibilities. One is that there is a danger, like in the second movement of a symphony, that it can claw you; it can become thick. And the other one is, you're frightened.

S: Maybe I'm both, you know? You see what it is, Reb Meire'le, when I am, let's say at *shalosh seudes* (the third meal of Shabbat) with my *chevre* (congregation / community), then we sing this first part a long time because they are on the level. Mostly, when I am at a concert, they don't have vessels for this kind of singing, so I sing the first part twice.

I'll tell you something, without bragging, the fact is the people steal my *niggunim*. Nobody ever records the first part. Right away they record the second part. Or with wedding bands [it's the same thing]. I say, "Who gave you the right to miss the first part?" You know I don't want to say bad things...one of the top singers today, or at least he thinks he's the top singer, the moment I came out with the Krakover *niggun,* he went right away and recorded the second part. I asked him, "What happened to the first part?" And he said, "I didn't even think that it was part of the *niggun*." That means he didn't get the message, because the second part without the first part is like half a sentence, and how could you just say half a sentence?

R: If you are telling me now that this is a conscious decision on your part because of the cadence or because of the receptivity of the people, then I understand it very well indeed. And from my learning with Mimi it seems to me that this is also a difference between the Baal HaTanya (first Lubavitcher Rebbe, R. Shneur Zalman) and the previous Rebbe (referring to the sixth Lubavitcher Rebbe, R. Yosef Yitzhak Schneersohn, aka the Freidiker Rebbe), whereas the Baal HaTanya was much more of, a sort of an introvert or only with a selected few, the previous Rebbe seemed to make a conscious decision that in order to deal with this generation there had to be a much more expansive, almost American approach.

S: They are (muffled)....

R: You think so?

S: 100 percent. You see, I had the privilege of being by the Freidiker Rebbe. By the Freidiker Rebbe, a good Shabbos was if you davened seven hours. I remember when I first got into Lubavitch, who would dare to start davening before 2 in the afternoon? You went to the mikveh, and then you learned your Chasidus (R. Shlomo shakes his head from side to side in the depth of the matter), and then you davened.... Today in Lubavitch you don't find this, except for maybe two or three individuals who I don't think they even exist anymore. Today Shabbos is the most important thing; you *daven* fast, then you grab someone who didn't make Kiddush yet...it's a completely different consciousness today. You are right.

R: I think, correct me if I'm wrong, if someone has been in music or art for over forty years, then you can actually analyze the *niggunim* from various stages. I think — maybe I should apologize to the *tzibbur* for all this business about music — I think I would like to introduce them to a Shlomo Carlebach *niggun*, "*Mimkomcha*" of about 40 years ago, which is unlike the sort of *niggunim* we sing now. You going to start or should I start?

S: You start.

R: You have to start [with a] low [tone] because it gets very high. (R. Meir starts singing "*Mimkomcha.*")

S: R. Meir, you are the best! Can I sing you something that is also [in a] major [key], it's also *hazzanus* (cantorial singing), but it's not so long. I need some good harmony. This was from just a few years ago. (Starts singing *"le'dor va'dor nagid godlecha, u-l'netzah netzahim kedushatcha nakdish"* 'From generation to generation and for all eternity we will sanctify Your Holiness'.)

R: Of course what you did there was to slip into a Viennese waltz.

S: (Cracking up, teasing R. Meir) *Moshiah* is coming with Johann Strauss and asks me, "Why did you ignore my teachings?"

R: I mean, in trying to be analytical about it, what you've done is you've put a limit on how internal you are prepared to be, almost as if you are not prepared to show yourself unless you are assured of who's there.

S: OK, Reb Meir, I'll give you a *kvittel* (petition) after; you are *mamesh* my Rebbe. (R. Shlomo gives a big wry smile and signals to the audience.) It's good, the nine days are cleaning days (the interview took place in the days before the ninth of Av, a time of repentance).

R: So I have something which I think is very important to ask you. I think one of your favorite, what you call "torahs" (teachings), is an Ishbitzer torah. You talk about the Torah of always, and the Torah of the moment. And you don't leave it open like that. I mean, you've got to say what is greater, and you're quite clear in your own mind what is greater. You think what is greater is the Torah of the moment. Presumably you would say that the Torah of the moment is in the context of the Torah of always. (Problem with volume.) So one of the favorite "*torot*" of Rav Shlomo is the Ishbitzer Torah. By the way, I don't think that Reb Shlomo is really [an] Ishbitzer. I think really he is a cross between Ishbitz and Kotzk. Or Reb Shlomo is a cross between Ishbitz and the Chozeh (the Seer of Lublin). I'm not quite sure. But I don't think he's completely Ishbitz.

S: Reb Meir, you are a *gevaldt.*

R: So one of his favorite torahs, and this is Reb Shlomo's, is that there is a Torah of always and a Torah of the moment...and it is quite clear that if you listen to Rav Shomo that he thinks that the Torah of the moment is the greater one. Within the context of the Torah of the moment there is a kind of take off where a human being is on the level and knows how to behave, even though it is not in the written books... and Rav Shlomo clearly identifies with the Torah of the moment. He is identifying with Pinchas (in the Bible). I am not talking about a particular action of Pinchas (laughter, referring to his killing of Zimri and Cozbi), but he's identifying with the Torah of the moment. But there is a difference. In the conscious act of the Torah of the moment, for a moment, but what you're doing is the Torah of the moment for a generation. A Torah of the moment for the always. I think that's what you're doing. That is to say that you think that in the world of Torah, this is how one should behave, despite what other people think, this is the road, this is the way to deal with the reality we're facing, but it's a continuum, it's not a moment, this... well, let me see how far I come with that one, if I come back.

S: You see, I'll tell you. You say such deep things, Reb Meir. You see, what it is, what made me turn from the always until the moment took more than a moment. Because I was watching all those generations before me, and I saw their married life, I saw the way they acted with their children, and I see, as a whole generation, they are so eager, for their children, for the always. But when it comes to the moment, I see the children are cripples. They don't know what to do. You see, all the Rebbes.... I'll tell you a story which cuts my heart. I realized that when it comes to the moment, there's nobody to talk to. Someone told me he was in the house of...without mentioning names...a great Rabbi. And a woman came and says, "I want you to help my daughter, she's leaving tomorrow night for India. And I know I will never see her again. Please come over to our house, please talk to her. Don't you have something to tell her? Make her go to Yerushalayim, why is she going to India?" The Rebbe was in the middle of eating, and it was *mamesh* glatt kosher. And as everyone knows, when you eat glatt kosher you are not permitted to be *mafsik* (to make an interruption), because glatt kosher is on the level of *Shmoneh Esreh* (the silent prayer where you can't stop and talk). (Reb Shlomo is making this up as a jab at the Rebbe's self-righteousness.) So he kept on eating, [thinking], "What can I do?" Meanwhile, his wife is bringing him the *knaidelech*, he keeps eating, [thinking,] "What can I do?" And the heat was boiling, he was boiling. Then suddenly, there's a phone call...again, I am not talking about a real great Rabbi, I am talking about [a phony]. I am not talking about the great Rebbes. Imagine someone comes to the Amshinover and says, "My daughter is going to India," he would go and talk to her. Or Lubavitch, I'm not talking about this kind of *tzaddikim*.

R: She wouldn't come to the Amshinover and say, "My daughter is going to India."

S: *Nebuch* (sadly), she wouldn't know the address. So anyway, suddenly there is a phone call, and the Rabbi is beside himself. There was a bakery on 13th Avenue in Boro Park, and they just found out that the oil they are using is not under *hashgacha* (rabbinic supervision). They are not sure if it is *mamesh treif,* but even if it's kosher, it's not under *hashgacha!* The Rabbi got wild. He stopped eating the *lokshon kugel* (noodle casserole), he was *mamesh* wild. The woman left. I said to myself, "If I ever become a rabbi, do I want to be like this?" You see, he knows always you have to eat kosher, that's 100 percent. But what do you do when one Jewish girl gets lost? I once asked a rabbi, "You are learning for five years all the laws of what happens if one *milchig* (dairy) spoon falls into a *fleishege* (meat) pot, but what do you do with all the meaningful Jews who are falling into a *treif* world? Why don't the Rosh Yeshivas ever talk about that? I see the way they were teaching in yeshivas. A yeshiva *bocher* (student) comes to a Rosh Yeshiva (Dean) and says, "Someone tells me a *shidduch* (match) about this girl," what would be the first question? The first question (of the Rosh Yeshiva) would not be, "Do you love her?" The first question is, "Is she *frum* (religious)?" Second question is, "Who's her father?" And then ten more questions. And loving? Who talks about it? What's going on here? So I realized that *Yid-dishkeit* needs something because I cannot imagine that God wants him to marry a woman just because she is *frum!* I don't even buy a tallis if I don't love the tallis. If I wear the tallis, I want to love the tallis. And I'll tell you something else. 80 percent of the yeshiva *bocherim* are leaving the yeshiva because there is no one to talk to. Sure, they could talk to the Rebbe about the kosher bakery, but they couldn't talk about everything in the world. You know, a yeshiva *bocher* came to me and said he came to his Rebbe and told him, "I'm so broken!" All the Rebbe said was, "Just learn stronger. Forget about your broken heart." But that's not the answer. You know what I realized, when a Yid (Jew) talks to you, at that moment, maybe he needs something from the Torah that nobody ever said before. And maybe he's not away from the Torah, but whatever happens to you in your life, the *Sefer* Torah (Torah Scroll) is open. Everything is part of the Torah. Everything which happens to me is part of the Torah. But this Torah is not the Torah of a kosher bakery. It may be the deepest. In our generation, I don't know if they ever met so many broken young people as there are today. So I realized that we need kind of a new Torah. I don't know where it's coming from, but we got to get it out. I'm still not saying the right thing, but it made me realize that when we talk to young people we have to give them the strength to know there is a Torah available for you when you need something for the moment.

R: This is very beautiful, Rav Shlomo. And I think everyone senses this about you. But it's almost between the devil and the deep blue sea. You seem to be agreeing that the Torah of the moment you have translated into the Torah, if not of always, then of your generation. This must make you very alone, and a very lonely person. I mean, who on earth would you discuss this with? Which Rebbe could you turn to and say, "I need to develop the Torah of the moment." The Amshinover?

S: I would come to you, Reb Meire'le. (Looks around the room.) Come to Mimi (Feigelson), come to Menachem (Kallus), come to Yehoshua (Rubin). You know, it's crazy, a lot of people ask me, "What's your reaction to Conservative and Reform Judaism, coming from Orthodox?" I want to tell you a way out story, a bit personal. In the good old days there was a Delta flight leaving San Francisco at one in the morning, arriving at 6:10 in Cincinnati, and 8:30 from Cincinnati arriving at ten after 10 in New York, a good flight. I would take it a lot of times, because I could stay all night at the House of Love and Prayer and then I could go back to New York. You know, Rabbi Gottshalk, who was the head of the Reform movement, happened to be [a] good friend to me because he was once a rabbi in San Francisco, and he would come a lot of times to the House of Love and Prayer. Anyhow, I'm going on this plane to New York, and in the second row there is a Rosh Yeshiva. I walked up to him and said, "*Gevaldt, sholom aleichem, vus hertzig?* How are you doing?" You know, I could see he was counting his fingers after I let go of his hand. He wasn't sure if I gave him five or four, or maybe six! He didn't ask me, "How are you?" and he knows me for so many years. Ask me how are you! Simple *shayla* (question), right? So I'm going further back, and suddenly I see the Rabbi Gottshalk, sitting in the last row. Rabbi Gottshalk got up, and we hugged each other and kissed for a half hour. And Rabbi Gottshalk says to me, "I love you so much because I know that you never let go of your dreams." I said to myself, "Isn't this heartbreaking? With this Rosh Yeshiva, we went to yeshiva together for so many years, and he doesn't have the faintest idea what I'm into, what I'm out of, what I want. And Rabbi Gottshalk, according to this Rosh Yeshiva, he's who knows what, right? And yet, he's so connected to the deep Torah I'm connected to. It's hard to know, but again, it's getting better. I want you to know that there is a tremendous awakening in the yeshiva world. Not by all of them, but by some of them. You know what Moshe Rabbeinu did: he brought the Torah down to the world. He didn't *shlep* us up to heaven to listen to God, but he brought God down. And you know, to bring God down to the world is not so simple. And the more you bring God down, the more you bring Mount Sinai to the world. And you know Mount Sinai is God to the world but doesn't compare to the way Yerushalayim is to the world. Yerushalayim is even deeper.

R: Now look what you've just done. I asked you for the name of one Rebbe who you would turn to, to be a sounding board in your loneliness for the Torah of the moment, and you've told an anecdote in which basically you are saying that the Reform Rabbi has more in common with me than this guy I learned with in the yeshiva.

S: On the moment level, yeah.

R: Which for you is the most important? Which is the moment in the context of the Torah of always? — And that poses a terrifying problem, which suggests that — maybe I shouldn't say this in public.

S: Why not? I said it already. It's already too late to go back.

R: Why doesn't the Torah of always appreciate the Torah of the moment? In fact, it's almost inhibiting the Torah of the moment.

S: The Torah of the moment for them doesn't exist.

R: Right, and for you it's the most important thing, and you're finding your commonality with someone who doesn't accept the Torah of always, he only accepts the Torah of the moment. That's your answer, via your story, to my question.

S: 100 percent. The saddest thing is...you know what it is...I'm sure you'd be angry for me if I said, no Meir, forgive me. You know, talking about drugs, I'm not saying everybody should take it, but there's some people I wish they would. (Laughter) They are so stiff! And their consciousness is so underdeveloped. I can't believe it! It is very strange, when I come and play for...I don't want to say anything bad... certain people, they only want to hear old *niggunim* which I made 30 years ago. And I for myself realized, the older I get, the more my consciousness is really developed. So *niggunim* which I made in the last ten-fifteen years are really meant for people with a high consciousness. They can't take it. You know, I'll tell you something. I played for (B'nai Brith) Hillel, somewhere. And everyone knows, without saying anything bad, that the consciousness of the Hillel Rabbis, maybe it's like the consciousness of the first twenty minutes when I was born. But after that (sees a Hillel Rabbi in the audience), Yossi is my man! Hey! Yossi is one of my super-top moment people. Stand up and wave at me, *mamesh!* Yossi and Devoreleh. I want you to know that Yossi is one of the only Hillel Rabbis who invites me. This is higher consciousness, right? (Laughter) Anyway, I am playing for this Hillel Rabbi, and there is an Ashram right next to it. It was not like next to Yossi, the Baba, next to the Hare Krishnas. It's a long story. You see I went with Yossi to visit the [Hare Krishna] Rebbe'le, I'll tell you later where it was, inner city. (Back to the Hillel concert.) The concert was awesome. After the concert the Hillel Rabbi comes to me and says, "I didn't like your concert. You didn't sing '*Esa Einai*,'" and he counted me five *niggunim* [that I didn't sing]. I want to share with you something. At that concert...and I was reminded because someone miraculously gave me a tape of that concert.... It was in about the year '72, '73. And there were a lot of yogis there, I mean, they were all *Yidden* (Jews), I mean, someone with the name Hooka Hooka or something, and what was your name before? "Moshe Korn." Or something like that. You ask a girl, and her name was Hannale.

Anyway, suddenly a young lady gets up; she was not a yogi, just a very fancy young lady, and someone told me that she was one of the top top rock stars in that neighborhood, wherever it was. And she says to me, "Can I sing a song?" So I say sure, I'd be so glad. And the song I was singing in the middle, you know it was (starts singing *Mizmor L'David, Havu l'Hashem B'nai Eilim*). So these days I am singing that *niggun* to *Mizmor L'Dovid*, but in '73, '74 I was singing it to the words, "*Shabbat Shalom U'Mevorach. Gut Shabbos, Gut Shabbos...*" (starts singing it again). So you have to help me — give me a good harmony. So this young lady gets on stage and begins singing (Shlomo tells this in a singing voice), "My name is Bashenyu, my name is Bashenyu, my name is Bashenyu, and my zaydie is Moishele the barber from the Bronx." Because I forgot to tell you before this *niggun*, she sang like this (sings, similar to his *niggun* for Moshe v'Aharon in *Kabbalat Shabbat*), and she was singing, "my zaydie is Moshe'le the barber from the Bronx. Moshe'le the barber, don't make me laugh. Don't make me cry."

And she was crying. And she said (singing the whole story), "Every Shabbos morning my zaydie would wake me up, and he would say, 'Bashenyu, my *yiddisher tayer kindt* (my dear Jewish child), let's go to shul.' And I would say, 'Go to shul? Don't make me laugh. Go to shul? Don't make me cry.' And my zaydie would take his tallis, and he would say, 'Bashenyu, *me'tayer kindt*, I want you to carry the tallis.' And I would say, 'Tallis? Don't make me laugh. My zaydie's tallis? Don't make me cry.' And then my zaydie would [take me to shul and] begin to *daven*, with so much heart, with so much soul. And he would cry and he would cry and he would hold my hand. 'My zaydie's tears, don't make me laugh. My zaydie's tears? Don't make me cry.' And after the davening, he would take me to the Rebbe and say, 'Rebbe, bless my *ainekel* (grandchild), Bashenyu.' *Ainekel*? Bless me? Don't make me laugh. Bless me? Don't make me cry.

"'Good Shabbos, Good Shabbos! Good Shabbos Good Shabbos! Shabbos? Don't make me laugh. Don't make me cry.'"

It was the best thing I ever heard in my life. (Closes his eyes. Deep silence.) The saddest thing in the world is that I was in touch with her for many years. And then suddenly I lost touch with her. And after I lost touch with her I stopped singing her *niggun*. Would you believe it that the person who drove me to the airport now to come to Eretz Yisrael told me, "You know, someone gave me an old tape of one of your concerts. Bashenyu is on it! So anyway, I got to put it on a record. It's awesome, no? You know what she says in those words, you could not write in a book. You couldn't say it; you can only sing it. And you know, I'm telling you this contrast without knocking him. Bashenyu sang at my concert — isn't that worth ten billion dollars?! And he comes complaining that I didn't sing *"Esah Einai."* I couldn't believe my ears. He's a cute Yiddele, you know. If he wants to be a shoemaker, *mazal tov.* But to be a rabbi, a Hillel Rabbi? Heartbreaking, right? Would you talk to him if you had a problem? I would ask him where's the nearest grocery store, that's what I would ask him. I would maybe call him up and ask him what time is *licht bentchen* (Shabbat candle lighting time). Anything more I wouldn't.

But you know what we need, and this is what is so special about Yakar, we need people with high consciousness to be connected to the Torah. You know, we lost a whole generation of *Ba'alei Teshuva* because of people who thought they could teach them...they can't, the kids who come back to Yiddishkeit, their consciousness is developed 2000 light years ahead, and the person who wants to teach them Torah is behind them millions of years. So, Meir, I want to bless you, you should have on the staff people with high consciousness, and if Bashenyu should ever show up at Yakar she should feel at home.

R: Reb Shlomo, maybe there are other people here who would like to ask you questions, but I just want to tell you that I have no doubt in my mind that if you had to choose between learning, teaching, and singing, that your *shoresh neshama* (the root of your soul) is in singing. And I think that through song you communicate something

God-like. And if you can communicate the God-likeness, then it's you. I have always felt that the reason why in *Tehillim* (Psalms) you have [the mention of] all these different types of instruments is because a human being in *Avodas Hashem*, the service of God, is like a musical instrument being played upon, where the most noble sound emanates from him just being a *kli* (vessel) while someone else is strumming.

S: Reb Meir, thank you so much.

R: Would anyone else like to ask Reb Shlomo questions?

S: *Die Heilige zisse Rav Yossele, gevaldt!* (The holy sweet Rav Yossele, wow!)

Yossele: (beginning of question missing)...how do you see storytelling as knitting together words of Torah and singing?

R: He's asking about telling stories (missing).... But I don't see telling stories as a *tipacacha* (a tiny drop of water — a simplification) for teaching, nor do I see telling stories as a *tipa* (a minute portion) of singing. But then I don't really have my question. I just think that if you have the gift of telling stories then it's just a very sensitive way of conveying an idea. And I think one has to move away completely from "Herr Rabbiner Professor" speaking from Mount Olympus down to mere mortals who are just going to receive words of wisdom. I think that's the beauty of Rav Shlomo. I believe that telling stories is the highest form of *kiruv*. I also think that there is another form of *chinuch* (education) that some people have developed, especially from the non-*frum* world, which is self-deprecatory humor. Making fun of yourself is a way of allowing people in.

S: Okay, I will tell you one of my favorite jokes. I think I shared it with you; it's a good one. You know, there's a Yid, a miser, and he never gives his wife money to buy fish for Shabbos. Finally his wife says to him, "Moishele, if you don't give me fish, then I am ready to divorce you." So he gives her 50 cents. She goes to the fish market. What can she get for 50 cents? A fish from 2000 years ago. It smells so bad, she cooks it, and fries it, but it doesn't help. Finally, the Yid comes home Friday night, he puts his teeth in it and, *chhhhh!* And she wants to go and throw it in the garbage pail. He says, "No, no no. In my house, you don't throw anything out." He goes back to the shul, and there is *nebuch* (alas) a *varmeh* (warm) Yid who *nebuch* (unfortunately) was not invited by anybody for the Friday night meal. He says, "Would you like to have some fish?" "Sure!" He is so hungry he eats the whole fish. As he finishes the fish, he faints. They call the ambulance, bring him to the hospital. The next day the Yid goes to visit him, *bikkur cholim* (visiting the sick) right? On Sunday they call him from the hospital, he died. So he goes to the funeral. Later he said to his wife, "See! You wanted to throw out that fish, and I took that fish and fulfilled three *mitzvos* with it. I fed the poor, I visited the sick, and I went to a funeral!"

I'll tell you, Reb Yossi, just because we are such good friends. It took me a long time to get through to the public that I could tell a story. Until today, I get invited to synagogues to give a concert, and I have to sign a contract that I will not tell a story. I'll tell you, Reb Yossi, without mentioning names, I got invited to a concert, this huge orthodox shul, and you know Sammy (Intrator) my man (his manager), so they call up Sammy and say we would like him to give a fundraising concert, there will be a thousand people, but I have to sign that I will not tell a story. Just sing one song after another. So the first part, you play for money, right? There's not much joy in it. I was singing one song after another and then there is intermission. During the intermission people came up to me and said, "Shlomo, what happened to you? You are not yourself tonight. You're knocking off one song after another." First of all, between one song and another, you need something, right? "And where are your stories?" So the president of the shul was sitting next to me, and I told the president that I had to sign that I'm not telling any stories. So he says, "Nah! I was only joking! I didn't mean it!" So the second half of the concert I told some *gevaldt* stories, and I hate to say bad things, but the president was sitting there and crying his eyes out. But you know even today, there are people who won't buy a recording if it has one story on it. And then there are other people who only want a tape with stories on it.

People with a very low consciousness, they can't stand my stories. Because I hope and I hope that my stories — they are not just stupid stories. Sometimes I listen to the so-called storytellers...meaningless, stupid, doesn't touch you. You don't cry, you don't laugh, and you just look at your watch and hope it's over soon. You know what a good story is? It's a story that when you look at the person telling it, you are praying inside, "Let it be a long story."

(Yossi makes a comment)

S: Yossi, you're the best!

R: I'd like to ask Mimi to help us sing this other *niggun* where Shlomo suddenly changes the mood.

S: The *niggun* I made for Tzvi? Ahh, this is unbelievable. For this I really need good harmony, really. Hey Devora'le you'd better sing with me. (Sings)

R: I just found one more, almost a crime. I don't think you have any image of someone you could follow. There is no image where you could say, "This is who I should be." You can think of certain aspects of individuals, but you are your own image. You are guided totally by *minei u'vei* (from within yourself), but it's coming through you. You have no one to look at and say, "That's what I should be."

S: Let me ask you. Is it a *chutzpah?* Or is it okay?

R: *Chas v'Shalom!*

S: No, I'm asking you.

R: I'm not here to make a joke. I'm here so people can understand the courage of what you are doing. I want to see how you would react to the question.

S: I don't know, I'm thinking to myself. You know one thing is clear to me. If I would have asked people what I should do, I would never do what I am doing. Although a few times I did ask Rav Moishe (Feinstein). I will tell you one of the things I asked Rav Moishe. I don't know why I had this "attack" that I should ask Rav Moishe. A *"frumie"* (religious) attack.

R: Only for the moment.

S: I got a call...you know today, Shomer HaTzair (Zionist youth movement) is not what it was. In the past they really hated religion. Crazy enough, I got a call from the Shomer HaTzair, it was the end of the '60s or the beginning of the '70s, to give a concert the night before Shevuos. At a camp in the mountains. It's a major breakthrough. But a concert in the 9 days right before Shevuos (when some forbid live music)! So I called up Rav Moishe. And Rav Moishe was a *gevaldt* Yid, he says *"L'man HaShem* (for the sake of God) you'd better go." But anyone else I would have asked...okay. Maybe today, you know the consciousness of the rabbis, I mean some rabbis have been growing up also. And you know, I'll tell you something. Would you believe how fanatic I was when I was growing up in yeshiva? When I was in yeshiva, maybe 16 or 17 years old, someone came back from Eretz Yisrael, I remember it like it was today, we were up all night, and couldn't listen enough to what he was telling us. He was telling us that in Yerushalayim the young people get together Friday night and they throw stones at the cars [that] drive on Shabbos. And I was praying inside, *"Ribono Shel Olam,* will I have this privilege, (laughter) when will I have *gevaldt Ribono Shel Olam* the privilege...?"* It was clear to me that until you throw stones at *mechalel*

*Shabbos* (desecrators of Shabbat) you don't really know what Shabbos is! But then I grew up, *baruch Hashem,* a little bit.

R: I thought you were going to say that when you were a young man you heard that someone came back from Yerushalayim, and he told you that a guy named Carlebach... sings to all sorts of audiences and you felt, "When will I have the *zechut* (merit) of throwing stones (at him)!"

S: I'm sure I would have. I'll tell you, it took me, personally, from being such a fanatic — I'll tell you how fanatic I was. I was in yeshiva, and I would *mamesh* not talk to girls. Simple as that. Not talk to girls. One time I saw my *chevrusa* (study partner) was standing talking to a girl. I stopped learning with him. (Laughter) I'm serious. I said, "You are not holy enough to be my *chevrusa.*" You know what it is? I checked on him what happened to him, he became a top therapist. And I am what I am. Then one time we met again, and I said, "You remember I stopped learning with you because you were talking to girls." And he says, "Ahh, *gevaldt!*" So he looks at me and says, "You know, I always had the feeling you need a therapist in the worst way. I mean, you are just so far gone I don't even think a therapist can help you. But I'll tell you, I cannot help you, I'm too close to you, but I will give you the name of one of my best friends." And you know, someone says to you, what do you know? Maybe he's right. Okay, I'm going to this therapist, *mazal tov,* and he says to me, "I'm so glad you came, I need a rabbi so badly." And he starts telling me, "My mother! You wouldn't believe what she's doing to me!" In my mind I'm like, *"Oy!"* I'm sitting there for an hour and then he says, "I'm so glad you came, but it's 75 dollars, special price for rabbis." So what a chutzpa, you know! He wants to unload on me! That was the last time I went to a therapist.

But it's very crazy, you know, a lot of my friends literally stopped talking to me. And you know, I have a very deep feeling that for every friend I lost, I gained at least a hundred friends. I'll tell you something, one time, many years ago, someone insults me so much, and I said, "Maybe he's right, I'm not God, what do I know?" I went to Petach Tikva, and I'm sitting in a coffee shop. And I was thinking, "*Ribono Shel Olam*, maybe I am really wrong, what do I know?" Suddenly an old Yid'ele comes and sits next to me. With a high consciousness. He says to me, "Shlomo, I want you to know something. Many years from now, everybody will do what you are doing because there is no other way. But," he says, "I just bless you that they should remember that you were the first." An *alter Yid*. You know. I wouldn't say *mamesh* the first, but one of the first.

Reb Meire'le, I don't know if you know how much good you are doing for the world. I'm telling you. I'm gonna interview Reb Meire'le now!

M: (Mimi) There are a few things I want to say. One is that in the class that I was teaching tonight, in the end of the class one of the students said, "So what's so special about this Carlebach? How is he different from other Rebbes?" And I said that today, if you want to see a Rebbe, you have to go to see him. But there is only one Rebbe in the world who comes to see you. And that's Reb Shlomo.

S: Pretty good! I'll have to remember it.

M: And there is a story that I wrote this year, and in one place I describe you. And one of the pieces of the description is that Reb Shlomo is the kind of person that if you were about to jump off a bridge, and all you had was a dime in your pocket, that you would use that dime to call Reb Shlomo. And you can be sure that he will walk you off the bridge safely. So when I open a *sefer* and I don't understand something, I think that you have taught me the questions to ask. And if I don't have a question to ask, then if it's the Mei HaShiloach. I say, "*Heilige* Ishbitzer, either you answer me, or you tell me what Reb Shlomo would ask." And I wait for the question or the answer. But when I walk the streets, I don't even know what questions to ask. And I was hoping that right now maybe you could teach us what questions to ask on the streets. And how can we learn to walk the streets the way you walk the streets? And where do we draw the courage to open our hearts, like you said this morning that opening our hearts is also a kind of *hachnasat orchim* (welcoming guests). And how can we learn to open our hearts to every person on the street? What do you do? We'd like to learn from you.

S: Listen, Mimi, I'll tell you what. You are one of the people who *mamesh* doesn't have to learn by me. God gave you everything in your heart; you *mamesh* don't need me. But since you asked me, let's assume that you didn't know and I'll tell you, but I know you know. You see, one of the things, which I realized when I was in yeshiva, which is missing. There is a torah, *"b'shivtecha b'veitecha,"* when you sit in your home, and then there is a torah of *"uv'lechtecha b'derech,"* when you walk on the street, or the way. When I was in yeshiva, the torah of *"b'shivetecha b'veitecha"* I learned. *Gevaldt,* did I learn it. But the torah of *"uv'lechtecha b'derech"* nobody taught me. Nobody taught me what you do when you walk on the street. The only thing is I had a great privilege that I had a father who was a street-walker. My father, when he walked down the street, everyone was eager to talk to him. I remember, when I was a little boy, three or four years old, and sometimes my father would take us to a restaurant. Every waiter, every waitress came running and wanted to serve the table my father was sitting [at]. And my father would ask every waiter, every waitress, "How are you? What's your name?" And when they were bitter, or downhearted, or broken, he would give them so much strength. I remember when I was four, and you know, I wanted so much to be a rabbi, so I thought that this is what I am supposed to be doing as a rabbi. So imagine when we would go to this restaurant, I remember one time really. You know, my mother was not so much into street walking. When you go to the street you go to the store, buy it, and come home, that's it. So we are in this restaurant. I don't know why I didn't forget it, and you know, little kids run around. So you know, my father orders soup, and until the waiter brings it, I walk up to every table and begin shaking hands of all the people, asking them how they are, what's your name, what brings you here? You know, like I was so happy, I'm learning how to be a rabbi. And then suddenly I hear my mother's voice, "Shlomo! Come *zie fort* here — come immediately here!" And then my father would say, "Let them...." You know, my father would never argue. But you know, I think I mentioned it last week, I will tell Reb Meire'le. A Yid told me he walked on Broadway with my father, and a completely broken person, a woman in rags, I'm sure [if] she would look in the mirror she wouldn't even recognize herself, she walks up to my father and says, "You really have God's image." So my father says to her, "You have God's image." And then the woman — suddenly she didn't wear rags anymore.

So you know what it is, we are learning it a lot of times, this lifetime, it's the heaviest lifetime we ever had. According to our tradition, according to the Zohar, you come down three or four times. In an emergency, five. But in this lifetime, we re-meet all the people from previous lifetimes. And when I walk on the street, I want so much [to see] if there is anyone I'm supposed to meet, please don't let me pass this person by. And a lot of times it takes a lot of guts, it takes a lot of courage to stop a person on the street and say, "Hey, who are you?" Because it's crazy, right? Crazy. But I would say that 99 percent we are living in a more open world. And you know it took me a little while to not be afraid to stop people. And if I could say that God gave me a gift besides making up *niggunim* or learning, that God gave me the courage, not because of people but despite people, to stop them. And you know like, Mimi, you remember in Poland? You know Poland is 200 years behind America. And we got to talk to strangers. And you know, in Poland, when I gave concerts, I mean there were some Jews there also but 99 percent of the people were non-Jews. And suddenly the first time they see a Jew they didn't know how to handle it exactly. So here I walked up and I kissed every person. And you know for the first split second I wasn't frightened. On the other hand — you know when I arrived in Poland, you remember, Mimi? Television asked me, "What do you want to do in Poland?" I said I want to embrace and kiss every single human being in Poland. And I said that I want you to know that basically I am bringing you a message from my great-great-grandfather, the *Heilige* Bach, who was the Chief Rabbi in Krakow in 1640. But the saddest thing is that when he was alive, without hurting your feelings, you Polish people were not interested in listening to him. So now, so many years later, I am his great-grandson, and I have a very simple message. The message is there is only one God. And we all are brothers and sisters. The next morning, Mimi, I told you, I had jet lag, and I woke up at five in the morning. And the hotel was four stars, and on the other hand, down the street at the Intercontinental it was five stars. There the coffee shop was already open. I'm going in there, and the woman, the manager of the coffee shop walks up to me and says, "Aren't you the person who was yesterday on television? And you said you want to embrace every person? Can I please have a hug?" And then all the waitresses came, and it was the cutest. And then one waitress came to me, you know, with broken English, "I hate to ask you, but it would mean so much to me. I have three children. Could you wait until I bring them?" And, *gevaldt*, right? Remember when we came in Lodz, and thousands of people came, and I was mamesh standing by the door and kissing everyone who walks in. And I had the courage to kiss them even if they didn't want to. Because after I kissed them, they realized, "Ah, it was so good!"

I want you to know that when I came to Soweto (in South Africa), our Black brothers, they definitely don't know, it's not their fault, right, they don't know how to handle a white man. And it's unbelievable, I'm on television, and I get a call from Soweto, and there is like a house for ex-drug addicts, for ex-convicts, and ex-prostitutes. Hundreds. And even if they are out of it, they are still broken. And they invited the whole community. I should have taken everyone with me. And after about ten minutes, after kissing most of them, then the rest were like.... I have to tell you this one cute thing. They could not pronounce my name. Shlomo, it's hard for them to pronounce. The only thing is they know one Jew, Jesus, right? So after each song, "Thank you, Jesus. Thank you, Jesus." It was unbelievable.

Anyway, *l'chaim, l'chaim.* Mimi, I just want to tell you. *U'velechtecha b'derech,* I just want to bless you that all the people that are connected to your neshama, I know they are in the hundreds and thousands, I bless you to have the courage to stop them, for just "Hello." You see, the world always thinks that when you stop someone, you have to have an excuse, "Didn't I meet you somewhere? You look exactly like my sister's friend." But you don't need any excuses. Talk straight. "How are you? Who are you?" You know, my beautiful friends, there is a Zohar HaKodesh which is awesome. There are two questions you can ask another human being. What are you? And who are you? When you ask, "What are you?" you are destroying the world. When you ask, "Who are you?" you are building the world. I ask you, "What are you? Are you white, are you green, are you Jewish, are you not?" I ask, "Who are you?" Here the Zohar HaKodesh says the deepest Torah in the world. When you ask God, "What are You?" he doesn't answer. When you ask God, "Who are You — *mi bara eleh* (who created these)?" then the *Ribono Shel Olam* (Master of the Universe) answers.

R: I would like to ask Alan if he would like to ask a question.

Alan: (A few words are missing)...and we followed you all over. And they suddenly all disappeared. So I really didn't search for them, but suddenly years later when I was like fifteen years old I discovered those people and they looked completely Chassidic, long *peyos*, black hats, and, you know, but they belonged to another club, so I never really go to ask them if you are still in contact with Rav Shlomo. I know a few of these people, at least two, one of them I think you were the *mesader kedushin* (wedding officiant) also, and he is really known, they give him a lot of respect, but I cannot mention names, you don't see them any more in the public media. And I want to ask you if you see them, if you still see them? And the music is filmed so you see them only in the mystery.

S: It's a good question. I have to tell you two things. First of all, a lot of people who know nothing, right? Sometimes I deal with them. I mean, they know a lot in their hearts but when it comes to Yiddishkeit they don't know so much. And let's say I'm their first kindergarten teacher, right? So they think that I'm giving them kindergarten stuff. But then they have to grow up and go to university, right? The only thing is they don't know that I gave them university stuff. And they go to kindergarten stuff now. You know, without bragging, my weddings... beyond, beyond university. My weddings are really *gevaldt.* You know, I was, a lot of people I was *megayer* (converting), and they were at a lot of my weddings, and then they get married and they ask you, "How was the wedding?" "Oh, the dancing! It was a *gevaldt.*" The wedding is the dancing? What about the *chuppa?* What can you do about the *chuppa?* You know, you drink wine, you make a few *brachos*, and you go home. You know what it is? They think they got higher. And then they look at me and they think that I was just the beginning. And then there are kids who maybe broke away from me a little bit because they thought I'm giving them kindergarten stuff and they are looking for something better. Eventually they come back and they realize that maybe your stuff was a little bit higher.

This is one answer but I'll give you the real answer. I met this Russian doctor; it's a good torah. *Nebuch*, he came from Russia, his wife was not Jewish, and when, *nebuch*, he wanted to go to Israel, she divorced him. OK, good. He comes to Israel, and he wants so much to get married. He was the head of the hospital in Moscow, really. The top surgeon. But you know, Israel, they should live long and happy, when a big doctor comes and they have to give him a big position, *nebuch* they reduced him to a male nurse. Okay. He's a male nurse. I meet him. He says to me, "You know something? Rosh Hashanah was Thursday, Friday, Shabbos. And there are a lot of Sephardim who prepare real heavy food, right? And it doesn't all go into the refrigerator. And on Shabbos it was very hot. So you can imagine that if on Shabbos you eat food that was cooked on Wednesday, or Tuesday, that was not in the refrigerator. Let's not even talk about it." He said, "I had hundreds of people to whom I had to pump out their stomachs." And without sounding coarse, it doesn't smell like Chanel perfume, right? He says, "I was pumping out the stomach of a young lady. And I'll tell you something, it sounds stupid to you," he says, "I fell madly in love with her. She was just an angel from Heaven. But I couldn't ask her address or anything. The next day I'm going to Bank Leumi, I don't believe it; she's in front of me. So I said to her, 'Do you remember me?' When she saw me, she ran out." And he says to me, "Do you understand? She identifies me with the smell of her stomach. Because I pumped her out. And I'm part of that pumped out." And it gave me so much strength. All of the people who I pumped out their *goyishe* stomachs, then they go to yeshiva, and they identify me with their own smell. *Mazal Tov.*

R: It's a beautiful answer. I think there is another angle. While yours is a psychological interpretation of identification, there is something more disturbing. There is to do, to become, and to be. And what you're talking about in all your torahs is to be. That's the goal. And for these, they are coming in from wherever they were, to do. So they're getting stuck in the "to do." And they identify the "do" as higher than the "be." But we know that the purpose of the "do" is to become. So I think that, maybe I shouldn't be saying this in public. It is the be-havioral life-style which isn't being explained as a structure in which to become, to be. It becomes an end in itself and it inhibits, unless it's explained, or can inhibit, and that's why they have to come to an understanding.

S: Reb Meir, it's a very deep Torah you're saying. You know, there were times when it really did hurt me a little bit. I'm walking down Meah Shearim Street, and there I see, he's now a *Chasiddishe Youngerman*, I picked him up in Chicago. A real pick-upper, I met him somewhere, started talking to him. And I said to him, "Aren't you ashamed?" If I would have given you a million dollars five years ago, you would lick me, right? Even if now you are a rich man on your own, I gave you the Torah, I gave you Yiddishkeit, how dare you pass me by without saying thank you? I know a lot of kids I met in America sometimes, and I sent them to Israel. Not only I sent them to Israel, I paid their tickets. Because I knew that if I wait until their parents paid their tickets they would never go. They are learning in yeshivas. I can't believe it, it's like I don't exist. It's really a *chutzpah*, you know?

You know, when I got married, *baruch Hashem*, I wasn't short on people who sent me telegrams or sent me letters. I said to one girl, I picked her up; she was mamesh in the dumps. She was a Zen Buddhist and in the dumps, both together. You know what? We picked her up. We made a *mensch* out of her, we paid her ticket to New York. And she joined a certain group, *baruch Hashem,* she got married. Then I saw her one time on the street, and I said to her, "You know something, how can you hear that I got married without wishing me a *mazal tov*?" What is going on there? The essence of Yiddishkeit is being thankful. You know what a Jew is, a Yid? It comes from the word Yehuda, *"ha'pam odeh es Hashem"* 'this time I will thank God' — Gen. 29:35. I'm thanking God. And if you don't have the feeling of thankfulness to someone who gave you something, so what good is the whole Yiddishkeit? But you see, whenever — Rav Yehuda, whenever I'm sad about someone who doesn't talk to me, *baruch Hashem,* God helps me to meet two new people who I hope will talk to me, until they decide not to talk to me.

(Audience member) Could I ask you to sing the Krakover *Niggun?*

S: What's your name? Dovid! Dovid HaMelech! But if you could give me a real good harmony. (Sings Krakover *Niggun*) *Heilige zisse* Reb Meir. You know who was with us in Poland? Brother Yachad'el (Witt). You know, since the Second World War there was one Bar Mitzvah in Warsaw (there was one before him, but the boy didn't know anything). So Yachad was the first Bar Mitzvah in Warsaw in the shul. And *mamesh* Yachad'el was the top man on television, you remember? He had long *peya'lach (peyot* — sidelocks), *gevaldt!* I have to tell you something funny. Anyways they were following Yachad all over. When he arrived, the television came and they talked to him. The whole time the photographer said to me, "slim, slim, slim." And I felt so bad, [thinking] that means he wants me to lose weight! And I felt so bad, I said to him, "I promise when I come back next time I will be thinner." It turns out he meant "Smile!" So anyway, Yachad'el didn't need any slimming because his *peyos* were *gevaldt!* Yachad'el, we have to go back to Poland.

Batya Kallus: (Beginning of question is missing)...how you give over. This year I have had the privilege with my *chevrusa* to be learning a lot. And we have been learning some Gemaras. And one of the things I have come to learn is that the most important thing is the question — about the Gemara, the *sefer* (book) or whatever you have been learning. And I wanted to ask you, when you are learning a *sefer,* what are the questions that you ask?

S: I want to taste the depths of it. I think, *"Gevaldt,* what is he saying?" You are talking more Rashi and Tosafot (on the Talmud). Sometimes it sounds so simple. It can't be. If it's simple, Rashi is not going to waste his words. And with the Mei HaShiloach (complex Hasidism) every word is [filled with depth and meaning]. Every word of our tzaddikim, *zichronam l'vrocha* (of blessed memory) is filled with so much depth. I had this Rebbe, Shlomo Hyman, when he would say, "one and one is two," it would throw you in the abyss of depth (whispers something). It's really true, one and one is two! And there were some people who were not so deep, they would say, "He didn't say anything." But for those who knew what he said, everything in the world is deep. And I can only bless you, if you have good questions, good. But the deepest question should be inside of you, "Have I tasted the depth of what the Torah says?" And you see, the moment you start asking for the depth, you are already knocking on the door. You know, every letter opens a different door. Can I tell them one more *gevaldt* story? *L'koved Shabbos* — it's Thursday night. It's *gevaldt.* I'll make it fast.

You know one of the biggest *geonim* (geniuses) in Hungary was named Rav Avram Aryeh. He became one of the greatest *geonim* in Hungary, and he became a big Sanzer Hasid. But here he was learning in Pressburg. He was 16 years old. And you know, the Chasam Sofer, they were not *misnagdim* (opponents to Hasidism), and they were not Hasidim, they were all great Kabbalists. So the Chasam Sofer saw he was *mamesh* into Shabbos, so he says to him, "Avram Aryeh, I see you are really into Shabbos. If you want to have a real Shabbos, you've got to go to Sanz." So Rav Avram Aryeh thought, in Pressburg, you know what is going on, *mamesh* two hours before *licht bentchen* (candle lighting time) the whole Yeshiva is there learning. Then they *daven Maariv* (the evening prayer), they eat, and then they learn all night. The next morning they *daven,* they eat, they learn, like one Shabbos you learn 48 hours. So he assumes that in Sanz, if the Shabbos is even better, that means they are learning 150 hours per minute. *Oy gevaldt,* was he mistaken. He is coming to Sanz two hours before Shabbos, it's chaos! One is falling over the other running to the *mikveh.* This one doesn't know where to eat, this one has no *kretchmer* (lodging). He says, *"Oy Vey!* Stupid me, why didn't I stay in Pressburg!?" Anyway, the chaos is over, they don't *daven* on time, it's already two hours after Shabbos [came in]. But you can't say that the *Maariv* wasn't a *gevaldt,* by the holy Sanzer. And *baruch Hashem,* they begin to learn! But the Sanzer's tisch (table) was perhaps 4 hours after Shabbos [began]. Everyone takes out a Gemara, and without being bold, but you have to watch me a little bit. So everyone begins to learn, so he also begins to learn. Suddenly he looks around, and sees that the Gemaras are not open! Everyone had a Gemara, and everyone was sitting with closed eyes. They are lunatics or something! They are sitting here, they have a Gemara and they don't open it! He keeps watching, and it's driving him absolutely crazy! Suddenly someone picks up a Gemara and starts saying, *"Heilige Shabbos! Zisse Shabbos! Heilige Shabbos, Zisse Shabbos!"* ('Holy Shabbat, Sweet Shabbat'!) And then someone from another corner of the *Beis Medresh* (study hall) also picks up a Gemara and starts beating it on the table (while chanting over and over again), *"Heilige Shabbos, Zisse Shabbos..."*. And finally, after two or three hours, everyone is banging on the table and saying, *"Heilige Shabbos, Zisse Shabbos!"* And he can't help it, but suddenly he himself is doing it, shouting, *"Heilige Shabbos! Zisse Shabbos!"* And he thinks, he can't understand himself, "I'm supposed to be a normal person, this is crazy." Okay, word got out around one o'clock at night that the Sanzer is coming to the table. And this is wild. He tries to stand behind the Sanzer.

Now the Holy Sanzer knows the souls of every person. After Kiddush the Sanzer turns around and says to him, "Hey, *youngerman* (Yiddish for young newly married man), let me tell you something. In the palace of the King there is so much light. Some people walk in, and the first door they open, the room is full of light, and they are so happy to stay there. Then someone opens another door, more light, and they stay there. And some people are looking for more light. It's all beautiful. But then there is someone who is not looking for light. He is looking for the King. He goes through all the doors until he finds the King himself. So do you understand, *youngerman?* During the week, we are all looking for light, for the light of the Torah. On Shabbos I am looking for God himself."

And then, something wild. The holy Sanzer put his hand on Avram Aryeh's shoulder, and he says, "*Der herst, youngerman?* (Did you hear, young man?) On Shabbos, "*zuch min der Heilige bashefer alayn*" 'looking for God Himself.' And many years later — this happened on *Parshas Balak* — and every year on *Parshas Balak,* Rav Avram Aryeh assembled his grandchildren, and they would be there for Shabbos, and he would tell them this story. Then he would say (pointing to his shoulder), "Can you imagine, just here on my shoulder, the Holy Sanzer touched me and said, 'You are looking for God Himself!?'" And then all the grandchildren would come and they would kiss that spot where the holy Sanzer told him. I want you to know that one of his great-grandchildren lives now in Williamsburg. And he came out with — I have to find it — a *toldos* (history) of his grandfather. And he writes in the foreword that his father was one of the grandchildren who kissed his grandfather's shoulder, where the holy Sanzer taught him that.

R: Reb Shlomo, I want to bless you that your answer to Batya was, sure the questions are a way of understanding. But real understanding is for the piece to become a part of you, what you would call, "it reached the inside of the inside," and what I would call internalized. And it needn't be said to you, that all the thousands of people whom you have touched, people who would appear to be at the edges of the Jewish people, you have produced people who have internalized everything that you have wanted [for them to be]. So it's no longer a question of knowledge, it's a question of being. You have *talmidim* (students) in Yerushalayim who live your Torah. Not necessarily consciously, I mean even the way they talk without realizing it, it's "Shlomo-ese," as it were. Yet on the other side they have totally internalized your torah, and we come here with great appreciation for what you have done.

S: Thank you so much, Rav Meir'el. Meir, you're the best! Let's sing one more time "*Yehi Shalom*" to connect to the beginning. (Sings *Yehi Shalom B'cheileich*) Carol, my cutest cousin.

Cousin Carol: I want to ask, since you're my Rebbe, Mimi taught me for so long...and when I hear Mimi speaking about you as a way, then I react against that, because it doesn't feel like what you taught me. So I want to ask you first if you really want it to be a way, and does it make it right, for everyone to be "*Gevaldt, mamesh.*" At that level, it's a mimicking way. If you were to ask us something about getting inside and holding something. But what I really feel, to be my own way is more daring. So I want you to bless all of us here, say yes to us. Say yes to us, "Yes, I want you to be your own way."

S: Listen, Carol. Sugar pie. Let me tell you something. You know, I don't want to say anything good or bad. I couldn't do it here, because it didn't come out. In my shul, you know my Shabbos, everyone who wants to say Torah says Torah. I want everyone to say their own, I don't want them to say over my Torah. I never asked anybody, "Can you please say over what I said last week?" I always ask, "What do you have to say?" If someone says "You said something, and I forgot it, maybe you can remind me." I don't want bagel *chevre,* where everyone looks like the other one. And 100 percent, we need everybody to have their own thing. And Rav Meir'el didn't mean to say that I want everybody to chew over my Torah'las. And whenever I say something that everyone should (roll their eyes heavenward) and say, "*Gevaldt, modim anachnu lach"* 'We are thankful to You, God'. But what Rav Meir'el meant that from our *chevre,* there is a certain sweetness. I don't know if I have it, but our *chevre* is *mamesh* sweet. And a certain openness.

You know, in my shul, *baruch Hashem,* I am sure in Yakar also, I can trust my *chevre.* People ask me, "How much do you trust your *chevre?*" I tell them, "I trust them so much that if I sent them to the Eskimos, then all the Eskimos would be keeping Shabbos next week." Not because they would convert to Yiddishkeit, but because if you gave them a taste of Shabbos, they would see that it is so good. What do you say, Rav Meir'el?

R: Rav Shlomo was explaining this morning the difference between *chochmah* (wisdom), *binah* (understanding), and *da'at* (knowing). And I don't know exactly what words he said. But what he was saying in my terminology is that there is a level of *da'at* where there is no gap between knowledge and being. One has an idea, and until the idea takes within — *niklat* (is absorbed, conceived) — still, one can give a big speech, say the ideas, but they are not the person. There is a level of *da'at,* after *binah,* way after *chochmah,* where there is no gap between the idea and the person. So what I was saying was that there are some people who have totally internalized *Chassidus,* where it isn't a question of, "I have knowledge," but that there is no gap between knowledge and being. When I ask myself, "Who was the stimulant, who caused that?" That must be the greatest confidence that what one is giving is *emes* (truth).

S: Listen, Carol, if you would just chew over what I said, you would be nothing. *Baruch Hashem,* God opens gates for you. You have a big *neshama,* and *mamesh gevaldt* ideas. I am sure you are again giving *chizuk* to (strengthening) a lot of people. So when I meet someone who you gave *chizuk* to, I wouldn't say, "it's an imitation of Carol." But I would still say, "it's a little bit a *hasid* of Carol, right?" Because you gave them *chizuk*. You know what Reb Nachman of Breslov says, the greatest gift that you can give to someone is self-confidence. And I just hope we are giving it to each other.

You know there was a time when the Rebbes thought that the more you knocked someone else off (the more you criticized, reproved) the *frummer* (more religious) you (they) would get. But the time for knocking people off is long over. What the world needs today is someone to tell them, "You are a *gevaldt* (you are great), you are good, you are sweet." Right? Rav Meir, what do you say? You are the expert.

R: I think one imitates to be reassured, and that must be the kiss of death. But I think that what you do project is very much the idea that one has to be real. And there is an almost anarchistic element in your teaching, which is [the idea of] not to be taken in by society. It's almost to be an outsider to society. Or prepared to be. It's clear to me that if you had only played a different tune the establishment would have adopted you, but then you wouldn't have been you.

S: (Almost asking in earnest) Do you think I missed out?

R: I generally believe...there was once a great Rabbi called Shakespeare. Shakespeare said, "This above all: to thine own self be true, And it must follow, as the night the day, Thou canst not then be false to any man." (*Hamlet*, I. iii.)

S: (Joking) And he was English, right? (Because R. Meir Rosen was British.) Remember the *Heilige* Rav Mordechai Lechovitcher, when he passed away? So his son, Rav Noach, became his successor. His father would say *hamotzi* (the blessing over the bread) over 12 challahs, and he would say it over two. Someone said, "You're not like your father!" He said, "No, I am exactly like my father. My father would never imitate anyone, and neither do I." But you know what really bugs you and me among the so-called religious people? They *mamesh* imitate each other. It's sometimes so far from real. A lot of Rebbes... everyone says the same thing. I just hope Reb Meir'el, I bless that all the people we meet will have the courage never to imitate anything. I bless you and me that we shouldn't imitate each other, we shouldn't even imitate ourselves. Because we are so easily imitating our yester-days. And it's stupid, right? I mean, yesterday was yesterday.

I don't know if I told you, my Rebbe, Reb Shlomo Hyman, anyone who learned *Kesubos* (in the Talmud) properly — Batya, you're learning Gemara? *Kesubos*, you learned already? No? Well, someday. Yachad'el learned already, Betzalel, hopefully you will learn *Kesubos*. It's the deepest, right? *Kesubos* is called, the "little *SHaS*" (the little Talmud). Everything is in there. So, *daf nun vav* (p. 56), it's the *sugya* (passage) called *tenai b'mamon* (conditions regarding money), it has one of the longest Tosafot in *SHaS* (*Sheis Sidrei Mishna* — the Six Orders of the Mishna). We learned that Tosafos for six weeks. And not chewing over yesterday's. But we learned that Tosafos like we had never learned Tosafos before. And finally, after six weeks, we got to turn the page. I had the privilege of being very close to him (Rav Hyman), I walked into his room. And behold, he's learning the Tosafos from the begin-ning again for himself. I said, "Rebbe, you learned the Tosafos now for six weeks. Now you're learning it again?" So he says to me, "Remem-ber what I'm telling you. If you ever want to be a *lamdan,* if you ever want to be a scholar, just remember, whatever you knew yesterday is meaningless today." Whatever I knew yesterday is nothing, I mean it's good, but today, I need so much deeper. God should bless us, we should be new every day. (Sings a *niggun*. Then R. sings a *niggun* that Reb Shlomo doesn't know.)

S: That is a beautiful *niggun*, whose is that, is that yours?

R: I'm a *kabtzan* (a beggar, a "collector"). You create, I collect.

S: It was a *gevaldt niggun*. Whose *niggun* was it?

R: This is a *niggun* you end off *Lecha Dodi* with — because it always leaves something. *"Habocher b'shirei zimra"* 'Who chooses song' *"Sheya'alei zimra"* 'that song should raise' what words cannot express.

S: It was *k'dai* (worth it) to sit all this time just to hear this *niggun.*

(Inaudible question)

S: Reb Shlomo Hyman? You know how much he was into learning? Anything that did not have to do with learning Torah, he threw out from his head. He didn't want it to occupy space. Do you know that he didn't even know his own address? A person who remembered *SHaS* backwards and forward didn't remember his own address! We heard it from a person...his eyes were half open (walking home). He knew it was the first right, the first left, and then it was his house. One day he got lost, and he finds himself in another street. He walks up to a Yid and says, "Do you know someone by the name of Shlomo Hyman?" The Yid says, "He's the biggest Rosh Yeshiva in the world." Rav Hyman says, "Do you know where he lives?" He says, "Would you please bring me to his house?" The Yid says, "Sure, I'd be very happy." He takes him to his house, and when the Rebbetzin opens the door, he realizes that it's Reb Shlomo Hyman. And he told it to people.

I have to tell you two things about him. Didn't I tell you last time about the way he was treating the *bocherim* (yeshiva students)? In the Beis Midrash there were a few hundred, but in his *shiur* there were forty or fifty. What happens if a boy asks a stupid question? What do you do? First of all you don't waste your time, because there are forty of fifty kids sitting there, so why waste time on something stupid? You try to answer it as fast as possible. Here is the story. I had the privilege of sitting right in front of him. I want you to know, *nebuch, nebuch,* his wife was in labor, Kremechuk was her name (the name of the town), and a pogrom broke out. And they were killing people left and right. He carried her *mamesh* with his hands to a wagon and a horse and they drove into the forest. But they had nothing there. And *nebuch,* the baby died. And she was injured for life so she couldn't have children any more. I want you to know, I have never seen a person giving his wife so much *kavod* (honor). But what he did every year, with two or three young men who were the best in that year, he would like adopt them. So I had the privilege, the last year of his life, I was adopted by him. I was always in his house. The Rebbetzin was like my assistant mother.

I want to share something special with you. In Yiddish you say, "a *holtz kop.*" His head is like wood, nothing goes in, nothing goes out. So I was sitting in front of him, and next to me there was a *holtz kop, mamesh* modeling for wooden heads. And you know, this boy was so sweet inside. And to open your mouth when Reb Shlomo gives a *shiur* takes a lot of courage. The boy doesn't open his mouth, and everybody knew he doesn't know anything. His parents paid for the yeshiva, and he was learning. Maybe he does know, maybe he doesn't know. One day we were learning something, and suddenly I couldn't believe my ears, he opened his mouth, like God opened the mouth of [Bil'am's donkey?]; he asked the most stupid question you could imagine. I mean you have to be a genius in stupidity to ask such a stupid question. I'm sitting there, I'm trying not to laugh. I look around, everyone's looking down. And I remember, he (Rav Hyman) didn't want people to laugh, so he's making like this (like he is thinking), beginning to eat the hair of his beard, so as not to put the boy to shame. Then he says to him, "You know something, it's an unbelievable question you are asking." And he says to them, "Let me explain to them what you are asking." And he fabricated a *gevaldt kasha* (challenging question). It had nothing to do with this boy. But *mamesh,* he was glowing, this boy, that he gave him so much *kavod* (honor). A few months later I left for Lakewood, but Rav Shlomo Hyman, *nebuch,* he had cancer; it should never happen to anybody, he passed away. You know what year that was?

'44. Forty years later, maybe '84, '85, I'm sitting on a plane going from Tel Aviv to New York. And someone says to me, "Do you know that this very big Rosh Yeshiva is on the plane?" Big Rosh Yeshiva, I want to see him. I get up and say hello to him, and it's my *holtz kop!* And we started talking to each other. He says, "Shlomo, let me tell you the truth. You know that nothing entered my head. It was blocked. You remember when I asked Reb Shlomo that question, and he was so good to me, treated me with so much *kavod?* He gave me so much strength, that I decided I really wanted to learn. And now I am, *baruch Hashem,* a top Rosh Yeshiva." He is a top Rosh Yeshiva, *mamesh* a big *lamdan* (scholar). Anyway, we need more Rosh Yeshivas like this. Reb Meir, what's the story, this is it? You're coming back? Okay, does anybody here want to ask me the most unbelievable question in the world?

Devora: What do you miss about that world (the Yeshiva world)?

S: You know what I miss? Anyone who has not really learned Gemara, Rashi, and Tosafos, cannot imagine the heavenliness of learning Gemara. Then you see the Rambam and the Ravad, and it's pushing all the buttons in your heart and your head. You know what I miss? I just told someone. You know the way I was living in Lakewood? I would go to sleep at quarter to twelve, try to go to sleep. At 2:30, my *chevrusa* would wake me up, and we would learn until seven. I have to tell you the sad truth, I davened fast, because the learning only began at 9:30, so I had a chance to sleep until 9:30. And they would bring me a little breakfast, I would somehow manage to eat, and we would learn until 2. By 2 I was at the end, I went to sleep until 4. I never ate lunch, I never had time to eat, because the *chevre* would bring me something to eat. Then at 4 I'm learning again until 9:30. 9:30, you *daven ma'ariv* and eat, and then we are learning until a quarter to twelve.

Do you know what I miss the most? We were up, learning, at 2:30, do you know how beautiful it is? You open the windows, *mamesh* you can hear the birds singing, you are singing a little gemara'la, you're singing their gemara, you know? It was so peaceful, so holy. And it was so holy that you cannot imagine you ever want to be without it. Or you know something? I don't know if any of you know how beautiful it is *mamesh* to make up a *torah.* You learn a Rambam which is *mamesh* the opposite of the Gemara and then you realize, you don't know how many nights I spent writing, writing, writing, writing. I have whole closets full of torahs. And I really do regret it, my father always told me, "Why don't you come out with a *sefer* already?" But it's so good. You know the Torah is so good, every Jew can make up a new torah. Every Jew can mamesh pave his own way in the Gemara. Pave his own way and compare, *"medame milsa le'milsa"* 'comparing one thing to another', I always knew that it would come to a point where…you can *mamesh* lose your mind over it.

I once had the privilege of hearing from Rav Yose Ber (Solovechik), and I really knew it before I heard it from him, because when I was in San Francisco, the kids, it was terrible, you know, LSD, blows your mind, I said, "Let me tell you something. LSD is *gevaldt.* But it does not compare to the way the Gemara blows my mind. God forbid, when you take LSD if you take one zillionth of an ounce more than you could take, you could injure yourself for life. It's *mamesh* dangerous. But let's assume you know exactly how much you can take, cleans out your *neshama*, lifts up your head. It doesn't compare to Gemara and Tosafos. It doesn't compare to Friday night. I want you to know that the top LSD man, brother Tim Leary, at one point I was very close to him. We were always talking to each other. You know, one of his torahs was in the *New York Times.* He said when you take LSD, and someone puts on some Beethoven, he starts yelling, "Ludwig, get off!" He says, "but I want you to know, a lot of times when I'm taking LSD I'm putting on your records. It's good stuff." But anyway, when I was in San Francisco, a lot of times brother Tim Leary came Friday night. And he said, "I want you to know, my whole life I am looking for something that would turn on people completely without drugs. You know something, I'm not Jewish, but I think you Jewish people have something. I see that Shabbos can turn on people completely, without drugs." I don't know if some of you remember, in the year 63-64, for two years brother Tim Leary would give lectures at the Second Avenue theater. Thousands of kids, it was a *gevaldt*, he considered himself a high priest. We were talking lots of times, I would tell him, you know, "Tim, you're a *gevaldt*, but I wish I could put in your heart how it tastes, when I'm learning, and I see the Rambam is saying the opposite, then suddenly, you know, it blows my mind a thousand times."

You know, when Rav Shlomo Hyman would give a shiur, it was 20 times LSD. But I'll tell you something else, my second Rebbe was Rav Aharon (Kotler), I mean Rav Aharon was bigger than Rav Hyman. You know, someone spoke to Rav Aharon, not a Jewish person, and he said that this man is at least seven times Einstein. It was awesome to talk to him. I learned by him for six years. And I was really like one of his closest pupils. So you would think I'd talked to him a lot of times, right? You are mistaken. When I would stand in front of him my teeth would chatter. Physically, literally. Here I am, seventeen years old, I learned by Rav Shlomo, and Rav Shlomo *nebuch gevaldt* he knew that he was very sick. He called up Rav Aharon because he didn't want me to get lost, because he knew he was *mamesh* not coming back, *nebuch, gevaldt.* So Rav Aharon calls up my father and he says, "I spoke to Rav Shlomo, and Rav Shlomo wants to send your son to Lakewood." Okay, I'm going there. My Rebbe said so and he was already in the hospital. He had no idea that he was so sick, he just knew he was sick. I come to Rav Aharon, Rav Aharon says, "You know, when you come to yeshiva you have to talk and learn, you have to say something." So Rav Aharon says to me, "Tell me something." Anything, you know! My teeth were chattering. I'm sitting there, and I don't know what to do with myself.

Then I *mamesh* begin trembling — I am talking to the biggest giant in learning! And he didn't want to put me to shame so he pretended like he's looking in the siddur, and from time to time he looks at me and I'm still shivering. So he says to me like cool it. He says, "You don't have to tell me anything. Because if Rav Shlomo says you should come learn with me, I trust his judgment. Just come. I want you to learn by me (*Fir durst by mir lern*)." You know the way he was saying shiur was 5,000 times Rockefeller Center. And he would talk so fast, if you missed out one minute, you could hang yourself. That's it, you lost it. And I have to brag, after a certain while, I was really so close to him. I had the privilege, by God's grace, I was so close to him that I *mamesh* knew his way in learning. And I have this kind of stupidity, where I'm sitting down, and I know already what was happening, I fall asleep. So a lot of times during his *shiur* I would fall asleep, I knew what he was going to say. Just for a second, I would fall asleep. And one time I had the privilege, I was tuned to him on his wavelength, and some rich man wanted to come and give money for the yeshiva, wanted to see one of his top students, so Rav Aharon pointed me out to him. Later the rich man says to him, "I saw him sleeping while you were talking." So Rav Aharon says to him, Okay, I don't want to brag about what he says. I was so close to him, he *mamesh* shaped my brains. Only from time to time I had the privilege that he would ask me, "So, did you like what I said today?" It's like Einstein asks me, "Did you like my theory?"

And really, if you ask me about my personal life, here comes the Lubavitcher Rebbe, and he asks me to stop learning and go out into the world. I mean, he didn't say, "Stop learning." But to leave the yeshiva and go out into the world! So I said, "What's going to be with my learning?" I'm training to be top learning. He says, "Forget about yourself." I can only tell you, I don't know what happened to me, but the Rebbe *mamesh* put a new *neshama* into my heart. Because until the Rebbe told me, "Go out," I mean, I loved people, but I really didn't care, I *mamesh* didn't care. I cared only to learn, learn, learn. I had this dream I had to be the biggest *lamdan* in the world. I was learning day and night. And I thought, *bezras Hashem,* when I'd be on the level of opening a yeshiva, I'd take the best best *bocherim* of all the yeshivas, and I'd be learning like crazy. Suddenly I walk out, becoming a clown — not really — like a holy clown. Talking to every person, every person I met, "Hey, what's going on?" When did I start going to Lubavitch? I must have been 24 or 25.

[Question] When we were in Vienna, before we left for America, we met one Yid, his name was Rav Moishe. Everyone called him Moishele Good Shabbos. I don't know if you know this *niggun* I'm singing, Moishele Good Shabbos. He was always like (sings) "Good Shabbos, Good Shabbos, etc." I got to put it on a real good tape, I didn't do it yet. And he taught us that he heard in Lublin that this was the *niggun* with which Rebbe Nachman davened. The sad truth is I asked a lot of Breslover Hasidim, and they never heard of it. So I don't know after the whole thing is over, if it's because all the big Breslover Hasidim are not here anymore. You know that after the First World War, the headquarters of Breslov Hasidim was not in Breslov, you couldn't get there, so they were homeless. Suddenly, in 1929, when Rav Meir Shapira made the Lubliner Yeshiva, he made it the headquarters of Breslover Hasidim. That means that on Rosh Hashanah all the Breslover Hasidim would come to Lublin. So this Rav Moishe said he heard it in Lublin. But on the other hand, maybe it was his own *niggun* and he didn't want to make himself so big. So then we were little, but slowly slowly, we heard Reb Nachman and again Reb Nachman.

I shlep a lot of Reb Nachman. Sometimes other *seforim,* Isbitzer, Tiferet Shlomo. Rav Yehuda, we *mamesh* have to become good friends again. You haven't spoken to me in so long.

[Question] You see, we met the old Lubavitcher Rebbe in Vienna when we were kids. And he told us three things. He told us to sleep with our *tsitsis*, *bentch* from a *siddur*, and he said, "Become Hasidishe kids, don't be German kids." So we considered ourselves already Lubavitcher Hasidim. And then, when the Rebbe came to America in '41, and my father was a rabbi in Crown Heights, at Young Israel, we went to *daven* in Lubavitch. And it was, to be absolutely honest with you, I was absolutely torn apart. Because on one hand I wanted to learn day and night, and on the other hand, Rav Aharon was the biggest *misnagid* (opponent) of Lubavitch. You see, he believed that the big *mistnagdus* (opposition) of the Vilna Gaon to Hasidus was only the Alter Rebbe (the first Lubavitcher). He said Lubavitch was *mamesh* paganism. He said according to *halakhah* it's *emes* (truly) *avoda zara* (idolatry). And here I'm learning in Lakewood, Rav Aharon is my Rebbe in learning, but *avodas Hashem,* how to *daven,* Shabbos…. So I was absolutely torn apart. My brother was with me in Lakewood, and he couldn't stand it, so he went to Lubavitch. I held out. Sometimes it's good for people to live with a conflict all the time. Anyways, finally I left Lakewood and went to Lubavitch, by the present Rebbe [R. Menachem Mendel Schneerson]. And only history will tell if I did the right thing or not.

And you know what bugs me? I look around and see what the Rosh Yeshivas are dishing up today. And without bragging, I know if I would have stayed learning, I would have said so much better. Not better, just so much deeper. So much wider. I'll tell you something — when I was learning by Rav Aharon, right, and I was talking to other big Rosh Yeshivas, without mentioning names, I remember I walked into one Rosh Yeshiva, and they were learning *Bava Basra.* He says, "Do you want to tell me something?" Okay, I said we were just learning now this Rambam. Rav Aharon had seven ways of saying *p'sak* on this Rambam. I am not comparing myself to Rav Aharon, but I was like, I had a completely different approach to Rambam. Thirteen ways.

I told this to the Rosh Yeshiva, who was supposed to be one of the biggest. After the third way he stops me and he says, "You know, you are a *talmid* (student) of Rav Aharon. I am not. I don't have the head to listen to all of this. I can't." I told myself, *gevaldt,* this is already a big Rosh Yeshiva. And I knew in my heart that if he is 50,000 feet high, then I'm five million feet high. It's a different kind of learning, like high school teaching and super graduate, something else, right? So sometimes it hurts me. I'm talking to *bocherim*, it's deep...ahh, it's not. And I think to myself, on the other hand, maybe, like Lubavitch says, you may not worship idols, but you can become an idol yourself. Who knows, I could have become a big *avoda zara* myself. Thinking, "Ah, I'm such a big *lamdan.*" It's possible, maybe God prevented me. But also, what happened to all the *chevre*? I would never have met them. I would never have had the heart to tell someone to keep Shabbos, I would have been in the yeshiva learning day and night, and I would tell my *bocherim* you have to learn day and night. And when you walk down the street, run fast, because the street is evil. Make it fast and come home. Maybe that's not what my *neshama* needs, I don't know.

[Comment]

Listen, Marilyn, you always say the best things, but I also wanted to learn so much. We all have complexes. But again, imagine, if I had stayed in Lakewood I would never have been in Yakar, right? I would have missed Reb Meir'el, I would have missed Mimi, I would have missed Carol, I would have missed Manchester. Anyway, I want you to bless me and I'll bless you back that whatever we are dreaming that we could have done, we should still do it. Because God can open gates in the most unbelievable way. And it's clear to me that the same way we have today airplanes and missiles, and a hundred years ago we didn't have it, you know the physical and the spiritual and the divine — it's the same. Whatever maybe our forefathers could learn in ten years, maybe we could learn in a few hours. Our *neshama.* What do you want to say, Menachem?

S: Because I was never thinking of getting *semicha,* I was never into it. I don't need papers. It may be a chutzpah to say so, but what do I need it for? So one day the Lubavitcher Rebbe says to me, when I was still working for him, "Shlomo, I don't want to see you until you get *semicha.*" And I was talking to the Rebbe every day; it means I need *semicha* in a few days. I went to Rav Moshe Feinstein, it was Chanukah time, and he told me that he wants to give me *semicha,* but until *Chol HaMoed Pesach* I don't have a minute to myself. You know, Rav Moshe would answer teshuvas day and night, it was a miracle he was alive because maybe he slept an hour a day. Not because he was learning, he was answering teshuvas for the whole world. He carried all of Israel on his shoulders. So I cannot wait from Chanukah until Pesach to see the Rebbe. So I walked in at the Lubavitcher Yeshiva, he doesn't live anymore, Bukowski, he was a big *lamdan* but he really didn't know what's going on in yeshivas. He says to me, and here I am already learning by Rav Aharon for six years, he says to me, "To tell you the truth, they will only give *semicha* to someone who has already learned at least three or four *masechtas* (tractates of the Talmud)." [break in film] Not that I didn't know him, I walked into Rabbi Hutner, Rav Hutner was a genius *sh'b'*genius *sh'b'*genius. He was not a Gaon, he never made it to be a Gaon, but he was an *Illui* all his life. Someone said to me, the three biggest *Illuiim* of the last generation were Rav Yosa Ber (Yosef Dov) Soloveitchik, the Lubavitcher Rebbe, and Rav Hutner. Rav Aharon was beyond Illui and Gaon, Rav Aharon was.... So anyway, I walked into Rabbi Hutner, he was very cute, but he liked very much to tell people what to do. And you know I'm sitting there and I don't know what to do, I'm putting one foot on the other like this. Then like this. I never spoke to him before, I said hello. And you know, to give *semicha* to a person is heavy stuff. You don't give *semicha* in the air. He says to me, "So what do you want?" I start stammering, "Would you maybe give me *semicha*?" He says to me, "Okay, tell me something." Then I regained my self-confidence. I said to him, "I should tell you something. I can chew over the outside Torah, maybe I have a good memory for saying what someone else said." So he said, "Okay, what would you do if you would be I?" That is one of his classic switch-overs to the other person. "Imagine you would be I and I would be you." He was sitting like where Mimi is and between us was a *SHaS*. I said. "If I would be you, I would close my eyes and take out one Gemara, put it on the table, and let it open by itself. And wherever it opens, I would tell you come back in three days and tell me some Torah on that page." So he says, "Okay, I'll do this." I don't know if he really closed his eyes or pretended like he did. He took out the Gemara *Chullin*, and it opened on *"ta'am k'ikkar"* That's a big *sugya*. If something is not *chazer*, but it tastes like *chazer*. Something is not shrimp, but it tastes like shrimp. That means every little part of the shrimp has to be taken out. But it still tastes like shrimp. It's a big *sugya* in the whole *SHaS*. So *mamesh* I am learning it like crazy. After three days I call him up. He says I want you to know that I *mamesh* have fever, but call me back in three days. In the meantime I was up day and night learning. I didn't want to get *semicha* for nothing. I brewed up a long torah, which was *mamesh* 72 Rambam and Ravads. So I'm coming to Rabbi Hutner, but also Rabbi Hutner was not a pupil of Rav Aharon. I mean he was a big Gaon, but he was not accustomed to this kind of learning. After twenty minutes he says, "I know already how much you know, I'll give you *semicha*." I said, "Rav Hutner, it's not fair, I am up day and night, day and night, I am making this whole torah, and you don't want to hear it?" So he says, "Okay, I'll listen to it." I'm knocking off the whole torah, left and right, and he says to me, "Come back in two weeks." This is really beautiful. I come back in two weeks, and his Rebbetzin opens the door, and he's sitting there at his table. And there were two candles on the table, and a little wine. The light was dim. And he says, I don't remember the words, but *semicha* is *mamesh* connecting you to Moshe Rabbeinu. Because he got *semicha* from his Rebbe, and from his Rebbe. In Ishbitz there is a lot of talk about *semicha*. When Moshe Rabbeinu gave Yehoshua *semicha*, it was the first *semicha*. *"Vesamach yadav — venasata me'hodcha"* 'and he placed his hands, and he gave from his majesty'. It's *mamesh* not to be believed. I could trace it back with names, Moshe to Yehoshua, Yehoshua to the *Z'keinim* (the elders), and Rabbi Hutner got from his Rebbe, Rav Moshe Mordechai, and Rabbi Hutner is giving me *semicha*.

I want you to know who was Rabbi Hutner's Rebbe. Rav Moshe Mordechai finished *SHaS* every two months. But not sitting by the Gemara; by the Gemara he was learning other things. He just knew the *SHaS* by heart, and he was saying it over like it's *Ashrei*, right? He finished the four sections of the *Shulchan Aruch* every six weeks. I mean, it was beyond. I remember Rav Moshe Mordechai once came to Vienna, and we lived at the outskirts, and he came to visit my father. And he was sitting in a chair, and hundreds of people came to see him. And he was so *aidel,* so humble. He answered everyone who asked him, but while the person was talking, his lips were moving. He was going over *SHaS,* fast, fast, fast. It was awesome, you know, I was five or six years old when I saw this. I can't forget it. This is a Yid who was like a living Torah. Can you imagine how often he finished *SHaS* in his lifetime? How often he learned *Shulchan Aruch?* So, take it or leave it, I got *semicha* from Rabbi Hutner. So it was *mamesh,* a very holy moment. You know, today some people get *semicha* by the mail. They ask you a few kashas in Yore Deah, and then they send you *semicha* in the mail. And *mamesh* he gave me *semicha,* and then he gave me this paper in my hands. Rabbi Hutner, he was very much, in a holy way, into *kavod* (honor). You talked to him, you don't turn around and walk out. You had to walk out backwards. And if you had the *chutzpah* to walk straight, he would call you back and say, "Wait." He said it angry but with a smile.

Then for one year I was very close to Rabbi Hutner. Talked to him all the time, talked to him about Lubavitch. You know, my Bubba lived in Berlin with my uncle, and every Shabbos afternoon she had three guests who would eat by her Shabbos lunch, Rav Yossa Ber (Soloveitchik), the Lubavitcher Rebbe, and Rabbi Hutner. I want you to know, who was leading the conversation? My Bubba! My Bubba was not a genius, my Bubba was a super-super-genius. First of all, she spoke five or six languages. She knew German literature, English, French, I mean, she was very *frum,* she had a big *shaytl,* but she was *mamesh* awesome. On the cultural level she was completely...and she was talking to them all the time. You have to realize that if Rav Yossa Ber and Rav Hutner were sitting all afternoon talking to her that she was an interesting woman. But my Bubba was very cute. By her, a man talking to a woman, unless they were married, just didn't go. And she was so sophisticated, a little bit too much. I tell you I couldn't understand my Bubba because she talked to everyone. But when any of her granddaughters would talk to any guests of hers for Shabbos, she would blow their mind. But anyway, all the grandchildren, excluding me, were *mamesh gevaldt.* I don't know if you remember them from London, you know, all my cousins.

Okay, Mimi, do you regret already that you invited me, or tomorrow after you wake up you'll regret it? Did you tell Rav Meir'el the theme I want to talk about in Elul?

M: *Teshuva me'Ahava.*

S: Celebrating my *aveiros,* right? *Teshuva me'Ahava* means I am thanking God for every *aveira,* for every mistake, because where would I be without my mistakes? I would have never learned anything. Basically it is all based on the *Sod Yesharim* on Yom Kippur. *"Ain omdim al divrei Torah ele im kayn nichshal baHem"* 'you only learn by mistakes'. What? She doesn't like mistakes? Okay, so then change it. It doesn't have to be. Do you want to call it, "How to be happy despite your mistakes?" Or just "How to be happy"? Rav Meir'el, are you inviting me to all your children's weddings? I am inviting you to all of my children's weddings. And all of us should come to everybody's weddings. Someone asked me, "How much do you have to wear in your shul?" I said, "Anything more than a bathing suit is highly appreciated." Hey, Yankele Sack, can you drive me home? *L'Chaim*, everyone. Unless Moshiach comes on Tisha B'Av, we have to fast, and we are making *Kiddush Levanah*.

*Reb Dovid Zeller, z"l, Professor Joshua Ritchie*
*and Reb Shlomo Carlebach, at David Ritchie's wedding in Los Angeles.*
*Photo by Rabbi Joe Schonwald.*

The Nameless *Niggun*:
http://youtu.be/nFwLkp1mbLI

# Reb Shlomo's Kislev Teachings

## Temple Beth Ami, Santa Rosa, CA, 22-23 Kislev, 5741 / November 30, 1980

Recorded and Transcribed by Reuven Goldfarb

*I dedicate this transcription to the complete refuah of Yitzchak ben Leah — Jerry Strauss, Shlomo's great friend and supporter — who organized the concert and learning at which these teachings were given over — and his equally dedicated wife and partner, who also needs a big refuah — Leah Belkala bat Chaya Sarah.*

## Part One — Dreams

Rabbi Shlomo Carlebach: I want to tell you something very deep. Let me ask you: what is higher? If G-d reveals himself to you face-to-face, like G-d spoke to Moses. Isn't it crazy? G-d never spoke to Moses in a dream — clear prophecy, right? To Abraham — clear prophecy. Isaac — Jacob also, sometimes — clear prophecy. And sometimes, it was in a dream. And Joseph, which is like an earthshaking dream that he'll be the King, you know — I mean besides getting involved now, without even thinking — how earthshaking that was! And besides everything else, like the first revelation of Jacob, when he leaves the Holy Land — he's so broken he has to leave the Holy Land, and everything, and everybody knows, when Jacob left the Holy Land, he didn't just feel his own personal feelings — him, Yankele, leaving the Holy Land. Jacob was so much one with all of Israel, he mamesh felt the pain of every Jew — till Mashiach is coming — leaving the Holy Land, right? So wouldn't it be more beautiful if G-d reveals Himself to him face-to-face and say[s] — "Listen, don't be afraid, Yankele, you'll come back, you'll make it back" — [instead of] in a dream?

Okay, now I want you to know something. The saddest thing is — without saying anything bad, you know — my luggage didn't make it, and I had brought about 200 books with me — the deepest depths — from the Ishbitzer on dreams. So anyways, I'll have to rely on my memory from last year, hopefully, or just make it up. What's memory? You make it up, right? *L'Chaim!* [Drinks some of the milk he had asked to be brought to him earlier.] From last lifetime.

I want you to know something very very deep. If someone talks to me face-to-face — I'll tell you as an example. Listen to this. Yesterday I walked on Broadway, and I met this absolutely beautiful girl, right? And she was just so cute and so sweet, and I just fell in love with her very madly — okay, mazel tov. Nothing happens before, nothing after, right?

But you know something else, yesterday I was — yesterday was Shabbos; I couldn't be on the subway — so Friday, I was on the subway, and for one split second I saw a girl on the other side sitting there and, mamesh, every night I dream about her. What's deeper?

Or I'll tell you something else. This is one of the deepest, deepest depths of Reb Nachman. How close do you have to be to a person to tell them something straight? Basically, a stranger can ask me, "How much is one and one?" I'll tell him "two". I don't have to love him; he doesn't have to love me — I'll tell him "two". There is [a] certain language which is only given when you love somebody very much, right? It's the deepest depths, right? On one hand, it's maybe not so clear. On the other hand, it's so much deeper, right?

You know how a Jew makes it in exile? A Jew in exile does not make it because [of] all the G-d revelations he ever had — or he will ever have. A Jew in exile, when he goes sobbing, is mamesh in the lowest depths, is crying, is broken, a Jew is making it because of all the dreams. You know what dreams are? You know, I can tell you a dream and you say it's stupid, right? If you are logic[al], if you are straight, it's nothing, right?

Joseph comes [to his brothers] and says, "I had a dream I'll be the King." Ha! You can laugh in his face, right? Imagine Joseph would have come — "I had a clear vision, a clear revelation — a prophetic vision — that I would be the King of the world." So that's what it is, right? Where would Joseph be? He would never become as holy as he is, as deep as he is. He had a dream. So the brothers consider him as if he is crazy, right? But can you imagine how deep the dream was, that he knew it's not crazy? How deep it is?

You know, I'll tell you, I had this absolutely crazy dream — I discussed it with my psychiatrist — I had this crazy dream that there's a ladder, you know, and like I'm lying on the floor, and there's a ladder going up from me to heaven. So my psychiatrist discussed it with me, right?

It's stupid, right? It's...*gevalt!* You know, I don't want to say anything bad, but imagine, G-d forbid, Jacob would have seen a psychiatrist the next day, you know? Where would you and I be? Where would we be? Where would we stand? He'd say, "Listen, you have some kind of complexes, you know, and all kinds of things — " A dream is so deep, and here I want you to know something. You see, what does it mean, "We are in exile"? To be in exile means that G-d cannot speak to us face-to-face, 'cause officially he's angry at us, and officially we're angry at him, right? But you know what's going on? When nobody's looking — when nobody's looking — we are sending love letters to each other, right? You know how deep this is? You know how deep this is? It's the deepest depth there is.

What's the whole world telling us? Listen, Jews, you're on your way out — forget it. What are they telling us now? Forget it. You're in Israel? It's a joke. Tomorrow morning the Arabs will drive you out. But *gevalt*, *gevalt*, every Yiddele knows — every Yiddele knows — it's not true, right? It's not true, right?

Imagine I would come to Yerushalayim, and there's this beautiful holy Temple, and it's just real, just, just renovated now by brother Max Cohen from Miami donated the paint. And it's just so beautiful, and we have an interior decoration, and we go there, and it's our pride. It's this beautiful building — how touching would it be? Honestly. And there Rabbi Goren has his office right on the first floor. Really, realistic. Would you shiver when you go there? No. You know why you shiver? 'Cause it's broken. It's broken. And the Zohar Kodesh says, even when the Holy Temple will be rebuilt, it will be both broken — and rebuilt.

How could G-d take away the holiness of the brokenness, right? You know what happened to the broken tablets, when Moshe replaced them? You threw out the broken tablets? We have both. Broken tablets? You know why the first tablets didn't last? Because they weren't broken. It has to be together — broken and not broken. So, dreams — G-d reveals Himself in a dream only to broken people. So deep, right? The deepest depths there is.

## Part Two — Yosef and Yehudah — The Tzaddik and the Ba'al T'shuvah

Okay, now I have to tell you something very fast. Why was Joseph the first one to be sold? The first Jew to be going into exile, being a slave, was Joseph. Everybody knew by prophecy — this was clear prophecy to Abraham — that "Your children will be slaves." And you know what Joseph was praying all his life? Let me be the one for all my brothers. Let me be it for all my brothers. Don't put it on my father.

And you know, everybody knows, basically the Gemara says that Jacob was supposed to go down to Egypt in chains. [*Shabbat* 89b] And, mamesh, Joseph did the whole thing for his brothers. But you see what's so crazy, imagine you walk up to somebody, and you tell them, "I love you the most in the whole world." And they think, they say, "Huh! I know what you mean. You want to manipulate me, you want to take advantage of me." Right? So you know, when Joseph said, "I'll be the King," what did he mean? He meant, "I'll carry the whole burden for you."

You see, an unholy king is someone who is really taking advantage. "You work for me, you're my slave, and I'm the king." What's a holy king? What's a G-d King? Not that "you're working for me" — he is working for you, right?

Let me ask you, sweetest friends, how did King David conquer Jerusalem? Everybody knows that Jerusalem belongs to King David — it's his personal property, did you know that? *Ir Dovid — Sukkos Dovid hanofales.* Why is Jerusalem King David's own property? The answer is very simple. Everybody knew that — you know, the seven nations who occupied all of Israel — and then the *Chiti, Yevusi* [Hittites, Jebusites] — they were such strong warriors, and they were living on that hill where Jerusalem is, and you couldn't get close. You know, they were waiting for two hundred, for three hundred years in Israel after Yehoshua, and nobody conquered Jerusalem. And do you know? Everybody knows — Hoshanah Rabbah, the seventh day of Sukkos, is the day of King David — right? If you remember. Why is this day, the seventh day of Sukkos — you know what happened on that Hoshanah Rabbah? King David decided, "I am going to take Yerushalayim all by myself."

One man — all by himself. Because really, if you trust God — does it matter to God if one man is going or if a thousand people are going? It's the same thing, right? Hoshanah Rabbah, King David walked up to Yerushalayim, and he conquered the whole city, right? That's a king, right? The king is not somebody who says, "Listen folks, let's go. I want you to be killed, and I am sitting in my office, and I'm directing traffic." Right? For that you don't have to be Dovid HaMelekh, right?

So you see, I want you to know that two people who carried the burden of all of Israel on their shoulders — already — were Yosef and Yehudah. You see, Yosef says, "Okay, you can go home." So all the brothers say, "No, we'll all be slaves instead of Binyomin." Yehudah stands up, and he says, "I want to be the slave." That means two people stood up, and they said, "We want to do it for all of you." This is two kings, right? This is a king!

And maybe some of you know, according to the tradition, it's called, *"Ma'an malka? Rabbonim."* 'Who are the great kings? Our teachers.' Why is it? Why is a real holy teacher supposed to be a king? (Always a king, hopefully.) It's not someone who puts it on you, right? A real holy king is someone who says, "I'll do it for you. I'll take it off you." *L'chaim, l'chaim.* [Drinks some more milk.]

So you see? Let me ask you something else. Why did Joseph tell the dream to his brothers? He couldn't control himself? Why, he was a yenta — or was he in analysis, and one of his brothers was a psychiatrist, you know? I mean, what was going on there? The answer is very simple. You know, Joseph knew one thing. If I am supposed to be the slave — if I wanna do it — the saddest thing in the world is I have to separate myself a little bit from my brothers. You know? I have to go by myself, right?

So Joseph knew one thing: the moment I tell this dream to my brothers, they'll be angry at me. But can you imagine? — I have to tell you one more thing, which is so beautiful and so heartbreaking. Let me ask you — what happened at that moment when the brothers saw Joseph? Were they laughing? Were they smiling at each other, you know, we're finally getting rid of this disgusting Joseph? Without getting involved — because I have to daven Mincha — for whatever reason they decided they have to sell him as a slave, what do you think was going on at that moment? [Long pause.] I want you to know something. Imagine you'd be up in heaven, right? Can you imagine if someone would have recorded the crying of the Jews when we went into exile? When the Holy Temple was destroyed when we went into exile? Can you just imagine it? Can you imagine the sounds of the crying? It does not compare to the crying of the holy tribes.

And here I want to share with you something which is so holy, that I just have to tell you, and I think if some of you remember — maybe Adina [Elana Friedman] remembers it. Okay, there are these two kings in the world. Joseph is the King of all the Tzaddikim, Joseph is the King of all the people who never did wrong in their life — and Yehudah is the King of all the people who went wrong — everything they did in their life is wrong. And they have the strength to fix it, right?

You see, Yosef is the one who gives you the strength not to do wrong, to keep yourself going all the time, and Yehudah is the one who gives you strength to fix it. And we need both, right? Those two kings [are] the pillars of all of Israel. Now listen to this — and remind me to come back to it, because we have to daven Mincha. I just want to tell you this. Okay, the brothers decide — basically it was Yehudah's decision — we have to sell him as a slave. Because they say like this: "We don't know if he is a Tzaddik or not. We don't know who he is. We give him a chance. If he goes to Egypt, and he remains a Jew, and he remains holy, he's one of us." Right? "If [he] gets lost, then he wasn't for real." Right? Okay, they're picking up Yosef from the pit, and they're telling him, "Yosef, this is our decision. If you are real, if you are one of the holy tribes — " You see, without getting involved, you know, they thought he is not one of the twelve tribes. Because if you're one of the twelve tribes, how can you separate yourself from your brothers? How can you separate yourself from your brothers, right? And they didn't know that he's only separating himself because he wants to take off the burden of being a slave [from them]. But anyway, that's what it was.

They said, "If you're one of us, you'll make it. But if you get lost — so you get lost." I want you to visualize — it's the deepest, deepest depths. But again, it's so holy, it's awesome even to think of it. How do you think the brothers said good-bye to Yosef? How do you think the brothers said good-bye to Yosef, right? Because deep down, can you imagine how much — how much love do you think was between the brothers and the house of Jacob? Unbearable, right? It was so deep and so holy, we have no concept, right?

Let me ask you, do you think, really, without knowing the depths, do you think there was jealousy between Rachel and Leah? Remind me to talk about it later. There [were] never two sisters in the world who loved each other more than Rachel and Leah, right? The deepest love, like Moshe and Aharon, right? Because everybody knows, Moshe and Aharon fixed the sin of Cain among men, and Rachel and Leah [are] fixing jealousy between women and hatred between women until Mashiach is coming, right? The two pillars — Moshe and Aaron, Rochel and Leah.

Okay, the brothers saying good-bye to Yosef. Okay, so Yehudah, who's the king, right? He says to Yosef, "Okay, we're selling you as a slave, and you'll have to prove yourself, if you remain a Tzaddik or not." So you know what Yosef says to Yehudah? He says to Yehudah, "My holy brother, please bless me I should make it." Right? "Bless me to be a Tzaddik." Now listen to this unbelievable thing: Yehudah blessed Yosef to be a Tzaddik. And you know why Yosef remained a Tzaddik? Because of the blessing of Yehudah, right?

What do you think Yehudah says to Yosef? 'Cause he's selling his brother as a slave, as much as he knows "I have to do it," so Yehudah says to Yosef, "Please bless me I should do *t'shuva.*" Right? So Yosef blessed Yehudah to do *t'shuva,* right? And Yehudah blessed Yosef to be a Tzaddik. Right? It's mind-blowing. Mind-blowing is not the word, right? So the two pillars of Yiddishkeit, the *Tzaddik* and the *Ba'al T'shuvah* — they blessed each other. It's unbelievable! Yosef is only a *Tzaddik* because of the blessing of Yehudah, and Yehudah is a *Tzaddik* [a *Ba'al T'shuvah*] because of the blessing of Yosef.

And you know, I want you to know something. *L'chaim* [sips]. You know — [someone stifles a sneeze] God bless you. [And again] God bless you. What's the holiness of the holy wall? You know what's so strange? It's a broken wall. And yet, you can see with an unclear prophecy the holy Temple, right? When you stand there, you see, mamesh, the *Beis HaMikdash,* right? But again, if you would see the *Beis HaMikdash* clear, it wouldn't be so deep. Because behind all the brokenness — like on a dream level — you see the *Beis HaMikdash* — therefore, it's so holy. Right?

I have to tell you just one more beautiful thing. When was the day that the wife of Potiphar mamesh really made it strong with Yosef — she says, [either] you do it, or I take you to prison. Which day was that? Everybody knows, it was Rosh HaShanah. But listen to this unbeliev- able thing. It was in the morning 'cause everybody — it was a whole big thing — it was a little thing in their pagan temple — and Yosef stayed home. Okay, I want to — [responding to someone's importunity] I'll daven in a minute — I want to share this with you. [Aramaic quota- tion] — it says, "he saw his father's face." [*Sotah* 36b] What — he saw his father eating breakfast? (They [had been] living together.) He saw his father waking up? What moment did he see? Which moment was revealed to Yosef? Which moment he saw his father? So the answer is very simple. He saw his father blowing the shofar.

You know, friends, I don't know if you have ever seen *mamash Tzaddikim*. I had the privilege of seeing the Lubavitcher Rebbe, I saw the Bobover Rebbe, I saw mamesh *Tzaddikim* the way they looked before they blow the shofar, right? When you remember that, it's something else, right? So I want you to know, Joseph went into prison on Rosh HaShanah, and everybody knows, he came out on Rosh HaShanah. *L'chaim, l'chaim.* [He drinks again.]

You know, the Ropshitzer says the portions of the winter wear heavy furs — you know? It's all covered up. It's all covered up. And it's such a privilege — you know, it's very crazy. Before Mashiach is coming, in our generation, really, we have such holy books; it's getting more and more open to us, and it's really more and more accessible to us — the deepest depths of the Torah, right? Let's say twenty years ago, nobody was sitting in Santa Rosa talking about Yehudah and Yosef, right? *L'chaim.*

[This the end of Part Two. May the tears that we shed over the Joseph story be transformed into drops of rain to moisten the parched land of Israel, fill her rivers, lakes, and streams, her reservoirs and aquifers. — RG]

## Part Three — Parents and Children

You know, I just want to tell you something very special. You know some people are — let's say the world — the outside world — the Greek world, the Greek civilization world. You know, when someone says to you, a father or a mother says, you know, "My children are the most beautiful children in the world," you think they're crazy, right? Stupid! They're subjective, right? It's true.

But I want you to know something. Do you know what that means? When I tell you my Neshamale is the most beautiful girl in the world, for me, you know what that means? That means G-d has revealed something to me about my child which nobody knows. And if I say I love my child like I love every other child in the world, I'm cutting myself off from G-d's prophecy, right? And, uh, you know, I'm sure you feel the same way. You know, sometimes, when I ask someone about their children, they say, "Yeah, they're okay, they're sweet, yeah." What's going on there?

Did I tell you? — I think I told Yitzchak [Muller] or one of you — one of my first experiences in the world. At that time I was crazy. I loved this one girl very much. So, it didn't work out. At that time I was in yeshiva. It's crazy, you know? At that time I was a little big shot in yeshiva, and some of you who know a little bit about what's going on in yeshivas, so if you're a good student, then a great rabbi wants you for a son-in-law, right?

So a super-great rabbi comes to Lakewood to talk to me about marrying his daughter. I tell you something — he told me all about his daughter: she's this, she's this, you know, like I tell you about Bermuda is beautiful — they have beaches and things. There was not tears in his eyes — he wasn't crying — it was like it was a business thing. He told me since I want to be a great rabbi, and she was fitting to be a good rebbetsin, you know? He gave me the whole thing. Left me cold like ice cream.

I want you to know, the next night I decided to visit the father of the girl I love so much. He was a little Yiddele, a Polish Yiddele, and he had a grocery store in Bensonhurst. What are you selling in a grocery store? You know, a little herring, a little corn flakes, a little leftover challah from last Shabbos, you know?

Okay, I walk in there; it was already maybe 10:30 because I was coming from Lakewood, and it was very late. All right, I took a chance. I know he's in the store till eleven o'clock. I walk in there; there were some customers. I'm standing there, so after all the customers left, he said to me, "Okay, what do you want?" So I tell him, "I'm a friend of your daughter." Obviously, she must have told him about me.

Do you know what happened? This little grocery store Yiddele — suddenly he had tears in his eyes. And he says, "My Tovele, my Tovele — " *gevalt*, right? So forgetting about the whole thing, I said to myself, if I would look for a father-in-law, I'd take him, right?

But now I want you to know something deeper. Not only that G-d reveals to parents something about their children, but it's going back also. It's a two-way street. G-d reveals to children something about their parents which no one else knows, right? Do you know, children — until they're disappointed — until their parents, *chas v'shalom,* disappoint them — think their parents are the most special people in the world, right? Do you know what's the most heartbreaking day in the world for children? When they find out that it wasn't true.

And you know, I'm one of those special blessed people that I had the privilege to believe until this very second how special my father was, you know? So special. Why? Because it was a two-way street. Because my father, you know? My relationship to my father was so special. So special. Unbelievable.

## Part Four — A Special Garment — The Seer of Lublin and the Yid HaKodesh

[Shlomo davens Mincha, then plays several songs. Now he's ready to tell a story.]

Listen friends, can we sit here for five more minutes? Let me tell you a fast, cute little story; then we'll take a little break-aleh.

[He catches sight of Aryeh Trupin] — Hey, brother, hey, I'm over-joyed to see you. [Changes his tone] You didn't bring your trumpet? [Aryeh plays clarinet and flute, but Shlomo didn't forget; he meant it generically.]

Aryeh: I did, but I was, I was sitting so entranced —

Shlomo: No, brother, I was sure you didn't have it. How could you hold back? But, you know, I'm so glad —

Chevra, can you get a little bit closer for two more seconds? I want to tell you a sweet story. Just to warm your bones with a good story.

[Confers with Jerry Strauss about the schedule. They agree, and Jerry makes an announcement. Shlomo compliments him.]

Okay, friends, let me tell you a fast story. Maybe some of you heard me tell it already, so you'll have to forgive me. And if you didn't, you'll have to forgive me I didn't tell it faster.

You know, some of us, friends, are doing someone a favor, and the saddest thing is that you regret it after that. You know? You do some-body a favor — you did — that's it, right? But to regret it after — what kind of *gesheft* [business] is this, right? Imagine I walk down the street, and I see a poor man. And at that moment, something touches my heart, and so I give him ten dollars. Next block, I think, "Crazy! Ten dollars? Five dollars wouldn't have been enough?"

The famous, classic UJA story about this Yiddele going on a bridge and [the bridge] begins to shuckle, and he's afraid he'll fall in, and he says, "G-d, I donate $100 for Israel." Okay, suddenly the bridge is okay. Nothing. It stops shuckling. He thinks, "$100 for Israel? Fifty wouldn't be enough?" It begins to shuckle again. He says, "G-d, I was only joking!"

But anyway, listen to this. This is a true story, a classic story. Everybody knows that the Yid HaKodesh, the Holy Jew, was the highest pupil of the Seer of Lublin. And one of the reasons he was called "Holy Jew" is that he had the same name like the Seer of Lublin, Ya'akov Yitzchak, and since you're not permitted to call anybody by the name of your holy master — so one way or the other — but the real holy reason is that one time all the pupils of the Seer of Lublin were standing in [the] marketplace of Lublin, and suddenly a Cossack passed by, riding on a horse, and he pointed at the Yid HaKodesh; he says, "He looks like a Jew." And he took off. So obviously it was Eliyahu HaNavi, and he told them that the Yid HaKodesh looks like a Jew.

Anyway, he was called Yid HaKodesh, and also everybody knows that if the Yid HaKodesh and the Seer of Lublin would have been always very close, they mamesh had it in their hands to bring Mashiach. So if you know, in the history of Chassidus, the saddest thing happened. Suddenly there was a whole group of people in Lublin, and they told stories to the Seer of Lublin about the Yid HaKodesh. It was like a little wall between them. So this took place at the beginning, when the other side was working for them not to bring the Messiah and to make a little anger between them.

Okay, now I want you to know, the whole time the Seer of Lublin was aware — he didn't believe anything they tell him, but he knew maybe really the time isn't there yet, you know? Maybe it's because the time isn't there.

Anyway, one Friday afternoon, the Yid HaKodesh — the Holy Jew — walks into the Seer of Lublin, and the Yid HaKodesh was so poor — his father-in-law was a baker, and you know — very, very poor. So his shirt was torn, and it was really dirty. So the Seer of Lublin says (you know — everybody knows — a *Talmid Chacham* — a scholar — is really not permitted to walk around dirty 'cause it's a desecration of G-d's name), so he said to the Yid HaKodesh, "You're not permitted to walk around with that shirt on Shabbos." Walks into his bedroom, takes out a beautiful shirt — and you have to realize the Seer of Lublin would not give a shirt to somebody unless he's completely holy, right? — because all the garments of my soul, of my body, are just one, right? And to wear a shirt which was worn by the Seer of Lublin — ah, your kishkes are turning over, right? I'd be afraid even just to go into the same room with the Seer of Lublin and his shirts, right?

Okay, the Yid HaKodesh takes the shirt, and he walks down the street. He wants to go to the mikveh. On the way to the mikveh, he meets Mosheleh the Shikker.

And Mosheleh the Shikker, you know, is a shrewd fellow, but mamesh his shirt is even more torn and is more dirty, so the Yid HaKodesh suddenly has a flash, "I wish Moshele the Shikker would look decent on Shabbos." He says, "Mosheleh, you want a good shirt? I just got a gift from the Seer of Lublin. Here, I give you the shirt." The Yid HaKodesh went to the mikveh, but in the meantime, Moshele Shikker — Moshele the drunkard — wasn't as stupid as that. He walks back to the bar, and he says, "Friends, I have here the most unbelievable thing, which nobody ever had. I have a shirt of the Seer of Lublin. Who's offering the most?" He auctions off the shirt for 1500 rubles, and the one who bought it was the bartender, and Monday, he went to the marketplace in Lublin — it was a real Jewish city — getting on a chair, and he says, "I have a shirt of the Seer of Lublin. How much are you offering?" And he auctioned it off for 10,000 rubles because someone had a thought, "I have no children," *chas v'shalom,* "and if I wear the shirt," you know, "G-d will help me." 10,000 rubles.

Word got back to the Seer of Lublin, and the Seer of Lublin, to tell you the truth, the Seer of Lublin was a bit angry — because he really gave it to him as a present, you know? Imagine someone loves me, gives me a gift, I'll say, "Listen, I gave it away" — "I gave it to YOU," right? I can understand both sides, right? And remind me, I want to tell you an Ishbitzer Torah on that, but I don't want to interrupt myself.

Anyway, the Yid HaKodesh was very downhearted. He thought, "Maybe it's really stupid. Maybe I shouldn't have given it. Maybe I should have — I don't know." Anyway, he walked down to the outskirts of the city, and he was sitting there, and he was mamesh crying 'cause he knew that means another war between him and his holy master. Sitting there and crying. Suddenly, another drunkard — but this time, mamesh, Elijah the Prophet. You know, when you're very broken, then the best thing is to tell your story to a stranger, right? So suddenly this drunkard comes up to him and sits next to him and he says, "Hey, why are you crying?" You know? Tells him the whole story.

He says to him, "Let me tell YOU a story." He says, "I want you to know, a few hundred years ago, in a city, there was a big thief, Yankele the thief. And he *mamash* stole, but he was so polished that you couldn't catch him. He *mamash* stole every penny out of the hands of every Jew in the city, until he was so rich, he decided to retire. Okay, he bought himself a beautiful house. Everybody knew it was stolen money, but you couldn't pin him down. And he lasted very happily after. But you know, if you don't continue to steal, finally your money goes out.

"One day, he was left with no money — listen to that chutzpah — he comes to the Jewish community, and he says, 'Folks, I'm poor. I want you to support me.' They said, 'What? Until now you ate of our money, and now you have the chutzpah to come we should give you more money?' You know? 'Give us back the money you stole from us and we'll support you.'

"Meantime, this *nebech*, Yankele the thief, has nothing to eat. One day, a very wealthy man, who was a neighbor, passed by the house of Yankele the thief — and by that time he was already an older man. He saw him sitting by the door of his house, so broken, and so hungry, and so desperate — so he said to himself, 'I don't care,' you know? 'I don't care if it's right or wrong. I gotta give this Yiddele something to eat for Shabbos.'

"Went back to his wife, and he says, 'Do me a favor. Send him a lot of *lokshen kugel* [noodle pudding], a lot of *cholent* [bean stew], and a gefilte fish so he can have enough to eat until next Shabbos. Send him a lot of food! We have enough.'

"To make it very short, from that Friday on, the rich wife sent food to Yankele the thief every Friday. This went on for many years. And now, you gotta open your hearts, like from here till the end of the world.

"One day there were two funerals: a big funeral — the rich man died; and a little funeral — Yankele the thief died. They both died at the same time, buried at the same time, coming up to Heaven — rich man goes first.

"Okay, the rich man — and you know, there's a huge scale. Okay, first they put on his good deeds; it didn't take much — a little briefcase — an angel brings the good deeds, puts them on one side, that's it. Now comes the bad side; trucks are coming, you know? The Yiddele sees there is no hope for him — you know? He's at the end. Okay, he's sitting there and shivering, and he knows, 'In a few more seconds they'll decree I have to go to hell, they'll push the button, and I'll be a barbecued rich man.'

"Now listen to this — at the very last second something happened, and suddenly the high court says, 'You're going to Heaven.' The high court says, 'You're going to Heaven.' The rich man looks at the scale — the bad side is so heavy, and the good deeds is nothing — suddenly he sees — something wrong with the scale. And he asks one of the angels, 'What's going on here?' They answered him, 'Don't you understand? Your friend, Yankele the thief, stole away all your *avayras*, all your evil deeds.'"

It's a *gevalt* story, you know? What a story, you know? Mazel tov, yeah. Such a holy story, you know? Good Yontif. Peace.

## Part Five — Introduction to the Birkat HaMazon; prelude to the concert

[The tape recorder gets rigged up again at the conclusion of the meal that followed the previous teachings and story. At first it's a scarcely audible jumble of words and phrases about how a human being gives help (reluctantly)] "...two hours later you bother me again?" "I'll tell you, listen to me now, Harry, we're such good friends, who cares about yesterday, today. Right now I need this money." "Okay, but I gave it to you." [The dialogue continues in this way, and eventually "Harry" gives his friend the loan — $2000 — but ends by saying,] "Please don't call me for another year." Compassion, right? This is a human being.

But you know the way G-d, when we deal with G-d? G-d *nebech* gives me a little piece of cake, a little bit...dinner. So I come to G-d with the holiest. I say, "*U-v'nai Yerushalayim*" 'Can you please rebuild Jerusalem?' "Can you please bring the Messiah?" [Does G-d say,] "What is this chutzpah?" You know? "I mean, really, because I gave you a little bagel, therefore you bother me right away about Yerushalayim?"

But now listen to the other side. I want you to open your hearts. Remember I told you I met this girl yesterday — can't say on Shabbos — it was Shabbos — last night I went out, I met this girl. And she was very sweet, she was smiling. And we walked into this coffee shop, and I said, "Can I take you out for coffee?" She says, "Why not?" You know? We're going in there, and I say to her, "Um...uh, you wanna give me the sugar, you know, for the coffee?" She says, "Okay." And I say to her, "Listen, you know, you're so beautiful. Maybe you can give me some more sugar. Would you like to marry me?" You know?

Now listen to this very careful. If she doesn't love me, you know? "Listen, what kind of chutzpah is this?" You know? "I didn't know you five minutes ago." Right? "Okay, you're taking me out for coffee, and I give you sugar, therefore? *Chutzpah!*" Right? If she loves me, do you know what she'll say? "You couldn't have asked at a better moment," right?

Now listen to this, sweetest friends. If you don't love a person after doing one favor, you say, "Really, I mean, really, take off, such chutzpah!" You know? "I just did you a favor — that's it! Don't talk to me for another year." If you love somebody very much, it's the other way around! If you do them one favor, you can't wait till you do them another favor, right? 'Cause it's so beautiful to do somebody a favor, right? When you love somebody — Listen, my Neshameleh, when she'll ask me, let's say in the morning, she'll say, "Daddy, give me apple juice." Ten minutes later, she'll say, "Give me this juice." I'll say "Chutzpah — I just — "? I'll say, "I'm so glad, *gevalt!*" I'm jumping out of my skin, right? Can you imagine, ten minutes later, she'll say, "Take me to Israel." So I'll blow my mind, my Neshama wants to go to Israel! Right?

So I want you to know, bentching is — bentching is, mamesh, that we are so close to G-d, we have just a little taste how much He loves us, that I can eat one bagel, and ask, "*U-v'nai Yerushalayim*. Please, *Rabeina shel olam*, bring the Messiah. Fix the whole world."

But again, you have to realize — and here I just want to tell you this one very important thing. This is one of the top torahs of Reb Nachman. You know, most of us think always of life in terms of, "What am I doing with my life? How much money do I make? What's my future? What's my past?" This is cute, right? It's the outside of it. Inside — life itself is so deep, right? [Long pause]

Chevra, I don't know what to say. Mamesh, my head doesn't work.

Anonymous helpful person: Reb Nachman. Top Torah.

Reb Shlomo: Ah, it's a *gevalt!* Thank you very much.

Same person: You're welcome.

[Shlomo continues] Reb Nachman says, at that moment, when you put food in your mouth, if you want to you can receive life on the highest level. Listen, I can take a bite of an apple and receive eternal life, right? Or I can just receive the apple. It's up to you.

So the story is that — all Breslov Chasidim were big shleppers, you know? Most of them. So Reb Nosson, the greatest pupil of Reb Nachman, was once invited by Reb Nachman's grandson, who was very wealthy. He didn't feel right to go there, but he was invited. The whole day he was crying inside, "*Gevalt*, my rebbe was so holy, and here this one is into money and everything." So he says, "I came to the house," and he regretted that he went. He wasn't accustomed to this kind of riches. And then he comes to the food. And he says, "*Oy vey.*" You know? "With this kind of golden plates and golden spoons, you're not gonna — who knows? Forget it!" But then he says, "Reb Nachman's grandson walked in, and he made a motzi," and he says, "the way he put the food in his mouth, I swear to you, I haven't seen it since Reb Nachman." Mamesh, the utmost — you know? With the utmost readiness to receive life on the highest level.

*Gevalt*, I'm keeling over. Yitzchak, can you start bentching? And I'll just bentch fast, yeah?

Jerry: Time for you.

Shlomo: Yeah, but I want to answer back, yeah?

Yitzchak: Okay, say *Rabbosai n'varech*. [Shlomo leads the call and response at the beginning of the bentching. And the *chevra* begins to sing....]

Quick segue to the concert, past the introduction by Rabbi Leo Abrami of Temple Beth Ami, the host congregation, in which he thanks Jerry and Linda Strauss and Linda's mother, Serena Yudel, who prepared the meal — and Jerry's introduction of Shomo and repeated thanks to Linda and Serena and to Yitzchak Muller who helped with the study group and songs and will be Shlomo's accompanist.

[Shlomo plays an opening number, then addresses the audience as follows:]

Shalom to you, my sweetest friends. Good evening. You know, friends, the difference between words and singing? It's very simple. Imagine if somebody talks to me, and while they talk to me, I also say the same words. It's crazy, right? Then I don't hear what they say, and they don't know what I'm saying — the whole thing is falling apart. Singing is the other way around. When someone sings, and I don't sing with them, then I absolutely don't know what they're singing about, right? The second difference is that words — if I go over them a hundred times — the more I utter those words, the less taste they have, right? If I say, one and one is two, one and one is two, one and one is [his voice trails off] — that's it, right? I know it already, right? Singing is the other way around. The more I sing the melody, the deeper I begin to understand the melody. As far as I'm concerned, a melody, unless you sing it at least 200 times, you — [end of tape]

## Part Six — Shlomo teaching about Chanukah

You know, my sweetest friends — Listen, I'm sure the children wouldn't mind if you tell them just to be a little bit quiet, without hurting their feelings. I'm sure they'll be with it. It's okay, it's okay, just — Friends, let's concentrate, okay?

Everybody knows, Tuesday night is Chanukah, the Festival of Light. And, you know, sometimes it's so obvious — you know, there's the book, "Who is Who in Judaism," you know? "Who is Who in the World," right? Sometimes it's so obvious who is real and who is not. For those who are not so real, they say, "Chanukah is a very unimportant holiday" — 'cause it really is, and what's so important about it, you know? Basically, on Chanukah you can do anything you want to. It's not like Yom Kippur — you're fasting, you go to shul. Chanukah, you can sell your herring. In the middle — in between one piece of herring and the other — you run to the window, you kindle a little light, so who cares, right? So it's not important.

But the truth is, the Holy Baal Shem Tov, the holy of holiest, told us that Chanukah is higher than the highest in the world. Yom Kippur is very special — Simchas Torah is special — it's all beautiful. But how does it compare to Chanukah? How does it compare to what a person feels when you kindle light?

Okay, now, sweetest friends, in a nutshell, I'd like to share with you what our holy rabbis teach us — what is light? What does it mean? Okay, I'm sure everyone has about ten million answers. Let me tell you the Torah from the holy Ishbitzer. I just want you, really, to open your hearts.

You know, I can tell you something — something very holy and exalted, which you didn't know before. And now you know it. So, you have an added [piece of] information. Imagine a person didn't know that there is one G-d. I meet this person. I explain to them, and I prove to them — there is one G-d. "Oh," they say, you know, "that's very nice, very beautiful. Thank you very much. I didn't know it." Now they know.

Or I'll tell you something. Did you think the whole world — the way it is now — that's the way it's supposed to be? People cheating each other, killing each other, hating each other? Let me tell you that our great prophets prophesied that tomorrow morning there'll be peace in the world. And you'll say, "Oh, I didn't know that. But it sounds good." You know? "Thank you for telling me. Where can I get that book?" "Oh, it's a dollar twenty-five." "So do you have any second-hand, where I can get it for seventy-five cents?"

Okay! What are they missing? What are they missing? They know the words. There's no light behind it, right? Let me tell you what light is. Light is that which lifts you up beyond you. Beyond you. Suddenly I'm reaching somewhere, to a place I didn't even know existed.

You know, let's put it this way. Imagine I didn't know there was one G-d, and suddenly somebody tells me, "There really is one G-d!" So, *gevalt,* am I reaching! Suddenly my soul expands two billion miles. Somewhere else. So, you know, sweetest friends, all the holidays, all our life is beautiful, but unless — unless there is light in it — you're dead.

You know, I always tell my friends, what do you think is happening in cemeteries? They have a committee — a cultural committee — they're having lectures, they have all the dead people get together, and they exchange ideas, you know? Without hurting anybody's feelings, if someone has a problem, he goes to a psychiatrist, right? Try one in the neighborhood, right?

What are they missing? They're dead, right? It doesn't change them. Doesn't lift them up to a higher place. You know what dead is? Can't move, right? Always the same. I'm the same when I say hello; I'm the same when I say good-bye. I'm the same when I eat an apple, and I'm the same when I kiss my child. Always the same.

You know what light is, sweetest friends? This is so precious. But now, one more step, friends. Light can only burn on pure oil. You know, the Maccabees came back, and they wanted to kindle G-d's light, and they realized, we need at least one drop of pure oil. Defiled oil — impure oil — doesn't produce light. Yeah, at the window maybe, but not in the heart, not in the soul.

I'm sure you share my feelings. Sometimes you hear a word from somebody, the same word you heard from a holy man yesterday — nothing happens to you. And the next time you hear the [same] word you heard from somebody unholy [from] somebody holy — someone who's operating on pure oil — suddenly a great light is shining inside of you. Such a deep light. So precious, so holy.

And you know, sweetest friends, do you know where we can reach? Does any of us know how high and how deep we can reach? Infinite, right? We're [made] in G-d's image. You know what's so special about the light of Chanukah? The Talmud says that basically G-d's light does not get that close to this world. There must be at least a little in-between of ten inches. [Ten *tefachim* — handbreadths. Shlomo is choosing not to get too technical here.] Chanukah, it goes all the way to the ground. You know what that means? All year long, without light, I understand "holy" is cute, sweet, beautiful, but let's face it — it doesn't reach down to this world, right? Really, let's face it. Do you really think you can sell herring and be holy? Do you really think you can be a stockbroker and be honest? Let's face it. You can't. You know why you can't? Cuz you have no light. If you have light? The lowest place [can be made holy].

And now, sweetest friends, listen to me. All of us know a lot of holy words. You know why it doesn't change us? Because we have this little in-between. I say, "You know, don't get too deep into me. Leave me a little space where I keep my unholy stuff. You know, really. Don't overdo it." So I never get anyplace. I never change. Chanukah is that moment when G-d's light reaches me in the lowest, lowest places in the world. The lowest.

And you know, friends, what's so beautiful about it? And here I want you to open your hearts. Do you think G-d wants you to be somebody else? Is there really such a thing as "low"? There is no such a thing. It is only because I had no light I thought there was high and there was low. Until the light of Chanukah reached me, I understood when I'm standing in the synagogue, I'm praying, I'm high. When I sell herring, I'm low. [On] Chanukah, I realize — what's wrong with selling herring? It's G-d's world, right? I can be the highest when I'm selling herring. Do you think I'm only close to G-d when I yell *"HaShem Echad!"*? G-d is one? A person can come into my store and buy herring, and I give him change from a dollar, but the way I give it to that person — that person knows there is one G-d.

So Chanukah is so good — so good. It's just the highest there is. And just one more thing, sweetest friends. You know what's wrong with the world? Any person who has a little bit [of] light in his heart, just a little bit [of] light — they always close the doors on you. [They] say, "Listen, face it. You are not as high as I am. I have a lot of light, but you can stay outside," right? "I mean, who are you? I mean, really. Let's face it. I cannot tell you all the great mysteries of the world, of the Bible — I mean, really, who do you think you are? You have no titles — " And whatever it is.

The holiness of Chanukah is that I'm putting the light right at the door of my house. Because if I have light, I'm just waiting for you, please, please come to my house.

One more thing, friends. G-d's light burns forever. G-d's light burns forever. Don't worry. Sometimes we think the world is going to the dogs, 'cause tomorrow morning nothing will be left. We don't have to worry. It looks to you like the oil is just enough for one night. What am I going to do the rest of the week? You don't have to worry. G-d's light is burning forever! If you have enough courage to kindle G-d's light for one night, I swear to you it'll last forever. It'll last forever.

Someone comes to you and he says, "Would you like to keep Shabbos?" You'll say, "Yeh, this Shabbos it so happens that I have time. But, really, next Shabbos, I can't." You just keep one Shabbos. But that Shabbos will burn inside of you until you keep the next Shabbos.

Someone will tell you, you know, "It's very bad to get angry." So, you say, "Today I just came back from my vacation in the Bahamas, and I am relaxed. Today I can manage not to get angry, but really, tomorrow, when I'm back in my business, don't tell me stories about 'not getting angry' — you cannot. You gotta yell at your secretary — you gotta yell at everyone; otherwise nothing is ever done." According to them, the way G-d created the word, first He yelled — and then He created the world. 'Cause otherwise nothing would have been done, right?

So you tell me you can just not be angry for one day. Okay. You start. You start for one day, for one minute, and G-d says, "I promise you — " Can I ask you why you're laughing? [Man he addressed answers:] "I was thinking to myself, when you said you were high selling fish, it's the idea that you did something that you liked...so much and it made you enjoy life so much. I was talking to a dealer in Puerto Rico — " [Shlomo interjects:] "He's saying good stuff, this man. Okay, let's hear it." [Man resumes speaking:] "I was talking to a dealer in Puerto Rico, and I said, 'What a job you have — you get to deal blackjack all day long.' He said, 'Not me. If you do it for a living it's just work.' And you were describing just how high you were, just on life." [Shlomo says:] "How about becoming partners with me, brother?" [Man responds:] "I didn't hear." [Shlomo repeats himself:] "I said, how about becoming partners with me and selling herring?" [Man replies:] "Not a bad idea."

[Shlomo strums his guitar and launches into another song.]

*Micha Taubman, who sponsored many of Shlomo's trips to the USSR and Poland,*
*and Shlomo Carlebach with R' Joe Schonwald at Shaarya Zeller's Brit, 1992.*
*Photo by Eli Moshe Klein.*

Shlomo Carlebach on the Road:
http://youtu.be/Qm3_aakne_w

# Reb Shlomo Carlebach on Children and Chanukah

## From the Archives of Steve Amdur

### Edited by Moshe Eliovson

SOMETIMES WE DO A MITZVAH, AND WE DON'T FEEL THE SECRET OF IT. May we be blessed that we should always feel it, but sometimes we don't. And there are moments when you do a mitzvah, you can't help it, but you feel all the secrets, all the secrets, all the holy secrets.

There is a torah from the Rizhiner Rebbe that it is not the parents who choose the children, but the children who choose the parents.... Why did our daughter choose us? Obviously, she saw that we loved her the most. How did my baby know that I love her the most? Not because I said so, but because she saw in my eyes that I was longing for her to be my baby. She saw me on the level of longing.

When do parents meet their children the way Avraham Avinu met Yitzhak? When they kindle the Chanukah lights together. When they see their children kindling Chanukah lights, that is when they meet their children. When children kindle Chanukah lights, the deepest depths of them are shining. Then parents realize, "My child not only has my light. My child has his own light."

There are three levels of walking. There is walking before some-body. There is walking with somebody. Then there is walking behind somebody.

Every mother and father is ready to walk before his child. "I will walk in front of you and tell you exactly what to do." Sometimes a parent is ready to walk with a child. But walk behind?

Sometimes you shake somebody's hand, and...*gurnisht,* nothing! It's nothing. Some people shake your hand, and they touch your soul. I learned this from my holy little Rebbe, from my baby.

Sometimes in the morning I take my baby and learn a little bit. From time to time my little daughter Neshama wants a little attention. So she starts pulling my clothes, she is pulling my *neshama* (my soul). All the hands of the world together won't reach where my Neshama's hands are reaching.

The Chanukah light is by the door. That means that I'm telling my children, "Even if you walk out the door, the light of this house should go with you." Eventually, all the children walk out of the house and make their own houses.

The holiness of children is that they're adding their own light. The holiest house is the house which makes a place for children to have their own light....

In Yehudah Maccabee's time, a whole generation was lost to Yiddish-keit because we didn't make a place for them.

When do children feel at home where they live? When their parents know what is special about them. If I live in a house, and nobody knows what's special about me, it's a hotel. In the hotel, I'm a number. In my house, I have a special place.

The holiness of a Jewish house is that two people and their two specialnesses get together. Out of their two specialnesses comes a little baby who is special and holy.

There is a very strong story: one of the earlier Lubavitcher Rebbes came to a city in Russia. There he saw old hasidim with long beards cleaning the house. He asked them, "What are you doing?"

They said to him, "Tonight the holy Toliner Rebbe is coming. We're cleaning the house."

He said to them, "This is beautiful, all of you old people cleaning the house. Where are your children?"

They said, "We wouldn't let the children do it. It is such a big honor."

He said, "That is why you should let the children do it!"

The Rebbe wrote in a letter, "I hope I am wrong, but I doubt very much that their children are still hasidim."

It is mind-blowing. Chanukah and Purim are the strongest holidays for the children. Chanukah and Purim are Mashiach's *Yomim Tovim* (Holy Days). When we celebrate the past, the adults know more. When we are celebrating the future, the kids know best.

I was privileged to see the way the old hasidim danced with their children when their children got married. I saw the old Bobover Rebbe dancing with his daughter. His tears of joy were flowing all the way to Jerusalem. That is the deepest, deepest teshuvah in the world. It is the deepest, deepest dancing in the world....

Imagine that my daughter says to me, "Can you get me some apple juice?" I jump up to get it. My face is shining from one corner of the world to the other. I think to myself, "There will be a time when she won't ask me for juice anymore. How precious is every time she still asks me for something!"...

If I am connected to her in the deepest way, then I am filled with joy when I can do something for her. If I am not connected that much, I wish that I didn't have to do anything for her even as I am doing it.

I have seen so many places where children walk through the door, and there is no one to open the door for them, to bless them with honor. If the President was at the door, knocking to enter, someone would be waiting by the door to greet him, to usher him through. But you don't wait for your own child, your own life? Who told you that you have the right to not stand by the door?

For me personally, when I wait for my daughter Neshama to return home from kindergarten, it feels like the waiting during Yom Kippur. What a blessing and what an honor to open the door for my child! Can you imagine what it means to know that a child is standing by the door, to know that his or her parents are also standing by the door with the same fervor?

Do you realize how deep it is to draw light upon each other? Can you begin to imagine how much everyone needs just a little bit of light? Just one drop of light is so deep.

Who teaches children to lie? Their parents. The Baal Shem Tov said don't teach your children to lie, because if you don't teach your children how to lie, it would never occur to them to lie. You have to tell them all the time that the holiest thing is the truth.

Then he says something very beautiful: If you're honest, then you won't be proud and you won't be arrogant. Because...arrogance comes from lying to yourself.

Sometimes the way parents relate to children, they think: I'm so great, I'm older than the baby, which is a stupid baby, what do I have to talk about to the baby? So when the children grow up, [they] let the parents know: I remember how you spoke to me when I was little, and to tell you the truth, right now you look little to me and I don't want to talk to you.

When children are born they need more than a little crib. They need a place in the world. Sadly enough a lot of parents think they can buy them everything, but children don't need that; they need a place in the world, a place of light.... And you know when you make place for your children, your children make place for you in places you never could get to on your own.

Reb Nachman of Bratslav says the woman has more *emunah,* faith in the world than man does.

Can you imagine how deep this is? Do you know how much faith you need in a baby, to bring it down to the world? You *mamash* have to believe in him, that he's going to make it. Because if you don't have faith that this baby will do it, you have no right to bring it down to the world.

There is a [teaching from the] holy Zohar which says that there are two questions in the world. There is 'mi' and 'ma'. 'Ma' means 'what'. And 'mi' means 'who'. The holy Zohar says, those who ask 'what' are destroying the world, and those who ask 'who' are rebuilding the world....

You know why children are so angry at their mothers? The children start to become angry when the mothers start asking, "What are you?" — Are you a good student? Are you beautiful? Are you not beautiful? — The child wants to cry out, "Why do you care? Ask me who I am!"

If a child has a sense, even a little bit of a sense, of this 'mi', of 'who I am,' this child can make it until the Mashiach comes. You know, if you tell a child all the time what he is, the child will be swallowed up and destroyed in the world. But if you can give a child this holiness, always to ask himself or herself "Who am I?" this child has unfathomable power.

I've told this story many times. I was in Russia [when it was dangerous to overtly identify yourself as a Jew]. It was Simchat Torah, so I was going to shul again. I saw a girl of 14 or 15 with a big Magen David [Star of David] walking toward the shul. So I pass by her and say under my nose, you know, "*Gut Yom Tov.*" Then I watch her and she goes to a little side street because in the big streets the police are too crowded. So she stops and I go over and say, "Gut Yom Tov." And she says — *mamash*, there were big tears coming from her eyes — "Aleph, beis, gimel, dalet, heh; *Sh'ma Yisrael, Ad—oi Elo(k)enu, Ad--oi echad.* That's all I know." And she says to me, "I want you to know that every Friday night I have to work in an office after I finish school. And I know it's Shabbos, and I wish I could kindle lights but I can't." She says, "What do I do, I find a place close to the window, and I watch the sun going down. And when I see it's Shabbos I sing to myself, 'Aleph, beis, gimel, dalet, heh; *Sh'ma Israel, HaShem Elokenu, HaShem echad.*'"

You know, when I heard this, it was as if she had taught it to me. The way this girl is kindling Shabbos lights — who knows where she is reaching...?

I had a Siddur in my hand that morning in Russia as I walked to the Beit Knesset. And I asked her, "Do you want me to show you an Aleph?" I've never seen anybody with so much simcha, such happiness — she was so proud that she knows what an aleph is, a beis, a gimel. I realized — let's say I know words, I know sentences — I even know Gemara. What good is that? I don't know anything. And I realized, I don't know one billionth of the Yiddishkeit of this little girl who knows the meaning of Aleph, Beis...I want to bless you that you should know the words, you should know the letters, the most important thing, I want to bless you to give over Aleph, Beis, Gimel, Dalet, Heh to your children. You know the world always thinks that with children, it's because they're so stupid that they begin with the letters, right? And then, they get more and more clever and then we teach them words. It's the other way around. Children, because they're so holy, they understand the letters. Then, *nebech,* they get older and they don't understand anymore, and we start to teach them words. Then they understand less, we teach them sentences. Then they understand less: they know a whole book. May you always know the letters.

The Volker Rebbe says: If each time when you are walking down the street you say, there goes one of G-d's creatures, an image of G-d, it's so beautiful. Then you love G-d more. But if each time you see a human being you say, there goes a disgusting creep, then you don't love G-d more.

I was waiting for a plane at LaGuardia when I noticed a sophisticated-looking woman, who had obviously just bleached her hair and was reading Reader's Digest, with a little girl of nine. Perhaps the little girl had done something wrong, who knows. But a little girl has nobody else in the world but her parents, and all the whole time I was waiting for the plane, her mother was yelling back at her, "Who needs you! Who needs you!" It struck me like the moment I heard that they had killed six million Jews. It's just the same thing. Telling a child, "Who needs you?" it's the same thing as saying, who needs six million. Believe me, I wanted to adopt this little girl and take her with me to the end of the world. But we are living in a world where the voice of the opposition is still so strong. It just broke my heart. I was *mamash* sick for a week after that. If you had seen the eyes of that little girl each time the mother said to her, "Who needs you?" She looked desperate. If this is what her mother tells her in public at the airport, who knows what she says to her at home.

So what we have to do, friends, is just believe more in human beings. Believe more in each other.

Why are parents ashamed before their children? It is because they know they are capable of so much more for them.

Children are so delicate. You have to know exactly what to say and what not to say. There are times you have to yell a little bit, but never too strong. It's absolutely forbidden to yell at children.

Imagine if you were to have holy eyes, you would see that when we yell at children we push them off two million miles. Sometimes you have to yell a little bit, from outside, never from inside.

I was once a Hebrew school teacher for two weeks. I didn't last too long. The top woman of the Hebrew school PTA didn't like me because I taught them aleph-beis with my guitar, and the third day they knew the whole thing. But this lady said, "All I hear going on is singing." Looking back, I'm really thankful. If I had been a good Hebrew school teacher I would never have started singing. I would have remained a little rebbele somewhere. To make it very short — there were two little kids in my class. And when I left it was really heartbreaking. So one of them, who was seven years old, said, "Thank you so much for teaching us. And thank you so much for not yelling at us."

There's nothing more degrading than excuses.... Parents who force their children to make two million excuses always cripple them. Then there are parents who have the holiness to say, "You did wrong. I'm sorry. I know you won't do that anymore. Let's talk about something else." These are the parents who surround their children with clouds of glory.

Imagine me sending a telegram to a friend, in Hawaii, "Come to New York immediately, I need you." This friend arrives, and he says, "What do you need me to do?" And I reply, "Please carry out my garbage."

And he says, "For that I have to come so far, all the way from Hawaii?" Children are coming from a faraway place. When they arrive, they ask their parents, what am I supposed to do here? And most parents answer, make a few dollars and have a good time. And the children answer, for that I had to come such a long way?

Our generation is a generation of disappointed children. But it is also our generation who have a G-d-given power to fix everything again. There is a great awakening in the world. The world is waking up to the realization that parents have to learn how to be parents, husbands have to learn to be husbands, and wives have to learn how to be wives — but not in schools or universities which only give you the fruit of the tree of knowledge.

Each time I hear a baby cry it sounds to me like the sound of the trumpet, announcing a better world. May your children and my children and all of the children of the world hold hands, and through them, you and I and the world become whole again.

Sometimes our holy sisters, our holy mothers, are just a little bit downhearted; they think, you know, we are spending so many hours feeding our children, diapering the babies, really in the meantime we could maybe write a book about loving children and here we are wasting our time on diapering them. But let me tell you something sweetest friends, let me tell you, if you would know, if you would know, how much light you bring into the world when you are taking care of children....

We need to teach ourselves and our children that they are the most beautiful candles in the world; we need them just to be here with all their joy and holiness.

*Reb Shlomo in a* farbrengen *with the Lubavitcher Rebbe, 1952*

*Teaching* Mei HaShiloach *at Yakar, Jerusalem, ~1985.*
*Photo by Rabbi Joe Schonwald.*

# Shlomo's Purim Teachings

### University of Florida, Gainesville,
### Sunday, 24 Shevat, 5746 / February 2, 1986

Transcribed by Reuven Goldfarb

I WANT YOU TO KNOW, ONE OF MY GREATEST MOMENTS, LAST YEAR, A day before Purim, I had the privilege to play in prison. You know how down-hearted people are in prison? When I came to them, I said, "Chevra, I came to teach you to say 'Good Purim.'" But, you know, little prisoners, you know, don't give a damn even about life any more. I want you to know — I never heard anything like it in my whole life. They were yelling, "Good Purim!" from the deepest depth of their souls, right? From the deepest depth of their souls. And after that, the dancing was to high Heaven, you know?

Let me ask you, friends, who is more important in the world, the guard or the prisoners? Obviously, the prisoners. But not on Purim, right? You know, the prisoners danced up to the guards and said, "Come, let's go and dance." And unbelievable — the guards danced with them! And who was the first one to kiss? Not the guards. The prisoners kissed the guards! *Gevalt!* It was *mamash emeseh* Purim [absolutely true Purim], right? It's *gevalt*, you know? *Mamash ad lo yada,* you know? *L'Chaim!* [crowd responds, *L'Chaim!*]

I hope — and bless me — this year I should have a chance before Purim to be in prison again. There was an old Breslover Chasid [catches on] — not me personally, but — [Question: "Where was this?"] In Israel. I have to tell you, just because you asked me, I'll tell ya, a fast prison story. It's my favorite prison story.

I don't want to say anything bad — um — in the blessed year before the Lord — 1969 — you know a lot of young people, really, as I said before, went into stuffing themselves with drugs. In a city, two hours away from New York — without saying anything — a very wealthy family — the grandmother died — and she left a quarter of a million or maybe a million dollars for her grandson to be given to him on his 21st birthday. But the parents — and he's also the president of a temple — and the mother is the president of Hadassah of New England — very outstanding people — felt the son isn't ready for the million dollars. And it's still better if she has it in HER pocket, than in his pocket, since she loves him so much. It was *mamash* ugly.

Okay, the boy was smoking a little hashish sometimes, you know. But he had his head on his shoulders as much as his father. You know what they did, on his 21st birthday? They called the police on him and had him arrested. The boy was so heart-broken. His parents got wild! They put him in solitary confinement. His girlfriend called me up. And she says, "I want you to know — you don't know my boyfriend, but he knows you. He was once in the House of Love and Prayer. The rabbis in that city — they all know his father, naturally, he's the president of the temple, I mean, how would they go against him? He just needs someone to talk to."

Listen to this. I had to leave the next morning — I had a plane [at] 9 o'clock to Paris. And the whole thing — I had to be there. I said to her, "I'll tell you something. If you can arrange for someone to drive me right now from New York there, I'm ready to sit with him all night. And drive me tomorrow morning straight to the airport."

Anyway, she came, picked me up, to drive me to the prison, but you know, I didn't know in order to go to prison, you need a written statement from the lawyer. You know, basically, a rabbi can go into prison any time. But I had no identification that I'm a rabbi, and I didn't have a letter from the lawyer! Anyway, you know, at night in prison, everybody sleeps — I'm getting there about 11 o'clock, and this *nebech, nebech* sad little guard sittin' there in prison, half asleep. I knock.

And he says, "What's going on here?" I say, "Listen, my dear friend. I am a rabbi, and I have to see one of my parishioners. His name is this — he's in solitary confinement — and it's a question of life and death. This boy needs me."

"Uh," he says to me, "Do you have identification?"

I say, "You crazy? Look at me! What do you think I am, a garbage collector or a shoemaker? What do you mean — I am a rabbi, and I wanna see him!"

I *mamash* put the fear of G-d in him. He says, "Okay, okay, okay!" [Laughs]

Anyway, I want you to know. You know what the saddest thing was — I forgot to tell you — his parents sent food to him in prison, and he refused to eat their food. You know? It's just — he says, "I have nothing to do with you anymore."

Anyway, I had my pockets, *mamash* — you know, I had a coat, and I had [it] *mamash* full of food. All kinds of things...vitamin pills — just for him. And he didn't — you know — he didn't investigate what I have. And also I had a package in my hand. And I had a lot of Reb Nachman — few things. Anyway, I want you to know, he brings him out and this boy was such a high person. I want you to know, I spent with him four hours. We didn't talk about the word 'prison,' about parents, about hashish, about nothing. I was *mamash*, I was learning Reb Nachman with him for four hours, just to give him strength.

Every few minutes one of the guards came in, listened a little bit, and walked out. I had to make that flight. Okay, about, let's say, 3:30, I finish, I give him all the food, and he was hiding it, you know, also like in a little coat or something. We walk out. And here is where the story really begins. And the guards are sittin' there, right? I said to him, "Tell me something." (I said it in front of the guards.) "Tell me the truth, brother. Are those guards still human beings? Or have they lost everything? Or is there hope for them?" So he says, "You know something? I think there is hope for them."

So I said to the guards, "You know something? I came all the way to spend a little time with you here in this prison. And this young man and I were just learning the deepest secrets of the Torah. Why don't you all join us for a few minutes?" *Mamash*, we made a circle — the prisoner, humble me, and the guards — and we were singing a little bit, and I was giving them Reb Nachman Torahs, and they were *mamash* crying *geferlach* [terribly], you know? They were *mamash* crying. *Mamash* got to them. And here was the most unbelievable thing. It was like after Mashiach has come. Okay, naturally, we hugged each other, I kissed them. They locked the door. I walk out. I look back. The prisoner and the guards were standing there waving. Unbelievable! Listen, I'm telling you, it was like after Mashiach had come. I couldn't believe it. Couldn't believe it. Anyway, good Purim. [The people respond, "Good Purim!"]

\* \* \*

Okay, Yossi, you tell me what you want me to learn about. Anything. [No answer] Okay, I'll tell you.

Let me tell you one beautiful thing. What is the greatest sign of love in the world? I want you to open your hearts to it.

The utmost evil is *lashon hara*, right? To say bad things about another human being. What's the other side? The other side is not, "I'm not saying anything bad." It's just, "I'm not saying anything bad," right? The other side is when you tell me somebody else did something wrong, I'll tell you, you know something? It's all my fault. It's all my fault.

I want you to know the deepest depths. When Aharon HaKohen, the High Priest, walked into the Holy of Holiest, he didn't ask for forgiveness; he didn't say anything. And there are millions of teachings on it. You know what the real truth is? According to the Gemara — the Gemara says, *"sh'tikah k'hoda'ah"* ["silence is like an admission," *Bava Metzia* 37b]. When you say nothing, it means you admit it. You know what? Aaron HaKohen walked into the Holy of Holiest, he says, "If there's anybody here who did something wrong, it's all my fault. Because if I would be better, they would be better."

And here I want you to know something so deep. You know why Adam was driven out from Paradise? Adam and Eve? You know, when G-d says to Adam, "Who did it?" — he should say, "G-d, it's all my fault." This is the way you love your wife? You tell G-d it's my wife's fault? You don't cover for her? Out of Paradise. Get out of here.

And I want you to know the deepest depths. This is really a deep Torah-le. The beginning of the wedding is that the groom covers the face of the bride. You know what he's telling her? "I will cover for you." Because every bride and groom is the fixing of Adam and Eve, right? He says, "I'll cover you up. I take it all upon myself." [Clears throat]

I want you to know the deepest depths. In the Sukkah — I want you to know, in the Sukkah, everybody knows — [on] Pesach, Abraham, Isaac, and Jacob, and the four mothers — maybe they're coming, if they want to, but it's not part of Pesach. In the Sukkah, after Yom Kippur, Avraham, Yitzchak, Ya'akov come — and the holy mothers.

I want you to know something. You know what Sukkah is? To cover, right? I want you to know, a rebbe teaches me right and wrong. You know what parents are all about? Parents standing before G-d and say, "It's all my fault. If I would be better, my children would be better." You know, Yom Kippur, I'm standing before God, and I say, "G-d, forgive me." On Sukkos, Avraham, Yitzchak, Ya'akov, and the four mothers come, and they say, "Master of the world, it's all our fault."

And here, I want you to know something even more awesome. On Simchas Torah, I dance with the Torah — but the Torah's covered. Do you know what it is? The Torah stands before G-d, and the Torah says, "G-d, it's all my fault." The Torah covers for me.

The Torah says, "G-d, if you wouldn't have written into me, 'Keep Shabbos,' then this person would be okay, so it's all MY fault," right? The Torah covers for me.

I want you to know something. You know why I dance with the Torah? 'Cause if the Torah is so holy that the Torah covers for me, then I really wanna learn that Torah, right? The Torah which only accuses me, makes me feel guilty, I'm not so eager, right? *Gevaldt* — I didn't know the Torah was so holy, right? [Whispers] I didn't know the Torah was so holy.

And I want you to know something awesome. It is based on a Torah from the Holy Kuzmirer. The Kuzmirer says, "Why did Moshe Rabbeinu break the tablets?" Moshe Rabbeinu comes down, and we made the Golden Calf. He broke the tablets. Why'd you do that? So he says like this, "Moshe Rabbeinu says to G-d, 'You want me to give the Jews the Torah which will make them into sinners? I'm not interested in giving them that kind of a Torah.'" He broke the Torah. [Whispers] Is that a *gevaldt*? Awesome. "I don't want to give them a Torah which makes them guilty and feel bad. I want a Torah which gives them strength." Awesome, awesome, awesome.

And here I want you to know the deepest depths. On Purim we're sending each other gifts, not face to face. On Yom Kippur it's just the High Priest, as I mentioned before. On Purim it's every person. You know what I'm saying to you? Not face to face. I'll cover for you. Don't worry about it. I'll cover for you.

And here I want you to know the deepest, deepest, deepest depths. In the whole story of Esther, G-d's name is not mentioned. You know what it is? [Whispers] 'Cause G-d is covering for us. G-d is not mentioned in there. I'll cover for you, right? *Gevaldt.* Do you realize? [Back to a normal voice] And you have to realize the Gemara says that on Purim we *mamash* received the Torah.

Because I always think G-d tells me, "Do this, do this." G-d is covering for me! Ah, it's a different G-d. I didn't even know. I didn't know what kind of a G-d I have, right? And I didn't know what kind of a friend I have.

Now listen to this unbelievable thing. The groom puts the veil over the face of the bride, telling her, "I'll cover for you. Don't worry about it." You know what the bride does? She walks around him seven times. "I'll protect you also. I'll cover for you." And *gevaldt,* you know, then we say seven blessings. If they love each other that much, they deserve seven blessings, right?

You know how deep this is, friends? *Mamash* it's clear to me. The Holy Baal Shem Tov one time came to a city, and there was this preacher there, and he was telling Yidden, "*Mamash,* you're sinners," you're this, you're that, "and you deserve to be wiped out — " He's *mamash* telling them — he's laying the fear of G-d upon them, and the Holy Baal Shem just went, "I can't take it any more," and the holy Baal Shem says to him, "Can't you make a living in another way than to say bad things to Jews?" [Laughs] I heard the story from the old Lubavitcher Rebbe [the Frierdiker Rebbe]. The Baal Shem Tov says — he went on the *bima*

— and he says, "G-d in heaven, I swear to you, he's lying. I swear to you he's lying. They are the best people in the world. The best."

And here I want you to know, why is Purim higher than Yom Kippur? [On] Yom Kippur, I'm standing before G-d, and I'm telling G-d how bad I am. Then, I need Aharon HaKohen to cover for me, Avraham, Yitzchak, Ya'akov to cover for me on Sukkos, and the Torah covers for me. You know, on Purim I'm standing before G-d and it's clear to me. *Mamash,* I don't have to say a word to G-d.

You know, I want you to know something. If I love my children very much — and I hope you all do — if my little girl says something bad about herself, I won't let her. I won't let her. I say, "How can you say something bad about my sweetest girl?" Right? So, you see, on [Yom Kippur] we are close to G-d — we are close enough to G-d to tell him everything we do wrong. But we're not that close yet. On Purim, we're so close, G-d says to me, "Don't tell me anything. Just tell me, 'Good Purim.'" GOOD PURIM!

[Musical interlude]

I wanna say one more thing. I want you to know something. If I love somebody a little bit, then, let's say, the girl I love the most, let's say, her name is Chanele, when you talk about Shprintzele, I talk of Shprintzele, right? And, you say "Rivkele" — it's Rivkele! If I love a girl the most — her name might be Chanele — and you talk about Shprintzele, I'm still thinking of Chanele. You say "Rivkele" — yeah, but I'm thinking of Chanele. You say "Sarale," and I think the whole time Chanele, right?

If you love G-d a little bit, when you mention G-d's name, it's G-d; when you mention somebody else's name, it's somebody else. On Purim, when you love G-d the most, whatever you say is G-d, right?

Every word is G-d. You say "Achashveros" — is G-d. Haman is G-d; Mordechai is G-d — there's nothing else. [Strums guitar a bit]

I have one more Torah, which is also beautiful. You know, the truth is, the Torah is G-d talking to us, right? Why do we mention G-d's name? Because we don't hear G-d is telling it to us — we read it in a book — and there it says, G-d said so. On Purim we are so high, I *mamash* hear G-d telling me the story of Esther. Our G-d doesn't say, "G-d"; He is telling the story, right?

So you see, it's clear, the real Kabbalos HaTorah — the real Receiving of the Torah, is when we read the Megillah of Esther. *Mamash*, I hear G-d talking to me. So sure, G-d doesn't say, "G-d did — "; I'm talking, right? If I tell you a story, and I say Shloime walked, Shloime ate, Shloime breathed —yeah, sure, I'm talking to you, right? [More guitar]

I have to tell you just one thing. Gerry, you know, I don't know how you handle [it] when it comes to making noise by Haman — you know what most people do? The noise is endless, right? And then they don't hear the Megillah properly, and then they stamp with their foot! I heard a *gevalt* Torah in Bobov. The first year the Bobova Rebbe came to America — I watched him. Comes to Haman [makes a thud], and he said a *gevalt* Torah.

Imagine — why do you do it like this? Because it's clear to you — you didn't do it the first time, right? [Laughter] So you think if you do it a hundred times you will do it? Or [Either] you can do it or you can't do it, right? And, you know, what is Haman, Amalek? — Takes away our self-confidence — says you can't do it anyway; I'm stronger than you, right? On Purim it's clear to me — Haman is in my hands; I wipe him out — that's it. So the Bobova Rebbe says that in Bobov, by his father, in Sanz, what are you doing it a hundred times? You give one *zetz* and that's it, right?

First of all, it's so much class, right? It's *mamash* class, right? [A clamor of laughter — this appeals to people] What? Yeah, that's it, you give one *zetz*, you know? I watched the Bobova Rebbe, you know, the way he was reading the Megillah — *mamash* like a prince, right? And us shleppers go [Shlomo gestures and mimes], and then you go like this, and the way they go like this — and they don't listen to the Megillah, and they make — get crazy. In Bobov, it's so beautiful. The people with their foot — one — and the kids with their gregger — one time. It's very beautiful.

I had the privilege — *Baruch HaShem* — of breaking through in my shul, you know? It's *mamash* beautiful. First of all, it's class, and second, it's *mamash* Haman — ch' — like an atomic explosion. [...strums]

Which one? Oh, you're talking to Denny [Shuman] now? Ahh. Yeah. I think last year they taped my Megillah reading, yeah. I heard it in Bobov when he came to America. But in my shul — Oh, you want to hear the Megillah reading with one *zetz*?! Okay, we'll have to do something.

Okay, and also something which is very important. You know, everybody's sending *Shaloch Manos* to friends. What about your own wife, your own children? You know, we are so busy doing things for the world, we forget the closest, right? Baruch HaShem, I got through to my chevra on the Moshav. You wouldn't believe how beautiful it is to watch them. Every little child brings *Shaloch Manos* for their parents, you know? It is so sweet! And so beautiful, you know? What?

You know what the cutest thing in the world is — last year when my cutest little Dari gave Neshamale *Shaloch Manos* for me, you know? And I gave Neshama *Shaloch Manos* back from my little Dari, you know? Oh, it was so sweet! Tch! I told you, this is deeper than the High Priest on Yom Kippur, you know, it's just — it is touching the deepest, deepest depths of our neshama, you know? It's not asking for forgiveness on Yom Kippur — it's just tch!...

Imagine husband and wife, all they talk about [is] forgiving each other — what a relationship is that, right? [Laughs] You see, I'm not — let me tell you something! Let me make it clear to you — I'm only saying this now because it's Purim, right? When it comes Yom Kippur, I'll tell you — *gevalt!* It's Yom Kippur — *Heilige* — *gevalt!* [Laughter]

And I have to tell you a Bobova Torah, which is true. Bobova Rebbe says, "By us Yidden it's like this: when it comes Pesach, Pesach is the greatest thing in the world. I mean, how can you compare anything to Seder Night? Really. You don't know what *Yiddishkeit* is. Comes Shavuos, you say, "What's Pesach?" Right? "Shavuos! *Mamash*, I'm standing on Mt. Sinai — this is it, right?" Then comes Rosh HaShanah. I say, "Listen, really, leave me in peace with Shavuos. Rosh HaShanah I blow the shofar! This is when I — when my soul is the deepest." Comes Yom Kippur, I say, "What are you talking about? Rosh HaShanah is cute. Yom Kippur! *Mamash*, it's the holy of holiest." Then comes Sukkos. "What's so big about Yom Kippur? Ach! Sukkos is — I'm sitting in the Sukkah, *mamash*, I'm sitting and completely surrounded by G-d's light — I mean, what are you talking about Yom Kippur?" Then comes Simchas Torah. I say, "What's Sukkos? They sit and they eat? It's nothing. Simchas Torah, when I dance with the Torah, that's the highest thing in my life." Then comes Chanukah. I say, "What's Simchas Torah? I mean it's cute — you're dancing — Chanukah, I'm kindling G-d's light in the world! On the darkest night I'm kindling Mashiach's light! So what are you talking to me about Simchas Torah?" Right? Then comes Purim. I say, "Listen to me — what's Simchas Torah? What's Chanukah? How dare you? Purim is *ad-lo-yada* — it's beyond everything, beyond everything."

And the Bobova Rebbe says, "You think we are lying? It is true. On Pesach, it IS the highest Pesach in the world. On Shavuos, it IS the highest Shavuos in the world. It's all true. It is *mamash* true."

And you know, someone asked me, "What's an assimilated Jew?" So I said to him, "I can say it in millions of ways, but an assimilated Jew [is someone who] who doesn't have the taste that Pesach is not Shavuos, Shavuos is not Sukkos — it's a holiday, right? It's not 'a holiday,' right? Pesach's Pesach — something else, right?" And you know what in a good — in most Hebrew Schools, sadly enough, they gave it over to the kids — it's a holiday. In most Hebrew Schools they tell the kids, it's a holiday, another holiday, another holiday. It's not "another holiday," right?

I'll tell you something — and let me give you over one torahle from my father before I say good-bye to you. You know, my father, *Baruch HaShem* — I mentioned it yesterday — I had the privilege — my father was just...Devorale, if you ever saw my father — no, you didn't — I'm sorry I didn't invite you to my house then for Shabbos — I should have. That time I wasn't into inviting guests so much for Shabbos yet. Took me a long time to learn. What? Yeah. Took me a long time to learn, yeah. Only when I went out to the House of Love and Prayer and realized it's the only way of saving Yidden — by inviting them for Shabbos. Now, today, everybody is doing it, but at that time I was *mamash* the first, you know? Like, it was revolutionary. Everybody was spitting in my face, even for saying it. At every concert I was begging, at every shul I was begging people, invite people for Shabbos — there was no other way! There IS no other way.

One rabbi says to me, "We'll never invite you again. You made us feel very uncomfortable." Anyway — [laughs, and people laugh with him] "We came here to enjoy ourselves, not to hear you preaching!" Okay, forget it. *"Shir HaMalot."* He lost the job also, *mazal tov.* So there. I'm not singin', he ain't a-preachin'. *Mazal tov.* I think he is selling horses now in Israel. I'm joking [more laughter] — I'm joking. I'm joking. But it's a good joke. [Laughs some more]

You know, the joke is like this. A rabbi went to Israel, and he is selling horses. So people are saying, "What's going on here?" He says, "In America horses tell the rabbi what to do. So why shouldn't in Israel rabbis — yeah. The horses — In America horses tell the rabbi what to do, so why shouldn't in Israel a rabbi tell horses what to do? You know?" [Dead air] No, I didn't say it right. Something — [laughter] something is missing. Anyway, I want you to know — [more laughter] who cares?

Okay, I want to tell you my father's Torah. My father was always giving over to my brother and me, you have *mamash* to take care of all the Jews, you know? So my father says to me, "There are two kinds of assimilated Jews. One you can help, and one — forget it. Maybe Mashiach will help them, but I don't think you can." My father explained it to me like this. "Imagine in B'nai Brak an assimilated Jew is driving his car" — or let's say half assimilated — I don't want to — it's not — I'm not judging them. I'm just telling it the way my father told it to me.

"A Jew is driving his car, and there is a red light. And he sees a Yiddele with a shtreimel, with seven children, crossing the street, right? And he thinks, 'I wish I could run them over, those disgusting Jews — khhh! Can't stand them.'" My father says, "This kind of a Jew, forget it." But then he says, "Someone is driving [on] Shabbos, and he sees a shtreimel and the seven children walking in the street, going to shul, and suddenly he has tears in his eyes. 'Master of the world, I wish it would be me and my seven children.' Ah," my father says, "all he needs is to be invited to a Shabbos. He wants to have Shabbos — he doesn't have it; give it to him. The other one doesn't want it, you know? So what are you giving it to him [for]? He doesn't want it, right?"

You know, in Netanyah, there is this big street now. One time my chevra and I stopped, and we bought pizza. And I said to the person selling the pizza, "Hey, *korei l'cha?* What's your name?" Chatzkele. I said, "Chatzkele, when are you coming to my moshav for Shabbos?" Do you know something? He put down the pizza, burst out crying. *Mamash* burst out crying. I said to him, "My Chatzkele, *ma kara l'cha?* What's happening?" He says to me, "Do you know, I'm in Israel for thirty years — and I'm waiting for somebody to invite me for Shabbos. And you are the first invitation I got." Isn't that unbelievable? He says, "I'm waiting for thirty years for an invitation." You never know, right? *Mamash,* you don't know.

[Begins strumming] Okay, let's sing one more song. [Launches into a melodic *"Dovid Melech Yisrael."* Plays for two minutes, then...] I heard one story in Bobov, which, like — I told it all over the world. You know, Bobov, they weren't so rich, in Poland. By the old Bobova Rebbe, Reb Shloimele, a hundred years ago. How much money did they have to buy beer? Though they had one big barrel of beer, and everybody was supposed to get a little drop. So there was one husky Chasid standing there, and drinking from the beer the whole time! Doesn't let anybody get close. So the Bobova Rebbe says, "Hey, Avramele. You're not the only person in the world. How about loving your neighbor as yourself? Somebody else wants beer also."

He says, "Rebbe, that's a good commandment for all year. But Purim I have to get drunk. So I gotta drink." The Rebbe looked at him for a long time. He says, "If you love your neighbor like yourself, you can get drunk by giving a glass of beer to somebody else." *L'Chaim! L'Chaim!* [Crowd calls back *"L'Chaim!"*] Good Purim! *Gevalt!* Thank you, folks. [Crowd calls back even louder, and clapping, too, "Good Purim!"] Hahaha. [Crowd laughs back] Peace. Peace to the pizzas.

# Another Purim Story and Teaching from Reb Shlomo

I would like to share with you, my beautiful friends, a story of the holy Vorke, the *Heilige* Reb Yitzchok of Vorke. One of his Chassidim, Moshele, was so poor, utterly poor, that he borrowed two hundred rubles from Reb Yankele, who was not rich and not poor — in between. He never paid it back. One night the holy Vorke went to visit Moshele, and Reb Yankele decided, "This is my time to ask him for the money back, because in front of the Rebbe he cannot — the Rebbe will do something to make him pay it back." He knocks on the door, and the Rebbe opens the door.

He says, "Hey, Reb Yankele, what brings you here so late at night?"

Yankele says, "Rebbe, I don't want to put Moshele to shame, but I have no other way. He owes me two hundred rubles for so many years, and he never paid it back."

The Vorke says to Moshele, "Moshele, it is just the three of us, so please don't be ashamed. Whatever money you have in the house, please bring it and put it on the table." And the holy Vorke said, "Oh, thank you so much. It is very, very beautiful."

He began counting: one, two, three...forty-one, forty-two...fifty-two, fifty-three...fifty-five, fifty-six. And he kept on counting the same pennies: fifty-eight, fifty-nine, sixty.... He counted until he reached two million rubles. Then he took the fifty-six pennies, and he gave them to Yankele, and he says, "Here is your money." It goes without saying, after a few weeks Yankele was a multi-millionaire.

You know, friends, on Purim, you know what I am doing? Whatever you did for me, I count it a million times when you are not looking.

You know, friends, when I love somebody very much, and I spend with them one moment? How often do I count that moment in my heart, in my soul, in my head? Millions of times.

You know, friends, each time I have the privilege of putting my children to sleep, is it one time? It is zillions of times. It is eternity times.

Each time I see my children *bentch licht* Friday night, was it one time? Eternity times.

Friends, I want you to know, each time I have the privilege of opening a Gemara, I look at these holy words. Did you learn this page one time? It is thousands of times, and you know, my beautiful friends, the Talmud always starts with page two. There is no page one. There is no one, a Jew never looks at a page one time; it is always more than one.

So I want you to know, my beautiful friends, on Yom Kippur I am standing before G-d, and G-d is counting exactly how many good deeds I did, and how many, G-d forbid, wrong things I did, and puts it on a scale, and then they decide. On Purim they can't judge me. You know why? Because on Purim, every good deed I did, G-d counts millions of time when I am not looking, when I don't know.

You know, friends, as long as G-d's name is only when it is written clear, it is one time. For me, G-d's name is a thousand times; everything is G-d.

# Reb Shlomo: The Specialness of Seder Night

### At Congregation Beth Israel in Berkeley, California, Sunday morning, 8 Nisan, 5754 / March 20, 1994; co-sponsored by the Aquarian Minyan

Recorded by David Miller; Transcribed by Reuven Goldfarb

Reb Shlomo: So can I ask all the good friends who want to learn with me a little bit, can you please move over here? Can you move? Can you move over here, friends? Come a little bit closer, so we won't have to be so far away from each other.

Okay, I want to learn a little bit, but just to warm up our hearts a little bit. [Shlomo begins to play. After the first run-through, he addresses those assembled.] Join me. [First song runs about three minutes. Then he segues into another song, at the climax of which he again says, "Join me." This song concludes in a little less than three minutes.]

Okay, thank you so much for coming. And — let's learn a little bit. I don't know where to begin and where to end, so I'll start right in the middle. You know, there are two ways of talking to children. Sometimes we talk to children baby talk, right? And we talk to them, like, on their level. But I'll tell you something — imagine, G-d forbid, there's a fire in the house, right? And I'm telling my children, "You better get out of here fast!" I don't talk baby talk. I talk to them straight, right?

I want you to know, G-d also sometimes, He talks to us baby talk, on our level, so we can understand what He's saying. And sometimes, G-d is talking to us on HIS level. But the truth is, we are just ordinary human beings; we are limited human beings. We don't have vessels for that kind of talk. We don't have vessels for this great, great, great light.

There's one night — one night — *mamesh*, when G-d opens all the gates. But you know, Seder night — Pesach — we need new vessels, right? It's not only because it's *chumatz*. The deepest depth[s] is that G-d gives us new vessels. G-d gives us — heavenly vessels. It's the light of Pesach — *ssss* — unbelievable light — unbelievable light shining into us.

You see, the world thinks free means I can do what I want to — this is kid stuff, right? Imagine you'll ask a baby — what's freedom? Freedom means, for me, is that I don't have to put on my diapers, right? This is what we are all into — I can do what I want to, right?

Freedom is that I am free to receive the deepest depths, right? The deepest depths. I want you to know — we don't have the faintest idea how much G-d wants to give us, right? And Reb Nachman says — even deeper — we have no idea how much is coming down from Heaven every second, right? G-d is not stingy, right?

But — I want to tell you something very, very deep. Sometimes you talk to somebody, and you want to pour out your heart, right? And you want to tell them something so deep; and while you're talking to them, suddenly you realize they don't know what you're talking about, right? Do you know how much that hurts? *Gevalt*, does it hurt.

And you know what it is, all year long, G-d wants to talk to us, and we pick up a little bit. Seder night — and you know, in the Zohar, Seder night is called *"mochin d'gadlus"* — completely different brains. You know what a slave is? A slave is somebody who has very petty brains.

I'll tell you something, as a far-out example — little bit — you know, in *Pirke Avos* — Sayings of the Fathers — it says the difference between the students of Abraham and the students of Bilaam (5:22), but in the Medresh, there's a different definition. The definition is that the students of Bilaam, let's say, buy something for a gold coin, and he [the shopkeeper] has to give them back change, a few pennies. So they stand there, and they count the pennies, and maybe one penny is missing. They're wasting their time and talk about the penny. The students of Avram don't count cash. The penny is not worth it to waste words on it or time.

You know, the Gemara says, a pagan, a pagan — and take it as it is — [Aramaic phrase] it means he could be killed over less than a penny. You know what that means? There are people who are ready to be killed over less than a penny, right? They'll start the biggest fight — and I don't want to say anything bad — sometimes when you go into a store and the cashier — she doesn't mean anything bad, and she doesn't get the money anyway — so she made the mistake of a nickel, right? Okay, so she made a mistake, so what? Then some people start up and say, "I'll call the manager" and "I'll have you fired" — they're ready to kill this girl for the one nickel, right? What's their problem? Their brains. [Titters] Yeah, their brains are defective. You know, and hopefully here you'll understand — a nickel is not a dollar, a dollar is not ten dollars, but if your brain is not really functioning properly, a nickel looks like a million dollars.

Seder night — *mochin d'gadlus* [expanded consciousness]. Look at the whole world — look at the whole world. And here I want to add something so deep, so deep. You know, the way we understand G-d all year long is so petty. Yeah, there is — I really don't know exactly what it is, but there is some being there, and he created the world, and he's spelled Gee Oh Dee — and if you're *frum*, it's Gee Dash Dee [laughter]

— I mean, I know it because I have my Ph.D. in Theology. Have you ever spoken to those people who teach Theology? I'm telling you, I know more about Chiang Kai-Shek's mother than they know about G-d. They know nothing — nothing.

Let me tell you something, and this is really the deepest. You know something? Imagine if a baby would be born, and the baby doesn't know who the parents are, right? So, he's taken by a nurse, grows up in a home for babies, and then, when the baby is eighteen years old, ready to understand the facts of life, then someone comes and teaches them how babies are created, and the door opens, and says, "Hah — meet your creator. Meet your father and your mother." What would the relationship be? I'm looking at my father and my mother — I would say, "Who cares?" Right? And here I know this is my father and my mother, right? Scientifically.

Why do babies love their parents so much? You know, every baby, every child, really believes that "My parents are the best people in the world." And blessing everyone we should never disappoint our children. You know what kind of knowledge the baby has about "These are my parents"? This is not petty knowledge you picked up in a book, *Facts of Life*. This is *mochin d'gadlus*. Something else. The deepest.

So the Zohar *kodesh* says, all year long we know G-d the way I know my parents because I took a course in Biology. Seder night G-d gives me back my G-d knowledge like the way when the baby is born. Oh, is that deep. *Gevalt*, is that deep. *Mamash*, I can't even bear it. My G-d.

You know, I want you to know something. Sadly enough, do you know how much we parents sometimes destroy this G-d knowledge and parent knowledge of our children? So they stop talking to us. Seder night, something happens, and suddenly between me and my children, it's back, just like they were born that moment. It's awesome, you know. Awesome is not the word. It's heartbreaking — I mean, not heartbreakingly sad, heartbreakingly beautiful.

I have to share something with you awesome. I know someone in *Eretz Yisrael*, in the Holy Land, and, you know, I'm blessing everyone never to go bankrupt, none of us, because when we came out of Egypt, we came out very rich. Why is he crying? He's okay? He's okay?

David Miller: He can't decide where he wants to be.

Shlomo: None of us, none of us can decide.

Reuven: There's child-care outside.

David: Yeah, I know, he doesn't want to go.

Shlomo: *Oy vey, oy vey, gevalt.* He needs Vera!

Shlomo: Okay, I didn't want to drop it. I just wanted to know why he's crying. Okay, give me your attention again. I met this Yiddele in Tel Aviv who was *mamash* a multi-millionaire, and then, it should never happen to anyone, suddenly he went — *mamash* — bankrupt. Then he disappeared, and I didn't see him any more. Then just some time ago, I walked down 57th St., and I see, *nebech*, somebody's pushing a little wagala with hot coffee and middle eastern cake — I look at it —ah! my Yiddele. My — *nebech* — bankrupt Yiddele. *Nebech, nebech* — *mamash* a *shlepper* now.

So I didn't know if he wants to talk to me. So I stood there, by a window, looking in, like I'm looking at the window of the store, but giving him a chance, and if he wants to talk to me, he can see me. He came up to me, he hugged me, he said, "Ah, Shloime, *gevalt!*" I said, "What's going on with you?" So he says to me, "Let me tell you something. You know, economically, I'm a little bit bankrupt. But let me show you a letter of my daughter."

It is actually the most beautiful letter I have ever seen of a child writing to her father. She wrote her father the letter on her eighteenth birthday, when she entered the holy army of Israel, and she writes to her father: "'Dear father, I want you to know, today I am eighteen years old. But I still love you as much as I loved you on the day when I was born.' So you see what kind of a millionaire I am?" He says to me, "Do you know how much would Rothschild give to get such a letter from his children?" *Gevalt*, right?

So Seder night — Seder night is the night when G-d restores our relationship to our children. And this is *mochin d'gadlus*, right? You know why most children are so sad? 'Cause their parents look at them, you know, "Listen, I'm a grown-up; I know how children are produced; I produced you — this man and this woman produced you — and also we paid for your diapers, we paid for your college — " This is not where it's at. This is all outside stuff. It's lower than outside.

So Seder night — unbelievable — but know one more very important thing. I want you to know, we give the way we receive. You know, the Maharal says — what's the problem of a stingy person? The world says, "A stingy person is somebody who doesn't want to give." The Maharal says, "No. The problem is he has never received anything." He has never received anything. He has no vessels to receive. He has it in his pockets, maybe, but inside he never received anything. So he can't give.

You know why, when I see a poor man, I pull out a nickel, and I tell him, "Listen, please stay out on the street — don't come to my house" — because even the house I'm living in I never received. Maybe I received the outside — I have my address, and I pay taxes, I pay the mortgage. Seder night — and I want you to know the deepest depths — we were learning it a thousand times — Pesach is one holiday where I need a house. You know, Chanukah I have to kindle the lights at the door of my house, but I can walk up to brother Dov and to his house and say, "Listen, here's a quarter. I want to be part and give you rent for the house for two minutes when I'm *bentching* Chanukah *licht*," and it's 100% *ba'al peh halacha* [legal according to the Oral Tradition]. For the moment it's my house.

But if I would walk up to Dov and say, "Here's a quarter. Can I walk around looking for *chumatz*?" He would say, "This is not your house," right? To look for *chumatz*, it has to be my house. And I just want to repeat — which most of you I'm sure learned — this is a classic Torah from Rav Kook. Sammy and I were learning it every year, and it's the deepest. The English — whatever it's called — when the English were still in Israel, they invited Rav Kook for Pesach, he should give a talk, about what's Pesach for us Jews? So he says, Every country wants to look for the *chumatz* in another country. He says, England is looking for *chumatz* in America; America is looking for *chumatz* in Russia. Russia is looking for *chumatz* in the whole world, right? Pesach is — look for *chumatz* in your house! *Gevalt*, right?

A slave looks always for *chumatz* somewhere else. You know how much freedom you need to look for your own *chumatz*? But you must have a house. And you know what it is? I want you to know the deepest depths. The night before the Seder — and I'm blessing you to have a taste in it — you know, a lot of people begin Pesach by the Seder. The Mishna begins *Pesachim*, "*Or l'arba'ah osar*" [by light of the 14th.] And the Ishbitzer says, on the fourteenth day, the night before Pesach, a great light is shining into me. Because unless a great light is shining, you'll never find your *chumatz*, right? Then you'll find, maybe, a little bagel you bought last year. But the real *chumatz* — the inside — and you know what the great light is? The great light is that suddenly it's shining into you what your real place in the world is, what your house really is. Then I look at myself — *gevalt*, am I far. *Gevalt*, am I, or am I destroying my own house, or I'm not even living in my house. In my house, in my four walls, my infinite space in the world — which is just four inches, but it's infinite, right?

So Seder night, when suddenly G-d gives me my house, my place in the world, I have no problem Seder night to invite the whole world to my house. You know why I didn't invite you yesterday? I didn't have a house. I can't invite you; I'm not in my house, right? Seder night — and now listen — open your heart, so deeply. Everybody knows that the angels came to Avram the first morning of Pesach, right? Avraham Avinu enters the covenant with G-d, and it says the next morning, the third day, "and he sat at the door of his house." And Reb Nachman says, if you want to know who is the master of the house, if someone's sitting by the table and eating, it could be the guest, right? How do you know who is the owner? The one who opens the door.

Let's say I'm visiting my friend Marvin — I mean, he knows I'm bringing *shleppers* with me — but officially, officially, I shouldn't, right? But I have no right to open the door and say, "Hey, *chevre*, come in!" It's not my house, right? The owner, right?

So Seder night, [it] becomes my house. And I want to tell you something so deep. Do you think my children are only my children because physically I brought them into the world? Oh, the connection is so much deeper. You know, you ask any holy sister who has the privilege of bringing children into the world — do they see the baby for the first time when they hold the baby in their hands? It's clear to them, I know this baby for thousands of years, right? I'll ask Yehudit, right? From before creation, right? *Mochin d'gadlus*, right?

You'll ask a scientist — that's crazy talk. I mean, you know, you got pregnant, you have a baby, and that's it, right? Without getting involved in the depths, you know what — what the Russians wanted, the Communists? They wanted to take babies away from their parents the moment they're born. This was their ideal. But there should be just a home for children, and just once a week they should see their parents, and maybe not see their parents until they are 16, 17 years old. Destroy this *mochin d'gadlus*.

You know what communism is all about? Do you think communism is to share everything you have with somebody else? No. That's the way they thought. I've been in Russia a few times, before. Communism is that you have nothing to do with another person. Parents don't talk to their children; children don't talk to their parents. You definitely don't talk to another person. You're afraid! I'm afraid to open my heart, right?

So Seder night — and again I want you to know something. What is the deepest relationship? Not that I can talk to you — that I can shine my whole *neshama* into you, right? My whole heart is shining into you. And your whole heart is shining into me, right? Infinite. So Seder night, when, humanly speaking, G-d — *mamash* G-d — is shining into me — we say, *"Ani, v'lo malach, ani v'lo seraph"* — G-d says, '...me, not an angel, not a seraph' — *mamash "ehla hakodesh boruch hu."* I want you to know, the Alter Rebbe — Lubavitch — when [he] would say Seder night *"ehla hakodesh boruch hu'* — *mamash* G-d Himself — he would always faint away — took a long time to revive him. You know, *mamesh* — G-d is shining into me.

You know, something you cannot reach in 2000 lifetimes, on Seder night, G-d is shining into me. And the moment G-d is shining into me, then — you know — all the slavery — I'm afraid of this one, I'm afraid of this one, and I think this one is my master, this one is my master — it's clear to me, nobody is my master — nobody is my master.

And here I want to share something with you, which maybe — maybe some of you don't know it, which is really so special. What do you think the Egyptians felt that night when we left Egypt? Do you know, they also had the highest G-d revelation in the world. Awesome. Just awesome. That night it was clear to Pharaoh that he is not the master. What do you think? Pharaoh let us go; he had a meeting with his congress, and they decided, okay, let the Jews go. It was clear — do you know, do you know how we walked out of Egypt? — like, in today's language? All of the rock bands of Egypt got together — the *medresh* says — Pharaoh invited all the musicians of Egypt, and they walked us to the border! They walked us to the border. Unbelievable, right? *Psss*.

I want you to know something which is not to be believed! — not to be believed. G-d says to Moshe, "Tell the Yidden to borrow gold and silver from their neighbors." And it says, *V'yishalu ish ma-es ray-ayhu* [*Shemot* 11:2]. You know, again, if you just learned the Torah from King James — and I always say, if you read the Bible, just King James' version, you better read *Peyton Place*; it's more interesting. At least it's a little bit exciting! Now listen to me, friends.

By the Torah, *ray'ayhu* means your equal — doesn't mean just your neighbor. It means like, crazy. Seder night, when you have the highest G-d revelation, I should walk in to the lowest Egyptian, who [is] hitting me and whipping me all his life? He is my equal? He is the lowest creep in the world. That night — that night — it was *mamesh* like after Mashiach had come. I want you to know we came out of Egypt — not only the Jews — I hope it's clear to you — not only the Jews walked out. All of the slaves of Egypt walked out with us. That's why Pharaoh got wise, after a few days. He saw the whole economy is falling apart 'cause there's no more slaves.

So you hear, friends, Seder night — Seder night — what is shining into me — what is shining into me? Something so deep, so lofty, so *gevalt*. You know what hurts you and me sometimes — you are invited to somebody's Seder, and their mind is so petty that G-d forbid — and G-d forbid — the wine is shuckling a little bit, and you make a stain on the tablecloth, then the hostess — I remember once I was — never again — I was by mistake by somebody's seder, and *nebech*, one of the guests — one of the guests, *nebech*, *nebech* — G-d should forgive him the eternal sin — a stain on the tablecloth Seder night. I want you to know, this hostess was mad for four days. I thought she's divorcing her husband the same night for inviting this person.

What's her problem? *Gevalt, gevalt* — was she far from the light of Seder night shining into her. You know, Rabbi Akiva Eger, one of the greatest in the world — he had this tremendous custom; it's really beautiful to tell you. Obviously, he was the Chief Rabbi of Posen — he was the Rebbe of the world, about 200 years ago. He was *mamesh* the greatest. He was so afraid if one of the guests makes a stain, then his wife — hopefully not, but you never know. So you know what he did when he walked in to the Seder? The first thing he did, he took the wine and poured it all over the tablecloth — forget it! Forget about the tablecloth. Don't be a slave to the tablecloth. Don't be a slave to anything. *Mochin d'gadlus*, you know? Do you think the table is only beautiful because the tablecloth is white? When your heart is dark, what good is it? Right? *Gevalt. Mochin d'gadlus.* So you hear, friends, Seder night, what is shining into me, like with Avraham Avinu, the moment, the moment you enter the covenant with G-d — you know what it means, "the covenant"? When I make a covenant with somebody — this is a Torah from the Izbica [the Ishbitzer] also — I cannot make a covenant with a dog. I might love my doggela, but I can't make a covenant with him — 'cause a doggela is a doggela, and I'm not, hopefully, right? You can only make a covenant with an equal.

When Avram Avinu entered the covenant with G-d, that means all of G-d was shining into him. And suddenly Avraham Avinu has the vessel for all of it, right? And those three pagans who came? Outside, they looked like three lonely pagans, but what he saw there were strangers, and *mamash* they need me to lift up their souls. And he was ready to do everything, right? Everything. Everything. So you see, friends, freedom for them is not holding back — receiving everything and giving everything — because the moment I receive everything, really, I can also give everything, right?

You know what Yosef HaTzaddik said to his brothers when they came to Egypt? He says, *"Anochi achalkayl es-chem"* [I will sustain you, *B'reisheet*, 50:21]. And if you know Hebrew, *Achalkayl* means to sustain you, support you, but I'm sure most of you speak Hebrew — *achalkayl* comes from the word *kol, kol,* right, to *kol.* It means the all of me to the all of you. You know, friends, most of us have friends to a little detail of us. How many of us have friends [to] whom you can relate on the level of awe? *Mamash*, awe. How many husbands and wives can relate on the level of awe? One married woman told me the most her husband had spoken to her in the last 20 years was, "What are we having for dinner?" "What are our plans for Sunday?" This is already a good marriage. Where's the awe? Where's the inside, right? Want to sing a little song. [The remainder of Side One is blank.]

[Side Two] Reb Shlomo: What a gift! The deepest, deepest, deepest gift there is. And you see, Pesach has to be before Shavuos. Because unless all of G-d is shining into me, how can I receive G-d's word? I'm sure it's clear to you — I can only talk to a person I'm really connected to. If I'm not connected to you, yeah, I can ask you, "How's the weather?" But I cannot talk to you inside talk, right?

So Pesach is this deepest connection. Just remember what the Rebbes say: On Shavuos we receive the Torah; on Pesach, *mamash*, we receive G-d — *"Ehla haKodesh boruch Hu beekh'vodo"* [But the Holy One, Blessed be He, in His Glory].

David: Shlomo, do you have time for a question?

Reb Shlomo: From you, brother? [Strums his guitar] What do you want to say?

David: Well, I'm troubled, the slaves.

Shlomo: Yeah.

David: They were never able to — forty years later, they were still slaves. Can you help us know, you know, and to open up our hearts?

Shlomo: Brother, you're the highest, the highest Jew in the world. Listen, let me tell you something. It's a deep question you're asking, but let me tell you something. So he's asked me, so if that light is so great that even later on we are not completely free yet, and they were not even really ready to go to the Holy Land. The answer is — *mamash*, thank you for asking me — the saddest thing about it is that this light is shining only Seder night. And then, sadly enough, it's up to you if you want to keep it or not.

You know why they count the Omer? Counting the Omer is making vessels — making vessels that this light should stay with us. Listen to me. If this light would be shining forever, Mashiach would come the next morning, right? And that's it! Obviously, it's not.

You know what it is? G-d gives us a taste of the way I could be — and G-d gives us a taste of how the world could be. And here I want to share with you, *mamash l'koved* Dovidl, an Izbica [this is the correct orthography according to scholarly sources; however, from here on I will spell it phonetically, to better convey Shlomo's pronunciation. — RG] Torah that's just awesome. Blessing you and me to learn, really, *mamash, Mei HaShiloach*, it's the deepest. You know, I heard from old Chasidim, we do not understand how did the world exist before the *Heilige* Ishbitzer.

You know, let me tell you, maybe some of you know who Ishbitz is — I didn't say hello to you, yet, brother. Hey! Ishbitze is a little town not far from Lublin. And there was this big rebbe, Reb Mordecai Yosef Leiner — and he was *mamash* the deepest. His grandson writes about him that a lot of people know the Torah, "but very few are privileged to know the Torah the way it was given on Mt. Sinai, which is my grandfather." In the long history, he was one of the few who received the Torah *ki n'see-nu-sum miSinai* — the way it was given on Mt. Sinai. And my personal privilege is that my great-great grandfather lived in Izbica, and he was a chasid of the *Mei HaShiloach*. Awesome. I could blow my mind already day and night, right?

But you know what happened? He moved to Germany, and then, I don't know what, they became German Jews [laughter] — nothing I can do about it, right? [More laughter] Yeah, they were Yekkes! A Yekke knows exactly when you have to *bentch licht*. A Yekke knows exactly — what time it is [laughter]. But he only knows what time it's down here; he never knows what time it's up there, y'know.

But then, my grandfather had eight sons and four daughters. The four daughters, three of them married rabbis, and the eight sons — three became really the leading rabbis in Germany, and the other three became — *mamash*, I need them now, but they're not there — multi-billionaires. Do you know that my father's oldest brother — my father's oldest brother — when he was eighteen, became an elevator boy in a bank. By 22, he was the owner of ten banks in Germany. And you know how rich he was? That the German Kaiser asked him he should give him one of his summer houses in the summer.

But let me tell you something. My uncle traveled all over Europe. (Back then America wasn't so strong.) So you would say my uncle most probably he's not so *frum* any more, he's a multi-millionaire. My uncle traveled with the whole *gescheft*. He traveled with people who are cooking for him, and — and — and — and — and he had his own Minyan. Yeah. My uncle was crazy like — he would never — he has to daven with a Minyan. So, let's say, he would take a train from Hamburg to Lubeck, he would take the train in such a way that he would have enough time to go to shul in Lubeck and daven with a Minyan. He would go to Frankfurt and he would take a Minyan with him in the train, you know? Awesome! Awesome.

I want you to know, my uncle was such a genius that even after the First World War, the Depression, the only bank in Germany which was still functioning was my uncle's. He was such a super-genius that he managed to keep the bank going. One day he had a cold. He told the people at the bank, "Please don't do anything without asking me!" And there was his assistant — I don't want to say anything bad — who was always jealous at my uncle that he is such a genius. So something came up; he decided that "I don't have to ask," and the bank was bankrupt within fifteen minutes.

*Nebech*, my holy uncle, when he heard this — and he was like the last hold for people who trusted him with millions of dollars 'cause they knew my uncle can be trusted. So when he heard that the bank fell apart, *mamash* he had a heart attack and died instantly. He couldn't bear the pain. And I'm sure, I could swear it was not the pain of his own money. It was the pain of all the thousands of people that trusted him with billions, billions, billions of mark[s].

Anyway — Ishbitzer, right? So the Ishbitzer says the deepest Torah in the world. You know, the first day of Pesach, when you bring also a sin offering, the *chatat*. So he asks, we just became Yidden yesterday — right? I mean, how much can you sin between the Seder and the next morning, *Shacharis*, unless, I mean you didn't meet us, we are experts on sin, right? We could have done a lot of things. But he asks, under normal circumstances, how much can you do? He says, we have to bring a sin offering because that night we could have brought Mashiach. We could have redeemed the whole world. We were so happy to get out of Egypt — we were so happy that it's a little bit better, that we forgot the world. Awesome Torah.

But you see, that night — you see, the way we are fixing it, that we hope maybe tonight, maybe we'll really fix the whole world. So we open the door, and we walk out, waiting for Elijah the Prophet — gotta sing a good song — we have such holy musicians here — the best — the best of the best.

So here, Dovidl — it's shining, and it's up to you to hold onto it.

Woman: How do you do that?

Shlomo: I'm sorry. What?

Woman: How do you do that?

Shlomo: So this is what the Counting of the Omer is. You see, basically, we don't have, really, vessels for this great light in our daily lives. But slowly, slowly. So the first night is *Chesed sh'b'Chesed*. Master of the world, shine into my facility of loving to this infinite light of you. Then the next week, I'm *mamash*, I'm praying for *Gevurah*, right? And, hopefully, by Shavuos — because the Torah is again all of G-d — but then, it's already up to me how much I received.

You see, Shavuos is up to me how much I receive. Seder, it's just if I want to, I get the whole thing. Shavuos is not a gift; Shavuos is like a business deal. You want to? 'Cause G-d asks us, do you want to have the Torah? Yeh. G-d didn't ask us, do you want to get out of Egypt? It's just shining into us. 'Cause you don't ask someone you love, do you want to give? You give it to them, right?

David M.: Last year at Yakar, you were giving the most *gevalt* learnings on the Four Sons — I think it was at Yakar.

Shlomo: Yeah?

David: Maybe it's too much to make the whole thing again, but I'm just thinking, trying to remember exactly the stuff you were saying about the son who doesn't know how to ask.

Shlomo: So, brother, if you're coming, then I'll have to learn it again. Brother, you're the highest.

David: We all need to know.

Shlomo [strums guitar]: F minor. [Begins playing — and, *mamash*, soon there is *freilich* dancing. Continues for seven minutes at that level, then goes softer and slower and gentler to its conclusion at the end of the ninth minute.] Okay, let's do something and learn a few minutes because stupidly, sadly enough, at 2 o'clock, *mamash*, I have to leave. So, let's — okay, we'll learn about the four sons — which is you and I, always. Thank you for getting up to dance.

All right, I want you to know, my beautiful friends, every year — *Barukh atah adonai eloheynu melech ha-olam, sh'hakol ne'heyeh bidvaro.*

David: Amen.

Shlomo [drinks]: Coming from Leah, it's straight from paradise. Another thing. You're the best.

Listen to me, my beautiful friends. Let it be clear to you that every year — you know, the Gemara says, G-d gives it, but he never takes it back. That light stays with us, and even if [we] don't have vessels on the outside of us to integrate it into our daily lives...we [still] have it.

You know, the *Heilige* Stepanefsha says — you know, sometimes you have a *gevalt* Shabbos, right? But then, right after Havdalah, you go right back to your old tricks. So you think you lost that Shabbos. You didn't. Shabbos is still there. And he says, the Stepanefsha says that every Yid, every person, has a little bank in their heart. And the

*Rabeino Shel Olam* puts it into your bank, into your account. And whenever you need it, you'll take it out, right?

The problem is, we never know how much we have, right? *Gevalt*, we have so much! Not only I have my own Shabboses — what happened to all the Shabboses of my Bubbes and Zeydes? They're in my account. They're gone, but they're in my account, right?

But anyway, you see, Seder night, what G-d gives me is awesome. And every year, I take a little bit — something. This is *mamesh* beautiful. The Ishbitzer says that every year, different flowers — new flowers which have never been before — come out. And he says those flowers are from that great light which is shining Seder night. It's filling the whole world. You think it's not much, in actuality, that maybe a tree can grow from it, but you know, flowers, something very soft, it just comes out.

I have to tell you something. When we were in Poland and Russia — you know how much sometimes we don't realize, you know, Poland, how much they are into flowers? You know, in America, someone gives a concert. At the end of the concert, if you like that person, you give them flowers. In Poland — after every song. I don't know how many people came — 10, 20, 30 — were full of flowers. And the most beautiful people. So I said to them, you know, it's crazy, when you want to show someone how much you love them, you should give them something which lasts longer than a flower, right? So one of the torahs they said was that when I love somebody very much, I tell them, even one minute with you is worth more than 2000 eternities without you.

Well, the Ishbitzer says that every Seder night, somewhere in the world, new flowers are getting born. It's not getting lost. And every year — you know, the Ishbitzer says, you also have to believe that you became better — you *mamash* have to know you really became better.

[Clears throat] And, uh, you know, I can change my relationship to my children, but the next morning I think, oh, I'm back where we were before — then it doesn't happen. It has to be clear to me that it really did happen. *Gevalt*, did it happen. *Gevalt*, did it happen.

So here we come to the Four Sons. And we learned it so often. And also Dovidl: you have to remind me — don't forget something — last year at Yakar we had — the whole week we were learning — so it was *gevalt*. And I don't have all the *seforim* with me.

You know, sadly enough, sadly enough, the world is so eager to minimize everything holy. I always tell my friends, do people ever say bad things about bad people? No, only about good people, right? If someone is bad, he is okay. If someone is good, we have to cut him short, cut her short, right? We're living, basically, in a world of tailors. Everybody cuts you short a little bit.

The way they translate — it's really crazy. One is a *Chacham*. One is wise. Okay, I say, thank you, G-d. My child is wise. Then I say, thank you, G-d. My son is wicked. You've gotta be an idiot to say that, right? Thank you, G-d — my son is a criminal. *Barukh haShem*, he's in prison. [Laughter] Anyway — I have to tell you something funny. A few years ago I really was a little bit sick. There was a hospital. Like, it was really a bad scene. I had a little bit of trouble with my heart. And, you know, in the emergency ward, so everybody's there together. But next to me was a patient, but he was actually in prison in Beersheva, but he was a little bit in the hospital. He was very cute. The whole night he was yelling, "In prison the bed is better than here in the hospital! [Laughter] And the food is better in prison than here. I demand better food!" And then, you know, little bit. Then he told me, he's so proud of his son, that his son, *Barukh HaShem*, is also a criminal [more laughter] and, *Barukh HaShem*, and both are sentenced to five years in prison. "*Ani — ani u-b'ni*" [I, I and my son] "*Ani u-b'ni bishvili.*" Do you understand what this means for me? — me and my son together in prison? *Gevalt*, right? [Laughter continues.] He was *mamesh* cute. I would have wanted to record this, you know, just, for eternity, the way a Jewish father is proud of his son. [Laughter. Shlomo coughs twice.]

And then we come to the *Tam*, right? *Tam* is, like, an idiot. [Greets another person] Hey, what's going on? Hey. But then, in addition, he's such an idiot, he can't even open his mouth. I'll say, thank you, G-d, *Barukh HaShem*, you know, I have a son who's completely underdeveloped. He's already 35 years old, and he can't read or write. The only thing he can do is eat. Thank you so much, G-d. It doesn't make sense, right? And one more question, which is the deepest: do you know that *Ma'alei b'Kodesh* — Everything holy is always deeper, deeper, deeper, deeper. And here we go down the drain! We start off with a wise person and end up with a complete idiot.

I want you to know, the first one — I don't know what happened before Levi Yitzchak — but the first one who like, *khh!* — who shot the arrow in the air — Reb Levi Yitzchak. So here it is. You know, G-d has many names. Sometimes G-d is called, called *Makom Ha-shel Olam*. G-d is the place of the world. You know what it means? It means that G-d makes a place for everyone. You know, the earth? Have you ever seen the earth saying, "Take your shoes off? Chutzpah, you're stepping on me?" The earth has space for everyone. G-d is called the earth of everyone. G-d says, you can always put your shoes on me, right? You can always stand on me. So we say, *Barukh HaMakom, Barukh Hu* — who blesses G-d, who makes space for everyone. Blessed is G-d who makes space for the *Chocham* — for the wise — for the wicked — and for the *Tam* — and *sh'eino yodea l'sh'ol* [for the one who doesn't know how to ask] — we'll make it fast — I'm going *b-r'shoot* [with permission].

What was it? Remember, we learned it. We learned that every year, it's just so good. What's the problem of the wise person? And you know that Seder night is a night of fixing. I say, "Thank you, G-d, tonight" — and also, you know, all of us — it's not only the outside. Inside sometimes I'm a *Choaham*, sometimes I'm a *Rasha* — so we go through all those phases ourselves. What's the problem with the wise person? The wise person is someone who knows everything but inside is dead 'cause he doesn't taste anything.

You know, friends, I can be married [and] have the most beautiful children. I can have the most beautiful house. But it doesn't mean that I really tasted — that I really feel inside what I have. So the *Chocham* is asking, "What's the Torah all about? I have a Ph.D. in Judaism" — so what? You know, it's like someone says, like asking the singing nun, "What is marriage all about?" You know — without saying anything bad about my friends, the singing nuns, right? They don't know what it is, right? But if you know what it is, if you know the words — do you know the inside?

So you know that so many moments in our lives we know everything, but *gevalt*, we don't taste it. I want you to know something. You and I, obviously, so many parents — just recently I was in somebody's house. They have the cutest kids in the world, and the little boy says to his father — he wanted to play with his father a little bit — so he says, "Daddy, I want to play with you a little bit." I'm telling you, the lowest person in the world would melt — the way he answered him so rough. "I have no time! I have some business to attend!" What kind of business did he have?

I was once in the office of a very big millionaire. His little girl called up. Then he says, "I told you not to disturb me in my office!" Bang. This girl is so cute. I wish I could have adopted her at that moment. Well, so he is wise. I'm sure he can write a book on marriage. But he doesn't know anything. So you know why we are not permitted to eat [anything else] after we eat the afikomen? So the taste of the matzah should stay with us.

Obviously, we are asking him, "Have you ever tasted anything in your life? Did you ever do anything and the taste stayed with you for a long time?" You know, friends, imagine I meet somebody I like. I meet them till six. Ten after six, I meet somebody else. When I meet someone I love very much, after the date, I cannot meet somebody else. Because I love them so much — the taste — I don't want to destroy the taste. Ah, it's so good. You know, when you come from the holy wall — you don't turn around and you go to a movie. Takes a long time to leave the holy wall. Taste.

Then we come to the *Rasha*. You see, the wise person is addicted — he is a slave to his mind. He says, this is all there is to life, right? I know my wife, I know everything about her. I know when she was born, and I know [what] she looks like, and I know how she cooks — what else is there to know? Nothing. So the fixing of the *Chacham* is — Seder night, G-d opens gates, that this *Chacham* suddenly realizes, "*Gevalt*, am I off! *Gevalt* am I off. *Gevalt* I need fixing."

Then comes the *Rasha*. You know, the *Rasha* is addicted to being bad. The *Rasha* is somebody who wants to be good sometimes, but he can't bring himself to be good, because he's supposed to be bad, right. You know, I know a lot of people — You gotta go, brother? *Mamash*, thank you. Give him the biggest hand — he's *mamash* the best [large applause]. Thank you a million times. Listen, beautiful friends, I'll make it fast. I want you to know something. What are the most heartbreaking moments in my life? I think I shared it with you already. I play sometimes in prison. Some time ago I played in this really maximum security prison. And, you know, you don't go there for a weekend. When you're sittin' there, you're there for a long time, you know? Anyway — and it has 2000 inmates. And, like, the director was afraid, if I played [for] all of them together, it would be too wild, so he divided, four times 500, with guards, everything. Okay, *Barukh HaShem*, it was beautiful, and at the end, I managed to kiss everyone and hug everyone, bless them to come out. There was, *nebech*, a little black brother, who was eighteen years old, he's in for life. Heartbreaking, right? In for life. But really a cute guy, you know? So I give him a big hug, and I say, "I bless you with miracles, you should come out of here." He walks up to the door, comes back to me, says, "Could you please give me another hug? I don't know if I'll ever get another hug again." *Nebech*, *gevalt*. You know what that means? And here let me tell you the two Torahs — three Torahs.

First of all, we tell the *Rasha*, "You think you're bad, right? So every time you meet people you think you have to bite them. You don't have to bite people." I'm knocking out his teeth. I'm saying, "Could you talk to me sweet? Can't you talk to me sweet?" And here comes the deepest depths of Torah. This is really a must. *Rasha* has three letters: Resh, Ayin, is the outside — is 'bad,' right? And Shin is the inside, and Shin, the three lines of Shin are our relationship [to] Avraham, Yitzchak, Ya'akov — what we inherited from our forefathers — something so holy — something indestructible. Indestructible. So you know what the Hagadah says? You have to do something for him. Cut out the Shin, that suddenly the inside should begin to shine. And I tell him, "You know, you don't need teeth. You don't have to bite people." Have you ever seen those people, when you want to hug them, they put on that frown, "Not me!" Why not? I'm your brother. I love you. You know, there are some people [who] are so rough on the outside, and they are so addicted — slaves! "I have to be bad!" I tell them, "You don't have to be." All you have to do is let your insides shine. And it'll be too long, but I want you to know the Hagadah. The truth is, by the *Rasha*, telling his father — not to the *Rasha*, to the father. What kind of father are you? You mean to say you never told your children how holy they are? You never gave them a connection to the inside? *Sssss.*

You know I think I shared with you. You know, I travel all the time; I come late at night to hotels. Once late at night, I'm checking into a hotel, and the woman at the desk is *mamash* beautiful, sitting there crying. I ask her, "Why are you crying? Forgive me for asking, but you're so beautiful. Why are you crying?" She says, "You know, I'm only 27 years old, and tomorrow I have my ninth divorce." *Nebech, gevalt.* Can you imagine the brokenness of this woman? Listen to me. I said to her, "Did your mother ever tell you how beautiful you are?" She says, "My mother would tell me constantly that I am so ugly that no man would ever want me. And whenever I did something wrong, she would take soap water, put it in my mouth, and lock me in a closet for three hours."

I'm telling the father of this *Rasha*, what did you teach him? *Li v'lo lo?* [For me but not for him?] Question mark. Just you and not him? You're a good man? [Inaudible] Then it says, "*Eelu hayah sham*" [had he been there]. I say to the father, "If you would have been in Egypt, you wouldn't have got out either." 'Cause G-d took us out of Egypt for our children's sake. But that is already far-reaching.

Then comes the *Tam.* The *Tam* is — everybody knows, the *Tam* is the same letters like *MaiS* [death] — Mem Tav, right? This is so deep, friends. You know what a dead person is? Everything is broken. Whatever I see, wherever I look, looks bad. In my father's shul was a Yid — he would come in Shabbos morning, and by the first five minutes, he already started a fight with seven people. And *gevalt*, a genius. This one is wrong, this one is wrong, this one hurt his feelings, this one could hurt his feelings — you know what a *Tam* is? Not broken, but you know, the *Tam* asks *Ma zos?* — he asks what gives you the strength — what gives you the strength to be so whole? You know what Egypt is? The slave is a broken person. I'm afraid of this one, I'm afraid of this one — and the *Tam* is the first one who tastes a little bit redemption. But he says, "*Ma zos?*" — *Gevalt!* Where is the headquarters for redemption? I need more, right? I need more all the time.

Ah, I'm telling him. Can you imagine? G-d created the world with his hands, right? But to get out of Egypt, even G-d had to stretch out his hand. That means, humanly speaking, ah, this was even hard for G-d! This comes from a very high place in Heaven. You can see the whole world as being beautiful, but what you need is something deeper than Heaven and Earth. Ah, from the highest — from the highest headquarters *b'chozek yad* [with a strong hand]. And then comes *sh'eino yodea l'sh'ol* [the one who doesn't know how to ask.] I want you to know something so deep. This is *mamesh* deep. Do you think we are praying for everything? There are certain things in life we are even ashamed to ask G-d. We are even ashamed to ask G-d. I want you to know something — the deepest depths. That our holy mother Sarah was praying all her life for children, right? What do you think our holy mother Sarah felt when she was 80? Do you think inside she thought, "I can't even ask G-d anymore"?

The plan was, for the whole thing, when G-d answered her, G-d says, "I want you to know — all the time that you were ashamed to ask me, I heard your prayer."

And you know, friends, this is the deepest, deepest depths. Sometimes [clears his throat], sometimes there are the deepest depths of our lives, deeper than knowing what the Torah is, deeper than being good or bad. We all have something deep, deep inside, and we are ashamed to ask G-d.

It says, *v'sh'eino yodea l'sh'ol* [and as for the one who doesn't even know how to ask] — he says, G-d, I want to ask you, but I don't even know how to ask you. It's too much of a miracle. You know, I always say, G-d, you know, I know you can do everything, but maybe this is too much, right? So the Baal HaGeula says, *"Aht p'sach lo"* [You shall broach the subject for him]. Tonight —

And you know why it says *"Aht b'lashon n'keva"* [the feminine form of "you"]? This is the deepest. Because our holy mother — if you re-member, the angel came the first morning of Pesach, right? [to an-nounce the birth of Isaac] And she opened gates, that there's nothing in the world you cannot ask of G-d. Even if it looks beyond hopeless — beyond hopeless.

So Reb Levi Yitzhak Berditchever says — he was always a *gevalt* — Master of the world, I am begging you, let me be the *sh'eino yodea l'sh'ol* — let me be the real one, the real one who knows deep, deep inside, I can ask everything of G-d. And, um, I want to bless you and me we should never give up hope, and, basically, this is the last thing, because, I mean, we went back after two thousand years to the Holy Land — isn't it stupid? Let me ask you something. A Yid is going to the gas chambers, and someone would ask him, "What are you praying for?" He says, "I'm praying to go to Israel." Crazy? *Gevalt.* It was their prayers that brought us back to Israel — the emeseh [the real] *v'sh'eino yodea l'sh'ol*, right? The ones, the ones who said to G-d, "I'm ashamed to ask you." I'm ashamed to ask you.

And also, I want to bless you and me and our parents and, as parents, husband and wife, they should be so close to each other that there should be nothing in the world that people we love couldn't ask of us — everything in the world — everything, everything.

Okay, friends, so right now we have about five more minutes. Five? We have two more minutes. And Reuven and Yehudit, *mamash*, and everyone, thank you a million times. And we gotta sing just one more good song. It's beautiful to be with you, friends. I bless you with the best Seder.

Jerry Strauss: Bless you back [murmurs of assent all around].

Shlomo: And I bless you with the highest *sh'eino yodea l'sh'ol*. And thank you, Jerry and Linda, for coming.

Leah Strauss: Oh, thank you so much for being here.

Shlomo: How long could I be without seeing you for so long? You know, everything has limits, right? [Strums and tunes his guitar] So one more song — praying for the Holy Land [launches into a lively, upbeat rendition of Psalm 23, with everyone joining in, then stops after only two minutes]. A chasid came to the Alter Rebbe; he was from Siberia, far away. He says, "Rebbe, you know, I live so far. Will I ever see you again?" He says, "Yeah, you'll see me again." He walked out, and he realized he forgot his handkerchief in the Alter Rebbe's room. And he went back to pick it up. Oy vey. How sad, right?

RG: That was it.

Shlomo: That was it. Okay, friends, I-I stop in the middle of the melody because I want to see you, I want to finish the song with you. Thank you a million times — have the best *Yontif* — and the most important thing is really, really, G-d should bless us to see the whole world opening their doors, *mamash* opening their doors for Eliyahu HaNavi.

I mentioned it last night — the Ba'al Shem Tov says, "G-d created the world, but to make doors and windows, it's up to us." Okay, good *Yontif*.

[Applause, then the usual hubbub of animated conversation. End of tape.]

# German, Polish, and Jewish Intercultural Healing

## German Civilization class, 24 Nisan, 5750 / April 19, 1990

### Transcribed by Reuven Goldfarb

[SHLOMO PLAYS AND SINGS THE MELODY FOR *"YEHI SHALOM B'CHEILEKH shalva b'armenotayikh"* 'May there be peace within your walls, serenity within your palaces' for a couple of minutes. Near the beginning, he says, "Join me," and after a while, "Open your hearts and sing."]

Okay, Shalom, my beautiful friends. Good morning. Thank you so much for inviting me. You see, I don't know exactly — I don't know exactly what you think I want to tell you. And I don't know myself what I want to tell you. But we gotta start somewhere.

Do you know the difference between a layman walking into a hospital and a doctor? Very simple. A layman walks into a hospital — really sick people — walks around and says, "Ah! Disgusting — *ach!* All those sick people. I don't want to stay here. Terrible." And the more sick they get, the more disgusted this person is. They walk out and say, "Nah, I don't like this hospital. Not for me." A doctor walks in — his eyes are glowing, right? "Hey — what a challenge!" And the more sick they get, the more he says, "I gotta stay here. I gotta cure them."

You know, the question is, are you looking at the world like layman or like a doctor? If you look like a layman, you say, "What a disgusting world. Newspapers bad, everything terrible." God bless you. "People hate each other, people kill each other. What a world!" You know?

"I'm looking for another planet." If you're a doctor, you say, "What a world! Hey, what a privilege to be alive in this world, where I can do so much." So I'm telling you from the very beginning, you'll tell me that the world is terrible, right? And, I don't want to say anything bad, but, as a Jew, as anybody who was persecuted in the world, I can tell you the world is disgusting. So I can say I want to check out, right? But, thank God, there's still some doctors in the world, and I hope and I hope and I pray to be one of them. So I look at the whole scene in a different way. I look at it like a doctor.

I want you to know something, that sadly enough, sadly enough, fifty years ago — I don't know why — I'm not God — the master of the world locked the doors of love between people. The doors were locked. Was no communication between people. Absolutely the doors of compassion were locked. And what you and I are witnessing — slowly, slowly — the doors are opening again. Doors are opening again — between people, between nations — and something is happening in the world. Something is happening in the world. And again, the people that are so accustomed that the gates of love are closed, when the gates of love are opening they don't feel comfortable. So they try with their last strength, you know, to prevent it. But who cares, right? Their time is over. They're bankrupt. They're bankrupt.

And I just want to share with you very fast. Like Rabbi [Gerry] Friedman says, it's fifty years later. Let's start from Germany. I want you to know that in Germany, the Protestant Church, every two years, they have something which is called "Day of the Church," *Kirchentacht*. They speak German, all the students here? Yeah? Real? Good. My German isn't as good anymore as it was supposed to be but pretty good. Okay, *Kirchentacht*. And miraculously, it's a whole long story, but it's not important. A few years ago, for the first time — you know, they had the *Kirchentacht* for maybe six, seven hundred years. I was invited. The first time — not to be believed — a Jew, humble Jew like me, was invited. And, um, I didn't even know myself what I'm letting myself into. And, uh, it's in Hanover, and they have a lot of things going on simultaneously. It's on the marketplace, and the big stage, and uh, I would say about 10,000 people are there, mostly young people between the age of, say, 18 and 30. And the Jewish community was supposed to supply me with a band, but somehow — stupidly — they forgot.

Okay, I'm just coming from America. In the morning I check into a hotel just to sleep a few hours. I'm supposed to start 6 o'clock; I'm getting there 5:30. Whew! I already regretted that I said yes. The Bishop is talking, and forgive me, not one person pays attention to him. He's talking for fire and for water, and there are about 10,000 young people sitting there drinking beer, telling each other dirty jokes, laughing loud, and, *nebech*, the poor Bishop is standing there talking, talking, and *oy vey*. Really, I felt bad for the Bishop, but what can I do? I felt even worse for myself! (Laughs) I realized in a few minutes brother me has to go on stage and it'll be the biggest joke in the world, 'cause I'm supposed to play for two hours, from 6 to 8. I mean, this is a joke, right? You know, it's a marketplace, and the band doesn't show up. I'm with a little guitar, and I play very bad — and what am I gonna do with them?

And you know what bothered me the most? If it's just me — but they didn't invite me for me. They invited me, a Jew. I'm representing the whole Jewish people. What a desecration of God's name. *Oy vey! Gevalt.* A few times in my life I really prayed, to tell you the truth. This was one of those times. I'm getting on stage, and I want you to know, I still shiver when I tell you it. I got on stage, and I said in German, "My sweetest brothers and sisters — *bruder und shvester* — I came to bring you regards from the Holy City, Jerusalem."* I want you to know, I

---

* The transcriber recalls that when Reb Shlomo told this story in Berkeley, he quoted himself as saying, "My sweetest brothers and sisters, I am bringing you a message of love and peace from the Holy City of Yerushalayim!" — RG

didn't expect it. They got up — like bitten by a snake — thousands of kids, rushing to the stage. Thousands of kids. I started singing — I'm telling you something — it was like after Messiah had come! It was like after the Messiah had come. I want you to know there were moments when I couldn't even move my hand because they were crowding me so much. With one heart and with one soul. And there were maybe two more Jews in the audience; the rest were all non-Jewish brothers and sisters. And just open your hearts.

And, you know, you don't sing all the time, you don't talk all the time. There's a few moments of silence. And suddenly like, at the end — they were all standing on their feet; there was nobody that was sitting. It was just awesome. A young man — you know — waves. I say, "My sweetest brother, what do you want to tell me?" It was heavy. You have to open your hearts. He says, "My grandfather killed your grandfather." It's heavy, right? So there was silence, like — it 's too gruesome.

So I held out my hand, and I said, "Brother, can you imagine how much the world became better in 50 years? That your grandfather killed my grandfather, and you and I are the best friends in the world? What a world — what a world." I said, "Brother, you better come here." So then the closeness got even stronger — was awesome, I'm telling you, was awesome. So I was telling them stories — what I was most interested in telling them. Okay, they know the Germans killed six million, but they don't know who they were! They don't know what Jews are all about! Told them stories about our great rabbis, our great people. It was awesome — awesome.

And then at the end we were dancing, and, you know, by the end, everybody was standing on their toes, holding out their hands because you could see they wanted to reach Heaven. I'm sure they did reach Heaven. I said to them, "You know something? I hope your hands will

392 — In His Own Words

reach the most desperate person in the world — because there is hope — there is unbelievable hope for the world — not to be believed."

You know, there was a rock band was supposed to go on after me, and this is not to brag, but I'm telling you stories. The rock band went on a quarter after 11 because every person there was kissing and hugging me. Everybody says, you know? "Where can we learn more?" And the rock band just couldn't get on stage, you know? Just imagine 10,000 kids on stage, on a small stage, you know? You can't throw them off, right?

Anyway, I want you to know, Sammy and I, my manager, we were in Poland, and I was — the whole time I wanted to go to Poland — and I have to — anyway, after a few years, thank God, last January, we were going to Poland. And I don't have to tell you, I get calls from everyone, you know, who is who in Judaism, and they tell me, "Don't go to Poland — it's the darkest place in the world — and they're all anti-Semites, it's just so bad, and so terrible, and I mean, just forget it — and I mean, I think you're even endangering your life — "

Anyway, I want you to know, it was like after the Messiah had come. It was so beautiful! And I could look at all those young people in the audience, and I could just close my eyes and imagine what their grandfather did — maybe to my uncle, maybe to my cousin, I don't know. But you know what it was? I was so glad that I have the privilege of kissing the grandson or the granddaughter of someone who did so much harm to the world. What a privilege! What a privilege!

I want you to know, friends, God is opening gates between nations which He hasn't opened in maybe in the history of the world. God is opening gates between religions. It didn't happen in the history of the world, right? [Someone sneezes] God bless you, darling. I want to share with you a *medresh*. *Medresh* [midrash] is commentaries on the Bible, which is — and if I'll sing it, it'll take too long. I don't know if you're in the mood for harmonizing, but I'll tell you what it says.

I want you to know that Cain never wanted to kill Abel. It's clear to us because Cain and Abel were the first two brothers on the planet, and nobody had ever died yet. Cain didn't know when you hit someone with a stone they die. Sadly enough, we know it because we watch television, right? But they didn't have a television then, and nobody had even died yet. Was Adam and Eve, Cain and Abel, right?

So Cain is angry at Abel; he took a stone and threw it on his head. And if you remember, Cain had the idea of bringing a sacrifice to God, but he only brought things which he didn't need. Then Abel picked it up from him, and he brought the best he had. So God accepted the sacrifice of Abel but not of Cain. So Cain was very jealous and angry — he's killing [Abel]. And just remember that God spoke to him after he did it. God doesn't talk to murderers. And listen to what the medresh says — it's awesome. Abel fell to the ground, and Cain did not know there is such a thing as dying — yet. *Mamash*, he sees his brother lying there. *Gevalt,* did he regret that he threw a stone at him.

You know, when you're angry, after you do it, the anger's over, right? He fell to the ground, and he began crying. He says, "Abel, you're my only brother. Please open your eyes. Please forgive me. Please open your eyes." And he was crying so much — and I want you to know, there was so much more connection between animals and human beings [than] we have today. The medresh says all the animals of the whole world came. They were also crying. They were crying. The first person dead in the world — they were crying for three days. And only on the third day they realized — he won't open his eyes. So here's the medresh — unbelievable. On the great day — let it be today; let it be tomorrow at the latest — all the Cains of the world will be lying next to the Abels they killed. They will fall down next to them, and they will say, "Please open your eyes. I swear I didn't want to kill you. I was just so angry at you." And they will cry and cry for three days. And a great miracle will happen — Abel will open his eyes. Abel will come back. And Abel and Cain will begin to dance. What a day. What a day.

You know what it is? Maybe some people hope that one day Abel will get back to life, and he will kill Cain. Okay, that's a different outlook. Thank God I'm not sharing it, and I hope you're not either. I just hope that one day the six million will open their eyes again. They have to open their eyes. There is no other way.

Can you imagine all the people who were killed in Siberia? Awesome. Awesome, awesome. Awesome, right? But you see what it is? You and I have the privilege of hastening — of hastening that day when Abel will open his eyes again.

I want you to know something very deep, friends. There are two things which we are taught in Heaven before we are born. Have you ever seen a baby when it's born? There is a therapist, and maybe a rabbi or priest, and they take the baby and they say, "Listen, baby, in this world, it's a custom for babies to cry. So we want you — don't overdo it, but let's rehearse a little bit, and baby, we'll teach you, you know, how to cry." You don't have to teach a baby how to cry. You know why? Because prayer is taught in Heaven. Prayer is not of this world. Crying is not of this world.

Have you ever seen a mother — the baby is born, and the mother says to the doctor and nurses, "I gotta have a little privacy with my baby." The mother says to the baby, "Listen to me, baby. I am your mother. Hm!" [Self-satisfied expletive] Mazel tov, right? "I'm your mother, and your father will be in soon. And I want you to love me."

Why not? You know something? Is there any way, any words to describe how much a baby loves his mother? Or her mother? You can write poetry from here to the end of the days. The way a baby loves its mother — we have no vessels even to fathom it. The only sad thing is later on we send those kids to school, and we have the privilege of destroying everything which is taught to them from Heaven.

Hatred is taught — because children, when they are born, they don't know that there is someone they are supposed to hate. Children don't even know there is such a thing as ugly. By children, everybody looks beautiful, right? Until I tell my baby, listen, this person — *chh* [grunt of enmity] is really ugly. This person? Just — this is a bad person. Don't talk to them.

So you see, friends, the question is, "What do we want to bring back to the world?" And you see what's so special — we don't really have to teach the world how to love. We...have to unteach them what the world has taught them. And if I can share something very deep with you, you know, we just had the holiday [of] Passover, and the matzoh we eat is called "the bread of healing." And without — [tape skips] — and you know, with prayer sessions, and all kinds of things, and we teach people how to love God. How does it sound to you? It's like I'm teaching the mother taking the baby aside, "Listen, I'm your mother! You better love me!" Right?

But you know what it is to be in exile? To be in exile is that you lose that heavenly teaching. You've lost it! And whatever you know is taught by us — even by your cutest teacher — pure slave! You're not real anymore.

You know what it is for us Seder night — Pesach — to become free? That God washes off all the dirt, all the dust. You know, friends, if I would relate to God like a baby when it's born, relating to its mother — what a relationship! What a relationship. I want you to know, according to our holy tradition — maybe yours, too — you know who is my soul mate? Did I tell you? I went to a singles bar last night; I met this girl — very beautiful. I think I like her. How does it sound to you? That's not so bad yet, right? You've heard worse.

According to our holy tradition, forty days before a baby is born, there's a voice in heaven calling out: "This man should marry this woman." And our holy rabbis comment on it — I mean, what's the hurry? Forty days before you're born? I would say even — I mean, you're eighteen years old — or seventeen — they decide in heaven whom you should meet — and this [is] what all the rabbis say: Just loving a person, love of this world, doesn't keep people together. You know what means "it's called out forty days before"? It's not of this world. Husband and wife — the connection — is heavenly! They have to be taught in heaven how to love each other.

So you see, friends, if you ask me personally. I want you to know — Yossi mentioned it before — I'm from Berlin. And I'm like the only, so to speak, living singer — Jewish singer — who was born in Berlin, that's also alive. So I was invited by the city of Berlin — if I can impose upon you and make it fast — It was very, very special. Very, very special. Okay, I'm arriving in Berlin, and I want you to know, television followed me for three days, day and night. And without bragging, it was shown on German television for weeks, every Sunday for one hour — for weeks! Like, every, every little thing. It was unbelievable. Okay, listen to this.

The first thing they do is take me to a prison. And there, about, five or six hundred — I would say — kids between the ages of 16 and 21 — thieves, dope addicts, dope dealers, prostitutes, you know, all kinds, and I'm playing for them. They wanted to see how I relate to them. *Gevalt*, was it beautiful! It was so beautiful. I still remember it. And I told those kids, "You know something? You think you're in prison? We all are in prison. We all are slaves. I mean, [when] you come out of here, you'll be the ones to teach the world how to become free again."

I want you to know—have you ever been in prison? I hope you never have to go to [there]. You know, every few steps there's a door with fifteen locks. Okay, there are these five, six young people, and they walk me out. You know, security gets a bit nervous, but it was so high, they didn't dare to stop those kids. It was unbelievable, right?

And they're a little — heavy criminals, some of them, right? They walk me, they open the door for me, they all walk with me. It was unbelievable. The whole they were telling me, "Please take me with you to Jerusalem. Please take me with you." It was just — I could see those kids need adoption in the worst way, you know? Maybe they're only criminals because no one ever hugged them and kissed them properly.

I want you to know, those kids walked me to the door of the prison, by the street, and nobody dared closing the doors on them. They stood by the open doors. I went to the car, and they waved. [End of tape]

*Reb Shlomo was often on the phone with his daughters. He never missed a call.*
*Photo by Rabbi Joe Schonwald.*

# Reconciliation with God

## Class in Jewish Mysticism, 24 Nisan, 5750 / April 19, 1990

### Transcribed by Reuven Goldfarb

Shlomo: [sings his melody for "*Shomer Yisrael*"] Give me harmony a little bit. [He sings again.]

Okay, I'll tell you the truth. I'm an innocent bystander. And I still don't exactly [know] what you want to talk to me about or what I'm supposed to talk to you about. Anybody can enlighten me? Or are you as innocent as I am?

Yeah? What does it say? [Someone evidently shows him a flier.] Where does it say 'mysticism'? Ah, Jewish Mysticism class. That means you all are mystics! [Laughter] It means you're here, but you're not really here, right? It's really good! [Chuckling] So how much of you is here?

You know, Seder night — without imposing upon you — you know, the third thing we're doing, we're taking a matzoh — the middle matzoh — and we break it. And the smaller part remains on the table, and the greater part we hide, meaning to say — two things. First of all, if you want to get out of Egypt, if you want to get out of slavery, if you want to save the world, the first thing that has to be clear to you is that every human being is heartbroken. We're living in a broken world. The world is broken. And second thing, which is actually the same thing —

You know, whatever I see of you [and] what you see of me is only a fraction — a small fraction. The greater part of us is so hidden — all of us. The greater part is so deep, so deep. You know, sometimes we see a person walking around smiling, laughing. Oh, the outside — what do you know what's going on inside, right? The other way around — sometimes we see a person *krechtzing*, crying, but maybe inside they're full of joy.

Okay, so I'm asking you again. The greater part of you is here or the smaller part? I hope, I hope, that just for this afternoon, it's the greater part of you that's here — because with the smaller part, you don't need me. With that you buy Coca-Cola, watch a little video. Talking about inside stuff, right? Inside. And inside is so deep.

You know, by us, when people get married, the beginning of the ceremony is that the groom covers the face of the bride. It's crazy, right? I marry her because I like her, but why do I cover her face? If I'm only connected to your nose, to your ears — that's sweet, but this is not what marriage is all about. I cover her face to let her know, you know what I've done? You know which part I'm connected to? To that part of you which I cannot see.

You know, what happens to you when you love a person? They might be six foot two or maybe five foot eight, but suddenly, when you love somebody, they're so big. They occupy the whole world. You know, when I like somebody, I walk on the streets of Paris — I see Paris, right? I walk on the street in Amsterdam — I see Amsterdam. When I love somebody very much, suddenly, I walk in Paris — I just see the person I love. I walk in Rome — it's crazy. Suddenly, they're infinite.

So, obviously, if you talk about reconciliation — I want you to know, everything G-d created is for the best purpose. Anger is an unbelievably good emotion — like everything in the world. The only thing [is] you have to know what to do with it. You know, most of us have so much in our hearts. The only thing is we don't know what to do with it. We don't know what to do with it. And we usually do it at the wrong time.

Anger is meant to be angry at yourself — not at somebody else. And I don't mean "angry at yourself" to tear yourself down — 'cause you have no right. Who am I to tear myself down? I was created by God! Can you imagine a Picasso painting would say to us, "Hey, I'm a lousy painting"? Chutzpah! Right? Picasso painted you!

We're talking about anger. Anger is meant to give you the strength to do better. Imagine, if we would never be angry at ourselves, I'd be the same creep all my life. What am I supposed to do after I make a mistake? I'm getting a little bit angry at myself.

I want you to know, there's an unbelievable teaching from Rav Kook; I don't know if Shelley mentioned it. Rav Kook was the last great Chief Rabbi in Israel. He passed away already over 50 years, but he, like, the greatest, greatest — Gerry, am I right? — the greatest — beyond greatest, right?

But you know what he said? Redemption will come to the world when the whole world, instead of being angry at each other, they begin to be angry at themselves.

You know, I can say about everything in the world, "It's your fault, it's your fault!" And here, I'm going right back to the beginning — why we were driven out from paradise. And I want you to take it on the highest level. And I'm sure you understand it's not just, "I ate the wrong apple." I mean, how many wrong bagels have we been eating for a long time, right?

You know what the problem is? God says to Adam, "Did you eat the forbidden fruit?" You know what Adam says? "It's not my fault. It's my wife." God says to Eve, "Is it true? You ate the forbidden fruit?"

Eve says, "Listen, God, I thought you knew everything. Maybe I'm mistaken. But let me tell you, it was the snake." So God says, "Listen, folks, I love you — you're cute and sweet — you just got married — but, I'm sorry, you have to rent a room somewhere else" — right? — "because there's no real estate available for a couple like you in Paradise."

I'll tell you a joke. How do you know that Adam and Eve were in Russia? Very simple. They had one apple and nothing to wear, and they thought they were in Paradise! Although I was just in Russia, it's gettin' better, *Baruch HaShem* — thank God! — God is opening gates. I want you to know something. It is so easy to be angry at another human being. It is just so easy to be angry at God. It's so hard to say, sometimes, "It's really my fault." It's the hardest thing in the world. You know, when we do something good, we don't say God did it. Huh! I did it! It's clear to you, right? Do you know how talented I am? Did I make myself clear? I mean, *gevalt!* I'm unbelievable, right?

Gerry, did you bring the latest article about me in the Jewish press? Unbelievable! A whole page [about] how talented I am, right? Stupid, right? When it comes to doing something wrong — when I do something wrong — it's not my fault! It should be the other way around. When I do something good, I should say, "Master of the world, why did I have the privilege to do something good?" What a privilege!

I want to share something awesome with you. Have you ever met this [couple]? I'm sure you meet them all the time — we all meet them. I ask the husband, "Does your wife love you?" You should see his expression. "I mean, how could she resist loving me? I mean, let's face it, right?" I ask the wife, "Does your husband love you?" It's worse. I mean, she looks at me, and like, "Are you blind or something? Don't you know how beautiful I am? I mean, Elizabeth Taylor is afraid to be in the same room with me" — right? Disgusting, right? Disgusting.

Let me share with you an unbelievable story. The Holy Reb Shlomo Karliner, one of the great luminaries about 180 years ago, they asked him, "Are you going to Heaven or to Hell?" So this is what he said — we should all live long — he said, "After 170 years, when I come up to Heaven, and I stand before the heavenly court, if they say to me, 'Okay, we have a place for you in Heaven,' I will complain. I will say, 'You know, Heavenly court, I'm sure you're good people, but you don't know me. I know me the best. I don't belong to Heaven. I never did anything good.' Okay, I'll make such a big *tumel*, they'll go to a higher court. And if the higher court says, 'Okay, go to Hell,' I'll go to Hell! I never expected anything else. If they tell me, 'Go to Heaven,' I'll complain again." And open your hearts. "I won't rest until I stand before God Himself, before the One, the real One, the real Judge.

"If God says to me, 'Go to Hell,' you know what I'll do? I'll be so happy. I'm doing God's will. God wants me to be in Hell, right? I'll dance so much in Hell until all of Hell falls apart. The walls of Hell will fall apart from my dancing. And if God says to me, 'Go to Heaven,' I will say to him, 'Is it because I deserve it?' And God will tell me, 'Hey. It's my gift to you.'" You know how deep this is, friends? If you sit in Heaven and you think you deserve it, you're sitting in Hell! You're not in Heaven.

You know what Heaven is? I don't know. I don't deserve it. Thank you so much. Thank you so much! You know, imagine if people would treat each other [from] this deepest depth. I don't know why I deserve that you're my friend, but thank you so much. Thank you so much.

I was always learning, you know? I don't know if I told you, Gerry, you know? I'm coming out with a book now, my talks at weddings. Yeh. Anyway, I'm calling it "The Fixing of the Broken Glass." One of the things I say there [is] why it is that two people have to walk the groom — two people have to walk the groom, and two people have to walk the bride, like pushing, right? Carrying. I said, "It's because when the great moment comes, when a man and a woman meet that really love each other, and the man says, 'I can't believe that she loves me. She is so beautiful! How do I come to marry her?' So people, *mamash,* have to push him."

Then it comes to her. She says, "My husband — tch! *Gevalt,* is he special! I can't marry him — I'm afraid! I don't deserve such a *gevalt* husband." So two...have to [push her]. Where [is] relationship based? This is so deep. And you know, this is not making myself a *shmatta.* This is so deep. This is so deep. Do you know why most people fail with their children? Because they think if I buy you a new car, you have to love me for it. I pay for your college — huh! You better lick my toes.

Imagine if parents would say to children, "I don't know how I ever deserved to have a child like you. I don't know how I ever deserved that you love me." And then the child would say back, "How do I ever deserve to have such parents?" What a relationship. What a relationship. That's Heaven.

So I want you to know, most people who are angry at people, who are angry at God — which is basically the same thing — think, "Ha! I deserve better. According to my talents, I should be the greatest person in the world." And you know what his problem is? "As you see, I'm not recognized" — right? It's heartbreaking, right? "The world doesn't know yet." Have you ever seen these people walking around? The unrecognized geniuses, right?

And one more thing I want you to know. If it's clear to me what I really have to do in the world, how deep this world is, how deep life is, then I realize I didn't do it yet. I didn't do it yet. You know, if I have to walk two million miles, and I walked five miles, I'm not *krechtzing* — I'm saying "*Oykh!*" I walked already five miles — yeah, you walked five miles. You have to walk two million miles. But if all I think I have to walk [is] ten miles, after five miles, I begin to demand, "You know, really, I walked already five miles. You know who I am? I'm very special, right?"

You see, if you're very, very deep—again, hopefully, if you have a little taste of mysticism — do you know what mysticism is? 'Mysticism' is not a Hebrew word. I would say — I don't want to say it's a pagan word, but it's not a Jewish word — it's not a God word. It's an English word. It's nice. I have nothing against it, but let me tell you. You know what a kabbalist is? What Kabbalah means? Kabbalah means to receive. Real Jewish mysticism is called Kabbalah, right? You what it means, Kabbalah? That I just received it; I didn't deserve it. What a privilege. And you know, being a kabbalist is not about how much you know. A kabbalist — I can give you a banana — and you can receive it like an intellect, or you can receive like a kabbalist. If you receive like a kabbalist, this banana gives you life forever.

You know, friends, someone can give you two million dollars and it's meaningless. Someone can give you a banana — not only a whole, a half — a bite. And if you receive it inside — the question is, where are you receiving it? How deep does it reach? You see, a true kabbalist is somebody whose vessels are so cleansed, who's so much in tune — you know, what does it mean to love another person? That means you touched the deepest depths of my heart. Touched the deepest, deepest depths of my heart. So this is a kabbalist.

You know, there's a non-kabbalist relationship. I love this girl; she loves me. She has money; I have money — and, what else? I covered everything. And we might as well get married; it's cheaper. No.

I saw this cartoon. A person walks in, and he says, "I'd like to buy a wedding ring." So he says to him, "How much would you like to spend?" "Ah," he says, "very little. It's my first marriage only." [Laughter from students] What a kabbalistic marriage, right?

But, you know, let me tell you. I want to tell you something very deep. This comes from the highest kabbalistic sources. I have no right to be angry at God for something which happens to me. But I have a right to be angry at God for something that happens to somebody else. For me, I have to assume probably God knows what He is doing. For somebody else, I say to God, "Master of the world, please don't do this. Don't do this. Master of the world, I want to be your servant, but you gotta take care of my friend." This is a true kabbalist.

I want you to know something else, since we only have a little time and you all are so precious. You know, we are angry at God sometimes, but the deepest question is, do you know what you did last lifetime? What do I know, right? Sometimes I'm angry at somebody else, and the deepest question in the world is, "Do I know what I did to you last lifetime?" You don't know. But you know, sometimes we come here to this world just to fix something we did last lifetime. There's a story — someone came to the Ba'al Shem Tov, the holy Ba'al Shem Tov — I hope everybody knows who it is. He was, like, one of the greatest luminaries in every way 250 years ago, and the whole Hasidic movement began with him.

A person came to him and he says, "I'm angry at God. Everything goes wrong. It's terrible. My life is really — " So the Ba'al Shem says, "Okay, I'll tell you something. There is one person who can explain to you what's going on in your life." Let's, just for the sake of a name, call him Reb Chatzkele. He says, "Go to Vitebsk, and there is a person by the name of Reb Chatzkele, and talk to him about it."

Okay, he's a poor shlepper — until he gets to Vitebsk, so much energy. He comes there, and you know, in those days, everything happened at synagogue. He says, "I'm looking for someone [named] Reb Chatzkele." They say, "There is no Reb Chatzkele here." He says, "Crazy." He says, "The Ba'al Shem Tov told me there's a Reb Chatzkele." He [another person] says, "I'll tell you. About 60 years ago there was someone here by the name of Reb Chatzkele — I mean, the lowest, the lowest. He denounced people to the police. Because of him, people were sent to Siberia. No heart, no soul — the worst! Thank God he's dead."

Comes back to the Ba'al Shem, and he says, "You know, I went there, and they told me the only Reb Chatzkele was someone who lived 60 years ago, [and he] was so bad." He says, "Don't you understand? *You* are Reb Chatzkele. You came back to fix something."

I want to tell you something awesome. Today in Israel, one of the greatest — again I'm throwing names at you — one of the greatest, absolutely highest, deepest, most awesome kabbalists — he passed away about six — seven years ago — his name was Baba Sali, from Morocco. Baba Sali means "the father of prayer." He had heaven and earth in his hands, you know? Heaven and earth in his hands.

I want you to know — you know, he lived in Netivot, and there are a lot of Jews, a lot of Arabs. And all the Arabs became his followers. I'll tell you how the story began. This has nothing to do with what I wanted to tell you.

One night, the *Heilige*, the holy Baba Sali has to go to the Holy Wall. And he would always go after 2 o'clock at night. And somehow they couldn't find a [Jewish] taxi driver; they only found an Arab taxi-driver. So the Baba Sali says, "Okay, take me to Jerusalem." He says, "I have no *gaz*. And the gas station is closed. I have no gas." Baba Sali says, "Trust me. Let's go."

Not only he took him to Jerusalem, he took him back — for three days after that he didn't need gas. So he told his friends, the other Arabs. So they became his great followers. But, I want you to know, one of Baba Sali's great pupils — his name is Moshe Ben-Tov — you heard of him? — Yerushalayim — something else. I had a long talk with him at one time. He says to me, "I want you to know, all the couples who get divorced today is only because last lifetime they did something against each other. They haven't fixed it yet." He says, "If people, instead of getting divorced, would *mamash* get together and really, really forgive each other, and say to each other, 'Whatever I did wrong to you last time, I'm begging you, forgive me a million times,' they would fix it."

You know, friends, we don't know. The only question is, if you're a little bit of a mystic, you still don't know, but you have a taste. There is something deeper than you'll ever know, something so much more. I have to tell you something — maybe stupid — one of my personal experiences — a few years ago — remember, Gerry? I was giving always at Purim a concert by Berkowitz? Gerry was there a few times. There must have been thousands of people, really mobbed. And, you know, after the Megillah, [after] a fast day, your stomach isn't so full yet. And if in the middle of my concert everybody comes and gives me a little *l'chaim*, a little whiskey, a little wine — after a certain time you're not in this world — you're really a mystic, right? You're not here.

Anyway, to make it really short — and this girl told it to me about five years later. I knew I met her that Purim night. She came and said hello to me, like hundreds of people come and say hello to me. Many years later she said to me, "I want you to know — I don't think you were aware of it — when I came up to you, between one song and the other, and I said hello to you, you *mamash* looked at me, and you said to me — " the girl says — "'I love you so much, I swear to you, in this lifetime I'll treat you better.'" It didn't come from my head. It didn't come from my head.

You know, let it be clear to you, friends, this lifetime is so awesomely deep. Why is it that we have a jet — they have Concordes — you think it's because we have a Concorde that we can meet so many people? It's the other way around! Because this lifetime is so precious — we have to meet so many people — so God gives us a little Concorde. You know [how many people] my grandfather met in — maybe — in one lifetime, you and I meet in one week, in one day. What a world!

You know, I'll tell you something. Thank God I had a little bit of training, so I'm so much aware of it. I remember a few years ago, I come to Australia — it was heavy. I'm walking in, and all the people say hello to me — I could swear by the living God I know them from last lifetime, from another lifetime — and I feel very close to them. And then, at the end of the concert, somebody else walked in, and I realized, wow, this is even deeper than that. This is even deeper than that.

And, you know, sometimes we meet a person, and we only have to tell them one word, which we forgot to tell last lifetime. You know, as far as I'm concerned — I'm sure you share my feeling — when you meet a person you have to tell them you love them 'cause maybe this is one [thing] you forgot to tell them last lifetime. You don't know. You don't know. It's awesome. It's *mamash* awesome, you know? Awesome.

So, you know, I can spend my lifetime being angry, or I can spend my lifetime fixing — fixing. This lifetime, today, you and I, we're here to fix. And, um, do we have time? Yeah, we have time. Let me tell you, fast, a Reb Nachman story. I'm sure Denny has it already on tape, but maybe not. It's a good story.

First of all, there are two things I have to give over to you before I tell the story. What is the medication against anger? Against hatred. Against (*chh!*) everything. There's only one medication, one little vitamin pill, and the vitamin is called joy. There is no other way.

You know, when you're sad, you hate everyone — yourself, God, your father, your mother, and everybody. When you're full of joy — [you] love the whole world! You know, if I'm sad, someone steps on my toes, my sad mind begins to work, "Oh, maybe this time he's stepping on my toes — I'm sure he hates Jews — who knows what he did? Maybe he's even a murderer, and I gotta be careful." You know? The way my mind wanders?

If I'm full of joy, I say, "Hey! You have strong feet," right? Unbelievable! You know, the Holy Sanzer said he only met one person who was completely out of anger. Takes a lifetime to work on it. You don't push a little button and it works. It's hard work. *Mamesh,* you have to fill your heart with joy.

You know, the *Heilige* Reb Herschel Riminover gave everything away. People came from all over the world and asked him for his blessings — he could have been a millionaire — but he gave everything away. And his *Shabbosdika challat* — his coat — was torn. The Chasidim come and give him 100 rubles for a new coat; he always gives it away. Finally, his followers decided they're gonna give him a coat — a long *Shabbosdika* coat made out of silver and with gold, and it's beautiful. They were so proud.

That Friday night, the person that brings in the soup is a little bit of a schmendrick; he didn't know how to balance it; he poured the whole soup over the rebbe's new *challat.* And the Sanzer was there, also one of the holiest rebbes. Do you know what the *Heilige* Riminover said to the waiter? "Hah. It feels warm." He was completely out — because — let me tell you something. If I'm standing in front of a bank, and I just took out 5 million dollars, and someone steps on my toes, what do I do? I start to argue? Who cares, right? I'm full of joy. Life is so beautiful.

So I want you to know, what makes a person most sad? When you think you can't fix it any more. What makes a person full of joy? When suddenly it's clear to you, you can always fix it. You can always fix it.

You know how much we can fix? Not only previous lifetimes. We can fix the world going back to Adam and Eve. You and I, we might be little nothings, but we're not. We have unbelievable powers.

So here's where the story begins, and I'll make it very fast.

Let's face it. The world is run by sadness. You know why there's no peace in the world? Because the people who want to make peace — they're sad people, right? Have you ever seen the peace meetings? Sad Mr. So-and-So meets Sad from So-and-So, and they should make peace. They hate each other! You gonna take two little holy hippies, you know, full of joy, and they'll have peace in two seconds, right? It's not even a joke — it's for real.

Anyway. So the King of the world, King Sadness, wants to see what's happening in the world, if he is still the King of the world. (And, please, just take it on the highest mystical level. This is really a mystical story.) So he walks around, all over the world, and it's not to be believed—everybody is sad! What a world!

What makes a sad person happy? When he meets another sad person. Have you ever seen this? What a joy, right? So one sad person says to the other, "Do you know how many people died since I saw you last? Let me tell you. Moshe died, Avram died, and Yitzchak is about to die, you know, and about 100 people divorced, and some other people are widows — " Unbelievable good news, right?

And then the other sad person says, "That's nothing. You only told me about 100 people who died. I have good news for you — 500 people died!" And they're just so happy with each other, right?

So the King of the world comes back to his capitol, and he's really elated. Everybody is sad! Everybody is *krechtzing*, everybody is complaining — it is unbelievable. What a world!

At the outskirts of the city — broken house, broken porch, broken chair, broken table, broken plate with some food in it — somebody is sitting there, playing the harp. And at the back of your mind, just remember, it's King David. He's playing the harp, and he's happy! The King realizes, "Hey — this is my arch-enemy" — because one happy person can turn over the world.

He walks up to him, and he says, "Hey, my friend, who are you?" He looks at him, and he says, "What? You don't know me? I AM THE GREAT FIXER! I am the great fixer. Do you know what I'm doing? I walk the streets of the world, and I yell on top of my lungs, '*I am the great fixer! Anything broken?*' People are bringing me their hearts, their lives, and I fix everything. Then people give me a few pennies, and I have a feast."

And the way you have to tell the story is — and Reb Nachman says — "And the feast was a feast." One person in the world — there has to be one feast with joy. The King realizes, "This is the end of me." He says, "Thank you so much." The next morning the Great Fixer walks the streets of the world, and he says, "I am the Great Fixer!" People open their windows and say, "Hey, Great Fixer, didn't you hear? No more fixing in the kingdom." No more fixing.

But the Great Fixer realizes there has to be a feast, so he walks and he sees a woman sweeping the floor. He says, "Can I do it? I'll do it for cheap." She says, "Sure, why not?" Gives him five pennies, [says] "Come back tomorrow." The King is back. "Hey, how did you make the money for your feast today?" He sees the King's getting crazy, you know? "No more fixing." He says, "Yeah, so what did you do?" He says, "I'm a floor sweeper. In fact, it's a steady job. I'm going back tomorrow."

The next day he goes back floor sweeping. They say, "I'm sorry. A new decree. No more floor sweeping." This goes on. Finally, to make it very short, every night the King comes to him, and whatever he does, he forbids it the next day.

The Great Fixer walks on the street. He is desperate. He sees that the King is hiring soldiers, and they're paid once in half a year. So he walks up, and he says, "Would you mind? Instead of paying me every half a year to give me five pennies every night?" "Why not?" Gets a uniform, gets a sword, walks up and down, pretends he is happy. At night he gets five pennies. The King is back.

He says, "Hey, how did you get your money today?" He says, "I'm a soldier, gettin' paid every night!" The next night he comes in. They tell him, "New decree. Only once in half a year." But this time was bad — it was already night. How do you make a few pennies to get a feast? He goes to a pawn shop, pawns his sword, gets enough money for half a year — and you know, he is a great fixer — takes some silver paper and puts it on top of the sword — looks like a sword — the King is back. And the King says, "How did you make your money today?"

He says, "I have money enough for half a year." But this time it was bad because for a soldier to pawn his sword is the death penalty.

The King doesn't say anything. The next morning he puts on all his medals — the King, I mean, *gevalt,* right? — goes down to prison. He says, "Is there any criminal here who has to be executed?" And you know, a King like this, who is sad, there are a lot of people [who] have to be killed. Anyway, so they find a little criminal, and the King says, "Let all the soldiers come, and I will appoint the soldier which should kill this criminal." Walks around and finds the Great Fixer. He says, "I, the King of the world, give you the privilege to kill this criminal."

But you know, my beautiful friends, only sad people are afraid of a King. If you're full of joy, you're not afraid of anybody. The Great Fixer says, "My dear King, brother King, or Mister King, I'll tell you — I never killed anybody, and I really have no plans of ever killing anybody. If you want this criminal to be killed, you have to do it yourself." The King gets mad, and he yells, "Aaah!" You know?

The Great Fixer realizes you cannot talk to the King. He turns to the world. He says, "World! Are you sure the criminal is really guilty? Let me tell you, I am the Great Fixer! I'm a magician. I'll show you a trick. I'll pull out my sword. If my sword is a real sword, that means he is guilty. And if, miraculously, my sword turns into silver paper, that means he is not guilty."

So Reb Nachman says, "The criminal walked home, the King walked home, and the Great Fixer walked home, and the feastele was a feastele."

I want you to know, friends, two things, what you and I have to do. We have to be filled with joy. What a privilege to be alive in our days. You know, friends, you know what's happening to the world? Miracles which have not happened in hundreds of years are happening right in front of our eyes. The world is getting together, even if it takes a little while, and even sometimes there's a little bit of cruelty involved — God is opening gates. God is opening gates between nations — between people. And the greatest thing is, God is opening gates for us [so] that we can meet people we haven't seen maybe in hundreds of years. And even if we don't know exactly why, what we can fix, I want you to know one thing, which is clear to me and to you, I am sure. When someone asks you a favor, don't ever say no. As much as you read some books on psychology — you have to be assertive, you have to say no — forget it. We are dealing with life here. When someone asks me a favor, maybe I asked this person the same favor last time. Maybe I'm only born to return the favor. You don't know! You don't know. We don't know.

And you know, friends, if you are aware, every split second, you're doing something in this world. If every person you meet is — is an earth-shaking event, then your relationship to people is completely different. Completely different. You look at people differently.

So you know, friends, you can spend your life being angry [or] spend your life being fixed. It's up to you and to me. And you know something else? Do you know how long it takes to fix another human being? Maybe just one feastele. One second of loving another person. One word of courage. One word of courage.

You know what Reb Nachman says? There are so many people in the world who could have brought redemption to the world. The problem was that at one moment in their life they needed one person to give them encouragement, and that person wasn't there. So when you meet somebody, you don't know. Maybe you are the one to — you are the one to encourage this person right now.

What do we know?

Okay, friends, let's hear something from you, holy mystics. Tell me a good reason to be angry. And let's hear from you something. Why am I so much aware of time suddenly? It's crazy. Who cares, right? Okay, let's hear something. Tell me something good or something bad — I don't care. It's crazy.

Friends, you know something? You are all so beautiful. It's so special to see you. It really is. And again, you see, I don't know. I don't know who is here who I met last lifetime. I don't know, you know? You don't know. And we don't know last lifetime, when we met, maybe we didn't give each other courage.

I want you to know something. When you meet a person, when you tell them something good, it's really like turning on the light for the whole world. When you say something bad? Turning off the light. And who gave you or me the right to make the world dark? We are here to put more light into the world — more light.

I want you to know something — I'll never forget it. A lot of times I have the privilege of playing in prisons. You know what a prison is? At one point in their life, they did something wrong, and they have to sit there a lifetime.

I was in this prison — without mentioning places — maximum security — that means they're not there because they forgot to eat bagels on Sunday — *mamash* murderers, right? 90% of them are murderers. The age, 18-28 — hundreds. You look at them? Heartbreaking.

You know what it means, sitting in prison your whole life? Do you know, in our religion, the Jewish religion, there is no such thing as prison — because this is more than death. Prison is dying a hundred times a second.

Anyway, I had the privilege of giving a concert, and it was unbelievable, because whoever tells them to be full of joy — they're only told, you know, "You're bad, you're criminals, you're terrible." It was a *gevalt* concert. After the concert, I had the privilege of really hugging and kissing every prisoner. And they walk out, and suddenly, one prisoner, *nebech*, in for a lifetime — he's 18 and a half years old — he comes back. He says to me, "Can you give me one more hug? Because I don't know if I'll ever get another hug again."

You know what that means? Maybe he's only a murderer because he needed one hug. You know, when people are desperate, they'll do anything, right?

You know what the craziest thing in the world is? I can go to a store and buy apples. I'm not ashamed to say, "I need apples." But people are ashamed to say, you know, "I just need a good friend for one second.

I need somebody to believe in me. I'm begging you. Just believe in me for one second." And what a privilege! What a privilege!

You know, friends, I'm sure you share my feelings. You know why the schools are no good? Because they teach [judge] you [in] every subject 'good' or 'bad'. But do the teachers know how to encourage their students? Very, very few, very few. You know, God blessed me with two little girls, and I have to tell you the sad truth: I didn't keep my vow. I nearly made a vow I will not send them to school — the way they are. I have to make a new school — my kids! Just — I couldn't. And I'll tell you, *gevalt*, do I regret it. *Gevalt*, do I regret it.

You know, we need teachers who look differently at children.... There was once a big panel — I didn't tell you, Gerry, in the good old days — [at] San Francisco State, [there] was a big panel on education. And I'm not an expert on education, right? But anyway, I was there. So, reluctantly, they asked, "You want to say something?" Okay, I said something. I said to them, "As far as I'm concerned, a teacher who is not kissing every student before they begin to teach is not a good teacher — is not a good teacher." How can you give over information — information is not the right word — knowledge, God knowledge, life knowledge, without loving the person?

You know something, when I call up Eastern Airlines — "When is your next flight to Atlanta?" — the girl doesn't have to be madly in love with me to tell me the next flight is 2:45. But when I send my child to a school and subject my child to a teacher for a year, if this teacher cares about my child like this girl from Eastern, what'll happen to my child?

You know, it's not that we have so many criminals — the miracle is that we don't have more! What a miracle! I'll tell you something — I mentioned it yesterday. I was talking to some young people. One young boy says to me — 16 years old — he says to me, "You know, my father hasn't kissed me since I'm five." Another young man — 18 — says to me, "You know something? I never see my father and my mother kissing." Heartbreaking. Heartbreaking.

So friends, I bless you — and I'm crying before you, and with you — the only way to get anger out of the world — to make clear to everyone, "You're angry about something? Yeah? So fix it!" Fix it. We have the power to fix everything. And whatever we see in the world wrong — because God would not show it to us just to make us miserable — when God shows you something — you know, when you see somebody else is terrible, so there are two ways of handling it. "Oh, this person's terrible." But again, maybe this person needs you to fix it. What do I know? *Gevalt*, what do I know, what do I know? But what a privilege to be alive. What a privilege to be part of a world which was created by God, and it's for us to fix it. Okay, friends, I bless you. I bless you and me, we should be great fixers. Thank you so much. Thank you. [Applause]

Okay, since you all are great mystics, Gerry, can I invite them tomorrow night to daven with us? Tomorrow night we'll daven, real good praying, 7 o'clock; then we'll eat together, and Saturday night, if you come, there'll be the highest concert. And, you see, maybe last lifetime you didn't come to my concert, so you have to fix it this time. Anyway, thank you a million times. And if you can say hello to me, I'd love so much to say hello to you.

[End]

Addenda: The following excerpt appears on the same tape, at the very beginning. However, as the voiceover clearly states that it is a continuation, I have decided to place it after the preceding, even though there is no clear transition between the two sections. Possibly there was another class session, though no such indication is made on the label or in the recording.

Voiceover: Religious Reconciliation tape continues.

Shlomo: Slowly, slowly, the world is fixing the sin of the Tree of Knowledge. And he [the Ba'al Shem Tov] said that the first sign will be that — that having babies will not be dangerous any more. Unbelievable. You know, thank God, today, you know it's — I mean, all our holy sisters should live long, but in former good days, you know, left and right, God forbid, women died [in] childbirth, and thank God, today it's not dangerous anymore. You know what? I have a very strong feeling — without sounding too Jewish — you know, the House of God — Jerusalem, right? — was destroyed. According to our tradition, the woman is making the house. You know, Reb Yose said — your name is Yossi? — Reb Yose said, when he was referring to his wife, he always said, "My house."

You know, let's put it this way. A bachelor lives in a house — it's not a house; it's a room. A woman makes the house. Since we came back to Jerusalem and are building the House of God, something happened to women all over the world. They are rebuilding the world again. They *are* rebuilding the world.

And one more thing. The Ba'al Shem Tov says something unbelievable, that before the Messiah is coming, everything holy will be in the hands of women. It's unbelievable. You know, today you walk into a spiritual meeting — there are more women than men. And something happens in our generation: most women have much higher souls than men. Yeah, in my synagogue there are so many beautiful women — I mean, not only beautiful, "Marilyn Monroe" beautiful, I mean "inside" beautiful — they have so much trouble finding a man. Because the souls of men today are not as great as the souls of women.

And, you know, sometimes people ask me, "Do you think a woman should be a rabbi?" So I always answer very simply. If the men rabbis would have kept our children in the synagogue, who needs our women? But thank God, us men drove them out — *gevalt,* did we drive our children out! I don't know about churches, but the synagogues [an expletive, the equivalent of "definitely!"]. They drove them out miles away. Maybe our sisters will bring them back.

But you see, there's one more thing. So let's say, in Reform, they accept women as rabbis, but with one sad, stupid mistake. So do you know what the women do? They do the same thing like men! You know, I saw last year, in *The New York Times,* the first woman rabbi speaking on *Kol Nidre,* the holiest night of the year. She talks about the Reagan administration — *oish!* What's going on here? For that I need a woman to become a rabbi — she should talk about politics?

I don't know how it is in the churches, but, sadly enough, by us Jews, you know, I hate to say bad things about Jews — most rabbis, instead of talking about God, about something holy, suddenly are politicians. And you know what they do? How they prepare themselves for a speech? They read *The New York Times* all Friday night. And the next morning they give a report, right? I mean, for that I need a woman, to do that?

But I'll tell you something. There is a tremendous awakening in the world. And, you know, women are not the same like men. And their vision of God — I don't know; I'm only a man — but when I listen to my wife and to my children — I have two daughters — God blessed me with two daughters — oh, it's so deep. It's a different thing. I don't know what it is. But I just know, it's so deep. And I know the world needs it in the worst way — in the worst way.

And what we have to do — again — is to give honor to each other. We men have to be big enough to realize that maybe our holy sisters have something to tell us which maybe we don't understand. And the holy sisters should know, maybe, the men have something to say. And, um, for my part — I don't know about other churches — but I know that we so-to-speak religious Jews really have sinned against our mothers and our sisters for the last two thousand years in the worst way — in the worst way.

You know, I was in South Africa — before my brother passed away — it was Friday night. Okay, this was a real religious synagogue — real *frum*, right? Okay, Friday night there are 175 people eating with me. Then I get up, and I'm dancing — suddenly the men are surrounding me — and what do the women do? They're excluded. They begin talking to each other loud, right? Suddenly I realized they talk louder than our singing! And again, you know, they are right. They are angry at us.

So I said to the men, "You know something? You think the women are so low, right? We are dancing, we are high on God. And the women are talking about earrings. It's our fault. Why don't we include them?" So what we did, we made half a circle men — I was standing in the middle — it was so beautiful! You know? And all the beautiful women and holy sisters, another half! Right? What a Friday night, you know?

You know, the rabbi — I don't want to say anything bad — a straight rabbi — he had planned the dinner, then I'll give a little speech — 9 o'clock it'll be over. 1:30 we barely, barely — they were ready to stay all night. It was so beautiful, you know? I mean the energies were so balanced and — it was so beautiful....

*Oy!* So what's gonna be? Let's hope for the best. [Conclusion]

[Recorded at The University of Florida Hillel Foundation on Thursday, 24 Nisan, 5750 / April 19, 1990. Transcribed by Reuven Goldfarb, 2003-2004, in Berkeley, London, and Tzfat. This tape, like the tape of the first Purim teaching (p. 345) and "German, Polish, and Jewish Intercultural Healing" (p. 388), was copied for me by Avraham and Leah Sand. An earlier, briefer transcript exists, the work of Steve Amdur, who worked from another copy of the same master but chose not to transcribe all of it. Like me, he was puzzled by the truncated (and apparently non-sequential) nature of the recording. Yet he also provided a clue to the proper dating of this material.

Shlomo refers by name to three individuals who are present with him in the class: Gerry Friedman, the Hillel Rabbi; Professor Sheldon (Shelley — now generally known as Shaya) Isenberg, at that time Chair of the Department of Religion; and Dennis Shuman, the sound engineer. — RG]

*Photo by Joan Roth.*

# *Parashat Metzora* — How Can You...?

FRIENDS I WANT YOU TO KNOW, THERE ARE SO MANY THINGS IN YIDDISHKEIT which you basically don't have to do. You can get away with so much; you can get away with a million things.

Let me ask you, does it say anywhere that you have to say good things about Israel? Imagine after many years, I finally made a trip to the Holy Land. I saw a few good things; I also saw a few terrible things. It's not *lashon hara* for me to say the bad things that I saw because let's face it, everybody knows it — it's public knowledge. But you know what? How could you? How could you?

Let's say you will ask me about my children, and I will tell you. There are a few good things about them, and there are a few things that are bad about them. I have a right to say it; I'm their father. But how could you? Let's say I ask someone about their wife or about their husband, and they tell me that a few parts are good and a few parts are bad. I have a right to say this — it's true. You asked me for the truth, and I'm so much into *emes*. I would die for the truth, I'm known in the whole world that I only tell the truth. Yeah, it's beautiful — but woe to that kind of beauty.

I want you to know, if anyone has ever learned *Hilchos Lashon Hara* of the Chofetz Chaim, you see that there are two million *heterim* [ways of permitting something] for saying whatever you want. You can mamesh learn the laws of *lashon hara* and find a *heter* for the worst thing. For instance, last week a boy asked me about a certain girl for a *shidduch*. Baruch Hashem, the Chofetz Chaim says that by a *shidduch* you are permitted to tell the truth about the person. Baruch HaShem, *gevalt* did I let loose, it was the greatest day of the week. Baruch Hashem, I mamesh had to tell the truth. So you know, it's beautiful for Dallas or for Houston, but it's not beautiful for Yerushalayim *Ir Hakodesh*. What level of truth is Yerushalayim all about? The Beis Hamikdash was destroyed because we hated each other. Let me tell you the sad truth, do you know what kind of *yiddelach* were around in those times? They were all *tzaddikim gemurim,* they were all holy people. Before they hated each other I'm sure they looked up in the *Shulchan Aruch* and they found out that *al pi halacha* [based on the *halacha*] you are permitted to hate this person.... But you know something? It's all cute and sweet but the Beis Hamikdash...the Beis Hamikdash is destroyed.

And here I mamesh want you to open your hearts in the deepest way. It's true, there are *yidden* in the world who I am permitted to hate. There are moments when I have the right to say *lashon hara* about everybody in the world...but how can you? Without sounding commercial, I have a little radio show on every Saturday night from 11:30 till 1:00. So one Saturday night on Rosh Chodesh Shvat, I was talking about hitting children. I said that maybe before Auschwitz it wasn't so terrible to hit children, but anyone who is hitting a Jewish child after Auschwitz belongs right there in Auschwitz because he is continuing Auschwitz. The time for hitting children is over, that's it. *Gevalt* did I have calls all night long! It was heartbreaking. People would call me up telling me I am saying something which is against the Torah. They were quoting *midrashim* left and right. I only said to them one thing. "You know friends, you can quote to me from here to eternity, but the question is how can you hit your child...? How can you?" Your child has nobody in the world, mamesh completely helpless. Sure you can hit them, why not, nobody will stop you, but *gevalt*, how can you? If you will tell me a whole Torah that is says *mefurash* [explicitly] in the *Shulchan Aruch* that you can hit your child, good. So you will go to Gan Eden, but I would rather sit in *Gehinom* [Purgatory] than sit next to you.

# Rabbi Shlomo Carlebach Teaching on Pesach Sheni

## Sunday evening, 14 Iyar, 5754 / April 24, 1994, in Newton, MA, at the home of Michael and Brenda Edwards

### Transcribed by Reuven Goldfarb

[Sings a jaunty melody, then the words come in: *"v'nomar l'fanav shira chadashah"* 'We will sing a new song before you' (from the Pesach Hagadah).]

I just learned last week an unbelievable story by Reb Shalom Shachna, the father of the Holy Rizhiner. And it would be too long to tell you all those names, but it's just a privilege to know that they existed in this world. He had hundreds of followers, but there were two: one of them had the most obnoxious wife ever — she was, like, really on his case — it was just — *mamesh,* he couldn't live! And each time he comes to the Rebbe, he says, "*Mamash,* I have to divorce my wife. I can't bear it anymore." He says, "Not yet, not yet, not yet."

The other one was a rich man. He had a lot of real estate, but he also owed a lot of money. But if he would sell the real estate, [with] whatever he has, he could pay off the bills. And they were *mamash* also on his tail. [Greeting a newcomer] Hey [inaudible name]! Good Yontif. So he says, "I want to sell all I have, to pay off." And he also tells him, "Not yet, not yet, wait, wait, wait, wait." Finally one day, the person who owes so much money couldn't bear it any more, he says, "You know,

I love my Rebbe, but I can't do it." He sold everything, paid off, and without saying anything bad — same night, he got *g'ferlach* [terribly] ill, he's just about taking off. He says to his best friend, the one who has this terrible wife, "Run to the Rebbe fast, and tell him I'm dying."

So Reb Shalom Shachna says — you know, basically, you know, especially in Rizhin, you don't say what you know. You know, it's clear to you and me, all the people who brag so much, tell you everything they know, they really know very little. 'Cause if you really know, you keep it inside. He says, "Basically, it's not my way of telling things, but I have to tell you."

You know, according to some other religions, you come back 2,000 times. According to us, you come back three times, maybe four times. Whenever it doesn't work, that's it. He says, "Both of you have been here already four times. You haven't fixed it yet. So the Heavenly Court had compassion [on] you. So they decided to send you back one more time. But it has to be in such a way that you're not really alive in this world. So your wife, *mamash,* makes you so miserable, that you're only half a life. And the other person, he owes so much money, he can't breathe. It was good for you. I wanted to keep you alive till you fix what you have to fix. Now, what can I do with him now?"

I'm telling you this story because everybody knows, today and tomorrow afternoon it's Pesach Sheni...actually, it's a holiday of the second chance. And just the words, "second chance," is already like — unbelievable words, right? That means it's never too late. You can always fix it. You can always fix it.

And before we go into details, I want to share with you something important. Today is also the Yahrzeit of Reb Meir, the Heilige Reb Meir. Everybody knows there were two giants in the Talmud, who are unsurpassed, Reb Meir and Rabbi Akiba, [masters of] the Torah *sh'baal peh.* You know, there's Torah *sh'b'ksav* — the written Torah. And the written Torah is so many words, so many letters, and that's it. Torah *sh'baal peh* is first of all the oral tradition — what God told Moshe not to write down, but to give over — and also, that everybody can add!

You know, take — let's say the last *parashah,* right? *Acharei Mos-Kedoshim.* We're reading the *parashah* already since Mt. Sinai, 3,300 years. Every year hundreds of new books are coming out, commentaries on the Bible. And good ones, *gevalt* ones, right? And not everything is printed, you know, *gevalt* what's not printed, right? And the masters of adding to the Torah [are] Rebbe Meir and Rabbi Akiba.

Something else happened [on] Pesach Sheni, which is awesome. Everybody knows, after we crossed the Red Sea, Amalek came and attacked us. You know what day Amalek came? Pesach Sheni. Unbelievable. Because the most anti-Pesach Sheni is Amalek. Amalek, everybody knows, is the nation who are the greatest enemies of Israel, but also, spiritually, Amalek is the arch-enemy of God, the anti-God.

Let's put it this way: you know, I shouldn't eat a hamburger on Yom Kippur. But imagine, I was very hungry, nobody was looking, going into a Doggy Diner, make sure nobody is there, especially the rabbi isn't there — hopefully. On Yom Kippur — and I knock in a little hamburger. So I'm not, let's say I'm not a very — very pious Jew, but I cannot say I'm against God, right?

Amalek is anti-God. What's Amalek saying? Amalek comes and tells you, "It's too late. You can't fix it any more. It's too late, forget it. It's not for you." Imagine I decide I want to do something absolutely beautiful. Amalek is the one who says, "I know you for so long. For you, it's like a little holiness attack. You'll do it for three days, and then you go right back where you came from. Forget it. It's too late to change." Everything is too late.

You know why there's no peace in the world? 'Cause Amalek is sittin' there, right? And [he says,] "Listen, they're killing each other for so long, and suddenly they'll change? Forget it!" Right? I always tell my friends, there's so many divorces in the world, and I could swear to it that Brother Amalek was standing under the chuppah and telling some — "I'd love to see how long this marriage lasts," you know? And the vibrations are — [out-breath expletive, like throat clearing]. I mean, you can see him when anybody starts doing something good. Right away, Amalek says, "Ahh. It won't last." Amalek.

So Amalek came to attack us on Pesach Sheni. And what's the most anti-Amalek? Anti-Amalek is, it's never too late because even if I fail, I have another chance. I always have another chance. I can always fix it.

And you know, this is really mind-blowing. Why is Reb Meir's Yahrzeit on Pesach Sheni? You know who Reb Meir was? You know, I hope you don't really take world history too serious[ly] — because they change it always [to make it] the way they like it. You know, I don't want to say anything bad, but us Jewish people, our history doesn't change. Let me tell you, that year was Mt. Sinai — it was Mt. Sinai. We don't have professors every year and try to change it a little bit.

You know, my zeide told my father — my father had a doctorate in Philosophy and in History — and my grandfather, he studied also History — he had a Ph.D. in History, but first in Germany and then in France. He says, "In France, why do they teach you a different history, right? What's good for France. And in Germany they teach you what's good for [Germany]." So what is the real truth? You'll never know, right?

According to world history, Nero, after he burned Rome, he got crazy, and he killed himself. According to our history, which is more reliable, he saw Rome burning, and he realized — can't live like this. He went to Yerushalayim, converted — became a Jew — and his grandson is Reb

Meir [*Gittin* 56a]. Unbelievable, right? You know what that means? That even the lowest human being, like Nero, also has a second chance. The world has a second chance. Whatever the world destroys — remember what Reb Nachman says, if you believe that you can destroy, why don't you also believe you can rebuild? And it's even deeper than that. God does not let you destroy more than you can rebuild. Suddenly the destruction stops because if you would go further, you couldn't fix it anymore.

Okay, now let's go down to — again — to the basics. Pesach Sheni is — you know, we have to bring a Paschal lamb on the 14th day of Nisan, and the people who carried the coffin of Yosef — if you remember, Yosef HaTzaddik told the Jews, "Take me with you when you come out of Egypt. I want to be buried in the Holy Land." So they were carrying the coffin of Yosef. But when you carry a dead person, then you cannot go to the Holy Temple. So they couldn't bring the Paschal lamb. So they came to Moshe, and they were very sad. "*Lama neegara?*" 'Why weren't we privileged also to bring the Pesach?' [Numbers 9:7] So Moshe Rabbeinu says, "Wait" — *eemdu* actually means, *mamash*, "Pray hard" — "and I will ask God what to do." So God says, "I'll give them a second chance — four weeks later, on the 14th day of Iyar."

You know, tonight is exactly four weeks after [Erev] Pesach. And, again, we have more time later. I just want to tell you fast. The second chance — you're not given a second chance just like this. You have to ask for it. If you don't ask, you don't get it. I don't have to ask God every Pesach, "Please let me make a Seder." I mean, I'm asking God, "Let me make a good Seder." But it's Pesach anyway. Pesach Sheni? I have to ask.

You know, I meet my wife, I marry her, and it's all beautiful. I hurt her feelings? Ah, I have to ask. Give me another chance. Certain things you have to ask. And certain things are given to you. So Pesach Sheni is the holiday of the second chance, but it's so deep — you know what Torah *sh'baal peh* is? It's my doing. Doesn't come down from Heaven unless I ask. So this is Reb Meir, right? Torah *sh'baal peh* — *mamash* asking for it.

And according to all the rabbis in the Talmud, the people who asked for it were those people who carried the coffin of Nadav and Avihu. If you remember, on Rosh Chodesh Nisan, when we initiated the Mishkan — the Holy Temple — Nadav and Avihu walked into the Holy of Holiest, and they didn't come out. You know, the High Priest walks into the Holy of Holiest once a year on Yom Kippur. Basically, you cannot just walk into the Holy of Holiest. And Nadav and Avihu were not told to go in. They walked in, and they left their soul there.

And again, I wish we would have all night. But let me tell you something — anybody here who studies the Bible — sadly enough, the English translation makes it like they did something terrible, and they were punished. God forbid, God forbid. But why did they go into the Holy of Holiest? And basically, because of them we have Yom Kippur.

And also — I'll start from the other side. You know, Moshe Rabbeinu came down from Heaven because we made the Golden Calf. And he asked for forgiveness, and on Yom Kippur God gave him the two tablets again. Why do I have to go into the Holy of Holiest? And if you remember, the High Priest walked into the Holy of Holiest — didn't ask for forgiveness — he just walked in there, didn't say a word, and he came out.

I'm sure Nehemia [Polen] was learning it in a million ways — and Brother Hershele, but let me tell you. There's two ways of asking for forgiveness. Imagine I'm yelling at my wife, and I *mamesh* hurt her feelings; then I say, "Listen, you know, I just learned that it is forbidden to hurt somebody's feelings, and also I read in another book it's very, very bad — so I want you to forgive me." How does it sound to you? "And I want you to know, I have a Ph.D. in Judaism, and also, really, *mamesh*, like, you know, it's really, it's against the Torah to yell at your wife." So my wife just melts away. Unless she is a shmendrick like me, right?

Let me ask you something — how would it sound to you? Let me ask you — why doesn't the Torah ever say you have to love your children? Would be beautiful. Imagine I walk up to my daughters and say, "Listen to me, I love you because it says in the Torah, 'You have to love your children.'" 'Cause the Bible says you have to love your children. How does it sound to you?

If I do something because I have to [someone sneezes] — God bless you — it's outside stuff. And you know what it is? And this is not to say I'm not doing it because — It's clear to me God wants me to love my children, right? But it's not on the level "you have to." It's deeper than "you have to," not less deep. It's so much deeper.

You know, I was talking to someone who had a little radio show in New York. Sometimes they talk about — sadly enough, there's still people who hit their children — it's disgusting. So someone called me up on the radio and says, "Where does it say in the Torah that you're not permitted to hit your children?" I said to him, "Let me ask you something— " [someone sneezes] God bless you — "You mean to say you can lift your hand and hit a little baby? Then you're not a human being, right? You're definitely not God's image, right?" You know it's deeper. "D'you mean you could?"

How would it sound to you? I will tell you if the Torah wouldn't forbid us to kill, I would walk around with a knife killing everyone. But then I read the Bible — the Ten Commandments [chuckles] — and I decided not to kill. Okay, you know, for some people maybe it's an emergency. You mean you COULD kill? I want you to know something awesome, awesome, awesome. The Ishbitzer says, when God spoke to us on Mt.

Sinai — God says, "Don't kill" — what was engraved on our hearts is not the words, "Don't kill." What was engraved inside of us: how precious life is. [Whispering] Life is so precious. It's not I SHOULDN'T kill — that's forbidden — I CAN'T kill, right?

You know, when God said to us, "Don't steal," it's not all — I saw, I saw *mamash* there written on the sky, "Don't steal." [A person evidently brings him something to drink.] What are you bringing me there, darling? You are cute! *L'chaim.* [People respond in kind] *L'chaim.* [Drinks] Thank you. What do I need my guitar for? [Puts it down.]

You hear, friends? Imagine if my little child says to me, "Can you give me some apple juice?" Am I giving her the apple juice because I have to? It's the deepest "I want to," right? Deepest, deepest, deepest.

You know the difference between serving God and serving idols? It's very simple. Serving the living God is "I want to." Serving a dead idol — by a lot of people, *gevalt*, God has become a dead idol — is "I have to." Anybody's doing things because he has to — it's pagan worship. [Whispering] I have to! Everything is forced. [Normal voice] Sure, when I serve God, I really have to — *gevalt* — it's the deepest, deepest, like I wanna, I wanna give my children apple juice. Sure, I have to. But I want to.

The Talmud says, "How did our father Abraham serve God before He gave us the Torah on Mt. Sinai? How did he know?" And the Gemara says, "It's inside." Inside. The deepest inside. The deepest, deepest inside. So I want you to know, until we made the Golden Calf, the Torah was so deep in our hearts. When we made the Golden Calf, something, God forbid, happened to us. [Whispers] I have to. [Normal voice] You see, when you serve the idol, even serving God becomes idol worship. I want you to know something. You know what idol worship is? It means God is dead. Doesn't move.

I'll tell you something I just shared with somebody. The first — you know, when they made Sha'arei Tzedek, so to speak, a Jewish hospital in Yerushalayim, they took a German-Jewish doctor, very religious, and he was like an idol-worshipper. When he was praying, he wouldn't move, even it's an emergency. 'Cause he'd say, "No, when I'm davening, I'm davening." What do you mean? Someone is dying! You'd better get your act together and come out — you're the doctor, right? What's his problem? Serving a dead God. Can't move, right? He doesn't know when yes and when no, right?

You know what's so special about the Torah? There is nothing, nothing, more alive than the Torah. Even when the Torah says no, maybe tomorrow it's yes. You know what it means to be a living person? To be in touch, to know exactly what does God want of me right now. Remember the children of the Heilige Strelisker came to the Heilige Rizhiner and [he] asked [them], "What was the most important thing by your father?" And they said, "For him, the most important is to know what God wants of him right now." What do you have to do right now, right?

You know, all those people — they have plans, and they know now already what they'll do ten years from now on Shabbos morning 9:20. They'll be in the synagogue and they'll be on page 35. It's idol worship. How do I know, right? I hope I'll be there, but what do I know, right?

I'll tell you something very deep — not only in doing good. The Heilige Rizhiner says to the chasidim, "Please, I would like to show you what is a real human being. Call me somebody in from the street." They call in somebody, and he says, "Listen, brother. Imagine you're walking behind me, and a thousand rubles are falling out of my pocket. What are you gonna do?" He says, "The truth? I'll keep it." "Thank you so much." He says, "What a thief! Call in somebody else." The next person comes in, and he asks him, "What would you do?" He says, "Rebbe, I'd give it right back to you." "Oy," he says, "What an idiot!"

[Crowd cracks up — even Shlomo laughs.] He says, "Call in somebody else." [They] call in the third person. He says, "Rebbe, I don't know. It depends what mood I am in." "Ah, that's the real one!" Right?

You know what it means, "the living God?" Not only that God is alive — I'm also alive! I don't know what I'll think tomorrow. I'll just hope. I hope I won't steal. But what do I know, right? You know, if someone says to you, "Are you keeping next Shabbos?" All I can say, "I hope." I hope. What do I know, right?

So in a nutshell, Nadav and Avihu were so afraid. So here we build a *mishkan,* and again the *mishkan,* God told us, "Build a *mishkan*" — again we did it because we have to (as much as we did it because we want to). They wanted to do one thing — "nobody told me — nobody told me — " "*shelo y'tsivu HaShem*" [paraphrase of Lev. 10:1]. I want to do it because I love God so much. I want to be so close to Him. I want to run into the Holy of Holiest. Oh, this is so deep.

You know, if my whole Yiddishkeit — my whole connection to God is because "I have to," it's a bad — it's a bad connection. But then I want you to know something deeper. When do I ever have the privilege to do something with my whole heart — with my whole heart. You know what holy is? I'm doing it. Sure, I'm doing it good. Even if one corner of my heart is not so much with it, it's still holy. You know what the Holy of Holiest is? "*V'chol adam lo y'hiyeh b'ohel mo-ed*" [Lev. 16:17]. There's nothing left in my heart which doesn't want to do it. There is not one billionth'l, zillionth'l ounce in my heart left which doesn't want to serve God. But this is not so simple.

You know, what's 'establishment'? What's bugging us about the so-called religious establishment? They know now that in fifty years from now, Kol Nidre Night, it starts 6:50. They know exactly ten minutes after eight the rabbi will make the Kol Nidre appeal. And about — approximately ten minutes after nine they'll announce how much everybody gave. And approximately nine minutes before ten — will be the closing prayer. It's all beautiful. No. [Whispering] It can't be. It can't be.

You know, imagine I get married, and I get myself a paperback book on marriage, and then I see exactly in the morning — ah ha, page 35, I know what to do. Then, after breakfast, I see my way in the reading, I need to turn the page, page 37, let's see what I have to do. It's all cute and sweet.

I have to tell you something. There are two stories which are actually the same. Reb Hanoch of Alexander — one of the biggest rebbes — there are two famous stories of him. But I'll tell you this one. He told the story: There was this idiot. And every evening when he undressed, the next morning he did not remember where he put his socks, where he put his shirt, where he put his pants. So he decided, *mamash*, one night he'll write down everything. So he wrote down, "My pants are under the bed. My socks are next to the bed. And I am in my bed." Next morning he wakes up. "Ah, my pants — under the bed. My socks are here." And then he sees, "And I am in my bed." He looks in the bed, and he's not there. He begins to cry. So he says, "Master of the world, where am I?" *Gevalt*, is that deep, right? *Gevalt*, is that deep. But where are you? Where are you? Right.

You know, friends, it is possible to do everything, but you never found yourself — completely disconnected from yourself. What do you really want? What do you *really* want?

You know what Aharon HaKohen — when he walked into the Holy of Holiest — you know what he brought back to us? Just the inside of us. Remember, we were learning it a lot of times — maybe not every person is holy. But every person is the Holy of Holiest. We have something so holy inside, so awesomely holy inside, right? But we're so disconnected from it.

So the High Priest, when he walked into the Holy of Holiest — and here, I want to share with you something I was learning yesterday, and that actually, it's the same thing. You know, my beautiful friends, let's again take a husband and wife. I hurt my wife's feelings. And then I ask her for forgiveness. So she says, "Okay, I forgive you." But you know what it is? Yeah, she forgives me, but sadly enough, those scars. Scars. Aye, *gevalt.* You know how many people hurt our feelings and we forgive them? [Someone sneezes] God bless you. Yeah, we forgave them. [Whispering] But the scar. It's heartbreaking, right?

I want you to know — I was learning it yesterday — the scar you cannot fix from outside; on the skin there's a scar. You can only fix it from [whispering] inside, behind the skin. [Normal voice] You know, from the holy to the Holy of Holiest was a *perochos* [curtain], right? Okay, so God forgave us for making the Golden Calf. But humanly speaking, there was a big scar, humanly speaking, even on God's heart. How do you — how do you get rid of the scar? Ah — the Holy of Holiest. Deepest. From behind the curtain.

You know, when I hurt somebody's feelings, and I ask them for forgiveness, we're still far from each other, still long distance. How many people make up, then forgive each other? — But *oy gevalt,* there's still long distance. Do you know, you can stand next to a person and be billions of miles away. Listen, God is everywhere, and how far are we from God, right? All those long distance calls. Holy of Holiest is — so close. It's just so deep, it's so deep. Suddenly, there are no more scars. Because it's this deepest revelation. *Gevalt,* am I one with you. I mean, if I did something wrong it was only my outside; it was never my inside. Deepest, deepest inside, right?

I want you to know something — everybody's asking. Basically, if I cannot do something good — it was not in my hand — it is considered in Heaven like I did it. *Ma aleh alav hakasuv k'ilu asah-oh* [*Berachot* 6a].

So everybody's asking, why are they *krechtsing* about [the Pesach sacrifice]? They couldn't do it, right? Because they were *tamei ha-mes.* If you touch a coffin you cannot go into the Holy of Holies. It was not their fault, right? But the answer is very simple. If all you're interested in [is] doing it because the Torah says you have to do it, so I did it, right? [But] I REALLY wanna do it.

Imagine Neshama says to me, "Can you give me apple juice?" And then I would say, "You know, I'll just — I'm so sorry — I'm just — I have a long distance call to Israel." So I really, I can't give her the apple juice, right? But then I say, "Neshama, you know something — " She says, "Yeah, I forgive you. I understand. You couldn't." "I'm so broken that I didn't give you the apple juice." I didn't do it, right? Nobody blames you. But I still didn't do it.

And here I want you to know something very deep. This is *mamash* very important to know, friends. Anybody who knows a little about Shabbos — you know, in Belz, the way they made Kiddush — ah, *gevalt. Gevalt* Kiddush, right? Bobover Rebbe — makes a different Kiddush; Satmar Rebbe — another Kiddush. So you would say, "Everybody makes Kiddush, everybody says the same blessing." Yeah, but the way they're saying it — everybody has their own individual way of saying it, right? Maybe on the outside it's all the same.

You know, take Yom Kippur, right? You know, sadly enough, there are some synagogues, the same service at 2000 synagogues, it's all the same because there's nothing inside in it, because the moment you put your inside — it cannot be that — two people don't do it the same way, right? It comes from inside. So they say, "Okay, so we won't be blamed for not doing it; we did it. But what we did, it's like all of Israel did it, right? But it was not my doing, my Korban Pesach," right? "Ah, you know, the way I bring Korban Pesach? The way I sing and dance when I bring the Paschal lamb, *gevalt!*" Ssss.

You know what Amalek does? You know what the greatest evil in the world is? When someone says to you, "Your own addition doesn't count. Whatever you do special is unimportant. Just do it!" I want you to know something. I watch sometimes — you know, in my neighborhood, a lot of homeless people — and *Baruch HaShem*, one of my greatest privileges is really, I'm very close to — I would say, to 98% of them. Okay, our chevra, *mamash,* you know, they know how to give a dollar to a poor man, right? You don't just take out the dollar, look to the other side, here, you know. Sometimes I watch my chevra, you know? Everybody's doing it in a sweeter way, right? In a special way, right? [Whispers] This is so special.

And here, I want to add something awesome. It was the people who carried the coffin of Yosef, who came to Moshe, and they said, "We need a second chance." How did they know? I was learning it yesterday, and it really blew my mind — myself. Everybody knows the story of Rachel and Leah, right? Rachel is engaged to Yaakov, and Yaakav and Rochel have a secret sign because they knew that Lavan — Laban — will put Lee-ah under the wedding canopy. So in the last moment Rachel saw — "Oh, my sister will be put to shame." She gave her over the secret sign.

So Yaakov didn't know it's Lee-ah; he thought it's Rachel, right? You know what that means? Rachel gave up her husband. Rachel gave up this world and the coming world because it was clear to her, "If I don't marry Yaakov, I have to marry Esau." Because everybody was saying, "Yaakov and Esau — and Lavan has two daughters — one is for Yaakov, one is for Esau," right? Do you know what it means to be the wife of Esau? Don't have to tell you. Not this world, not the coming world. Give everything up, for what?

Lemme ask you something: imagine this young lady stands under the Chuppah, and then suddenly the groom says, "I don't want you," and she'll be put to shame. She'll get over it! A few years later she'll meet somebody else, she'll get married, right? But you know what? [Whispering] The scar. The scar. You know what Rachel did? She gave up her life for the scar of Leah. Ah, that is awesome. "I don't want any scars on my sister's heart." So here they come to — Yosef, the son of Rochel — they come to Moshe, and say, "You know something? Unless we do Pesach Sheni, there'll always be a scar on my heart — why I didn't have this Pesach. Why didn't I have the privilege to do this?"

[Normal voice] So someone says to me, "You know, it's okay. You'll still go to Paradise." I'm not asking you about Paradise or Hell — [whispers] I want so much to do it! [Normal voice] You know, friends, when you want to do something for your best friend, for God, and you don't do it — there's this deep scar on your heart. And if it was the coffin of Nadav and Avihu, obviously it's even easier. You know what's Nadav and Avihu? *Kodesh Kedoshim* [Holy of Holies]. And *Kodesh Kedoshim* is only when I *mamash* do it, with all my heart, with all my soul.

So you hear, my beautiful friends, today is a holiday when it's clear to us — it is never too late. Not only it's never too late; it's never too late to fix even the scars.

— Transcribed in Tzfat, the first week of Iyar, 5761. Completed 8 Iyar, 5761 / May 1, 2001.

I am living proof of the essential truth of the words I've transcribed. I was with my family in Newton on the very day that Reb Shlomo gave over this teaching. I knew that he was in town, but I didn't make an effort to find out where he would be and when. The fact that someone else had made a tape, and that I could obtain a copy of it from Betzalel Edwards, made it possible for me to have a second chance — and to share this teaching with you. — RG

# The Doors We Go Through

Transcribed by Emuna Witt-Halevi

## Introduction

We all felt that the torah Reb Shlomo gave over was just for us; exactly what we needed to hear, precisely at the right moment. We were privileged to host Reb Shlomo wherever we lived; I'd spend the whole day preparing the house. Reb Shlomo would finally come late, after a full day of many events, bless each and every person, and then sing a few beautiful *niggunim.* By that time I'd be the first one to fall asleep, with a bunch of my little ones on top of me even before he began to teach (the room was packed with a hundred people on cushions on the floor). In the middle of his discourse, he'd explain to us that children didn't want to go to sleep; we needed to tell each child how beautiful he is, how much we love him and need him, and how much Hashem loves and needs him even more! I'd wake up immediately and hear those words and take them into my heart. (I'd be frantic every morning getting lots of little kids off to school, and then I'd remember the words of Reb Shlomo reminding us to send our holy children to school with great *simcha* [joy] and sweetness!)

Even though I slept through many teachings, we taped it all, and the next morning I'd listen to Reb Shlomo and transcribe every word. It kept my sanity for all those years raising 14 children; Reb Shlomo's torahs got into our bones, our blood, our souls. It is still my work in the world, and I can't believe that after 30 years of transcribing I am still finding the most mind-blowing torahs that I never heard before.

I am sharing a torah here that Reb Shlomo gave over in a Hebrew School in Palo Alto in 1978. It will change your life and answer your questions; Reb Shlomo is talking directly to you.

\* \* \*

Special moments. Special people. You know who is a special person? A special person is somebody who has something special in their life. If you have something special in your life, everything becomes special. A person who has five minutes of "special" in their life — if you have one person who is special to you — wherever you go, you make everything special.

You see, sweetest friends, G-d wanted us to build the Holy Temple, and in order to build the Holy Temple, it has to be special. Isn't G-d's Holy Temple all over? Isn't the whole world G-d's Holy Temple? It begins by building a holy little tabernacle. And from there it expands all over the world. If I have five minutes I'm learning, it's so special, so special. So holy. Whatever I do with the rest of the time becomes so holy also. So special.

Sweetest friends, what the world is so hungry for is something special. You know what it means [that] the Holy Temple is destroyed? It doesn't have a special light anymore. Things are the same. Going to the synagogue, going to the office, serving G-d, writing out a check, it's all the same. Playing a baseball game with my children, it's all the same. It's all the same.

Now I want you to know something very, very deep, in a nutshell. These two months we are living in now, Chodesh Adar, the two Chodesh Adars, it's the time when we celebrate Purim, which is the ultimate wiping out of evil from the world. You know, after the story of Purim was over we went back to the Holy Land and we rebuilt the Holy Temple. But what's going on there? There's retail evil and wholesale evil. Retail evil is I walk down the street; I see a poor man, my little boy says, "Don't give charity. Keep it." Someone asks me a favor — how stupid, he asked me last week. Let him go to someone else. This is retail evil.

Wholesale evil is something else. Wholesale evil is the snake who tells you there is nothing special. One more thing. Can you explain to me why something is special and why something else is not special? On Purim when we are drunk, it doesn't mean I'm drunk with wine. On Purim I am filled with all the things I have no words for — with that thing which is so high, but I can't explain it to you. It's there; I know. You know what I'm doing when I am giving to my friend who is so special to me? On Yom Kippur I can't return to G-d without being special. Purim is so special, so deep.

Let's learn for five minutes. Where's the *Lekutei Moharan*? Okay, what I need is the highest concentration. Open your hearts. G-d opens gates for me. The first time G-d opens one gate most people are afraid to go in and just stand there and smile and go away. Okay, they have enough guts to go in. You go through and there are two doors. It's up to you to decide which door you want to go through. Open your hearts. I'm going through one door and the next room has four doors. Then I'm going through another door, I'm going in there, and there are eight doors. Now listen to this deepest depths. Imagine I'm already in that room with eight doors. Do you know that only one door goes to the next room? All the other doors go outside. Only one door goes deep; you are out again. You are out [in the] cold, have to start all over again. *This goes on all the time. This explains so much of our life.* We were in there, getting stronger, stronger. Maybe the first three doors, I went through the right doors, then one day I made a mistake and took the wrong door. Out in the cold again.

What does it mean to be out? Listen to this deepest depths: nobody ever goes through where you were before. Nothing happens twice. You know what it means, "the door out"? It looks like you are going somewhere. Okay, Reb Nachman says the most important thing is, I'll ask you, I'm already in the eighth room. There are about 64 doors, maybe I shouldn't go through any doors anymore. I'll stay here. The moment you think that, you're out the door. So you don't need a door, you are out. Any way you are out. So what do you have to do? Just keep on walking. *The most important thing Reb Nachman says, even if you went through the wrong door, you learn something from it also. Each time you learn more about the doors; it's a very deep* torahle, *the teaching of the doors. Someday we'll know exactly how to do it. You know, friends, someday we won't have to go through doors. Because only outsiders need a door to get in. If I live in the house, I'm inside.*

I want to learn with you one more thing, very important also. When you come to those doors, everyone tells you which door to take. *Let me tell you from my heart to your heart. Whatever people tell you is always the wrong door. You know what the right door is? The right door is the door that nobody points out to you. Your heart tells you, this is my door. Because how can anybody else know which is your door from G-d?* How could anybody know?

*Sometimes you can meet somebody on the street anywhere in the world and you feel very close to them. You never met before. You know what it is? Maybe last night you went through the same door.*

Every person has two sides. One side is what I have, the other side is what I don't have. That side which I don't have is not so simple, I don't have it. I'm longing for it so much. There is one part of me that is completely unfulfilled, not fulfilled yet. There is a part of me which

I have, then there's a part of [me] which is *mamash* longing. I want you to open your hearts. If I'm longing for 100 dollars, that means I don't have it. If I'm longing for something holy, how come I'm longing for it? If I would not be connected to it, I would not be longing for it. I'm only longing for it because I have it already. I'm not longing for a person that I have no connection to, I'm only longing for a person I'm connected to.

Reb Nachman says, the passage says, *Ani tefillati* [*Psalms*, 69:14], I am my prayer. You know the difference between a world level and a G-d level? If someone were to ask you, "Who are you? Where's your 'I'?" They would say the part of you that is already fulfilled. That part of you which is longing, which is not there yet, this is not your real "I"; this is your missing "I". David HaMelech says, *V'ani tefillati* — you know what my real "I" is? The real "I" is the part of me that is praying, praying so hard. Listen to me, sweetest friends. We connect to people on two levels. With some people we connect on a  level, and we know, this is not sweet. *When that part of me which is longing for something connects to somebody who's also longing for the same thing, this is the highest meeting between people.*

I want you to open your hearts. There is Torah and there is *tefillah*. When I'm learning something I know it. I'm praying for something I don't have. There is no law that says when you study there should be ten people. It's beautiful if there are ten people. If there are 100 people, 1000 people, it's beautiful! But it doesn't change the learning. Davening, praying when ten people are together; when there are three people it's something else. Ten people is something else. Do you know what it means — the connection of ten people praying? So deep.

Har Sinai is the "I" which knows; G-d gave it to me. He tells me what to do, what not to do, everything is there. Yerushalayim, the Holy City, King David's House, G-d's House, *Kee Beit tefillati, kee Beit Tefilla* (this is the House of my prayer, the House of Prayer), Yerushalayim is praying. It's very strange; Mount Sinai is only us Jewish people. When you know something and somebody else doesn't know it, you don't turn them on. Yerushalayim, we're praying; soon, soon, the whole world will come to pray here. When you pray, you can turn on the whole world. You *mamash* can turn on the whole world. Because this is the deepest "I" of me. The deepest deepest part of my *neshama*; the utmost longing, the utmost longing for something so holy to happen to me, something so special to happen to me.

You know, sweetest friends, when children are born, what's the first connection to their parents? They are privileged to hear the baby cry. What a privilege! You know how I judge people? Sometimes I stay in people's homes. At night the baby is crying, please be quiet! What do they know about this prayer of this child? When children are crying, it's so deep. It's *Mashiach* davening, it's *Mashiach* davening, Yerushalayim davening. You see what it is, the portion of this week and next week, almost Purim time, we are learning about building the Holy Temple, building a house. Have you ever walked into a house and feel like a stranger or have you walked into a house and feel so beautiful. It's very simple. If the people who live in the house, if their "I" is what they are and what they know, what is there? The house is empty. If the house is filled with prayer, *gevaldt*, do you feel at home.

I want to bless everyone to have children, and those who are expecting children to have them in the right time, with great joy. One of the holiest rebbes, the *Heilige* Reb Dovid'l — a chasid came to him and said, "I'm married eighteen years and I don't have children; please bless me." So he says, "You know something? Ask one of my chasidim, the holy Tosha, Rav Shraga Feivel HaLevi of Kosov." "How should I ask him?" "Invite him to your house." So the next time the Tosha comes, the rich Yiddele goes up to him and says, "Could I invite you to my house for lunch?" "Yes!" He was delighted. Before he sits him at the table he starts walking around the house. They had a lot of respect, but finally they asked, "What are you looking for? Maybe we can help you find it." "I'm looking for a crib for a baby." "Rebbe, I'm sorry, we don't have a baby, so we don't have a crib." "Then I can't eat here. I only eat in a house where there are children." "But Rebbe, you promised you'd eat here!" "That's okay, I'll have to come back next year." *Mazal tov!* You know what kind of house it is with children? It's really G-d's house. It really is. Children are crying.

What do you do before you go to sleep? You are praying, I should wake up tomorrow. Everybody knows that the highest connection between people is at night. At night, two people connect their prayers. They should wake up tomorrow. Our children should wake up tomorrow. The world should wake up. Thank you, *shalom!*

— Kol Emeth Weekday Religious School, Palo Alto, California, 1978

*Reb Shlomo and Neila with baby Neshama in Griffith Park, Los Angeles, 1975.*
*Photo by Rabbi Joe Schonwald.*

# Two Stories:
# The Gypsy Musician
## and
# The Poor Woman's Blessing

Transcribed by Tzlotana Midlo

TODAY WE ARE LIVING IN A WORLD WHERE PEOPLE DON'T HONOR ANY-thing that is holy. Holy has no *kavod*. If people meet a very holy man who is also very successful in business or something else, they will give him honor. He'll receive a write-up in the *New York Times* and get invited to speak in Madison Square Garden. But people won't be respecting him for his holiness. They honor him because he is so suc-cessful that he draws a tremendous crowd. Rebbe Nachman says that in exile, all honor originates from the "other side." *Kavod* is no longer connected to holiness. Even the honor that people give to each other is completely without life....

Reb Dovid of Dinitz told this story about a trip his mother made to Vienna. His mother was walking along the street when she met a friend who told her that the greatest violinist of the gypsies was giving a concert in the city that night.

Reb Dovid's mother decided she absolutely had to go to this concert. So she went to the ticket office to get a ticket for the performance. And as she walked in the door she noticed a poor gypsy sitting on the floor against the wall, playing his violin. None of the people who passed him bothered to listen to what he was playing. They were all too anxious to buy their tickets to hear the famous musician who would be performing in the concert hall.

That night, the concert hall filled up quickly with thousands and thousands of people. The lights dimmed. Everyone directed their attention towards the stage to see this great performer. Finally he appeared on the stage. And suddenly everybody recognized him. This great musician was the same gypsy violinist who had been sitting against the wall in the ticket office. And they realized that he had been playing beautiful awesome melodies, and no one had paid any attention to him.

The whole audience was absolutely silent. Then the violinist spoke. "You know," he said, "I had the impression that you respected me for my music. But when I was sitting on the floor in the ticket office none of you cared to listen to what I was playing. I performed the entire concert that I was going to play here tonight. But not one of you listened to me — because I seemed to just be a poor gypsy, not a famous musician; because I was sitting on the floor instead of standing on a stage; and because you didn't have to pay twenty rubles to see me. Now I understand. You don't respect me; you only respect fame and your twenty rubles. And you think that I should now play the music that comes from the deepest depths of my soul, that is the holiest thing that I have in this life, for you and your twenty rubles? Forget it! I don't want any part of this!"

And the gypsy violinist walked off the stage and out of the concert hall, with everybody staring after him in awe and shame. He walked out, and he was never heard from again. He disappeared...

\* 　 \* 　 \*

One year, before Yom Kippur, the *Heilige* Reb Levi Yitzchak gave notice to the whole city of Berditchev that he wanted everyone to come on *erev* Yom Kippur to receive his blessing — but it would cost one ruble. And one way or another, everybody came. They either had a ruble or borrowed a ruble, but they all managed to come to receive the Rebbe's blessing.

Finally all the people left, and Reb Levi Yitzchak was left alone with his closest *chassidim*. It was getting later and later, but the Rebbe still wasn't going to *shul*. It kept getting closer and closer to the time for Kol Nidre. His *chassidim* kept saying, "Rebbe, it's late — it's so late." But still Reb Levi Yitzchak didn't move. Obviously he was waiting for somebody...

It kept getting later — it was so late. And, you know, all of us are so late. *Gevalt,* are we late! But the secret of life is to know that it's never too late...

Finally a very poor woman came, with a little girl hanging onto her skirt. The woman said to the Rebbe, "*Heilige* Rebbe, here is my ruble. Please bless me." So Reb Levi Yitzchak blessed her.

But the woman didn't leave. She stood before Reb Levi Yitzchak for a moment, and then she said. "Rebbe, believe me — it was so hard for me to get that one ruble. But here is my little girl with me, and I don't have another ruble for her. Please Rebbe, could you bless my daughter for free?"

Reb Levi Yitzchak shook his head. "I'm sorry," he said. "The price is one ruble. If you don't have another ruble, I can't bless your daughter."

The woman burst into tears. "Rebbe, I don't have another ruble. But I already paid for one blessing. So please, Rebbe — take away the blessing you gave me. I don't care what happens to me. But please bless my child, please bless my child!"

Reb Levi Yitzchak couldn't control himself. He got up, ran to *shul*, opened the holy ark and cried, "*Ribbono Shel Olam,* did you hear what that woman said? She said to me, 'I don't care what happens to me, but please bless my child....'

"Master of the World, please be more generous than I was with the poor woman. If You want me to bless her daughter, how can You not do the same? I don't care what happens to me, but please bless Your children. Please inscribe all Israel in the Book of Life!"

*Teaching in Jerusalem in the 1980s.*
*Photo by Rabbi Joe Schonwald*

# Cry Over Every Stitch

as told by Rabbi Shlomo Carlebach

THE *HEILIGE* REB YERACHMIEL OF P'SHISCHA HAD A TAILOR WHO MADE just enough for bread and herring. A nobleman came to his shop, took a liking to him, and appointed him his tailor. When you are the tailor of the nobleman, you don't need a Rebbe, and you don't eat bread and herring anymore. He kept away from Yidden, kept his nose in the air, and was a very outstanding tailor.

One day, the nobleman came with material from Paris, and he said to the tailor, "This is the best material I ever bought, and I want you to make me a suit like you never made before." The tailor thought, "I am the best tailor in the world. I once was a chassidisher Yid; all I had was bread and herring, and now, thank G-d, I have bagels and lox."

He made the suit, and it really was beautiful. He brought it to the nobleman, who put it on and couldn't get it off fast enough. He yelled at the tailor, "This is the most terrible suit I ever wore." Cursing him, he took out his pistol and said, "If I ever see you again, I'm going to kill you," and he took the suit and threw it out of the window. The tailor picked it up and ran for his life, thinking it's time to go to the Rebbe again.

He said to the *Heilige* Reb Yerachmiel, "Rebbe, believe me, it's a beautiful suit. What did I do wrong?" The *Heilige* Rebbe replied, "I'll tell you what. Undo the suit, and then put it together the same way. Just put it together, and tomorrow night take it to the nobleman, and G-d be with you."

The tailor was up all night, crying over every stitch. The next day, he brought it to the nobleman and said, "Please give me just one more chance." The nobleman put it on and said, "This is the masterpiece of the world. I never had such a suit. You outdid yourself!" The tailor went back to the Rebbe. "Rebbe, what's going on?"

The Rebbe said, "I want you to know, arrogance smells so bad. Even for a low person like the nobleman, the smell was so bad he couldn't stand it. There was no other way; you had to start all over again. This time, when you put the suit together, you cried over every stitch, all your arrogance was gone, and you pleaded: 'Master of the World, have compassion on me. I have a wife and children. Please God, let the suit be beautiful.' And anything you do with great humility, with tears and with prayers, is so beautiful, so good."

You know, friends, once a year the *Ribono Shel Olam* tells us, take everything apart and put it together again. On Rosh Hashana and Yom Kippur, when you do teshuva, you take everything apart. The whole world is falling apart, everything is wrong. And then comes Succos. I build the Succah and put my life together again. But do you know what I do over every stitch? I yell, "Master of the World, this is the best I can do for You, but I'm begging You to help us." And on Simchas Torah, I put on this new suit and go back to my house. Suddenly I realize, the world is so beautiful; there is no day when there is more humility in the world, for this is Moshe Rabbeinu's day.

On Simchas Torah, every Jew dances with children, and the biggest Rosh Yeshiva dances with Moishele the water carrier, and it's clear to him: "Maybe Moishele knows the Torah better than I do. Maybe the way I put my sefer together was with a little bit of arrogance, and this smells so bad." So on Simchas Torah, everybody is taking the sefer apart and putting it together again — and *gevalt*, what a Torah it is.

# Notes on Contributors

**Steve Amdur, *z"l*,** was an itinerant Jewish Sufi. He was an early resident of the New Buffalo commune in New Mexico, a preserver and protector of recorded teachings at the Abode of the Message in New Lebanon, New York, and an internet pioneer who helped to build the listserv GeoCities. com. In later years he divided his time between Camp Zenith in the Swiss Alps; the Island of Rhodes; and his favorite places in Israel, including the Moshav, Kibbutz Ha'On, and Yerushalayim. He devoted considerable energy to transcribing Reb Shlomo tapes, always adding his editorial comments and impressions. His instincts were sound: to preserve and to annotate that which would otherwise have been ephemeral. In that spirit he issued brief weather reports for wherever he was lodging. His last residence was on Monhegan Island, off the coast of Maine. He left this world in 2009. To read the obituary penned by his brother Nicholas, visit http://lcnme.com/obituaries/stephen-benjamin-amdur.

For 40 years **Barry Barkan's** mission has been to restore the role of *elder* to our contemporary world. With his wife Debora, he co-founded the Elders' Guild, which is seeding an elder culture based in community, wisdom, and championing the future. In 2011, they planted their Regenerative Community elder care approach in Israel where it was dubbed *Kehila Tzomachat* and quickly spread to over 100 communities and continues to grow. An Ashoka Fellow, he was given *s'micha* as a *Baal Bracha*, Master of Blessing, by Rabbi Zalman Schachter-Shalomi, *z"l*.

Since Reb Shlomo left this world, **Neila Carlebach** has devoted her creative time to teaching and writing. Her inspiration is derived from

Reb Shlomo Carlebach's deeply moving spiritual teachings, which she absorbed over her 22 years of learning from him. To this bank of knowledge she has infused her studies and insights on Torah and Jewish Mysticism, as well as her own life experiences, which include her years as a therapist/healer and a theatre arts teacher and actor. She and Shlomo have been blessed with two daughters, Neshama and Nedara, and five grandchildren.

**Rabbi Yehonatan Chipman** is a translator who specializes in Judaic studies. He writes a weekly commentary on the *Parashat Hashavua/Haftarah* entitled *Hitzei Yehonatan*, which he sends out via email to hundreds of subscribers. Following Shlomo's death, Rabbi Chipman began writing a reflective essay about him each year as part of his commentary on *Parashat Hayyei Sarah*. A founding member of Havurat Shalom in Somerville, MA, he and his wife Randi have made their home in Jerusalem for several decades.

**Betzalel Edwards** is a Torah scholar, rabbi and translator. After studying music at Boston University, a trip to Auschwitz and Israel inspired him to focus on Hebrew and Arabic studies, Islam and Judaism. He made *aliya* to Israel in 1993 in order to make peace between the Jews and the Arabs. It didn't work. But he did join Reb Shlomo Carlebach's band on its last Israeli Tour in 1994 and performs on the "Od Yosef Chai" recording and the documentary Givalt 1/6 (on YouTube). Between 1997 and 1999, while living in the Old City of Jerusalem, he translated the Ishbitzer — Rabbi Mordechai Yosef Leiner of Izbica (*Living Waters: The Mei HaShiloach*), largely inspired by Reb Shlomo. He has taught at many yeshivas and is a regular Scholar-in-Residence at the Carlebach Shul in Manhattan. For three years he was an editor and translator with the Koren Talmud Bavli project (Steinsaltz Talmud in English). He is currently the lead guitar player for Chopped Liver Enigma, a Jerusalem-based 70s and 80s cover band. He has no privilege or honor greater than the merit of raising a family and learning Torah in Jerusalem.

**Moshe Eliovson** is an Adjunct Instructor of T'ai Chi at Yeshiva University.

**Rabbi Doctor Reb Mimi (Miriam Sara) Feigelson,** the first female Orthodox rabbi, grew up in Israel and was ordained by Rabbi Shlomo Carlebach. Reb Mimi serves as the *Mashpi'ah Ruchanit* (spiritual mentor) and Lecturer in Rabbinic Literature and Chassidic Thought at the Ziegler School of Rabbinic Studies, The American Jewish University in Los Angeles. (www.zieglertorah.org).

She is an international teacher of *Chassidut* and Spirituality and a storyteller. She has taught in many Jewish communities and organizations throughout North America, Canada, England, and the former Soviet Union, and has been engaged in interfaith dialogue for many years in India.

Prior to arriving in the U.S., she was associate director of the Yakar Institute for Tradition and Creativity in Jerusalem and director of its Women's *Beit Ha'midrash*. She was adjunct faculty at the Ma'aleh Film College and published regularly in the *Ha'aretz* Literary Supplement. When returning home to Jerusalem she continues to teach in institutions across the Jewish denominational spectrum.

In 2011 Reb Mimi was accepted as a member of the Board of Rabbis of Southern California as an independent Orthodox rabbi. In 2016 she received a Doctorate from HUC-JIR. Her dissertation is entitled: "On the Cusp of Life: From Scared to Sacred — Reclaiming the Jewish Funeral." It is an exploration of redefining Jewish funerals and burial rituals.

**Ruth Fogelman** was born in England and came to Israel as a teenager. She worked on a kibbutz for a year, served two years in the army, and holds degrees in English literature from the Hebrew University in Jerusalem and Bar Ilan University. In 1979 she and her late husband, Dr. Yakov Fogelman, moved to Jerusalem's Old City, a setting which has inspired much of her poetry and photography (all her books contain photographs as well as poems), in a spirit of "to raise Jerusalem above my chief rejoicing." Her first book, *Within the Walls of Jerusalem — A Personal Perspective,* was released in 2000, and her first full poetry collection, *Cradled in God's Arms*, was released in 2009. Her chapbook, *Jerusalem Awaking* (Sifrei Bitzaron), was released in 2010. She won the Reuben Rose Poetry Competition in 2006, and received an honorable mention in the Lindberg Peace Foundation Poetry Contest 2010. Her poems have appeared widely in anthologies, literary journals, including *The Deronda Review, Poetica Magazine,* and *Arc,* and e-zines, including *International Literary Quarterly* — http://www.interlitq.org; *Cyclamens and Swords* — http://www.cyclamensandswords.com; and *New Vilna Review* — http://newvilnareview.com. She heads the Jerusalem writing workshop, *Pri Hadash.*

**Rabbi Yoel Glick** is a renowned teacher of Jewish meditation and spiritual wisdom who has been guiding seekers on the path for over thirty years. He is the director of Daat Elyon (daatelyon.org), an online center for spiritual training and wisdom, and has taught audiences of all denominations and faiths in locations across the globe.

Yoel was the first person to receive *smicha* from Reb Shlomo. He also has received rabbinic ordination from Yeshiva University. Rabbi Yoel is the author of *Living the Life of Jewish Meditation: A Comprehensive Guide to Practice and Experience* (Jewish Lights) and *Seeking the Divine Presence: The Three Pillars of a Jewish Spiritual Life* (Trafford).

**Reuven Goldfarb,** a former member of San Francisco's House of Love and Prayer, co-founded and edited *AGADA,* the illustrated Jewish literary magazine, taught English at Oakland's Merritt College, and received *S'micha* from Rabbi Zalman Schachter-Shalomi as *Moreinu, Maggid,* and Rabbinic Deputy as a consequence of his years of work with the Aquarian Minyan, a vanguard Jewish renewal community in Berkeley, where he and his wife Yehudit raised their family. His poems, stories, and essays have appeared in scores of periodicals and anthologies and won several awards. He now serves as copy editor for books and manuscripts and coordinates monthly meetings for the Upper Galilee branch of Voices Israel. Residents of Tzfat since 2001, he and Yehudit co-founded *Bayt Maor HaLev* Center for Movement, Healing, and Language Arts. They host classes, workshops and a weekly *Chug Pirke Avot* in their home. "Walking to the Kotel" previously appeared in *Poetica Magazine* and won First Place in its 2004 Annual Contest. "Potiphar's Lament" appeared in *The Deronda Review* in 2008.

**Ari L. Goldman** is a professor at the Columbia University Graduate School of Journalism, where he directs the Scripps Howard Program in Religion, Journalism and the Spiritual Life. He teaches a variety of courses, including the popular Covering Religion seminar that has taken students on study tours of Israel, Ireland, Italy, India, and Russia.

Goldman is the author of four books, including the best-selling *The Search for God at Harvard.* His newest book, *The Late Starters Orchestra*, was published by Algonquin Books in June 2014. In it, he describes his efforts to relearn the cello after a lapse of 25 years. His obituary of Reb Shlomo in the *New York Times* was one of the first public notices about Shlomo's demise.

**Alon Goshen-Gottstein** is acknowledged as one of the world's leading figures in interreligious dialogue, specializing in bridging the theological and academic dimensions with a variety of practical initiatives, especially involving world religious leadership. He is both a theoretician and activist, setting trends and precedents in the global interfaith arena. He is the founder and director of the Elijah Interfaith Institute, and its rich website is testimony to his many and varied activities. A noted scholar of Jewish studies, he has held academic posts at Tel Aviv University and has served as director of the Center for the Study of Rabbinic Thought, Beit Morasha College, Jerusalem. Stanford University Press published his *The Sinner and the Amnesiac: The Rabbinic Invention of Elisha ben Abuya and Eleazar ben Arach,* and the Littman Library published his co-edited volume *Jewish Theology and World Religions.* His *The Jewish Encounter with Hinduism — Wisdom, Spirituality, Identity,* has just been published by Palgrave-Macmillan. He is the editor of a series entitled "Interreligious Reflections," published by Lexington Books.

**Yossi Klein Halevi** is an American-born journalist who has lived in Jerusalem since 1982. He is a Senior Fellow at the Shalom Hartman Institute in Jerusalem and a contributing editor to the *New Republic.* His writing frequently appears in the op-ed pages of major American newspapers. He is the author of *At the Entrance to the Garden of Eden: A Jew's Search for God with Christians and Muslims in the Holy Land,* and *Like Dreamers: The Story of the Israeli Paratroopers Who Reunited Jerusalem and Divided a Nation,* which won the National Jewish Book Council Jewish Book of the Year Award. He lives in Jerusalem with his wife, Sarah. They have three children.

**Rabbi Sam Intrator** was born in Baltimore, MD, to Holocaust survivors. His early education included an old-world style *cheder* and the Talmudic Academy day school. He then studied at Ner Israel Rabbinical College and Yeshivat Derech Chaim. He subsequently earned a degree in political science from Queens College and worked closely with New York City Council member Susan Alter for 16 years.

Rabbi Intrator received ordination from Rabbi Shlomo Carlebach, *zt"l*, and Yeshivat Kol Yaacov. He assisted and learned with Rabbi Carlebach for many years, traveling widely with him in the U.S., Israel, and Communist Poland and Russia. He served as Assistant Rabbi at Congregation Kehillat Jacob (The Carlebach Shul) on the upper west side of Manhattan from 1992 until the untimely passing of his mentor. He then became the Senior Rabbi of the synagogue, serving from 1994-2000.

Rabbi Intrator has been a guest speaker and rabbi at various universities, including UCLA, NYU, Oxford, and Amherst and Smith Colleges. He has participated in interdenominational panels with other spiritual leaders in New York City and been featured in many newspapers, including the *New York Times.* He has also appeared on the television show *Extra!* Rabbi Intrator is head of Kavanah Life, an organization dedicated to raising spiritual consciousness in prayer and ritual, and is currently writing about the deeper meaning of prayer. He serves as Rabbi of the Ocean Pavilion Synagogue in Miami Beach.

**Rabbi Dr. Menachem Kallus** was born to parents who survived the Holocaust and resettled in Brooklyn in the 1950s. Though he grew up with Reb Shlomo's music (as did the entire New York 'Yeshivishe' world of the '60s), he met Reb Shlomo, z"l, only in the mid-'70s when he was well on his way out of the Haredi community. Upon his presenting a litany of what was wrong with Judaism, Reb Shlomo told him: if you can see what's wrong, you can also help fix it. It was this remark that kept him from entirely abandoning Judaism.

In the mid-'80s, Kallus moved to Jerusalem to attend graduate school in the Department of Jewish Thought at Hebrew University, which in 2003 awarded him a doctorate for his dissertation on the practice of contemplative prayer in Lurianic Kabbalah. Once in Israel, he attended Shabbatot with Reb Shlomo as frequently as possible. In the late '90s, Kallus received rabbinic ordination from Rabbi Zalman Schachter-Shalomi, z"l.

In 2011, in honor of the 250th anniversary of the passing of the holy Baal Shem Tov, z"l, Kallus published a bi-lingual, annotated edition of the 'Amud haTefillah' from *Sefer Baal Shem Tov al haTorah*, entitled *Pillar of Prayer*, augmented with over 300 teachings. For the past decade, he has had the z'chut of facilitating the annual 'Aliyah la-Kever' of Reb Shlomo, z"l, at Har Menuchot.

**HaRav Yisrael Meir Lau** is presently the Chief Rabbi of Tel Aviv and Chairman of Yad Vashem. He was the Ashkenazi Chief Rabbi of Israel from 1993-2003, and in that capacity, and as a personal friend of Reb Shlomo, he delivered the stirring eulogy that appears in this volume, in the lucid translation by Rachel Ebner. He also served as Chief Rabbi of Netanya from 1978-1988, where he developed a reputation as a popular orator. A survivor of Buchenwald, he is the 38th generation in an unbroken family chain of rabbis. Known as a bridge builder between factions in Israeli society, he was awarded the Israel Prize in 2005.

**Chaya Lester** is a Jerusalem-based psychotherapist, writer, and performance artist. She is Co-Director of the Shalev Center, which melds Jewish wisdom with advanced psychological tools and technology.

Chaya holds a BA in Religious and Jewish Studies from the University of Pennsylvania and an MA in Clinical Psychology from the California Institute of Integral Studies. She also did extensive doctoral work on the theme of "Experiential Torah Learning" at Oxford University. In addition to her private practice, Chaya regularly performs her one-woman show, *Babel's Daughter*, to enthusiastic audiences in Israel and abroad.

**Rabbi Itzchak Marmorstein** is an Israeli-born rabbi whose teachings integrate the depths of the ancient teachings and the breadths of the contemporary unfolding. As a passionate student of the teachings of Rabbi Avraham Yitzchak HaKohen Kook (1865- 1935) for over 30 years, he is doing pioneering work in bringing Rav Kook to the public through classes and creative musical and dramatic presentations.

He teaches the Torah of Rav Kook in a variety of settings, most notably at Beit HaRav Kook — Rav Kook's historical home in downtown Jerusalem. He is the gabbai of the renewed Shabbat minyan at Beit HaRav.

Itzchak also presents/performs the extraordinary poetry of Rav Kook with leading jazz and spiritual folk musicians in Israel and North America. His Tzadik Records CD "HaOrot-The Lights of Rav Kook" presents the poetry of Rav Kook with Rabbi Greg Wall's ("the Jazz Rabbi") Later Prophets.

Itzchak was ordained by Zalman Nechemia Goldberg ShLIT"A, in 1989 in Jerusalem. In 1992 he received semicha from Rabbi Shlomo Carlebach, *z"l* and in 1996 from Rabbi Zalman Schachter-Shalomi, *z"l.*

**Tzlotana Barbara Midlo** is the compiler and editor of *Lamed Vav: A Collection of the Favorite Stories of Rabbi Shlomo Carlebach, ztz"l.* This book has become a favorite of Shlomo chevra everywhere.

**Rabbi Micha Odenheimer** was born in Berkeley, California, and grew up there and in Los Angeles in the Orthodox Jewish community. He graduated from Yale University, *Cum Laude,* with a B.A. in Religion in 1980 and received his rabbinic ordination in 1984. A student and close friend of Rabbi Shlomo Carlebach, and fascinated by Jewish mysticism as well as Jewish ethics, Micha made *aliyah* in 1987 and ever since has been working in social activism in Israeli society and has lectured and written extensively on Judaism and social justice. Soon after his arrival, he became a co-founder of Elul, the first joint secular-religious bet midrash. He spent much of 1990-91 in Ethiopia, where he covered the *aliyah* of Beta Israel, including Operation Solomon, as well as the civil war and the rebel entry into Addis Ababa. A prolific journalist, Micha has reported on poverty, globalization, and human rights from around the world, and written for *The Washington Post, The Guardian, The London Times, The Jerusalem Report, Haaretz,* and *The Times of Israel.* In 1993 he founded the Israeli Association for Ethiopian Jewry and served as its director until 1998. It became, and remains to this day, one of the most instrumental and valued organizations dealing with the absorption of Ethiopian immigrants into Israeli society. That year the Joint Distribution Committee granted Micha the Boris Smolar Prize, based on his work covering Ethiopian Jewry.

His strong interest in the Jewish right and responsibility to participate in shaping a vision for humanity and a desire to engage Israeli and Jewish youth led him to found Tevel (www.tevelbtzedek.org), a Jewish Peoplehood project meant to engage the next generation in the struggle to end extreme poverty and environmental destruction on a global level, from a place of profound commitment to Jewish identity and tradition. Tevel currently works in Nepal, Haiti, and Burundi. He and his Tevel colleagues have developed a unique approach to transforming their service-learning participants into cutting edge, agriculture-based community development specialists, who aim at helping rural villages remain or become sustainable. In appreciation of his pioneering work, Hebrew University awarded him the Simon and Ethel Flegg Prize in 2011. His acceptance speech — "Can Global *'Tikkun Olam'* Bring the Jews Together?" — can be viewed here: http://youtu.be/NLvxbYgdr0c

**Dr. Nehemia Polen** is Professor of Jewish Thought at Boston's Hebrew College. He is the author of *The Holy Fire: The Teachings of Rabbi Kalonymus Shapira, the Rebbe of the Warsaw Ghetto* (Jason Aronson, 1994, 1999), and is a contributing commentator to *My People's Prayer Book,* a multi-volume Siddur incorporating diverse perspectives on the liturgy (Jewish Lights). He received his Ph.D. from Boston University, where he studied with and served as teaching fellow for Nobel laureate Elie Wiesel. In 1994 he was Daniel Jeremy Silver Fellow at Harvard University and has also been a Visiting Scholar at the Hebrew University in Jerusalem. He is an ordained rabbi and served a congregation for twenty-three years. In 1998-9 he was a National Endowment for the Humanities Fellow, working on the writings of Malkah Shapiro (1894-1971), the daughter of a noted hasidic master, whose Hebrew memoirs focus on the spiritual lives of women in the context of pre-war Hasidism in Poland. The research culminated in his book, *The Rebbe's Daughter* (Jewish Publication Society, 2002), recipient of a National Jewish Book Award. His most recent book is *Filling Words with Light: Hasidic and Mystical Reflections on Jewish Prayer* — with Lawrence Kushner (Jewish Lights Publishing, 2004).

**Melinda (Mindy) Ribner** is the author of *New Age Judaism, Kabbalah Month by Month, Everyday Kabbalah,* and *The Secret Legacy of Biblical Women: Revealing the Divine Feminine.* A licensed social worker by training, she offers individual and couples spiritual psychotherapy, utilizing kabbalistic wisdom and meditation as part of treatment. A teacher of kabbalistic meditation for over 25 years, she offers workshops and classes on meditation, healing, Kabbalah of Intimacy, Kabbalah of the Feminine, and performances from her recent book, *The Secret Legacy of Biblical Women,* throughout the United States. She is single and divides her time between New York, Florida, and Israel. To be on her newsletter or to contact her personally, contact her at beitmiriam@msn.com. Her website is http://kabbalahoftheheart.com.

**Carol Rose** is a writer, educator, and spiritual counselor. She teaches courses in the use of imagery for healing, creativity, and personal growth. Her poetry and essays appear in Canadian, American, and Israeli journals. Her books of poetry include *Path of the Mothers* (2015) and *From the Dream* (2013), both published by Albion-Andalus Books, Boulder, Colorado, and *Behind the Blue Gate* (Vancouver, BC: Beach Holme Publishing, Ltd., 1997). She co-edited the anthology *Spider Woman: A Tapestry of Creativity and Healing* (Winnipeg, MB: J. Gordon Shillingford Publishing, Spring 1999).

Her awards include The Henry Fuerstenberg Award for Poetry (1998); a nomination for the John Hirsch award for "most promising Manitoba writer" (1996 and 1997); and Second Prize in The Stephen Leacock International Award for Poetry (1994). In addition, she has given lectures on Women and Spirituality in Canada, the United States, Israel, and Copenhagen, Denmark (for the Danish Writer's Guild and the Folkevirke Arts and Cultural Organization in 1995 and 1996).

Carol currently lives in St. Louis, Missouri, with her husband, Rabbi Neal Rose. They are the parents of five children and the grandparents of fifteen. "Reflections" previously appeared in *Kol Chevra*.

**Rabbi Michael (Mickey) Rosen, *z"l*,** will forever be associated with the Yakar Center for Tradition and Creativity, the Modern Orthodox community he founded in London in 1978 and later established in Jerusalem (1992) and Tel Aviv (2007). The Jerusalem Yakar features "soulful, Carlebach-inspired prayer services" and has long served as a magnet for English and Hebrew-English speakers and been a popular venue for classes and workshops, advanced study, lectures by controversial public figures, and cultural events. Rabbi Rosen, along with his colleagues, Rabbi Doctor Mimi Feigelson and Rabbi David Zeller, created a space in Jerusalem for Shlomo to teach. The public conversation between Mickey and Shlomo that begins on p. 255 is one outstanding example of their collaborative work.

In 1997, Rabbi Rosen's colleague, Benjamin Pogrund, started Yakar's Center for Social Concern, "dedicated to fostering thinking about current events, and creative contact between Jews and Arabs." It serves as a concrete expression of Mickey's desire to apply Torah concepts to pressing ethical, social, and political issues.

Another major contribution was Rabbi Rosen's book on Reb Simhah Bunim (1766-1827), a non-conforming Hasidic master. *The Quest for Authenticity: The Thought of Reb Simhah Bunim* (Jerusalem and New York: Urim Publications, 2008) provides in-depth descriptions and analyses of the various courts and schools of that era, the influence of Reb Bunim's teachers upon him, and the effect his approach had on his contemporaries and successors. Due to Mickey's engagement with the world outside of Orthodoxy and of the Jewish world itself, he was often severely criticized, as was his spiritual hero, Reb Bunim. Mickey was truly a Simhah Bunim of sorts, an iconoclast and a consummate gentleman, exceptionally erudite and deep.

In his *sefer*, he writes, "R. Bunim lived within the paradox that truth often brings one into dissonance with one's community. Once the teacher accepts that he has to accept and practice the options that 'common consciousness' lays before him, he becomes a lost man who has died before his body dies, or is at least asleep." Such was not the fate of Bunim, nor of Mickey, nor of Shlomo. In Mickey's case, it was a cruel disease, ASL, that captured his body but not his soul. He left this world on December 7, 2008.

Rabbi Rosen and his wife, Rabbanit Gilla Rosen, who succeeded her late husband as Dean of Yakar, raised their six children in Jerusalem, two of whom, Rabbi Chananel Rosen, Co-Director, and Rabbi Dr. Shlomo Dov Rosen, are integral members of the Yakar faculty, seamlessly continuing their father's legacy, and nourishing his vibrant centers of prayer and learning in Jerusalem and Tel Aviv.

**Joan Roth** is a photographer whose work has been published and exhibited throughout the world. Her passion lies in visually conveying the grandeur of ordinary women. Born and reared in Detroit, Joan Roth came to New York in 1962. During the early years of the women's movement, she was part of several important consciousness-raising groups in East Hampton, New York, and in New York City, and started other groups across the country. Roth has photographed the women's movement since its early days. She photographed the UN International Conferences on Women in Nairobi and Beijing, and in 1994 she began documenting Veteran Feminists events. Roth traveled worldwide to publish *Jewish Women: A World of Tradition and Change*, the first book about Jewish women — including in cultures such as Ethiopia, India, and Yemen — by a Jewish woman photographer. She also photographed women in Baltimore and Seattle for the Jewish Women's Archive's oral history project, Weaving Women's Words. (Source: the Jewish Women's Archive). Joan was a close friend of Shlomo and often photographed him. Many of the truly enduring and familiar images of Shlomo are part of her artistic legacy.

**Rabbi Zalman Schachter-Shalomi,** *z"l* (1924-2014), and Reb Shlomo met in Vienna when they were boys. In 1949, when they were students in the Lubavitcher Yeshiva in Brooklyn, the Frierdiker Rebbe, Yosef Yitzchak Schneersohn, sent them out as *shlichim* to college campuses, the beginning of outreach to acculturated and assimilated Jews. Reb Zalman inspired the Chavurah movement and is known as the father of Jewish Renewal. Although their paths diverged, he and Shlomo remained close friends and colleagues. For a fuller profile of Zalman's life and accomplishments, visit https://aleph.org/Reb-Zalman.

**Rabbi Joseph Schonwald** was born in Haifa in 1947 to Holocaust survivors from Czechoslovakia. The family lived in Israel, Australia, and California, where he spent his youth. Returning to Israel after the Six Day War, he studied at the Diaspora Yeshiva and was ordained in Jerusalem in 1971. He subsequently earned a Master's degree in Education from Loyola University in Los Angeles and another Master's in Counseling Psychology from Arizona State University, while serving as a congregational rabbi in California, Kansas City, and Arizona.

Since returning to Jerusalem with his family in 1991, Rabbi Joe has served as Executive Vice President of the Abraham and Sonia Rochlin Foundation, which funds relief and educational projects in Israel, Eastern Europe and the Former Soviet Union. He was the founding president of the Shlomo Carlebach Foundation, begun after Reb Shlomo, z"l, left the world.

Prior to the fall of the Iron Curtain, R. Schonwald visited Russian Jews in the Soviet Union who had been denied exit visas, bringing books, vitamins, hope, and comfort. After the fall of communism, he traveled throughout the Former Soviet Union and Eastern Europe, to teach Jewish college students in various programs.

Rabbi Schonwald was instrumental in assisting the aliya effort to bring the Jews of Quara, who had been left behind in the Operation Solomon airlift, from Ethiopia to Israel and has supported their integration into Israeli society. He currently consults with foundations about programs for youth-at-risk, education, immigrant absorption, programs for the elderly and disabled, higher education, and community development.

Rabbi Schonwald and his wife, Rolinda, live in Jerusalem. They have three daughters and five grandchildren.

**Rabbi Avraham Arieh Trugman** has been involved in Jewish education for over thirty-five years. He is the director of Ohr Chadash, a dynamic educational program based in Israel. Rabbi Trugman is the author of eleven popular books and has produced five CDs of original music. He appears at Shabbat programs and lectures extensively worldwide.

**Charles Yeshayah Vernoff, Ph.D**, *A"H*, emeritus professor of religion at Cornell College, helped to reshape the curriculum of the religion department by adding depth and intercultural breadth to the course offerings, and brought a thoughtful, acute voice to faculty deliberations. Best known for his courses Mysticism East and West, The History and Theology of the Holocaust, and Contemporary Jewish Literature, Vernoff was also a scholar whose work appeared in the *Journal of the American Academy of Religion, Journal of Ecumenical Studies, Jewish Civilization: Essays and Studies,* and many others. Vernoff was also known on campus for his classroom teaching, his embrace of One Course at a Time, his fierce intellect, and his commitment to community. "Uncle Chuck," as he was affectionately known, was an early member of Havurat Shalom in Somerville, MA, and a co-founder of Havurat Or Chadash in Los Angeles, together with R' Joe Schonwald. He passed away on March 11, 2013, at the age of 71. To read Hillel Goldberg's *hespid*, go to http://www.ijn.com/soil-still-moist/ and for Tehilla Goldberg's reminiscences, to http://www.ijn.com/angels-tears/.

**Emuna Witt-Halevi** met Reb Shlomo at the age of 14; it changed her life. She made her way from the High School of Performing Arts to Yeshiva High School of Queens and came with her graduating class to Israel, married young, and had 14 children in Israel and continued her acting career in the role of mother! She has been transcribing Reb Shlomo torahs for 30 years and teaching them world-wide and has edited the *Kol Chevra Yahrzeit Journal* for Reb Shlomo for over 20 years. Please be in touch when you come to Israel, emunawitt14@yahoo.com.

**Rute Yair-Nussbaum** teaches Chassidut in Matan (Jerusalem), Midreshet Nishmat, Maale (the Jewish film school), and in various other places, including Havruta — the Hebrew University Bet-Midrash — and Midreshet Ein Prat. She is an alumna of Ramat Gan Hesder Yeshiva and earned a BA in Jewish Philosophy and Jewish History from Hebrew University, and an MA from NYU. She is presently pursuing a Ph.D. in Jewish Philosophy at Haifa University.

# Afterword

by Reuven Goldfarb, Redactor

WHEN RABBI JOE INVITED ME TO JOIN THIS PROJECT, I CAME ABOARD AS proofreader. We soon saw that copy editor would be a more appropriate title, and in that capacity I have worked intermittently yet diligently and intensively over the past several years. I have kept in touch with the more than 30 contributors and sought their approval for any changes I might suggest. Throughout, I have had their full cooperation. We exchanged ideas about proper phrasing, historical accuracy, sources, references, spelling, transliteration, punctuation, capitalization, line breaks, and the correct use of italics, quotations, and quotation marks.

The project moved ahead in fits and starts, delayed by personal scheduling conflicts and other distractions. Creative options for making the book maximally effective were developed. Deadlines dissolved and were reinstated. In most cases, the delays actually allowed new ideas to germinate and solutions to production problems to be found.

I followed the same methodology as I practiced as editor of *AGADA*, the illustrated Jewish literary magazine, eleven issues of which I published in the 1980s. I did not impose a house style, preferring to allow each author his or her own voice and mode of expression. As you have seen, if you have read this far, there are a multitude of possible approaches to Reb Shlomo's life and work. Many, but certainly not all of them, have been included here — a tribute to Reb Shlomo's broad appeal and universal message.

From a technical viewpoint, some of the trickiest decisions involved how to transliterate — and even to translate — Hebrew, Aramaic, and Yiddish terms in common use and among specialists, and here, too, I did not seek uniformity. There are many different accepted spellings for key words in our lexicon, which is another way of saying there is not a single correct orthography for every term. I have sought to achieve consistency within a single essay, poem, or story. And as for a word like *niggun* — a wordless melody — is it necessary to italicize all of its multiple appearances in this book? And aren't most readers likely to know it and need no glossary to define it for themselves? And doesn't context supply sufficient clues?

The same applies to the names of Rebbes, their hometowns, and the names of their books. Legitimate scholarly differences exist between them. Ishbitz or Izbica? God or G-d? T'fila or Tefillah? *Gevaldt* or *gevalt*? And so on.

I consulted many modern Jewish books in English and found a diversity of spellings in their texts and definitions in their glossaries, reflecting the preferences and background of each author or compiler. It seems to me that every alternative carries with it a singular flavor and resonance, which I would not like to eradicate. I decided against compiling a glossary of our own because these words, titles, and place names of non-English origin are easily available online and in even a modest Judaica library. Rather than pose as an authority, I refer the reader to other, more astute, scholars.

I am grateful to my wife Yehudit for her overall support throughout this project and her invaluable assistance during the final proofreading. She supplied not only the proverbial fresh pair of eyes, but she brought to the task her superb editorial skills and depth of understanding.

I would like to express my gratitude to my friend and colleague of over 40 years, Rabbi Joe Schonwald, the publisher and final editor of this volume. Our collaboration has been enhanced by our mutual respect, and our love and appreciation for our esteemed teacher. The work has been rewarding beyond measure, in large part due to the spiritual benefit I derived from the closer connection to Reb Shlomo, of blessed memory, that came with it. It is a privilege to be able to share his legacy with the world.

— 13 Tammuz, 5776 / July 18-19, 2016 / Denver, CO
— 20 Kislev, 5777 / December 20, 2016 / Tzfat, *Ir HaKodesh*

*Reuven Goldfarb (left) and Rabbi Joe Schonwald.*
*Photo by Rolinda Schonwald.*

# Titles of Internet Links

P. 6  Memorial service for Reb Shlomo's 22nd *Yahrzeit*

P. 20  Reb Shlomo tells the story of the blind Chazan in Krakow

P. 43  Od Avinu Chai — Reb Shlomo sings on an Israeli TV show, 1973

P. 81  Rare Footage of Shlomo Carlebach in the 1970s — Le'ma'an Achay Ve're'ay

P. 88  Rabbi Shlomo Carlebach – In Concert Toward *Slichot*

P. 94  Reb Shlomo with Reb Yehuda Katz in Leningrad 1989

P. 116  Eulogy for the Rebbe of Lubavitch;

Teaching at the Carlebach Shul in New York, October 1988

P. 127  Barry Barkan on meeting Shlomo for the first time

P. 150  Boi B'Shalom – Reb Shlomo sings on an Israeli TV show, 1973;
Pe'er VeChavod – Reb Shlomo sings on an Israeli TV show, 1973

P. 203  Interview with Neshama Carlebach

P. 212  How many songs have you composed, Shlomo?

P. 223  Modzhitzer tune for B'Motzaei Yom Menucha including "Kra Yesha";
Shlomo Carlebach – Singing Modzhitzer Rebbe's Hallel

P. 226  The Soulful Melodies of Shlomo Carlebach with Neil Seidel

P. 233  Neshama Carlebach – "The Krakow *Niggun*" at March of the Living 2013

P. 236  The Rizhiner *Niggun*

P. 238  Shlomo Carlebach – Yehi Ratzon

P. 251  Shlomo's funeral in Jerusalem

P. 307  The Nameless *Niggun*

P. 334  Shlomo Carlebach on the Road

## In the late 1990s Rabbi Joe Schonwald and Yehuda Katz produced these CDs for the Shlomo Carlebach Foundation – "Shir L'Shlomo"

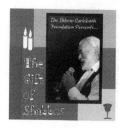

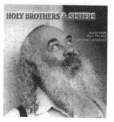